The EU in the 21st Century

David Ramiro Troitiño · Tanel Kerikmäe ·
Ricardo Martín de la Guardia ·
Guillermo Á. Pérez Sánchez
Editors

The EU in the 21st Century

Challenges and Opportunities for the European Integration Process

Springer

instituto de estudios europeos
Universidad de Valladolid
Centro de Excelencia
Jean Monnet

TAL TECH

Editors
David Ramiro Troitiño
Tallinn University of Technology
Tallinn, Estonia

Tanel Kerikmäe
Tallinn University of Technology
Tallinn, Estonia

Ricardo Martín de la Guardia
University of Valladolid
Valladolid, Spain

Guillermo Á. Pérez Sánchez
University of Valladolid
Valladolid, Spain

ISBN 978-3-030-38398-5 ISBN 978-3-030-38399-2 (eBook)
https://doi.org/10.1007/978-3-030-38399-2

This Springer imprint is published by the registered company Springer Nature Switzerland AG
The registered company address is: Gewerbestrasse 11, 6330 Cham, Switzerland

Hegoak ebaki banizkio
nerea izango zen,
ez zuen aldegingo.
Bainan, honela
ez zen gehiago txoria izango
Eta nik...
txoria nuen maite.

To Ossu, Anne Maria, Hugolin and Stella Marella

Contents

The Current Position of the Union in Terms of Integration and Development

EU in Twenty-First Century, Does Crisis Mean Opportunity?

David Ramiro Troitiño, Tanel Kerikmäe, Ricardo Martín de la Guardia and Guillermo Á. Pérez Sánchez

Abstract This book analyzes the long-term problems of the European Union from a multidisciplinary approach. The European Union is facing numerous challenges in the twenty-first century. Some of them can be an opportunity to advance in the integration process; others can be even a threat to the existence of the organization. Nevertheless, all of them are a fascinating combination basic to understand the current state of the European integration process, how the European Union was created, what it is now, and what could be its future shape when these problems are addressed in the coming future.

Keywords European integration · European Union · Future of the EU

The structure of each chapter must follow a neo-functionalism approach: Basically, how the situation was before, how the previous situation was improved, how the situation is now, and what to do to improve the current situation (spillover effect).

1 Introduction

The European Union is a long-term peace project started in order to avoid confrontations between its members. The first successful attempt, the European Coal and Steel Community, set the path of the integration, for the further development of the organization. The Schuman Declaration publicly reflects that Europe cannot be built at once but gradually. The further the member states are integrated, the less the possibilities for a confrontation between them. Since then, the integration has been based on two different slopes:

- Regular improvements in the working system of the European Union based on the daily expertise and necessities.

D. Ramiro Troitiño (✉) · T. Kerikmäe · R. M. de la Guardia · G. Á. Pérez Sánchez
Ehitajate Tee 5, 19086 Tallinn, Estonia
e-mail: david.troitino@ttu.ee

D. Ramiro Troitiño et al. (eds.), *The EU in the 21st Century*,
https://doi.org/10.1007/978-3-030-38399-2_1

- Treaties and other important measures including important novelties in the area of influence of the European Union.

This book focuses on the second option, more spectacular, from the perspective of integration as a necessity of the own process. There are other possibilities, as an ambitious political leadership, but mostly the great steps further in the integration process are the consequence of fulfilling communitarian necessities.

Currently, the European Union has gone beyond the national barriers without achieving a state status. It is a consequence of the actors involved in the process, as the governments of the member states. Systematically, they want to solve the problems generated inside the organization, but with the less sharing of national sovereignty as possible. It has generated tensions inside the process of integration because deeper integration is seen as the solution for most of the problems of the European Union. Nevertheless, the necessity of compromise between the different actors involved in the creation and development of the European Union means the influence of three main paths of integration: neo-functionalism, cooperation, and federalism.

The structure of each chapter has followed a neo-functionalism approach: Basically, how the situation was before, how the previous situation was improved, how the situation is now, and what to do to improve the current situation (spillover effect), but without forgetting other influences as already mentioned. The whole understanding of the process and solutions comes from the inclusion of different perspectives and proposals to reach the compromise between all the participants in the process of integration.

This work is for students and researchers, as we believe the different chapters have been developed in a way that a general reader can understand it and a researcher can use it. It has implied several restrictions in order to combine the general interest of the publication and its scientific value. It is divided into several chapters that can be read independently providing an accurate inside sight on the topic. Nevertheless, the general analysis of the whole work will provide the reader with a wide perspective of the current situation of the European Union in terms of challenges and possible outcomes.

The topics have been selected thinking about the main challenges for the European Union in the coming future, understanding challenges as opportunities. Crisis is period of change; these movements from the European perspective can have three different outcomes, included in all the chapters selected:

- Deeper integration: The European Union solves its problems increasing the common management of a problem in order to solve the previous distortions, wrong functioning or just new necessities that did not exist before.
- Stagnation: The different interest of the different actors involved in the European Union cannot reach a common position and nothing is done. Normally, it happens when the solution to the problem or answer to the challenge needs a sacrifice that some actors are not willing to make. In other words, the solution is known, but the priorities are others. Once the problem becomes a priority, an agreement is reached.

– Less integration: This is the less common approach in the European Union integration process, but it is important to keep it in mind as the Euroscepticism grows during the crisis periods. Currently, the Brexit is a good example of this option, but also the call from different political parties and even member states to renationalize some European policies.

2 Content of the Publication

All the chapters are selected according to their influence in the development of the European Union in the twenty-first century. Their importance comes from different sources, as economy, politics, public opinion, or just potential benefits for the European Union. Obviously, there are not included all the challenges but those the editors considered crucial in the coming years.

The starting point of this ambitious work is a detailed description of the current position of the European Union in terms of integration and development, analyzing from general approach the complete thematic of the book developed by Guillermo Pérez, an outstanding scholar with the needed long-term vision to develop such a delicate thematic. This chapter also includes an overview of other important challenges for the European Union not included in this publication for practical reasons.[1]

The concerns of the European citizens are a basic necessity for the development and success of the European Union because without the support of the people the organization will just collapse in the coming years. The European Union must answer the necessities of its people if it wants to gain their loyalty. Any transfer of loyalty can be made by the states, but will not last without the support of the citizens, real holders of the sovereignty in our European societies.

Hence, Ricardo Martín de la Guardia discusses populism, new political parties in Europe, governments and ideas and their support for a less integrated Europe.[2] Religion and identity are a part of these concerns of the citizens, as the previous homogeneity of Europe based on Christianity or secularism is not a reality. New obstacles and challenges have risen for the development of the Union in the context of internal cohesion, masterly described by Luis Domínguez Castro and José Ramón Rodríguez Lago. They have been able to provide a clear vision of an issue really controversial in Europe and crucial for its social and educational development.[3]

The preoccupation that migration generates among Europeans is higher than ever, and it affects the development of the European Union and its survival. Lara Sansus has presented this problematic challenge discussing the role of the EU in the migration crisis and in relation to the member states. Her research analyzes how migration will affect the internal and external affairs of the European Union and why it is a

[1] Martin and Perez (1995).

[2] De la guardia and Sánchez (2003).

[3] Castro and Lago (2018).

key question regarding integration or multiculturalism as options for the future.[4] Migration is becoming a main concern for the European population and it will affect the EU. Therefore, it is crucial to foresee what the EU can do to provide the right answers to its citizens.

Terrorism and criminality are becoming a concern for the European Union citizens. The free movement of people included in the treaties has brought some negative side effects as the free movement of criminals. Nataliia Oliievska focuses on this problem and proposes different alternatives in order to solve the necessities of the citizens in this field from the less restrictive approach to the integration perspective.[5]

There are challenges linked with the internal development of the European Union, and the integration has generated some benefits, but also some new obstacles that need to be solved in order to improve the global performance of the European Union. Brexit, as a failure in the integration process, is a fundamental issue in the coming years as it can threaten the own existence of the organization if the British succeed in the process. The success of the British secession will not be decided by the performance of UK outside of the European Union, but the combined perspective of, on the one hand, the British performance and, on the other hand, the EU performance.[6] If UK grows more than the EU, Brexit would be an option for other member states; if the EU grows more than UK, Brexit will be a failure. Hence, it is a fundamental work led by Essi Laitinen to understand the possibilities lying ahead of the Brexit and how they will affect the UK and the EU.

The Brexit understood as a part of a bigger process outlines the structural contradictions of the communitarian framework and the inevitabilities to reform the structure of the European Union to avoid future problems. The topic is masterfully dissected By Celso Cancela outlining the problems created by the own architectural development of the European Union and how the EU should face them.[7] As the EU is a moving project in a constant evolution, its structural framework needs to adapt to these changes.

The use of new technologies will be vital in the reform project as the EU needs new tools for increasing effectiveness and closeness with its citizens. It is necessary to improve how the citizens interact with the structures of the state. Tanel Kerikmäe, as main researcher, focuses on the participation in the EU democratic process and EU elections[8]; the way they can help with the democratic deficit of the European Union; and how the EU can shape the world with its normative power in this field.

This influence can be seen in the exceptional research presented by Carlos Aldereguia; the EU has a great opportunity to create high standards of environmental protection in the world, saving the planet from its current degradation. The specific topic chosen is related to fishing, given that the EU is the main world market for fishery and aquaculture products. Facing the magnitude and urgency of the

[4] Kerikmäe (2014).

[5] Ramiro and Pando (2017).

[6] Troitino et al. (2018).

[7] Outeda (2001).

[8] Kerikmäe et al. (2019).

problem of IUU fishing, the EU decided to intensify its action and adopt additional measures derived from the current international framework.

The normative power of the European Union has been long discussed, but it is basic enforcing the communitarian law inside the European Union with high effectiveness. There is still space enforcing law in the European Union. Ondrej Hamulak's research covers the rule of law principle as two-way (general) provision addressed to the EU itself[9] and the member states, and it will cover all thinkable alternatives of the promotion to this constitutional cornerstone of the EU.

Iwona Pawlas addresses a problematic topic, the economy inside of the European Union. It has been a very successful field, and the integration is going beyond the economy. Nevertheless, as a dynamic system, it cannot be forgotten. There are many challenges ahead that need to be outlined, and proposals are needed for perfecting the system and decreasing the negative aspects of the economic union of Europe.[10]

The European Union needs to reform internally for facing twenty-first-century challenges successfully, but there are also external incentives. David Ramiro Trotino leads a research group on the external projection of the European Union from a wide perspective, presenting a coherent map of an intricate system. If the EU wants to have some responsibility and influence on the external world, the whole system should be reformed.[11] The current globalization reduces the independent capacity of the individual states, so the union of the European States is a necessity to keep their international influence. European understanding of the society alive.

The eastern border of the European Union presents the higher challenge from the external point of view; the crisis generated in Ukraine has already tested the performance of the European Union in the international arena. The European Union has not cleared its position, to stand firmly on these principles or being pragmatic. Iurii H. Barabash and two more colleagues from Ukraine present this idea by representing the controversy in Ukraine between European human rights and path dependency with Russia.[12] The European Union has an excellent opportunity reassuring its ideals in the world, but its position is still not clear, as there are different positions between the communitarian actors involved in the process.

The conflict in Ukraine challenges the external relations of the European Union with Russia, main priority for many members of the European Union. The benefits and losses of this cooperation are highly important for the European Union because it will shape its own essence in opposition or collaboration with its biggest neighbor, Russia. Alexander Antonov discusses it brilliantly in the context of the NATO Russia Council.[13]

Russia is also a main character in the last topic selected for this work, the challenge presented by cybersecurity. Agnes Kasper and Holger Mölder provide the perfect

[9]Hamuľák (2016).

[10]Pawlas (2014).

[11]Troitiño et al. (2017).

[12]Барабаш (2004).

[13]Antonov (2018).

example of new necessities of the European Union.[14] The Common Foreign and Security Policy was not thought for cyber defense because in its origins it was not a priority, but now the organization must react fast to face a challenge that could threaten the working system of the European Union and its member states.[15]

3 Conclusions

The European Union is facing multiple challenges in twenty-first century; some will be solved with deeper integration, creating new structures and policies and sharing a new level of sovereignty between the member states. Some will be temporally addressed with higher level of cooperation, delaying the negative consequences or even unravelling their complex implications. However, some of these challenges will require efforts the member states are not willing to do and will remain unsolved.

Nevertheless, the European Union will move forward as a living process that cannot be stagnant for a long period or its own existence is in danger. There will be changes related to society, politics, law, economy, and international relations. The capacity of the European Union to address successfully described in this publication will determine the future of the organization in the close future and its success internally, in terms of social, political, and economic development, but also externally where the competition between world powers could decrease the effectiveness of the European Union.

Literature

Antonov, A. (2018). Russia's aggression against Ukraine: State responsibility, individual responsibility and accountability.

Барабаш, Ю. Ю. (2004). *Тарас Шевченко: імператив України: Історіо-й націософська парадигма*. Києво-Могилянська академия.

Castro, L. D., & Lago, J. R. R. (2018). Educación y diplomacia cultural en la primavera de Europa (1948–1954) = Education and Cultural Diplomacy in the Spring of Europe (1948–1954). *Revista de educación, 383*, 63–84.

De la guardia, R. M. M., & Sánchez, G. Á. P. (2003). Hungría y España ante los retos de la cooperación en la Europa unida del siglo XXI. Introducción histórica. *Revista de Estudios Europeos, 35*, 3–12.

Hamuľák, O. (2016). *National sovereignty in the European Union: View from the Czech perspective*. Berlin: Springer.

Kasper, A. (2014). The fragmented securitization of cyber threats. In *Regulating eTechnologies in the European Union* (pp. 157–187). Cham: Springer.

Kerikmäe, T. (2014). Protecting human rights in the EU. In *Controversies and challenges of the charter of fundamental rights*.

[14] Kasper (2014).

[15] Mölder (2010).

Kerikmäe, T., Troitiño, D. R., & Shumilo, O. (2019). An idol or an ideal? A case study of Estonian e-Governance: Public perceptions, myths and misbeliefs. *Acta Baltica Historiae et Philosophiae scientiarum, 7*(1).

Martín de la Guardia, R. M., & Pérez Sánchez, G. Á. (1995). La Europa del Este, de 1945 a nuestros días.

Mölder, H. (2010). *Cooperative security dilemma–practicing the Hobbesian security culture in the Kantian security environment* (Doctoral dissertation).

Outeda, C. C. (2001). *El proceso de constitucionalización de la Unión Europea: de Roma a Niza* (No. 3). Univ Santiago de Compostela.

Pawlas, I. (2014). Rozwój polskiej gospodarki na tle pozostałych krajów Unii Europejskiej w okresie niestabilności w gospodarce światowej. *Prace Naukowe/Uniwersytet Ekonomiczny w Katowicach.*

Ramiro Troitino, D., & Pando Ballesteros, M. D. L. P. (2017). Churchill's European integration model. *Revista de Occidente, 433*, 57–71.

Troitiño, D. R. (2017). Jean Monnet before the first European community: A historical perspective and critic. *Trames, 21*(3), 193–213.

Troitiño, D. R., Färber, K., & Boiro, A. (2017). Mitterrand and the great European design—from the Cold war to the European Union. *Baltic Journal of European Studies, 7*(2), 132–147.

Troitiño, D. R., Kerikmäe, T., & Chochia, A. (Eds.). (2018). *Brexit: History, reasoning and perspectives*. Berlin: Springer.

The European Union Crossroads: Current Situation and Future Challenges

Guillermo Á. Pérez Sánchez

Le bilan reste positif.
Robert Schuman, *Pour l' Europe.*

Abstract This is a description of the current position of the European Union in terms of integration and development wherein the subject matter is analysed using a general approach.

Keywords EU XXI century · EU integration · EU challenges

1 Initial Note (as an Introduction)[1]

From a historical perspective, it can confidently be affirmed that the European integration process was fundamental to the peace-building work this "savage continent"[2] needed to eradicate the ill will the end of the war had foreshadowed. As is pointed out below, the alternative to this "savage continent" was proffered by Robert Schuman, despite the fact that it may initially have seemed as if the process to be attempted were

[1]This section serves as an introduction to the rest of the chapters.

[2]Lowe (2016) and Zweig (2017).

The author is the Principal Investigator (PI) of the "*Europeísmo y redes transatlánticas en los siglos XX y XXI*" ["Europeanism and trans-Atlantic networks in the twentieth and twenty-first centuries"] research project: PGC2018-095884-B-C22 (Spanish Ministry of Science, Innovation and Universities/EU-ERDF).

G. Á. Pérez Sánchez (✉)
Institute of European Studies, Universidad de Valladolid, Plaza de Santa Cruz 5-1 Planta, 47002 Valladolid, Spain
e-mail: guiller@fyl.uva.es

D. Ramiro Troitiño et al. (eds.), *The EU in the 21st Century*,
https://doi.org/10.1007/978-3-030-38399-2_2

a kind of "leap in the dark"[3] or "an uncertain road"[4] (according to Ian Kershaw[5]) that must be taken in order to restore Europe. Thus lays the land almost seventy years after the European project that started with the Schuman Declaration[6] on 9 May 1950 and the creation of the European Coal and Steel Community (ECSC) the following year (Treaty of Paris, 18 April 1951).

With the 60th anniversary of the 25 March 1957 Treaty of Rome now past, two questions arise: does the European community stand before a crossroads now, a particularly decisive moment since its founding? Or, on the contrary: without denying the crossroads in front of the European community project begun in the 1950s, could it be said in the latter half of the second decade of the twenty-first century that Schuman's proverbial balance sheet still positive? To answer either question, we must first analyse the European project from a historical perspective to see whether it could be concluded, paraphrasing a certain Enlightenment thinker, that "If the European Union didn't exist, it would be necessary to invent it". Since it has already been "invented", we must subsequently assess its present situation and future challenges. In the words of Araceli Mangas Martín: "Nevertheless, it is thanks to the existence of the European Union—with all of its faults—and of other international organisations that this brutal economic crisis [2007–2014] did not lead us to war, which is the way in which similar situations were resolved in the past". In this regard, Mangas herself indicated the following in a later article: "The European Union, despite its problems and circumstantial flaws, is the only conceivable context for the continent's communal well-being. The only thing we Europeans have to fear today is the advance of 'revived local tribalism'. Just like in 1914 and 1939".[7]

As things stand, and with all data in hand, this is a reflection on whether the European Union stands before a crossroad leading to nowhere, or rather whether, with its many vices and virtues, this unifying project—to borrow a valuable descriptor from Ortega y Gasset, pioneer[8] and champion of the European ideal (as he defined himself after giving his speech, *Europa Meditatio Quadem* [Meditation on Europe], on 7 September 1949 at the newly created Free University of Berlin)—continues to be worthwhile. We explore whether the scales tip towards the positive in the same way they did when presented by Schuman fifty-six years ago in his missive "*Pour l'Europe*" (in English, "For Europe"), a volume published posthumously.

Taking this into account, a review of the present situation leads one to the conclusion that perhaps the European Union stands not just at one crossroads, but at many. It faces the task of choosing a road from amongst at least four possibilities. No matter which path it chooses, the European Union will have to respond to a series

[3] Martín de la Torre (2015).

[4] Translator's Note (T.N.). A reference to the title of the Spanish translation of Kershaw's book, "*Ascenso y crisis. Europa, 1950–2017. Un camino incierto*", originally entitled "Roller-Coaster: Europe, 1950–2017".

[5] Kershaw (2019).

[6] Becerril Atienza (2018, 41–50).

[7] Spanish periodical *El Norte de Castilla*, 18-V-2013, pp. 22–23; *El Mundo*, 6-I-2014, p. 17.

[8] Ortega y Gasset (1986).

of compromising and even critical situations that loom on the horizon: the immense challenges to be resolved now and in the near future.

2 The European Union Facing the Twenty-First Century

At the end of his life, Robert Shuman wrote in his "European will", "*Le bilan reste positif*": "The balance sheet remains positive".[9,10] His words faithfully match our reality: finally, the new possible Europe was underway. According to Luis Suárez, "Sixty years [referring to the 60th anniversary of the Treaty of Rome]. A very small number, given the dimensions of the goal that we strive for. Yet, it is evident that we have made considerable achievements. War in Europe has been put to an end. A good deal more: armies are restoring their moral order now that they consider themselves to be humanitarian instruments called upon as a sorrowful remedy to defend victims of hate".[11] This is a new Europe in which, thanks to peace amongst Europeans, its nations have reached their greatest levels of development and socio-economic well-being at the hand of good democratic governance. Herein lies its essence, in the form of three great ideas that are the bedrock of the European ideal.[12] For George Steiner, the essence of Europe is represented by its *cafés* and human-scaled cities.[13] This is the differentiating factor which gives the Old World its distinct personality within the global world. This is a new Europe, in conclusion, one able to prevent the final catastrophe so many times approached: "We leave the twentieth century behind, which many historians have called the cruellest in history with an abundance of arguments. (…) Beyond the negative experiences, we are compelled to remember its creative efforts. These three founding fathers of the new Europe born out of the post-war period, themselves emanating from a politically active Catholicism, proposed that moral values should be carried over into political terrain, thereby erasing the hate that had separated countries".[14] The three fathers Luis Suárez refers to are Schuman, Adenauer and De Gasperi, cited by name by Suárez as he reflected on the 60th anniversary of the Treaty of Rome:

> An important point: what the Treaty of Rome abolished was nothing less than a prolonged and dour track comprising more than six hundred years of periods highlighted by increasingly cruel wars that were capable of extending their plague-like reaches across the entire globe. That said, while the voices demanding peace resounded from many and diverse planes, it is impossible to forget that they united only when Adenauer, Schuman and De Gasperi took the matter into their own hands and delved to its deepest roots.[15]

---

[9]Schuman (2006, 98).

[10]T.N.: Own translation from Spanish.

[11]Spanish periodical *La Razón*, 9-IV-2017, p. 5.

[12]Pérez Sánchez (2001, 15–55).

[13]Steiner (2012, 64).

[14]Suárez Fernández (2003, 338).

[15]*La Razón*, 9-IV-2017, p. 5.

As subsequently developed, and with Robert Schuman's political generation no longer present, this new Europe followed in the footsteps of the Declaration of 9 May 1950: "Europe will not be made all at once, or according to a single plan. It will be built through concrete achievements which first create a de facto solidarity". Thus, it was gradually perfected, strengthened and expanded with time. And so, the new Europe had to be everyone's; it would only reach fulfilment with the membership of all European nations, joined amongst themselves by the same values. In this regard, and despite a lengthy wait, its expansion process finally reached the eastern end of the Old World. In effect, fifty years after the start of the integration process that forged the European Communities and coinciding with the collapse of the Soviet socialist system in former Eastern Europe,[16] the pro-Europe example was set by the 1950s generation, specifically their commitment to peace, freedom, democracy, social justice and human rights, as they arduously and resolvedly impelled that the continent's central and south-eastern countries come "back to Europe" and to the "common European house"[17] through their integration in the European Union. As Michael Zantovsky relates it:

> Within weeks of the revolutions in Central and Eastern Europe, the slogan 'Back to Europe' emerged, spontaneously and independently, in Czechoslovakia, Hungary and Poland. Already in January 1990, Havel spoke of the joint 'return to Europe' to the Polish Sejm and Senate. In May 1991, in Aachen, on the occasion of receiving the Charlemagne award for his contribution to the European idea, Havel spoke of the ambition to win full membership in the EU. It took another thirteen years for the Czech Republic and other countries of Central and Eastern Europe to get there.[18]

The above segment is, in fact, part of the chapter notably titled "Back to Europe" from Michael Zantovsky's book on Václav Havel, entitled "Havel. A Life" (Great Britain, Atlantic, 2014). It was clear that without the old Eastern European countries, the EU integration process underway would be incomplete.[19]

But the task is not finished. To paraphrase Kant, "We must continue cultivating our garden". In other words, the never-ending task is to preserve and align the European legacy to the times without which the new, united Europe would get off track. To avoid straying adrift, there could be nothing better, thought Robert Schuman, than to educate the new generations of Europeans in the classroom.[20] "We never tire of repeating it: the unity of Europe will not be achieved by European institutions; it will only be possible to the degree that mindsets evolve. Herein lies the importance of the free movement of ideas and people among European countries; countries that oppose this on principle will exclude themselves from Europe".[21] Deepening his analysis ("Europe is a Cultural and Spiritual Community", analysis presented by Robert Schuman at the "The European spiritual and cultural problem, considered

[16]Pérez Sánchez (2007, 191–217).

[17]Martín de la Guardia and Pérez Sánchez (2017).

[18]Zantovsky (2017, 134) and Zantovsky (2016).

[19]Martín de la Guardia and Pérez Sánchez (2009, 153–221).

[20]Troitiño (2017).

[21]T.N.: Own translation from Spanish.

as a historical entity, and the means by which to express this unity in contemporary terms", round table discussion held by the European Council in Rome during October 1953), he wrote, amongst other things, the following:

> In the first place, it is necessary—imperative—for Europeans to become conscious of what unites them (…) "Europe divided has not known how to provide the modern world with the "spiritual message" that it needed. (…) Europe will re-forge its spirit from the diversity of its traits and ambitions. The unity of these fundamental concepts is reconciled through the plurality of its traditions and convictions, and with the responsibility of private initiative. Contemporary Europe must be constituted by this co-existence, which will not be a simple conglomerate of rival nations who are periodically hostile, but instead an organised and collaborative community of action.[22]

With the impetus of the European ideal—a way of understanding and making Europe—the new possible Europe inherited now and passed from one century to the next will thereby be able to continue along its path in the framework of an evolving European Union in an attempt to "overcome what we have inherited, integrating it in a revitalised way".[23]

2.1 The European Union at Its Crossroads

To reflect on the present circumstances of the European Union also means to think about everything that has been achieved, taking into consideration the circumstances of its founding, as has been mentioned, in a Europe destroyed and divided by two wars—both of them Armageddon-like—during the first half of the twentieth century (the 100th anniversary of the start of the first, as well as the 80th anniversary of the start of the second now behind us). Be as it may, Europe's present—and here we may indeed speak of Europe, the Europe united in the early days of the twenty-first century—or that of the European Union, can be said to be at a crossroads. The outlook should appear much more optimistic to Europeans now than the past of precisely one hundred years ago.[24] In any case, a look at the present situation leads us to affirm—as has been mentioned before—that the European Union possibly faces multiple crossroads[25] and must choose a path from among—at least—four possibilities.

These issues will be contemplated through the study carried out by the Friedrich-Ebert-Stiftung Foundation (associated with German social democracy) regarding the four possible process scenarios that could arise at the heart of the European Union at this time and until the year 2020. Between their extremes, Europe would find itself in an indefinite dead-end crisis or, conversely, on a path towards a sort of federal union aimed at creating the "United States of Europe". The study's key findings were presented to the Spanish public through an interview with its coordinator, Bjoern Hacker.

---

[22]T.N.: Own translation from Spanish.

[23]Beneyto (1999, 127).

[24]Coudenhove-Kalergi (2002).

[25]López-Aranda (2017, 68–82).

Another analysis entitled New Pact for Europe will be used to address the premises of the above study. Reflecting on "a European future in five scenarios", this study was presented in a Spanish forum organised by the *Fundación para las Relaciones Internacionales y el Diálogo Exterior* [Foundation for International Relations and Foreign Dialogue] (FRIDE).[26] In any event, in 2019 (and therefore, more than sixty years after the Treaty of Rome[27] and nearly seventy after the Schuman Declaration, as has been mentioned), the aim is to continue advancing, always keeping Goethe's words in mind: "You and yours may remain idle, but he whoever follows me will always have tasks at hand". Let us, therefore, place the possible courses upon the table for analysis as delineated by the crossroads that the European currently faces.

The first of these paths, and the initial crossroad on the horizon with regards to the economic crisis that reared its head starting from 2007 to 2008, would establish a dead-end scenario for the European Union which neither EU institution leaders nor the government leaders of the Member States most affected would be able to effectively stave off. They would be reduced to "muddling through" it, which would have a negative effect on the proper function of the EU monetary and economic processes currently in place. In addition, Member State economies would cease to be as competitive as other more vigorous economies of the moment, such as China's, due to "stagnation, deflation and debt", in a situation that would be sustained over time. For the team of analysts coordinated by Bjoern Hacker, this description would define "the phase" in which we found ourselves at the peak of the last crisis and to which we could again return if we relapse into another similar situation. This would undoubtedly spark general unrest in European public opinion to the point of even raising questions about the Eurozone and therefore the aforementioned monetary and economic union process. On this point, Ana Palacio, ex-Minister of Foreign Affairs for Spain, emphasised that "The internal European market continues to work, but it has lost its magic", during a forum organised by the aforementioned FRIDE in order to present the New Pact for Europe. "The legitimacy it had then among citizens in terms of guaranteeing prosperity today no longer exists". However, she rejected the idea that introducing the euro had been a crass error, explaining that the common currency "was conceived in the 1980s at a historic moment when no one could have imagined today's world. The euro has its flaws, but it is a fundamental pillar of the European Union, which is humanity's greatest project following World War II". In the same debate, ex-president of the European Parliament Enrique Barón "rejected the idea of either renouncing the euro or rethinking the entire debate on Europe".

The second path outlined by the aforementioned Friedrich-Ebert-Stiftung Foundation—based on the first, but much more traumatic—would lead to a hypothetical "Yugoslavia-like" rupture of the Union,[28] which could entail a scenario that would not be devoid of violence, or even, albeit less dramatic, a "Soviet-like" rupture.[29] Truly, Dantesque to pro-European idealists, this scenario would come about as the

[26]Spanish periodical *XLSemanal* (14 April 2013). Spanish periodical *El País* (21 February 2014).

[27]López-Aranda (2017, 68–82) and Khader (2017, 94–103).

[28]Martín de la Guardia and Pérez Sánchez (2007).

[29]Martín de la Guardia and Pérez Sánchez (2005).

result of divisions and hostilities fuelled by populist radicalism from the extreme right and extreme left, as well as sickly nationalism, both forged in the heat of European politics. Contrary to the values of the European ideal mentioned above, this would certainly dilapidate the inheritance of nearly seventy years of European integration from which Europeans from the four corners of the Old Continent currently benefit. (The association between the UK and the European Union may expire, part of the quintessential nature of divisive national-populism, after forty-six years, which, for some analysts, may signal the beginning of the collapse for European integration.[30]) Thus, the old spectres of ancient hatreds, confrontations, conflicts and even war amongst Europeans could again be revived.

> The success of Brexit corresponds to the rise of the nationalist populism that has spread across Europe for the last decade. At the end of the twentieth century, it was a rarity in the form of small factions the political analysts and historians identified with radicalism or as simply bizarre. Today they have turned into mainstream movements that leave their mark on political agendas and language. Not only has there been UKIP in the United Kingdom,[31] the French National Rally and Spain's Unidos Podemos, but other parties of the same fabric with the same ability to govern have arisen in Austria and the Netherlands under the names of the Freedom Party and the Party for Freedom, as well as the *Fidesz*—Hungarian Civic Union in Hungary (and especially, *Jobbik* [For A Better Hungary]), Alternative for Germany, the Swedish Democrats, the True Finns, with populism in Greece between *Syriza* and the Independent Greeks—National Patriotic Alliance (ANEL), having also seen the victory of the Five Star Movement in Italy, as well as the populist party in Denmark, to top off the list.
>
> Populism is a virus that resides "ab initio" (from the beginning) in the organism called political society. Once it has appeared, the most normal turn of events is that the contagion of its words, ways, agenda and aims spreads to other political stakeholders. It does not simply arise due to political corruption, economic crisis or refugees. This is the left's explanation. There are other factors that explain its ascent. First, adequate ideological foundational support must exist, a mentality if you will, in order for populism to be successful. Evident, for example, in the hearts and smiles of the Podemos campaign, the growing sentimentalism in politics, gestated in the hyper-protective society of the welfare state and nourished by the transformation of politicians into media-broadcast spectacles, has generated what could be called "emotional democracy." This has made effective political discourse turn to a focus on moving emotions, especially hate, anaesthetising the intellect and reason, and appealing to simple moral-laden proposals that are comfortable for citizens. The more emotional and infantilised politics is, the easier it becomes for the populist to navigate the terrain: "The phantom haunts Europe again".[32]

To prevent this from affecting the European community process underway, José María Beneyto, participant in the aforementioned FRIDE forum organised in order to reflect on a New Pact for Europe, advocated for teaching values (cited above) that give meaning to the European Union. Whilst it is true that "what has been done up to now has been essential", it is absolutely necessary to keep up the "fight to continue spreading the word", to which all pro-Europeans should be committed.

The third of these foreseeable paths—likewise formulated according to the first alternative laid out above—may be similarly contrary to the pro-European pursuits

[30]Leonard (2017a, 10–11).

[31]Ramiro Troitino and Pando Ballesteros (2017).

[32]Jorge Vilches: *La Razón*, 26-VI-2016, p. 34.

formulated by the fathers of the European Community after the end of the Second World War: the transformation of the European Union into a kind of "German private club". "Germany and the most stable economies" would belong to this "exclusive club" (the antithesis of the Europeanism spearheaded by Robert Schuman and the political generation of the 1950s) as its own fiscal and economic union. Thus, in this third scenario, a "smaller and more stable" European Union would drive a fiscal, monetary and economic union, where less stable or "periphery" economies would remain outside, unable to participate. However, the first question to answer would be to establish which economies would be considered the "periphery". Are we talking about the southern European countries that have suffered the ravages of the economic crisis more intensely? Or should "sick" economies such as France's and Italy's economies also comprise the "periphery"? The creation of this third scenario would mean nothing less than the oft-evoked "two-speed Europe". This scenario currently appears to be the most plausible one for overcoming the European community's current situation, according to the leaders of the most significant member states: Germany, France[33] and Spain[34] (no longer Italy, now lingering at the far edges of the system in holding with its militant anti-Europe, nationalist-populist government). Europe has remained burdened with persistent effects of the economic crisis since 2007–2008, which, according to certain analyses, has degenerated into a European identity crisis. In any event, and as indicated by Jordi Sevilla, Spanish ex-Minister of Territorial Policy and Public Function, in the aforementioned FRIDE forum,[35] the European Union's current situation should be monitored with more calm and "lower expectations about what this could effectively offer us, as well as try to implement the provisions established in treaties" without interestedly forcing the any of the variables of the integration process underway with respect to some Member States.

The fourth and last scenario amongst the possible alternatives (to bring to a close a process that would present new derived situations unendingly) would set a course towards a kind of federal union, that is, a "United States of Europe". This option is already well known, having been discussed in the mid-nineteenth century by persons with European convictions such as Victor Hugo. According to statements in the cited study conducted by the Friedrich-Ebert-Stiftung Foundation, this scenario is considered "the most difficult, yet most desirable scenario" by experts. They are not wrong about its difficulty, considering the even-more-utopian-than-possible nature of the goal of creating a "United States of Europe" in the short to mid-term. The prospect does not appear to be on the agenda for European nations, especially those most implicated in the integration process, such as France. The stated goal—more utopian than possible, we repeat—enjoys sympathies from a certain sector of pro-European idealists, as demonstrated in the aforementioned FRIDE forum; when asked a question in this regard by María J. Rodríguez, Portugal's ex-Minister of Work, the majority of the audience "supported the most complex and ambitious option: creating a United States of Europe".

---

[33] Demesmay (2017, 38–44) and Gutiérrez-Peris (2019, 76–85).

[34] Leonard (2017b, 16–22).

[35] Kerikmäe (2019).

Having outlined the possible crossroads that lay before the European Union in our day and time, the first option should be discarded as undesirable, since it would lead to the dead end of permanent economic crisis. We would likewise reject the second option discussed amongst the scenarios as destructive because it would incite a "Yugoslavian"- or "Soviet"-like end (notwithstanding, Brexit has placed the assertion that the integration process underway would be "irreversible" into question, albeit the contagious effect predicted by some analysts has not come to pass[36]). We would moreover discard the third of the courses open to us due to its characteristic lack of solidarity and thereby reject the EU's conversion into an "exclusive club" only for "privileged countries" (although, as has been noted, the "two-speed Europe" presents itself as a realistic option nowadays). Thus, only the fourth possible crossroad remains open to us, but with the caveat that, beyond a route to federalism, from our point of view, the most desirable option would be to slowly and steadily strengthen the monetary and economic union currently in place.

2.2 The European Union and (Some of) Its Future Challenges

Reflecting on the future of the European Union means thinking about the challenges ahead[37] as the first two decades of the twenty-first century come to a close. As stated before, the European Union must respond to at least (not to restrict the list) five compromising, perhaps even critical, situations that loom on the horizon: the immense challenges to be resolved now and in the near future. First, the euro-scepticism that never fails to make a dent in the European ideal must be met head-on[38] with renewed faith in European integration. In this regard, it is worth recalling what an article entitled "*De los euroconvencidos a los antieuropeos*" ["From Euro-Convinced to Anti-Europe"] expressed, quoted here:

> Until now, euro-scepticism had developed at the margins of the system, both at the ideological extremes and among parties that did not occupy government positions (Araceli Mangas refers to an article entitled, "*La resistible ascensión de la anti Europa*" ["The Resistible Ascent of Anti-Europe"[39]]). Hence, it is not surprising that the clans considered to be euro-sceptics have been the populist radical right, the radical left, agrarian parties and protestant parties. Meanwhile, the main clans—socialists, liberals, Christian democrats—have converged in pro-integration positions (…). So, while it can be confirmed that the new wave of euro-scepticism has permeated all Member States with an electoral decline in euro-believers, euro-scepticism has diverse faces. While anti-European parties are the ones winning electoral gains in the north (the populist radical right), in the south, the alter-Europeans (the radical

[36] Troitiño et al. (2018).

[37] Fernández Navarrete (2018, 324–370).

[38] Soto Carmona (2019).

[39] Spanish periodical *El Mundo*, 06-05-2014.

right) are particularly successful. Considering the current power balance within European institutions, what future awaits the European Union?[40]

The immediate future was recently outlined upon the close of the 26 May 2019 elections to the European Parliament. The most significant aspect of the results was not the loss of weight carried by the two traditional powerhouses, the popular parties and socialists, but instead the consolidation of groups contrary to the European community process, from euro-sceptics to openly anti-Europeans, from both the right and left ends of the political spectrum. (British European parliamentarians were amongst them, the UK being obliged by legal imperative to participate in voting whilst Brexit has still not been made official.) Whilst the number of these groups' seats did increase, their totals were insufficient to create a minority block that could paralyse parliamentary action.

Secondly, the economic situation must be addressed resolutely—without overlooking the consolidation of the euro on the international market alongside the dollar—in order to restore European Union citizens' trust in the maintenance of socio-economic welfare right now, which is still in question due to the hardships of the economic crisis that started in 2007–2008. This is the thrust of some analyses, for example, the one put forward by Salvador Forner and Heidy-Cristina Senante: "Until rather recently, a complaisant tale (to a greater or lesser degree) concerning monetary unification was the norm, within which a variety of narratives relating to European integration converged, including institutional, political and academic ones. These narratives had been based on the acceptance of a supposed internal logic concerning the evolution of economic integration, which should have resulted in a monetary union, as well as in the multiple advantages associated with the single currency. These advantages were fundamentally economic, but also related to identity, strengthening the international profile in other areas, and even the creation of rapport and peace between the two eternal rivals, France and Germany. The recent crisis has served to relativize this perspective and has given credence to an alternative narrative that questions those foundations, envisaging the single currency as a factor provoking inequality among the euro area countries and even the disintegration of the European Union".[41] Nevertheless, we see contributions that are clearly positive in relation to the euro at this point in time and thus with the monetary and economic union process, according to which "'Failed experiment' and 'error' are regular definitions of the euro by economists and politicians both in and outside the EU. The support of Eurozone citizens, however, continues strong fifteen years after the euro's introduction. Why? Fear doesn't explain everything".[42]

Thirdly, the transcendental challenge of the UK's departure from the European Union must be confronted. Known as Brexit,[43] the British authorities activated Article 50 of the Treaty of Lisbon on 29 March 2017, based on the results of the 23 June 2016 referendum (albeit, it is true that currently—more than two years later—we find

[40]C. Plaza-Colodro: *El Norte de Castilla*, 28-04-2017 and Rodríguez-Aguilera (2012).

[41]Spanish periodical *Ayer*, 103 (2016-3-), pp. 213–214 and Márkaris (2012).

[42]Otero-Iglesias (2017, 84–93).

[43]Ruiz Navarro Pinar (2018, 393–394).

ourselves in what could be the last extension before said withdrawal, the extension expiring at midnight on 31 October 2019, in a pitiful example of negotiations on fruitless agreements).

> Article 50. /1. Any Member State may decide to withdraw from the Union in accordance with its own constitutional requirements. /2. A Member State which decides to withdraw shall notify the European Council of its intention. In the light of the guidelines provided by the European Council, the Union shall negotiate and conclude an agreement with that State, setting out the arrangements for its withdrawal, taking account of the framework for its future relationship with the Union. That agreement shall be negotiated in accordance with Article 218(3) of the Treaty on the Functioning of the European Union. It shall be concluded on behalf of the Union by the Council, acting by a qualified majority, after obtaining the consent of the European Parliament. /3. The Treaties shall cease to apply to the State in question from the date of entry into force of the withdrawal agreement or, failing that, two years after the notification referred to in paragraph 2, unless the European Council, in agreement with the Member State concerned, unanimously decides to extend this period. /4. For the purposes of paragraphs 2 and 3, the member of the European Council or of the Council representing the withdrawing Member State shall not participate in the discussions of the European Council or Council or in decisions concerning it. A qualified majority shall be defined in accordance with Article 238(3)(b) of the Treaty on the Functioning of the European Union. /5. If a State which has withdrawn from the Union asks to re-join, its request shall be subject to the procedure referred to in Article 49.

As things stand, the vote for Brexit indeed generated a strange feeling amongst analysts from the time of the decision forward, given that it can be interpreted by some as the failure of the integration process,[44] whilst for others, this option opens up the possibility of re-orienting the European Union without the British burden.[45] In this sense, the UK has been perceived similarly to a rock in the shoe of the European process. Furthermore, it should not be forgotten that for the UK itself, the withdrawal process from the European Union may necessarily be fatal to its own existence as we now know it, given that in Scotland—where the majority voted to remain—the all-too-apparent possibility of a new referendum to leave the UK has again been raised so as to later request admittance to the European Union as a sovereign state. In any event, and as Jorge Dezcallar has explained, "The first aim of Europeans is to ensure that Brexit is an exception and not a precedent. That will depend on the way in which negotiations with the United Kingdom proceed inasmuch as how the new northerly-southerly balance and the Franco-German balance within the EU are articulated".[46] With regards to Spain, one should not overlook the new situation concerning Gibraltar,[47] this being the moment, as Rock of Gibraltar analysts have pointed out regarding its co-sovereignty, for a first step towards resolving an age-old and inadmissible colonialism issue.

---

[44] Mangas Martín (2016, 427–437).

[45] Fernández Navarrete (2018, 326–342).

[46] Dezcallar (2017, 104–114).

[47] Mangas Martín (2016b, 3–16).

In fourth place, the territory of the European Union should continue to be known as a place of freedom and safety through effective action against Salafi jihadist terrorism,[48] which currently troubles, and in many cases, provokes terror in Europeans. This is why ensuring its utter defeat must be a priority. "In general, jihadist-Salafism affirms the duty of jihad for all Muslims. This is the core idea of their doctrine. There are local jihadists, such as in Palestine, who do not seek to establish a worldwide caliphate, and international jihadists, the idea to which members of Al-Qaida ascribe. The latter fight for the establishment of Islam throughout the world".[49]

Right now, the former is especially obvious in countries including the UK, France, Belgium and Germany, not to mention Spain. As indicated by experts, this is the reason why a more effective relationship between police and intelligence, security and media services in both European countries and their non-European allies is unquestionably necessary. In the words of Fernando Reinares, "As of right now, the jihadist threat in western Europe springs from two general sources: on the one hand, the so-called 'Islamic State' (ISIS), and on the other, Al-Qaeda and its branches and like-minded entities. A threat directly or indirectly related to Al-Qaeda existed up through 2013, the organisation having formed in 1988. For approximately twenty-eight years, this was the only framework for global jihadism. However, since 2014, the jihadist terrorist threat in western Europe has also stemmed from ISIS, comprised of what had previously been the Iraqi branch of Al-Qaeda, although now it is a competing organisation that has become its rival for hegemony in global jihadism".[50] This is the state of affairs. As Judy Dempsey states it, "Protecting [European] values and dealing with war [seem] almost a contradiction in terms. However, this is the challenge set before the European Union in the light of terrorism on the continent".[51,52]

Fifth and lastly (so as to avoid making this list an endless one), the members of the European Union must together find a coherent common solution to which all Member States agree on the migration—and therefore, necessarily and foremost, humanitarian—crisis.[53] It is estimated that one million people arrived abruptly to European territory in 2015, taking advantage of Turkey's laxity and the virtual power vacuum in Greece at that time. It is calculated that this number may have doubled through 2017. In the words of Michel Agier, "Today, the planet is home to 65 million refugees and displaced peoples. For want of reception policies, many of them are compelled to live in camps, as something akin to open-air prisons whose residents are deprived of basic rights".[54] The root of this need is found in the conflict scenarios experienced in the Middle and Near East (Afghanistan, Iraq, Syria ...), not to mention northern Africa (Libya) or the Sahel (Mali and other countries in the region). The latter are considered the southern border of Europe and therefore are the highest priority zones

---

[48] Balázs (2017, 26).

[49] Larroque (2016, 38).

[50] Reinares (2016, 52–53).

[51] Dempsey (2016, 28–31).

[52] T.N. Own translation from Spanish.

[53] Balázs (2017, 26–30) and Letta (2017, 147–159).

[54] Agier (2017, 15).

in terms of common security and defence policies. All of this directly affects all EU community countries, whose half-hearted resolve is generating much criticism and perpetuating a situation of intolerable suffering for migrants and refugees.

As explained in the Commission's July 2016 document,[55] "The European Union and the Refugee Crisis", we are reminded that "In the last 2 years, Europe has experienced the greatest mass movement of people since the Second World War". In such a difficult situation, the European Union has enacted a series of measures that address the root causes of this diaspora in order to focus the problem and resolve it to the degree possible. The European Union would thereby be providing "humanitarian assistance and development aid", be committed to the "rescue at sea" of displaced persons in the Mediterranean, and to "protecting the borders of the European Union" and fighting "criminal networks". It would also be promoting Member State actions to "relocate and resettle" asylum seekers and, likewise, "return irregular migrants with no right to stay in the EU to their home country", in addition to permanently supporting "agreement with Turkey" in order to prevent undesirable situations such as the one that took place during the summer of 2015. Additionally, the European Union is considering a reform of its rules on asylum, thus explained in the aforementioned factsheet: "Although the EU started to develop a common asylum policy in 1999, the rules were never designed to cope with a massive number of people arriving in a short space of time. New proposals are now on the table from the Commission to revise the existing laws in line with current and future needs. The basic principle will remain the same [meaning, pursuant to Regulation (EU) No. 604/2013, also known as the Dublin III Regulation, in force since 1 January 2014]—people should apply for asylum in the first EU Member State they enter unless they have family elsewhere—but whenever a Member State is overwhelmed, there must be solidarity and a fair sharing of responsibility within the EU".

3 Final Note (as a Provisional Conclusion)

The crossroads the European Union is facing having been presented together with the possible scenarios or paths forward, and the European Union being committed to responding to the great challenges of the present as well as those of the future, it can be asserted that the most desirable action would be, as has been stated before, to slowly yet steadily deepen the monetary and economic union currently in place. This is the great challenge to which all twenty-seven Member States must be committed, omitting the UK (although the threshold of thirty may be reached sooner than later considering the proposed integrations currently under negotiation). It should also be noted that this step would be in consonance with the aspirations of the founding fathers of the now almost 70-year-old European Community to found a community that guarantees peace amongst Europeans, is open to all states in Europe, is institutionally stable, promotes improved social and economic development and is

[55] Pinyol-Jiménez (2019, 68–74).

committed to democracy and human rights. This would be a European Union whose leaders, like Robert Schuman in 1963, would be able to continue to affirm to the Europeans of their time in 2023 (to create a round number) that "the balance sheet remains positive".

In this regard, and thus committed to said scenario, the open letter promoted by the University Institute for European Studies/CEU and presented to the Spanish and European public together for their opinion during the first quarter of 2017 in order to assert the European ideal on the 60th anniversary of the Treaty of Rome should be mentioned. Said letter, entitled "A genuine European Union to ensure welfare, security and democracy", states that "Democracy and the core values of the European modern civilisation are under attack. The European Union itself is questioned, although it ensured peace, democracy and welfare for decades", later exhorting EU leaders to "(...) match the vision of the Founders. They should open the way to the re-foundation of the EU on the basis of the European Parliament proposal (...)". In any case, beyond the words—re-found, reinvent, etc—the aspiration must be, as exemplified by the aforementioned open letter, to replenish and renovate the European ideal as it was founded, upon the three ideas that underpin the integration process: peace amongst Europeans, socio-economic well-being and good democratic governance. If we are determined to question the European Community process in progress since the 1950s (which, by the way, is about to celebrate seventy years in the making), everything we have achieved together—and that is no small amount if you look at it—would be destined to loss. In an atmosphere of collective amnesia, this could lead us to dust off the old spirits of division and conflict and—who knows?—re-concoct the brew that would push us towards a new collective catastrophe, a third Armageddon, when but one hundred years have passed since the first one. As stated at the outset of this work, to eradicate our worst thoughts and deeds, "If the European Union didn't exist, it would be necessary to invent it". Yet, it has been "invented", and it is on its feet. That it remains so is the task of all Europeans committed—in good faith, as has been said—to the European ideal in operation for nearly seventy years.

References

Agier, M. (2017). «Un mundo de campamentos». In *Le Monde diplomatique–en español*.

Balázs, P. (2017). «Trilemas europeos, de Schengen al crecimiento económico». Vanguardia. Dossier: *Unión Europea: refundación o desintegración*, no. 64.

Becerril Atienza, B. (2018). «La Declaración Schuman y la comunidad Europea del Carbón y del Acero: un nuevo modelo». In E. Nasarre, F. Aldecoa, & M. A. Benedicto (coords.), *Europa como tarea. A los sesenta años de los Tratados de Roma y a los setenta del Congreso de Europa de La Haya*. Madrid: Marcial Pons.

Beneyto, J. Mª. (1999). *Tragedia y razón. Europa en el pensamiento español del siglo XX*. Madrid: Taurus.

Coudenhove-Kalergi, R. N. (2002). *Paneuropa* –«Estudio preliminar» de R. Martín de la Guardia and G. Á. Pérez Sánchez. Madrid: Taurus.

Demesmay, C. (2017). «El tándem franco-alemán en una Europa en crisis». *Política Exterior, 177*.

Dempsey, J. (2016). «La paz europea hecha añicos; los valores amenazados». *Política Exterior, 171*.
Dezcallar, J. (2017). «El Brexit, una oportunidad para Europa». *Política Exterior, 176*.
Fernández Navarrete, D. (2018). *Historia de la Unión Europea, de los orígenes al Brexit*. Madrid: Ediciones UAM.
Gutiérrez-Peris, D. (2019). «Francia ante el reto europeo, ¿"chevalier seul"?». *Política Exterior, 188*.
Kerikmäe, T., Troitiño, D. R., & Shumilo, O. (2019). An idol or an ideal? A case study of Estonian e-Governance: Public perceptions, myths and misbeliefs. *Acta Baltica Historiae et Philosophiae scientiarum, 7*(1).
Kershaw, I. (2019). *Ascenso y crisis. Europa, 1950–2017. Un camino incierto*. Barcelona: Crítica.
Khadesr, B. (2017). «1957–2017: el futuro ya no es lo que era». *Política Exterior, 176*.
Larroque, A.-C. (2016). *Geopolítica de los islamismos*. Madrid: Rialp.
Leonard, M. (2017a). «El futuro de Europa», Vanguardia. Dossier: *Unión Europea: refundación o desintegración*, no. 64.
Leonard, M. (2017b). «El papel de España en la próxima UE». *Política Exterior, 180*.
Letta, E. (2017). *Hacer Europa y no la guerra. Una apuesta europeísta frente a Trump y el brexit*. Barcelona: Península.
López-Aranda, R. (2017). «La Unión Europea, entre lo deseable y lo posible». *Política Exterior, 176*.
Lowe, K. (2016). *Continente salvaje. Europa después de la Segunda Guerra Mundial*. Barcelona: Galaxia Gutenberg.
Mangas Martín, A. (2016a). «*Posbrexit*: Una Europa confusa, entre el desánimo y la incertidumbre». *Revista de Derecho Comunitario Europeo, 54*.
Mangas Martín, A. (2016b). «¿Brexit? Escenarios internacionales y Gibraltar». Working paper 9/2016 dated 17 June. *Real Instituto Elcano*.
Márkaris, P. (2012). *La espada de Damocles*. Tusquets: Barcrelona.
Martín de la Guardia, R., & Pérez Sánchez, G. A. (2005). *La Unión Soviética: de la perestroika a la desintegración*. Madrid: Istmo.
Martín de la Guardia, R., & Pérez Sánchez, G. A. (2007). *La Europa Balcánica: Yugoslavia desde la Segunda Guerra Mundial hasta nuestros días*. Madrid: Síntesis.
Martín de la Guardia, R., & Pérez Sánchez, G. A. (2009). «Las sucesivas ampliaciones. De la Europa de los Seis a la Europa de los Veintisiete». In J. Mª. Beneyto Pérez (Director), J. Maillo González-Orús, & B. Becerril Atienza (Coordinators), *Tratado de Derecho y Políticas de la Unión Europea* –Volume I: *Desarrollo histórico y caracteres básicos de la Unión Europea. Naturaleza, valores, principios y competencias*, Pamplona, Aranzadi-Thomson Reuters.
Martín de la Guardia, R., & Pérez Sánchez, G. A. (2017). *La Unión Soviética ante el espejo de las comunidades Europeas. De la Europa sovietizada a la «casa común» europea (1957-1988)*. Valladolid: Ediciones Universidad de Valladolid.
Martín de la Torre, V. (2015). *Europa, un salto a lo desconocido*. Madrid: Encuentro.
Ortega y Gasset, J. (1986). *La rebelión de las masas*. Madrid: Espasa-Calpe.
Otero-Iglesias, M. (2017). «El euro como vínculo social». *Política Exterior, 176*.
Pérez Sánchez, G. A. (2001). «El ideal europeísta: de la modernidad a la contemporaneidad». In R. Martín de la Guardia, G. A. Pérez Sánchez (coords.), *Historia de la integración europea*. Barcelona: Ariel.
Pérez Sánchez, G. A. (2007). «La "nueva Europa": de la caída del comunismo a la integración en la Unión Europea». In S. Forner (Ed.), *La construcción de Europa: de las «guerras civiles» a la «unificación»*. Madrid: Biblioteca Nueva.
Pinyol Jiménez, G. (2019). «Deconstrucción de la política europea de inmigración». *Política Exterior, 187*.
Ramiro Troitino, D., & Pando Ballesteros, M. D. L. P. (2017). Churchill's European integration model. *Revista de Occidente, 433*, 57–71.
Reinares, F. (2016). «Amenaza yihadista en Europa, ¿qué hacer?». *Política Exterior, 171*.

Rodríguez-Aguilera de Prat, C. (2012). *Euro-escepticismo, Euro-fobia y Euro-criticismo. Los partidos radicales de la derecha y la izquierda ante la Unión Europea*. Barcelona: Huygens Editorial.

Ruiz Navarro Pinar, J. L. (2018). «El futuro de Europa: hacer mucho más todos juntos». In E. Nasarre, F. Aldecoa, & M. A. Benedicto (coords.), *Europa como tarea. A los sesenta años de los Tratados de Roma y a los setenta del Congreso de Europa de La Haya*. Madrid: Marcial Pons.

Schuman, R. (2006). *Para Europa*. Madrid: Ediciones Encuentro.

Soto Carmona, Á. (coord.). (2019). *La democracia herida. La tormenta perfecta*. Madrid: Marcial Pons.

Steiner, G. (2012). *La idea de Europa*. Madrid: Siruela.

Suárez Fernández, L. (2003). *Cristianismo y europeidad. Una reflexión histórica ante el tercer milenio*. Pamplona: EUNSA.

Troitiño, D. R. (2017). Jean Monnet before the first European community: A historical perspective and critic. *Trames, 21*(3), 193–213.

Troitiño, D. R., Kerikmäe, T., & Chochia, A. (Eds.). (2018). *Brexit: History, reasoning and perspectives*. Berlin: Springer.

Zantovsky, M. (2016). *Havel. Una vida*. Barcelona: Galaxia Gutenberg.

Zantovsky, M. (2017). «De vuelta a Europa». *Política Exterior* (January/February).

Zweig, S. (2017). *La desintoxicación moral de Europa y otros escritos políticos*. Barcelona: Plataforma Editorial.

The Concerns of the European Citizens

Nationalist Populism: New Political Parties in Europe. Their Ideas, Governments and Support for a Less-Integrated Europe

Ricardo Martín de la Guardia

Abstract The rise of nationalist populism during the last two European parliamentary elections calls for a rigorous analysis of these new political forces. From Euro-scepticism to Euro-phobia, they criticise a large portion of the underpinnings and policies fostered by the EU.

Keywords Populism · European integration · European politics · European Union · Euro-scepticism

1 Introduction

The prominent advance of nationalist-populist groups stirred commotion among the Old World's traditional political parties during the 2014 elections to the European Parliament. Euro-sceptic forces won out in three countries with solid democratic histories: France, the UK and Denmark. The French National Front was accorded 24 members to the European Parliament (MEPs) with nearly 25% of the vote, while the UK Independence Party (UKIP) won the same number of seats with 26.7%. The Danish *Danks Folkesparti* (People's Party) won the same percentage as UKIP and sent four representatives to the EU Parliament. Putting aside the differences among them, around 120 of the newly elected MEPs across Europe represented Euro-sceptic or clearly Euro-phobic parties.

In the election held five years later, on 26 May 2019, which drew a 51% voter turnout, fear of an even larger increase in these parties was eased, but they managed to maintain their positions: the nationalist-populists were here to stay. In Germany, *Alternative für Deutschland* (AfD)'s numbers receded compared to their general elections, but they still won 10% of the vote. On the other hand, and despite the fierce critiques of its adversaries and the European political "Establishment", 9.1 million Italians supported Matteo Salvini's *Lega* party, which won 34.3% of the vote. The extreme right in France, now called *Rassemblement National* (National Rally), remains under the same direction, that of Marine Le Pen, who came out

R. M. de la Guardia (✉)
Instituto de Estudios Europeos, Universidad de Valladolid, Valladolid, Spain
e-mail: guardia@fyl.uva.es

D. Ramiro Troitiño et al. (eds.), *The EU in the 21st Century*,
https://doi.org/10.1007/978-3-030-38399-2_3

on top again with 23.3%. The Brexit Party likewise won, having been founded just shortly beforehand by the impervious Nigel Farage. With 30.5% of the vote, his party sought to break with the EU as soon as possible and take back their country's full sovereignty.

Turning to the central-eastern section of the European map, Hungarian President Viktor Orbán's *Fidesz* party squarely earned 52% of the vote, an only slightly lesser percentage the one gained five years before. In Poland, the *Prawo i Sprawiedliwosc* (Law and Justice) party similarly won 45.6% of votes and 27 seats.

The specific stances of some of these groups aside, the most significant parliamentary group on the political spectrum in this regard is unequivocally the Europe of Nations and Freedom group, which moved from 36 to 57 seats, supported by Le Pen's Rally and Salvini's *Lega*.

The first question that comes to mind is how parties with a generally short lifespan, that were marginal groups on their countries' political playing fields until recently, that are sometimes linked to an extreme right much reviled by the media, and that do not enjoy economic resources significant enough to create dependent networks have managed to weave themselves so tightly into the fabric of their respective communities. However, this analysis does not address these groupings' development in relation to their respective national contexts. It is, instead, a study of their discourse concerning the European Union. These groups are characterised by their constant criticism of the institutions in Brussels. They fluctuate between Euro-scepticism and Euro-phobia with nuances that sometimes come to be their distinctive hallmarks. As will be observed, some nationalist-populist organisations aspire to change the competencies and workings of EU organisations yet accept the prospect of maintaining the EU, while others would like to leave as quickly as possible or even dismantle the EU from within.

In short, the latest parliamentary elections have established the nationalist-populists, but they have not achieved the necessary proportion of 33% to block normal European legislative processes. On the other hand, and as occurred in 2014, the variety of positions among the Euro-sceptic faction is an obstacle to their acting in unison. During the last legislature, the parties from this spectrum arranged themselves into three groups as well as other formations that voluntarily chose not to join them.

The Europe of Nations and Freedom group is currently the leader within this ideological family, occupying 69 seats. Matteo Salvini's *Lega* and Marine Le Pen's National Rally lead the alliance of nationalist-populists with 22 seats, followed by 11 MEPs from AfD, three from Austria's Freedom Party, the representatives associated with Belgium's *Vlaams Belang,* and two members from the Czech Republic's Freedom and Direct Democracy party. In turn, the Europe of Freedom and Direct Democracy group unites the 29 representatives from the Brexit Party with the 14 representatives from Italy's Five Star Movement. Other MEPs are considered "non-attached" and yet others belong to different groups. For example, Poland's Law and Justice party is associated with British Conservatives, together with the Netherlands' radical right-wing Forum for Democracy within the European Conservatives and Reformists group. Meanwhile, Viktor Orbán's *Fidesz* continues to be affiliated with the European People's Party.

2 Nationalist Populism: Ideological Foundations and Critiques of the European Union

Since at least the end of the 1990s, and more clearly since the 2008 crisis, Western Europe's system of political parties has shown signs of burnout. The main political forces that had comprised governments since 1945 were connecting less with populations that were progressively more critical of its programmes and performance. The traditional discourse of the liberals, conservatives and social democrats clashed with a reality distinct from that of decades before. Structural problems such as unemployment and corruption in some countries combined with other issues, such as mass immigration, lack of opportunity, and detachment from local culture associated with globalisation, problems which—whether real or perceived as real by citizens—created uncertainty, if not angst.

In the light of these issues, nationalist-populists launched into the political arena with simple manifestos that were bereft of solid theoretical grounding. Their easy slogans and formulas have very significant repercussions among a part of European society that is very concerned that its way of life and purchasing power may disappear owing to the failures of an economic and political elite whose sole north star is the maintenance of its own privilege.

The climax of this race to the abyss is perceived in the ineptitude of Brussels' bureaucrats. It has been quite simple for nationalist-populists to identify the European Union as a super-state whose only aim is to sustain itself and provide advantages for civil servants and political leaders, all the while citizens endure the onslaught of recurring crises. If, as claimed by these extremist organisations, said crises create an intolerable increase in inequality that widens the gap between rich and poor, the globalisation promoted in Brussels is useless to mitigate socioeconomic disparities. *Au contraire*, economic globalisation would have itself induced the dismantling of European industry and, in consequence, an end to the labour market regulations hard-won by decades of fights for the security of the working class.

Globalisation would also have provoked cutbacks in the welfare state which, according to nationalist-populist discourse, would have been accepted by European State governments under pressure from Brussels. Industrial outsourcing, increased unemployment, the loss of rights that had been won, austerity policies—in sum, the most negative consequences of the latest economic crisis—would frame the European Union as the guilty party and the leaders of Member States as its essential accomplices. Even though these elites avail of the invaluable support of media power (whose main function has been to justify their actions), new communications technologies have opened doors for alternative information formats that dwindle the monopoly-like control of news media. Thus, intense use of social media and alternative mass communications tools by populist groups has made their messages reach the public. In the meantime, they accuse journalists, radio broadcasters and television stations of being complicit in the system.

It is, therefore, thanks to these extremist parties that the general public is acquiring a critical sense of awareness that is very distinct from conservative discourse in the lax example provided by conventional political groups ranging from the liberals to the socialists. In response to the anxiety-inducing uncertain future driven by far-flung, assimilationist institutions based in Brussels that are obsessed with austerity, the populist right renationalises policy, thereby returning to the familiar and reclaiming competencies for the national States so as to correct the erroneous direction urged on by EU institutions.

While part of their discourse continues in synchrony with the tradition of the old-guard far-right, nationalist-populist groups have made a qualitative jump with respect to the old parties' manifestos and attitudes. Most of the new radical right does not reject the democratic system but instead uses it to criticise some of the system's own foundations in order to modify its structure. Nevertheless, it should be noted that their programme does not reject the established order (e.g. economic foundations). Rather, it desires to enact profound reform. Strong criticism of European Union functioning lies along precisely this line of action.

We agree with Mudde and Kaltwasser on their characterisation of national-populist movements, whose primary characteristic is the *nativism* that these movements believe the State should preserve via the maintenance of national homogeneity. Only the country's nationals would enjoy the full rights of citizenship, thus preventing the loss of the values identified with the country in contrast with foreigners. The enemy may be found inside the state, but they are outside of the nation. The second characteristic is *authoritarianism*, both in terms of these parties' argument for maintaining social order as the supreme good and in terms of being guided by strong, charismatic leaders. Finally, they share *populism* to the extent that they divide society into conflicting groups that are always opposed: the people and the corrupt elite.[1] These parties would champion the *authentic* interests of the common people as opposed to the manipulative actions of economic and political elites. It is the latter who have controlled the system to their own exclusive benefit up to now.

In this sense, the populist right uses inclusion/exclusion as one of their basic criteria for political action. The "we" (the "true nation") stands in opposition to everyone else (the "other"), defined as those with a different vision of reality than the one espoused by the populists, whose perspective is therefore rendered unnegotiable. As a result, illegal immigration (and sometimes legal immigration), as well as multicultural principles, become the focus of constant criticism because these are the factors that disrupt the supposed homogeneity of the homeland nation. Ultimately, and despite their adaptation to the current day and age, the main point of reference for these parties continues to be defence of the fatherland and its cultural traditions. Language and even religion, on occasion, serve as the cement that glues the national community together. The defence of identity and sovereignty justifies the reproach of the European Union as a power structure that is alien to the true interests and concerns of European countries and whose objective is to sustain perks for the politicians and civil servants who have shaped Brussels around their own privileged lifestyles. Flaws and weaknesses are blamed on this "European super-state", whose poor performance has a negative effect on the daily lives of citizens. Excessive bureaucracy, centralist

[1] Mudde and Kaltwasser (2013).

decision-making, irresponsible meddling in national economic policy and cultural homogenisation are some of these negative consequences.[2]

3 Islamophobia and Anti-multiculturalism

While Islamophobia was certainly a component of the radical right before the attacks on the Twin Towers, it undoubtedly intensified from 2001 forward. These parties easily relate Islam with the loss of rights for women, the gay community and other parts of society in order to prove how Muslim communities in Europe not only fail to integrate into Western culture but that they furthermore isolate themselves voluntarily, all the while benefitting from the generous resources made available by governments. Muslims are transformed into Trojan horses who slowly mine the ability of European civilisation to live together in harmony. In other cases, this immigrant group is converted into a breeding ground for terrorist groups. Likewise, the populist right flatly rejects the integration of Turkey into the EU, viewing this country as heir to the Ottoman empire, whose values and lifestyle are foreign to European sensibilities, as can be demonstrated by the majority of the millions of émigrés who live in Germany. This is, anyway, the way in which *PEGIDA (Patriotische Europäergegen die Islamisierung des Abendlandes)* [Patriotic Europeans Against the Islamisation of the Occident] understands things. This organisation arose in Dresden during the autumn of 2014 with the overriding aim of demonstrating their radical opposition to what they understood as the destruction of harmonious co-existence in Germany. Increased Muslim immigration, together with émigrés who arrived decades before, endangered community life and even the continuity of the German nation. This group vehemently criticises the asylum policy chaired by Angela Merkel and promotes the selective expulsion of immigrants as well as a freeze on the entry of new contingents. This is undeniably the most exemplary instance of how rejection of the Muslim population can turn into a nationalist-populist movement.[3]

Reminiscent of the events transpired due to public pressure with regard to the fall of the German Democratic Republic, their organised marches in Dresden, Berlin and other cities won the support of thousands of citizens from a wide variety of social backgrounds: a unique mix of youth with extreme-right identities from traditional families or individuals with no particular defined political affiliation. The *PEGIDA* phenomenon was very influential in the creation of the AfD nationalist-populist party.[4]

Dutch Islamophobia has been particularly consequential in the growth of the extreme right, which had been virtually irrelevant in the Netherlands at the end of the 1990s due to prevalent multiculturalism in society, among other reasons. In this case, the ascent of a party adhering to the ideology in question is strongly linked to the personality of its leader, Pim Fortuyn. Openly gay with a background in the

---

[2]Rodríguez-Aguilera de Prat (2012), p. 138.

[3]Çakir (2016), pp. 149–162.

[4]Speit (2016).

leftist tradition, his unique progressive aura partially protected him from acquiring an image based on his criticism of Islam, to which he attributed a wholistic elimination of freedoms in addition to an inability—and refusal—to integrate into Western society. He was assassinated in 2002, a tragic turn of events that assuredly influenced the 17% vote won by the "Pim Fortuyn" list during the legislative elections held that year.[5]

Years later, former liberal legislator Geert Wilders founded the *Partij voor de Vzijheid* (Freedom Party) in defence of the rights and freedoms threatened by the invasion of non-Europeans. With robust rhetoric, he advocated to close Muslim schools, stop the entry of Muslim immigrants and eliminate financial assistance to Muslims so that these resources would return to the social classes most affected by the crisis. Not unlike similar parties, his manifestos pushed for the return to a domestic currency as opposed to the euro and strong support for national industry.[6]

In the 2014 European elections, his party won 13% of the vote, a result that was essentially repeated in the domestic legislative elections of March 2017. It garnered fewer votes than the number predicted by surveys, but in the light of the leader's xenophobic discourse, the result cannot be regarded as a failure.

As has been stated, it is precisely the defence of national traditions with a central focus on language that constitutes a substantial part of nationalist-populist discourse, along with a fight against multiculturalism, which expunges the nation's own characteristics. The universalism preached by parties maintaining their liberal roots is considered a pernicious doctrine that refutes the essential nature of distinct national communities. Regional and local diversity, customs and traditions, as well as respect for ancestral legacies all demonstrate the ways in which unity is not incompatible with diversity when the latter respects the nation's spiritual foundations.[7] Instead of defending autochthonous peoples, both European institutions and their Member States spend countless resources on sponsoring failed integration policies for immigrants who, instead of integrating, take advantage of these programmes in order to strengthen their own identities. That is, when they aren't propitiating Islamic terrorism.

It is undeniable that immigration from outside of Europe—especially from parts of Africa associated with the Near and Middle East—have meant a qualitative leap, inasmuch as they are discordant with both the image and the internal composition of the population of many European countries. Muslims are used by nationalist-populist discourse as a paradigm of non-integration in a host society. They are the disruptive element that inserts foreign behavioural patterns into Western values.

In Germany, the success of right-wing populist groups had not found their footing before the AfD's gains in the 2014 European elections. Just months after their appearance on the public landscape in the spring of 2013, they won 7% of the votes cast in 2014. Likewise and despite the media's caustic campaigning against them on national and local levels, as well as the criticism launched at them by the rest of the parties on

---

[5]Camus and Lebourg (2016), p. 234.

[6]Troitino and Faerber (2019).

[7]Poirer (2007), pp. 57–58.

the left and the right, AfD managed to enter many of Germany's regional parliaments with results hovering around 10%, and even higher in Saxony and Thuringia. This nationalist party, averse to immigration and the mass arrival of refugees, emphasises economic policies in their programme even more intensely than very similar groups within their own ideological field, such as the Dutch Freedom Party.[8] AfD's discursive components comprise a patriotism based on reinstating the family as Germany's focal point, boosting the national production economy, warding off the threat of international outsourcing, strengthening its agrarian and industrial power, and reinstating the Deutsche mark as the national currency. Their call to return to traditional societal and political formulas effectively carves out space among CDU/CSU voters. However, it is not just this group, but youth and people in the middle class who are disenchanted with the direction the Christian democrat government who have responded favourably to the party's proposals.

With respect to European politics, AfD vehemently excoriated the economic bailouts, arguing for the prevention of an even greater economic burden from falling upon the shoulders of German taxpayers. To reverse these situations, AfD proposes the transfer of competencies from Brussels to the German federal parliament, thereby thinning out EU bureaucracy.

The most revealing example of militant anti-Europeanism is the UK Independence Party (UKIP). Founded in 1993, the party arose from dissidents within a conservative sector, such as university professors and economists, among others. In other words, this was a group of intellectuals who openly censured the consequences of becoming party to the Treaty of Maastricht. They grew from a small faction to a burgeoning voter base until their zenith in the 2014 European elections, when they won the most votes of any party in the UK. The cornerstone of their message: leaving the EU. They built a populist discourse based on rigid anti-migratory policy to preserve and extend the national values being diluted in the welter of British multiculturalism.[9] According to experts, the British electorate succumbed to such a simple proposal—one with plenty of "anti-" and sparse theoretical foundation—primarily because of the profound chasm between conventional parties' promises and attitudes.[10]

Nigel Farage, UKIP's controversial leader, left the party at the end of 2016, having achieved his fundamental goal: the UK's exit from the European Union. However, with the delay induced by the extension of negotiations between London and Brussels, Farage propelled the creation of a new organisation at the start of 2019. With the unequivocal name "Brexit Party", he again won the European elections held May of that year. Having gained 30.5% of the vote, he increased the next five years' EU representation to send a total of 29 representatives to the European Parliament.

Meanwhile, Marine Le Pen's success was remarkable in the 2014 European elections in France, in which she campaigned with a very eloquent slogan: *"NON à Bruxelles, OUI à la France!"* ["NO to Brussels, YES to France!"]. Her triumph cannot be attributed (as simplistically as much of the media would have it) to the

---

[8]Bebnowski (2015).

[9]Ramiro and Pando (2017).

[10]Goodwin and Milazzo (2015).

disenchantment of European Union citizens after the economic crisis or to the unquestionable charisma of the party leader. A very significant percentage of the French population opted for a party that would curtail legal immigration, pressure Brussels to harden border controls outside the EU and promote the national economy. Apart from nostalgics and chauvinists, her vote was extraordinarily varied: the youth vote, unemployed people, the intellectual middle class, etc. all attracted by a project to reinstate the social well-being lost in the name of putting an end to the austerity policies fostered by EU and civil servant elites. Neither party activists nor the electorate were mere one-off anti-system neofascists. They encompassed diverse strata of French society. After this victory, the 15th National Front Congress at the end of November 2015 symbolised the culmination of Marine's ascent, which led to a very significant changeover of personnel in France's highest offices, backed 100%.[11]

4 The Populist Influence on Centre-Right Parties

It is helpful to note how part of the radical right's discourse has influenced centre-right parties, who have modified some of their policies on extremely important questions for European citizens accordingly. The fear of a progressive loss of their electoral base to more radical alternatives has, to a certain degree, conditioned the centre-right, forcing them to shift to more extreme positions on challenging subjects such as emigration, security and identity loss.[12] The consequence of the pressure exerted by a loss for centrist and conservative forces in favour of nationalist-populist parties is increasingly hard-line rhetoric (and even legislation) on these issues in order to prevent an even greater decline in support for conventional parties.

Events in Finland serve as a recent example. The leader of the True Finns Party has displayed his ability to play with ambiguity, a skill that allowed him entry into the Finnish government after their 2015 elections. On the one hand, Timo Soini's discourse was radical when it came to denouncing immigration and the loss of the country's identity and influence in the European Union. However, he delved deeply into a social programme, advocating proposals for improvement based on an increase in social expenses. His aim was to spread his influence in the mid- and low social strata. Reducing expenses in the form of multi-cultural initiatives and assistance, as well as the bailout to Greece, were amalgamated into Soini's political discourse for that purpose. He did not go so far as to request an exit from the European Union when he became Minister of Foreign Affairs, instead working together with former European Commissioner Olli Rehn (Minister of Economic Affairs). In fact, Soini's social proposals in the coalition government achieved important gains: liberalism in economic affairs and strict immigration policy.[13]

---

[11] Martín de la Guardia (2018), p. 181.

[12] Hamulák (2018).

[13] Arter (2010), pp. 484–504.

In some post-communist democracies, specifically Hungary and Poland, a number of nationalist-populist movements' focal points (immigration, relationships with EU institutions, etc.) have been carried over into the government plan. In Hungary, *Jobbik (JOBBoldali Ifjúsági Közösség)* [Association of Right-Wing Youth], was started in 1999. It developed into a political party in October 2003, when Hungarian nationalism voiced its proposals to reinstate the country's Christian roots and return to the idea of community based on the pillar of family as a national value. They wanted to reclaim competencies from the EU in order to create domestic economic policies capable of propitiating the prosperity of companies with Hungarian capital that use national energy resources. The 2008 crisis made the intrinsic deficiencies of globalisation plain to see; its most damaging consequences were felt in the most economically vulnerable citizens, whereas large capitalist corporations came out of the crisis even stronger. So it is that association with the European Union is another key point in *Jobbik*'s discourse; the most radical critiques aimed at Brussels attack its bureaucratic nature, distant from people's daily problems.

The party took its first step forward during the European elections of June 2009, when it won nearly 15% of the vote and three seats. This is where the influence of the far right's advances on the governing political party is most evident; the centre-right ended up adopting some of *Jobbik*'s proposals to prevent a possible drain of votes to the nationalist-populist group. National-populist "contagion" radicalises the traditional parties' discourse and political activity, thus reducing the distance between their positions.[14]

With Hungary on the edge of collapse in 2010, the country's serious economic problems coincided with *Fidesz*' return to power. The party led by Viktor Orbán was first created as a moderate centre-right organisation in line with the rest of European parties ascribing to this ideology. However, some of its opinions were gradually radicalised. With a victory at the polls in 2010—a particularly difficult moment for Hungary—*Fidesz* adopted a more Euro-sceptic stance, shifting the blame to Brussels, and therefore escalating the party's nationalist tone. This was also how it tried to compensate for *Jobbik*'s entry into the Hungarian national parliament, one of whose stickling points from the very start had been criticism of the European Union. Suddenly, *Fidesz* had an electoral competitor who was simplistically using the EU as a scapegoat, but who yielded success for *Fidesz* among an electorate who were generally unaware of the importance of European aid. Moreover, *Jobbik* played the European Union withdrawal card, in response to which the incumbent felt the need to take a more critical stance regarding the economic crisis itself and the challenges it faced in redefining institutional architecture amidst the confusion in Brussels. President Orbán pushed for the approval of a new constitution—the standing document in effect since the start of 2012—whose authoritarian features astounded European colleagues.[15]

The authoritarian trend is clear. Despite the dissent voiced both in and outside of Hungary, *Fidesz* remains a member of the European Popular Party. Over recent years,

[14]Van Spanje (2006), pp. 563–586.

[15]Krekó and Mayer (2015), p. 195.

Fidesz has adopted a discourse that overlaps with *Jobbik*'s distinctive principles as they have been declared to date, and according to *Jobbik*, Europe's decadence can only be overcome by a return to Christian roots, traditional family and by preventing the arrival of Muslim immigrants to Hungary, which could erode the Hungarian nation's true values.

At odds with cosmopolitanism and multiculturalism, the fanatical defence of language is an integral part of "border politics". What better than the language—and especially so with a language as distinctive as Hungarian—to affirm the essence of a homogenous culture as the substance of the nation-state? That is why linguistic policy is an essential part of both *Jobbik's* and *Fidesz'* discourses and activities.[16]

In Poland, the ultra-conservative Law and Justice party won out in the 2014 European Parliament as well as in the presidential elections the following year. The way in which the party's manifesto has developed since their start reflects the enormous and unique weight of Catholicism in the discourse of the Polish radical right. They depict their country's traditional values as inextricably united to the Catholic faith and Church, together with the idea of traditional family as the bedrock of society. In response to the triumph of secularisation in Europe, Italy's *Lega* and Poland's Law and Justice party believe that the moral and spiritual decline of the Old World are evident in the merely mercantile-minded European Union.[17] They believe that the EU's moral relativism has infected the Polish nation, which must remain on its guard to avoid succumbing to decadence.

The traumatic history of Poland demands a special sense of patriotism from its leaders. They must be committed to traditions and use them as the basis for actively developing and enacting policy. In effect (albeit to a greater or lesser degree depending on the specific point in time), the polarisation between traditionalism and liberalism has forged one of the ideological debates of our time. Poland's nationalist-populist right has reacted to the controversy by reinforcing the social section of its programme (in line with the social doctrine of the Church and John Paul II's encyclicals) and juxtaposed it with the fragmentary liberalism of its opponents to the centre and the left.[18]

Together with powerful leaders' criticism of the media's "excessive" freedom of information and attacks on university autonomy, the advance of authoritarian policies put into place by the Law and Justice party as the current Polish government leader is cause for much concern in Brussels. Ever since the legislative elections of October 2015, authorities in Poland—a country generally considered to be one of the most exemplary success stories after European integration spread eastward—have defended significant discrepancies with the EU. The European Parliament even met in a single-issue session on 13 September 2016 to debate what it considered to be the Polish government's "authoritarian drift". Moreover, the European Commission reminded Warsaw ten months later in July 2017 that it was studying the option of activating Treaty Article 7, which allows for the temporary suspension of a country's

---

[16] Wodak (2015), p. 74.

[17] Kerikmäe et al. (2019).

[18] Martín de la Guardia and Pérez Sánchez (2019), p. 207.

membership to the EU. Said law may only be applied upon a "serious breach" of the rule of law, a phrase which expresses the severity of the situation. In the end, unanimity was not reached in the European Council after Viktor Orbán's administration declared their support for Warsaw.

5 Conclusions

The loss of trust in politics in the conventional sense, as an instrument by which to resolve problems and improve people's living conditions, was underscored by the economic crisis triggered in 2008. Because of their failure to supply a precise and effective answer, European institutions lost the little confidence that millions of Europeans entrusted in them. Euro-sceptic and Euro-phobic parties to the right of the political spectrum that had hardly been relevant in European countries except in very specific cases grew quickly, gaining popularity among a public that was very willing to entertain criticism of Brussels. Corruption, bureaucracy and removal from citizens' real problems were the centrepieces of nationalist-populist discourse, one that attempted to discredit the EU as a system that already lacked transparency. In the interim, these parties opposed these hapless practices named with proclamations of the return of politics to the common streets. They spoke of direct contact between people and their representatives that would supersede a mere ballot count every four or five years.

In general, all nationalist-populists advocate open-market economies, but always with some restrictions. They criticise the cross-border neoliberalism of the EU and assert welfare chauvinism. The globalisation accepted and promoted by the competent EU community institutions would fly in the face of the solvency of various national economic sectors, instead favouring the illogical and grim competition of EU State economies among themselves, with a consequent loss of economic muscle. In exchange, there would be scandalous profits for international corporations, well-removed from the suffering caused by unemployment and the loss of purchasing power for citizens. The solution for these problems and the rest of the challenges created by Brussels' intrusion into the public spheres of the countries in question resides in the recuperation of economic policy-making competencies by each respective government.

The losers of globalisation constitute a social stratus that is susceptible to manipulation by the simplified discourse of populism. Marginalised from the benefits of the EU process, their gaze returns to the domestic State, to whom they look as the sole possible protector of their interests; the local wins out against the global. The protector-State gathers the vulnerable with open arms and rebuilds the national identity that has dissolved amidst the anonymous corridors in Brussels. As a counterpoint to this loss, nationalist-populists are proposing a "Europe of fatherlands" that can supplant the homogenising centralism of European institutions.

The idea of nation is consequently an essential central point in these movements' discourse. A set of eastern European societies felt the need to rediscover their identity after decades of submission to the USSR. The fallacy of internationalism and the solidarity of brother nations preached by the communist parties having broken down, their transition to democracy opened the doors to the recovery of strong nationalist sentiment. That transition contrasted with these countries' quick integration into the European Union, a power structure that seized competencies from States that had so recently recovered full sovereignty.

The identity dimension is therefore fundamental to these parties. The external enemy (globalisation, the EU) and internal enemy (émigrés, ethnic minorities) attempt to minimise the natural essence of the nation so that it can be subjected to the spurious interests of the economic and political elite, who only seek to perpetuate their power through their conventional interpretations of reality. The constant invocation of "nation" contrasted with "establishment" means that right-wing populists construct both physical and mental walls to protect what they identify as distinctly their own. Likewise, they appeal to fear in order to align stereotypes of enemies, whether internal or external, and strengthen the sense of belonging to a national community.

In any event, nationalist-populists do not negate the validity of democracy. They understand elections as the path to power or, if unsuccessful, as a way of influencing decision-making from within parliament. Legislative changes should allow the system to be modified to fit their policies and interests; even if said legal modifications are radical, they would comply with law. In this sense, it seems undeniable that these parties have influenced the transformations that have taken place in post-communist democracies, specifically in Poland and Hungary. Some of their most visible concerns (immigration, identity policy, relationships with EU institutions, etc.) have become part of government agendas to a greater or lesser degree, as has been observed. Not only that: their attitude has obliged conventional forces to take stances on especially delicate problems that they had hitherto glossed over to avoid making defined statements.

However, observation of the nationalist-populist parties that have become part of coalition governments reveals that they have softened their anti-systemic positions in terms of economic policy and adapted to liberal policies, while still true that these policies are nuanced with attacks on international outsourcing and budgetary support for social programmes. On the other hand, their profoundly nationalistic discourse has remained unscathed as a primary distinguishing badge, one that is opposed to immigration and critical of the transfer of competencies to Brussels. In conclusion, it has been shown that criticism of the European Union is one of the main elements of the nationalist-populist discourse framework.

References

Arter, D. (2010). The breakthrough of another West European populist party? The case of the true finns. *Government and Opposition, 45*(4), 484–504.
Bebnowski, D. (2015). *Die Alternative für Deutschland. Aufstieg und gesellschaftliche Repräsentanz einer rechten populistischen Partei*. Berlin: Springer.
Çakir, N. (2016). PEGIDA: Islamfeindlichkeit aus der Mitte der Gesellschaft. In A. Häusler (Ed.), *Die Alternative für Deutschland. Programmatik, Entwicklung und politische Verortung* (pp. 149–162). Berlin: Springer.
Camus, J.-Y., & Lebourg, N. (2016). *Les droites extrèmes en Europe*. Seuil.
Goodwin, M., & Milazzo, C. (2015). *UKIP. Inside the Campaign to Redraw the Map of British Politics*. Oxford: Oxford University Press.
Hamulák, O. (2018). La carta de los derechos fundamentales de la union europea y los derechos sociales. *Estudios Constitucionales, 16*(1), 167–186.
Kerikmäe, T., Troitiño, D. R., & Shumilo, O. (2019). An idol or an ideal? A case study of Estonian e-Governance: Public perceptions, myths and misbeliefs. *Acta Baltica Historiae et Philosophiae scientiarum, 7*(1).
Krekó, P., & Mayer, G. (2015). Transforming hungary-together? An analysis of the *Fidesz-Jobbik Relationship*. In M. Minkenberg (Ed.), *Transforming the transformation? The East European radical right in the political process Routledge*.
Martín de la Guardia, R. (2018). Hacia una Europa incierta: el avance del nacional-populismo. In R. Martín de la Guardia, G. Pérez Sánchez (Dirs.), *La integración europea e iberoamericana. Actualidad y perspectivas en el siglo XXI* (pp. 171–189). Thompson Reuters Aranzadi.
Martín de la Guardia, R., & Pérez Sánchez, G. (2019). Democracia sin liberalismo: el nacional-populismo en Hungría y Polonia (1990–2018). In Á. Soto Carmona (Coord.), *La democracia herida* (pp. 179–217). Marcial Pons.
Mudde, C., & Kaltwasser, C. R. (2013). *Populism in Europe and the Americas: Threat or correction for democracy?* Cambridge: Cambridge University Press.
Poirer, P. (2007). Les nouvelles droites et le régime politique de l´Union Européenne de 1979 à 2004. In P. Delwitt & P. Poirer (Eds.), *Extrême droite et pouvoir en Europe. The extreme right parties and power in Europe*. Belgium: Université de Bruxelles.
Ramiro Troitino, D., & Pando Ballesteros, M. D. L. P. (2017). Churchill's European integration model. *Revista de Occidente, 433*, 57–71.
Rodríguez-Aguilera de Prat, C. (2012). Euroescepticismo, Eurofobia y Eurocriticismo. Los partidos radicales de la derecha y la izquierda ante la Unión Europea. Huygens.
Speit, A. (2016). Bürgerliche Scharfmacher: Deutschlands neue rechte Mitte- von AfD bis Pegida. Orell Füssli Verlag.
Troitino, D. R., & Faerber, K. (2019). Historical errors in the initial conception of the euro and its subsequent development. *Brazilian Journal of Political Economy, 39*(2), 328–343.
Van Spanje, J. (2006). Contagious parties: Anti-Immigration parties and their impact on other parties. Immigration stances in contemporary Western Europe. *Party Politics, 16*(5), 563–586.
Wodak, R. (2015). *The politics of Fear: What right-wing populist discourses mean*. Sage.

The Religious Factor on the European Political Agenda—Old Paradigms and Future Challenges

Luis Domínguez Castro and José Ramón Rodríguez Lago

Abstract The motto "United in diversity", which officially began to be used by the EU institutions in 2000, still seems to have been a wise choice that, honouring the classic adagio *Pluribus Unum*, makes a present commitment with a project for the future. Nevertheless, almost two decades after the beginning of the third millennium, uncertainty hangs over the balance between the two terms of the binomial. In fact, the European continent is destined to become more diverse in the next few decades, also from a religious perspective, even though there are some clouds of doubt on the horizon about how such pluralism will affect its degree of unity. It generates a problem of integration for the European Union that should be addressed properly.

Keywords Religion · Secularism · European integration · Common identity

1 Introduction

As stated by Enzo Pace, democratic societies need a certain level of organic solidarity among their citizens. However, solidarity seems to be under the threat of *"a double contingency: a tetragonal and intransigent secularism, on the one hand, and on the other, policies of identity that instrumentally mobilise symbols and religious codes to erect new ideological walls"*.[1] The siren songs intoned by those in favour of an exclusive narrative are reappearing in today's Europe; similarly, centenarian clichés serve as fuel to light new bonfires which worship their own gods, exorcise the others' and persecute pagans and heretics.[2]

[1] Pace (2019), p. 86.

[2] Apart from the Polish and the Hungarian governments, which firmly advocate these policies, the level of support in countries such as Italy, France and the UK has considerably increased, as confirmed by the results of the European Parliament elections, held in May 2019. For more details, see https://www.election-results.eu/ (27/05/2019).

L. Domínguez Castro · J. R. Rodríguez Lago (✉)
Facultade de Filoloxia e Traducion, Universidade de Vigo, Campus Lagoas/Marcoende, 36210 Vigo, Spain
e-mail: jrlago@uvigo.es

D. Ramiro Troitiño et al. (eds.), *The EU in the 21st Century*,
https://doi.org/10.1007/978-3-030-38399-2_4

Throughout history, religion has played a key role in the configuration of the national states of the European area.[3] Moreover, it significantly contributed to the creation of an image of Europe which is directly associated with the West and with Christianity.[4] In contrast to the teleological paradigm of secularisation which prophesied that religion would play a residual role in contemporary societies, traditional confessions have proved capable of continuing to play a relevant role, while competing against new communities with transcendental aspirations by getting support from the most diverse spiritual movements.[5] Remaining united in diversity means that integration principles of market and citizenship must be given priority over exclusive postulates of war and tribe. This aim can only be achieved with a great deal of effort and resources in order to fight phobias and atavistic impulses, which have so often resulted in brutality.

Europe has never been isolated from the global dynamics which, one way or another, have affected the continent. The transatlantic, trans-Mediterranean and trans-Ural networks which, for centuries, contributed to build its identity are nowadays noticeably increasing their influence on a territory that is characterised by a clear population ageing process, by demographic decline and by difficulty in maintaining economic growth.[6] In a global world where, once again, the dispute over supremacy is resolved in the Pacific Ocean, migration and capital flows will have a strong influence on the future of the European Union. Therefore, it is highly advisable to reflect on the role of confessional transnational networks in both spheres.

In the twenty-first century, the traditional paradigms which served to build collective identities around nation states and European unity are questioned by new social—and also epistemological—realities that make it necessary to review some principles. Secularising modernisation firmly spread since the 1960s; however, it was ousted in the last decade of the twentieth century by the so-called resurgence of religion, as well as by a more in-depth analysis of the capacity for survival, transformation and regeneration shown by such identities.[7] The narrative on the European integration process was also temporarily subjected to a strictly secular perspective.[8] We now know that the narrative on European unity, under the strong influence of the disaster caused by the two World Wars (which had originated within Christianity) and of the distress at the Nazi and Soviet totalitarian regimes (with their extermination camps and gulags), also intended to overcome the fratricidal conflicts among the different nations and churches. This narrative, under the auspices of the Americans,[9]

---

[3] Barker (2009) and Spohn et al. (2015).

[4] Perkins (2004), Leustean (2013) and Chaplain and Wilson (2016).

[5] Helas and Woodhead (2006), Rosati (2015) and Stolz et al. (2016).

[6] The population of the 28 states which are currently members of the EU represented 13.5% of the global population in 1960. Nevertheless, it does not even reach 7% nowadays and it is expected to be under 5% by 2050. European Commission (2017), p. 24.

[7] Casanova (1994) and Berger (2014).

[8] The exaltation of Jean Monnet over the "Catholic fathers" of Europe (Schumann, De Gasperi, Adenauer, etc.) was also present in that narrative. Cohen (2007), pp. 14–29.

[9] Dolan (2002) and Pollard (2014), pp. 379–383.

described the above-mentioned regimes as "political religions" and considered that Christianity was at the foundational core of democracy, by guaranteeing individual freedom.[10]

In line with the Peace of Augsburg—which established the *Cuius regio, eius religio* principle in 1555—and the Peace of Westphalia—which inspired a certain degree of tolerance of minorities in 1648—The Hague hosted, in the spring of 1948, a gathering of international leaders who, still in shock after the Czechoslovak coup d'état, agreed that Europe should be built on Christian values. The Secretariat of the Cultural Committee of the Congress of Europe was composed of Salvador de Madariaga and Denis de Rougemont (who promoted ecumenical Christianity), Étienne Gilson (a Catholic intellectual), Joseph W. Hunkin (an Anglican bishop) and Paolo Giobbe[11] (an internuncio of the Vatican in the Netherlands). The initial lack of trust in the project on the part of Protestants was quickly overcome after the foundation in Amsterdam, a few months later (in August 1948), of the *World Council for Churches*, which had the support of North American John Foster Dulles.[12] The solution to the sempiternal "Jewish question" (the creation of the state of Israel in the Promised Land) and the establishment of an alliance to fight a common enemy (the Soviet regime, which supported atheist materialism) contributed significantly to the reconciliation of Christian churches. The Second Vatican Council and the official recognition, on the part of the Catholic Church, of religious freedom as a fundamental right, were the culmination of this virtuous circle.[13] Nevertheless, the final outcome cannot be understood without taking into account the role played by transatlantic ecumenical networks since World War I as well as the success of Christian democracy (not just Catholic) in the European Union.[14]

The resolution of the "Jewish question" and the construction of a Western Europe which would come to the aid of the Eastern Christian churches—silenced by Soviet oppression—made it possible to ensure diversity in unity from the very beginning of the unification process.[15] Such diversity was supported by the consensus reached by the Christian, classic and illustrated heritages, but relegated religious minorities to the background, regardless of their historical importance. It will not be easy to keep this idea of Europe in a place which is subjected to increasing external influence, most notably in urban areas and among young people.[16] The creation of a European identity in line with the dynamics of both market and citizens requires a broader concept of *diversity*, which, until then, only referred to "real Europeans".[17]

[10]Hayes (1926), pp. 93–125, Voegelin (1938), Hayes (1960) and Warren (1997).

[11]Canavero and Durand (1999) and Coupland (2006).

[12]Mojzes (2018).

[13]Melloni (2016), Horn (2015), Menozzi (2009), pp. 230–251, and McLeod (2007).

[14]Leustean (2014) and Durand (2013).

[15]Sachar (2000) and Leustean (2010).

[16]In 2016, the average age of the Muslim population was 30, in contrast to that of non-Muslim population, which reached 43. Pew Research Center: *Europe's Growing Muslim Population*, 29 November 2017, pp. 36–37.

[17]Heyller (2010).

The institutional strategies designed by national states to deal with religious minorities—which were actually gaining more and more followers—were very diverse. Indeed, they depended on the social context and the traditions of each particular form of government. The French secular model[18] coexisted with the Anglo-Saxon multicultural model and with the degree of tolerance in traditional mono-confessional countries. In any case, the rapid changes which took place in the spiritual sphere resulted in a need for more attention from European institutions.

2 The Veils of Sancta Sanctorum—Affiliation and Religious Practices

The traditional distinction between church and state, clearly represented by the French Republic, initially reached those community institutions which had been founded when the paradigm of secularisation, and the theses which connected religion with the private sphere were at their peak. In fact, the EU still does not offer any information about the religious affiliation of its citizens in its official statistics, even though those theses are weakening due to the emergence of more complex integration perspectives. The analyses carried out by official community institutions—for instance, the European Union Agency for Fundamental Rights (FRA)[19] and the European Commission, which publishes its Eurobarometer on a regular basis—still do not give much importance to religion, which is always neglected, to the extent that it only seems to be taken into account in a collateral manner. The same applies to those surveys conducted by private organisations, such as the European Values Study, published by the Leibniz Institute for the Social Sciences,[20] and those carried out by the European Social Survey (ESS), created in 2001 by the European Science Foundation and coordinated by the European Research Infrastructure Consortium (ERIC) since 2013.[21] The use of different methodologies adds to diversity; nevertheless, it also implies certain contradictions when dealing with such a complex issue as identity in the confessional field.[22]

Two institutions provide us with a more systematic view of the role played by religion in Europe. It is revealing to find out that their headquarters are located in the Swiss Confederation and the USA, as both countries have been making a major

[18] Since 1872, the French legislation does not allow to reveal information about the citizens' affiliation, their identity or any other personal data connected to religion, neither in the census nor in any other study carried out by the government. The legislation of 1978 also imposes constraints on the collection of data concerning race, ethnic group or beliefs unless explicit consent is given by participants. Baubérot (2017) and Poulat (2010), pp. 113–129.

[19] https://fra.europa.eu/es (27/05/2019).

[20] Bréchon and Gonthier (2017). https://europeanvaluesstudy.eu/education-dissemination-publications/education/atlas-of-european-values/ (27/05/2019).

[21] https://www.europeansocialsurvey.org/ (27/05/2019).

[22] Hill and Hood (1999) and Billiet (2002), pp. 339–383. https://www.europeansocialsurvey.org/ (27/05/2019).

contribution to dialogue between the different confessions since World War I and still seem to be its most important promoters. The Swiss Metadatabase of Religious Affiliation in Europe (SMRE), whose headquarters are located at the University of Lucerne, offers the most accurate statistics available on religious affiliation in the 28 states which are currently part of the European Union as well as in the 47 full members of the Council of Europe.

Religious affiliation in Europe (2006–2015)

%	Christians				No. of Christians			No. of religious affiliation
	Catholic	Protestant	Orthodox	Other	Jew	Muslim	Other	
EU (28)	44.5	11.8	7.5	2.3	0.2	3.0	1.5	28.9
COE	28.6	8.4	21.7	1.5	0.2	13.6	1.8	23.9

Sources https://www.smre-data.ch/en/data_exploring/religious_affiliation# /mode/majority_religion/period/2010/dataset/1562/presentation/Table (27/05/2019) and Metadatabase—Religious affiliation—Degree of pluralisation. https://www.smre-data.ch/en/

Catholic: Christ Catholic Church, Greek Catholic Church, Mariavite Church, Old Catholic Church, Roman Catholic Church. **Protestant**: Anglican Church including Church of Ireland, Arminianism, Baptists, Calvinists, Dutch Reformed Church, Evangelical Church, Lutheran, Presbyterianism, Protestant, Silesian Evangelical Church of the Augsburg Confession. **Orthodox**: Albanian Orthodox Church, Armenian Apostolic Church, Greek Orthodox Church, Old Believers, Old-Rite, Old Orthodox, Russian Orthodox Church. **Other Christian**: Adventist, Apostolic, Brethren Church, Charismatic Episcopal Church, Evangelicals, Fraternity Church, Free Lutheran Church, Free Presbyterian, Hussites, Mennonites, Methodist, New Apostolic, Pentecostalism, Quaker, Unitarians, URC/Congregational. **Jew**: Jewish, Judaism, Mosaic. **Muslim**: Bektashi, Shiite, Sunni. **No religious affiliation**: Agnostics, atheists, no denomination, no religion

It is much more complicated to establish how religious affiliation is connected to beliefs and religious practices. Indeed, the former is strongly influenced by cultural and national identity, whereas the analysis of the two other variables—beliefs and religious practices—requires the use of the data sets which have been published since 2004 by the Pew Forum on Religion and Public Life (Think Tank Pew Research Center), whose headquarters are located in Washington, D.C. The latest reports provide useful data for studying a range of religious issues in 25 EU states (it should be noted that no data is available from Cyprus, Malta and Slovenia).

2017	Believe in God		Religious practices			
%	Absolute certainty	Do not believe	Adults highly religious	They pray daily	Services at least monthly	Very important in their lives
Romania	64	4	55	44	50	50
Greece	59	6	49	29	38	55

(continued)

(continued)

2017	Believe in God		Religious practices			
%	Absolute certainty	Do not believe	Adults highly religious	They pray daily	Services at least monthly	Very important in their lives
Croatia	57	10	44	40	40	42
Poland	45	8	40	27	61	29
Portugal	44	13	37	37	36	36
Slovakia	37	27	29	31	31	23
Italy	26	21	27	21	43	21
Ireland	24	26	24	19	37	23
Lithuania	34	11	21	15	27	16
Spain	25	31	21	23	23	22
Bulgaria	30	17	18	15	19	19
Netherlands	15	53	18	20	18	20
Hungary	26	30	17	16	17	14
Latvia	28	15	15	17	16	10
Austria	13	29	14	8	38	12
Finland	23	37	13	18	10	10
France	11	37	12	11	22	11
Germany	10	36	12	9	24	11
UK	12	36	11	6	20	10
Belgium	13	54	10	11	11	11
Sweden	14	60	10	11	11	10
Czech Republic	13	66	8	9	11	7
Denmark	15	46	8	10	12	8
Estonia	13	45	7	9	10	6

Source Pew Research Center. Eastern and Western Europeans Differ on Importance of Religion, Views of Minorities, and Key Social Issues, 29 October 2018, pp. 21–22

The above data shows that there is a clear difference between Western and Eastern Europe, and also between the north and the south. These discrepancies are not only due to the coexistence of various confessions, as they also depend on other variables such as the degree of urbanisation, democratisation and material development. Furthermore, apart from the differences between states and the differences between confessions, it is important to take into consideration the emerging plurality of confessions within the borders of each state, as well as the relation with those citizens who have no religious beliefs. Besides, a significant number of participants adopt volatile positions, since they describe themselves as non-practising believers.[23] Europe's multiplicity of identities deserves a more detailed analysis.

[23] Pew Research Center: *Being Christian in Western Europe*, 29 May 2018, p. 7.

3 Perceptions and Phobias from the Myths of the Past to the "Fake News" of the Present

> No one will be able to stop the trend towards a multiracial and multicultural society in Europe … this large-scale immigration will turn modern European cities into something similar to the current New York, which began as a WASP city, and now is a melting pot of ethnic, cultural and religious communities[24]

These words, pronounced by Umberto Eco in 1997, seemed to be prophesying the imminent arrival of a cosmopolitan Europe, but they were perhaps more of a reflection of his own wishes rather than a historical reality, always more complex than simple acts of will. Only a few months before, the above-mentioned Italian intellectual had made public, along with Carlo María Martini—a Jesuit cardinal with a good reputation in the cultural field, and also the Archbishop of Milan—a fruitful epistolary exchange on faith and unbelief.[25] Almost a decade later, another prominent cardinal in the theological field, Joseph Ratzinger and, his German compatriot, the political scientist Jürgen Habermas, resumed that dialogue.[26] Revealingly, the debate on religion in Europe was still dominated by the dispute—more or less moderate—between the representatives of the Catholic Church and the scholars who called themselves agnostics. As for the other confessions, they were still relegated to the background, even though their influence had been growing progressively.[27]

The methodologies used for the analysis of religious phenomena in Europe still show deficiencies when dealing with the role played by Orthodox Churches, Islamic communities or new spiritual movements, on account of their extremely complex and diverse nature.[28] Nevertheless, this task cannot be abandoned, for the sake of science. Indeed, it is actually urgent, as it is necessary to fight against the existence of recurring clichés, spread by the wars of religion and encouraged "ad nauseam" by the media, only interested in engaging audiences. The feeling that a hypothetical paradise has been lost generates anguish, resulting in a suitable framework for Islamophobia and anti-Semitism.

The international networks which contributed to pacify the spirits in the previous decades now promote hatred: Trump's USA, Modi's India, Erdogan's Turkey, Netanyahu's Israel, Bolsonaro's Brazil, etc. In spite of difficulties, the European Union seems to have become the last bastion of diversity and tolerance. In 2017, The Movement opened its doors in Brussels, inspired by a North American, Steve Bannon. In other words, the strategist who led Trump to presidency in 2016 began a war against community institutions. This cultural war has targeted the guidelines established by Pope Francis as the head of the Catholic Church. The Dignitatis Humanae

---

[24] Umberto ECO: speech at the congress *Los desafíos del tercer milenio*, Valencia, 23 January 1997.

[25] Eco and Martini (1996).

[26] Habermas et al. (2005).

[27] Ramiro Troitino and Pando Ballesteros (2017).

[28] Recent research in this field includes Hämmerli and Mayer (2014), Iner and Yucel (2015).

Institute, chaired by British ultra-conservative Benjamin Harnwell and emeritus cardinals Renato Martino—former permanent observer of the Holy See to the United Nations and president of the Pontifical Council for Justice and Peace—and Raymond Burke—former nuncio of the Vatican in the USA and last Cardinal Patronus of the Sovereign Military Order of Malta—leads the opposition to the current pontiff and sponsors the creation of a Judaeo-Christian Western Academy intended to defend the essence of tradition and to start a new crusade.

The internal battle within the Vatican Curia will have a significant influence on the future of an institution, the EU, which has always borne the mark of Catholicism. Pax Christi encouraged, since 1945, the reconciliation of European Christians who were in a conflict during World War II. Furthermore, some renowned Catholic leaders—such as Schumann, De Gasperi and Adenauer—were the founding fathers of the different European institutions. Finally, after the signing of the Treaty of Rome, Pope Pius XII explicitly stated his support for the European project: "*If it is true that for Europe the message of Christianity was like the leaven in dough... The most valuable of treasures with which she has been charged... This message can maintain the vigor and integrity... in a supra-national community, can guarantee respect for cultural differences and a spirit of conciliation and cooperation, along with an acceptance of the sacrifices which it will entail and the dedication which it will demand*".[29]

The Catholic Office of Information and Initiative for Europe (OCIPE)—whose headquarters moved to The Hague in 1965—and the Council of the Bishops' Conferences of Europe (CCEE)—officially established in 1971—served as tools to make progress towards ecumenical dialogue and the Vatican Ostpolitik, while Pope Paul VI was the head of the Catholic Church.[30] The papacy of Pope John Paul II brought the restoration of conservatism in the Curia as well as the emerging influence of secular Catholicism, whose representatives included Opus Dei and noticeable movements such as Communion and Liberation, Regnum Christi or the Neocatechumenal Way.[31] It also supported the creation of the Commission of the Episcopal Conferences of the European Community (COMECE),[32] the most important mediation tool to deal with the community institutions since 1980. A few years later, the majority of votes obtained by the natural heir to Christian democracy—the European People's Party—in the European Parliament encouraged the battle to give Christianism a significant role in the Constitutional Treaty[33] project and, in 2003, the apostolic exhortation *Ecclesia in Europa* became a real living will of the Polish Pope—who was shortly after succeeded by a Bavarian pontiff—with regard to the European narrative.

Nevertheless, the election of Bergoglio—from Argentina—as Pope, made it possible to appreciate the global dimension of an institution whose interests exceeded

[29]Discorso di Sua Santità Pio XII ai partecipanti al Congresso d'Europa (13/06/1957). https://w2.vatican.va/content/pius-xii/en/speeches/1957/documents/hf_p-xii_spe_19570613_congresso-europa.html (27/05/2019).

[30]Fejérdy (2016).

[31]Menozzi (2009), p. 240.

[32]http://www.comece.eu/religious-freedomcomece-the-catholic-church-in-the-eu (27/05/2019).

[33]Färber (2017).

the European boundaries. The most recent edition of the *Annuario Pontificio* reveals striking data.

Catholics in each continent (2017)					
%	Europe	America	Africa	Asia	Oceania
Baptised	21.8	48.5	17.8	11.1	0.8
Priests	42.6	28.6	10.9	15.9	1.1
Major seminarians	14.9	27.3	27.1	29.8	0.9

Source Presentation of the *Annuario Pontificio 2019* and the *Annuarium Statisticum Ecclesiae 2017* https://press.vatican.va/content/salastampa/es/bollettino/pubblico/2019/03/06/pres.html (27/05/2019)

The number of Catholics in Africa will soon exceed that of European Catholics, who have already been clearly surpassed by Americans. Similarly, the evolution in the number of aspirants to the priesthood suggests that the European clergymen—to date, the majority group, but with a really high ageing rate—will be soon less numerous than the American, Asian and African clergymen. This change will affect the largest global corporation in charge of dealing with all spiritual issues.[34] Nevertheless, Catholicism will still be the main religion in Europe in the next few decades. Not only are a majority those citizens who declare themselves to be Catholic, but also they are much more numerous than those who do not profess this religion, both in the EU and in the member states of the Council of Europe.[35] Indeed, its influence will still be crucial, on account of its dominant position (the number of Catholics represents more than 80% of the inhabitants in Poland, Malta—96% and 94%, respectively—Croatia, Italy, Ireland, Portugal and Lithuania[36]) and of the persistence of its networks in civil, political and military institutions. Its hierarchical and centralised nature, along with the fact that it is considered both a confession and a state recognised by the international community, gives it a privileged position if compared to other confessions.

Another key aspect which should be taken into consideration in order to carry out an adequate analysis is the presence of citizens who do not identify with any religious groups (71% in the Czech Republic; 69% in Estonia; 51% in the UK and France).[37] In fact, a very large percentage of those brought up in the Christian faith also become agnostic or atheist in their adult life, especially in the Netherlands (39%), Belgium (34%), Sweden (30%) and Spain (28%).[38] The battle between Christian and secular principles gave rise to an intense debate during the drafting of the European constitutional project and is still open in all of the states. The relationship between

[34] Lynch (2018).

[35] Kerikmäe et al. (2019).

[36] Liedhegener and Odermatt (2018), p. 93.

[37] Liedhegener and Odermatt (2018), p. 96.

[38] Pew Research Center: *Eastern and Western,* 29 October 2018, p. 19.

Catholics and those who support a secular Europe will continue to be the keystone of the European spirit, even though it will also be under the influence of the role played by the other traditional confessions and the new spiritual trends.

Orthodox Churches, which represent more than 75% of the total population of Greece (91%), Romania, Cyprus and Bulgaria,[39] remain shrouded in uncertainty due to the bitter dispute between the patriarchates of Constantinople, Moscow and Kiev. The foundation of an autocephalous church in Ukraine in 1995, along with Constantinople's recent official recognition of the Patriarch of Kiev, has led to the most important schism in the history of the Orthodox Church.[40] Meanwhile, on the Protestant side, the progressive decrease in the number of believers in traditional confessions (representing more than 50% of the population only in Finland, Denmark and Sweden)[41] coincides with the expansion of the independent Christian Churches and the multiplicity of providentialist Evangelical and Pentecostal movements, which are under the strong influence of America and Africa.[42] The evolution of the different Christian branches will significantly affect Europe; therefore, it is indispensable to monitor it carefully in order to ensure the peaceful coexistence of all religions.

In spite of the dominant position of Christianity and secularism, the alert generated by the terrorist attacks carried out by various jihadi cells in Europe has resulted in a disproportionate perception of a hypothetical assault on the fortress of Christianity.[43]This hyperbolic image, nurtured by the sensationalism of the media and by the interests of those who desire to spread fear, stigmatises Muslims and makes people associate them with terrorism, massive immigration and uncontrolled reception of refugees.[44]

Out of every 100 people, about how many do you think are Muslim?			
Country	Actual	Av. guess	Factor
France	7.5	31	4.13
Belgium	7.0	23	3.29
Netherlands	6.0	19	3.16
Germany	5.0	21	4.20
Great Britain	4.8	15	3.12
Sweden	4.6	17	3.70
Denmark	4.1	15	3.66

(continued)

[39]Liedhegener and Odermatt (2018), p. 95.

[40]*The Holy Synod of the Russian Orthodox Church has considered it impossible to remain in the Eucharistic communion with the Patriarchate of Constantinople*, 15 October 2018. https://mospat.ru/en/2018/10/15/news165259/ (27/05/2019).

[41]Liedhegener and Odermatt (2018), p. 97.

[42]Kay and Dyer (2011), Butticci (2016).

[43]Troitiño et al. (2018).

[44]Pew Research Center: *Europe's Growing Muslim Population*, 29 November 2017, pp. 16–25.

(continued)

Out of every 100 people, about how many do you think are Muslim?			
Country	Actual	Av. guess	Factor
Italy	3.7	20	5.40
Spain	2.1	14	6.66
Czech Republic	<0.1	3	30
Hungary	<0.1	6	60
Poland	<0.1	7	70

Source Perils of Perception. A 40 Country Study, Ipsos, 2016. https://www.ipsos.com/ipsos-mori/en-uk/perceptions-are-not-reality-what-world-gets-wrong (07/05/2019)

A survey conducted in 2016 in twelve of the most important states of the EU raised the alarm about the dangerous breeding ground for Islamophobia generated by citizens' perceptions, not only in those countries where Muslim communities are becoming considerably large (France, which is the country with the highest number of Muslim citizens, does not exceed 8%), but also, especially, in those where their presence is negligible (for instance, Poland, Hungary and the Czech Republic[45]). Moreover, it should be noted that there has been an increase in xenophobia against traditionally stigmatised communities.

Negative opinions about Muslims, Jews and Roma (Gypsies)			
%	Muslims	Jews	Gypsies
Hungary	72	32	64
Italy	69	24	82
Poland	66	24	47
Greece	65	55	67
Spain	50	21	49
Netherlands	35	4	37
Sweden	35	5	42
France	29	10	61
Germany	29	5	40
UK	28	7	45
Median	43	16	48

Source Pew Research Center: *Europeans Fear Wave of Refugees Will Mean More Terrorism, Fewer Jobs. Sharp ideological divides across EU on views about minorities, diversity and national identity,* July 2016, p. 9

Contrary to the sensationalist narrative of a Western Christian civilisation threatened by barbarians and rooted in the myths spread by crusades, a more realistic,

[45] Allievi (2009) and Göle (2014).

moderate analysis confirms that the relationship between Christians and citizens with no religious affiliation will continue to play an essential role in Europe. Indeed, both will be required to meet the needs of a post-secular society characterised by its heterogeneous and pluriconfessional nature, where religious freedom and active dialogue are destined to be crucial in order to ensure peace and safety. Therefore, the challenge to be faced in the next few decades will focus on the adaptation process of a group of states, defined either by an only religion or by the paradigm of secularisation, to new societies, more and more multicultural, where religion will remain under the influence of migration flows and liquid identities.[46]

It costs a great deal of time, blood, sweat and tears to overcome prejudice and to establish a fruitful dialogue between Catholics and Protestants, but after World War II it was finally possible to replace conflict with concord.[47] It will be necessary to create new networks between the different European religious communities and their neighbours so as to avoid further confrontation.

4 Wills and Resources—the EU and the Challenge Posed by Religious Diversity

As a response to the threats which seem to be looming on the horizon, the most recent work carried out by the EU institutions has been following three different courses of action: the defence of freedom of conscience in the EU, the promotion of dialogue and of interconfessional cooperation and, finally, the support of the initiatives launched by academic institutions in order to analyse these issues. We firmly believe that it is necessary to draw attention to the significant work which has been accomplished in these three directions, as it will be useful for facing future challenges.

In November 1950, the member states of the Council of Europe approved the *Convention for the Protection of Human Rights and Fundamental Freedoms*, which was incorporated to Community Law in 2009 and dealt with freedom of thought, conscience and religion in article 9. In a context characterised by the effects of the holocaust and also by the Cold War, religious issues were in line with the protection of individual rights to fight genocide and oppression under totalitarian regimes. In 1999, the European Commission approved three directives aimed at fighting all forms of discrimination. One of them (more precisely, the directive on equal treatment in employment and occupation) explicitly dealt with discrimination on grounds of religion and established a jurisprudence which is currently supported by the Court of Justice of the European Union.[48]

If cooperation between Protestants and Catholics had served the purpose of reinforcing the European project in its early years, cooperation with Orthodox Churches

[46] Vilaça et al. (2014).

[47] Pew Research Center: *Five Centuries After Reformation, Catholic-Protestant Divide in Western Europe Has Faded*, 31 August 2017.

[48] Leustean and Madeley (2009), Maioli (2011), Verhelst and Frederiksen (2017).

will play a key role with regard to integration in the East. In May 1989, the Ecumenical Assembly held in Basel under the motto "Peace and justice" gathered representatives of the East with representatives of the CCEE (Catholic) and the Conference of European Churches (KEK), which included the main Protestant groups. Similarly, the Ecumenical Assembly which took place in Graz in June 1997 under the motto "Reconciliation: a gift of God and a source of new life" represented an improvement in terms of cooperation between Christian confessions.

Inter-church cooperation led community institutions to pay attention to this course of action and to integrate it into their policies. In 1994, the last European Commission chaired by Jacques Delors launched the initiative "A Soul for Europe" and created the European Ecumenical Commission for Church and Society (EECCS). It should be noted that this was the first time that an institutional status had been given to gatherings of representatives of the different confessions with the presidents of the commission and the European Council.

The Constitutional Treaty of 2004 finally certified the initiative launched by Delors, by supporting the need for a transparent, open dialogue between the EU institutions and the different religions and philosophical doctrines.[49] Article 17 of the Treaty of the Functioning of the European Union (TFEU), in force since 2009, confirmed this purpose and supported a series of actions[50] to be taken in accordance with the guidelines published by the council.[51] Moreover, the European Parliament regularly hosts all kinds of events and seminars on intercultural dialogue and religious pluralism.[52] As for the commission, it has appointed a *Special Envoy for the Promotion of Freedom of Religion or Belief outside the EU.*[53]

Finally, the progress made in the academic field with regard to the analysis of the religious factor has also drawn the attention of the EU. In September 2001, we witnessed the creation of the *European Association for the Study of Religions* (EASR),[54] established in The Hague and connected to the *International Association for the History of Religions* (IAHR)[55]; in 2016, under the auspices of the European Parliament, it was the turn of an ambitious initiative, the *European Academy of Religion* (EuARe). To date, this institution—established in Bologna—has held three important international conferences.[56] Lastly, in April 2017, the European Commission approved,

[49]Biedenkopf et al. (2004).

[50]The European Parliament Intergroup on Freedom of Religion or Belief and Religious Tolerance (FoRB and RT): *Annual Report 2017;* Martina PRPIC: *Religion and Human Rights*, European Parliament Research Service, December 2018. http://www.religiousfreedom.eu/ (27/05/2019).

[51]*EU Guidelines on the promotion and protection of freedom of religion or belief,* Foreign Affairs Council meeting Luxembourg, 24 June 2013.

[52]http://www.europarl.europa.eu/at-your-service/es/be-heard/religious-and-non-confessional-dialogue/events (27/05/2019).

[53]Jan Figel, Special Envoy for the Promotion of Freedom of Religion or Belief: *Overview of country visits: main meetings and activities*, October 2016—March 2019. https://ec.europa.eu/europeaid/special-envoy-jan-figel_en (27/05/2019).

[54]http://www.easr.eu/ (27/05/2019).

[55]http://www.iahrweb.org/ (27/05/2019).

[56]Cadeddu (2019), pp. 7–12.

under the Horizon 2020 programme, the credit line *Religious diversity in Europe—past, present and future*, which materialised in the Religious Tolerance and Peace (RETOPEA) project, with a budget of 2.4 million euros.[57]

5 Conclusion

In the last few years, the EU institutions have been assigning a more and more relevant role to the religious factor with the aim of guaranteeing a future of peace and freedom. The narrative of the European spirit alluded by the founding fathers must now be invoked within new parameters. A more diverse, pluriconfessional Europe requires a post-secular European Union, capable of integrating different religious communities, facing new challenges and repelling the dangers of intolerance and exclusion which affect a section of the society. The different states, churches and emotional and intellectual communities are facing a dilemma nowadays: they need to choose whether they recognise diversity as a value in itself or fight against it by supporting exclusion policies and clinging to traditional myths and paradigms. Just like in the case of the origins of the EU, only unity within those in favour of transconfessional dialogue—regardless of their diversity—will serve as a guarantee of the motto "United in diversity". Cooperation between the different agents of the civil society will contribute to demolish the walls erected by prejudice. Nevertheless, the most decisive role is reserved, once again, for the will of the states and the material and institutional resources assigned to the dissemination of a more inclusive European narrative.

Acknowledgements This work was carried out under MICINN research project PG 2018-095884-B-C21. Translated to English by Macarena Muradás Sanromán.

References

Allievi, S. (2009). *Conflicts over Mosques in Europe*. London: Alliance Publishing Trust.
Barker, P. W. (2009). *Religious nationalism in modern Europe. If God be for us*. New York: Routledge.
Baubérot, J. (2017). *Historie de la laïcité en France*. Paris: PUF.
Berger, P. (2014). *The many altars of modernity: Toward a paradigm for religion in a pluralist age*. Boston and Berlin: De Gruyter.
Biedenkopf, K., Geremek, B., & Michalski, K. (2004). The spiritual and cultural dimension of Europe. Reflection group initiated by the President of the European Commission and coordinated by the Institute for Human Sciences. Vienna/Brussels: European Commission, Community Research.
Bréchon, P., & Gautier, F. (2017). *European values. Trends and divides over thirty years*. Leiden: Brill.

[57] http://retopea.eu/s/start/page/home (27/05/2019).

Billiet, J. (2002). Proposal for questions on religious identity. In *Development of the core module*. European Social Survey. https://www.europeansocialsurvey.org/.

Butticci, A. (2016). *African Pentencostals in catholic Europe. The politics of presence in the twenty-first century*. Cambridge (MA): Harvard University Press.

Cadeddu, F. (Ed.). (2019). *EUARE Lectures. Ex nihilo and 1. Annual Conference 2017–2018*. Bologna: European Academy of Religion.

Canavero, A., & Durand, J.-D. (1999). *Il fattore religioso nell'integrazione europea*. Milano: Edizioni Unicopli.

Casanova, J. (1994). *Public religion in modern world*. Chicago: University of Chicago Press.

Chaplain, J., & Wilson, G. (2016). *God and the EU. Faith in the European Project*. Routledge, London and New York.

Cohen, A. (2007). "'Le "Père de l'Europe". La construction sociale d'un récit des origines. *Actes de la recherche en sciences sociales* 166–167.

Coupland, P. M. (2006). *Britannia, Europa and Christendom. British Christians and European integration*. Basingstoke: Palgrave Macmillan.

Dolan, J. P. (2002). *In search of American Catholicism. A History of Religion and Culture in Tension*. New York: Oxford University Press.

Durand, J.-D. (2013). *Christian Democrat Internationalism. Its Action in Europe and Worldwide from post World War II until the 1990s* (Vol. 2). Bruxelles: Peter Lang.

Eco, U., & Martini, C. M. (1996). *In cosa crede chi non crede?*. Roma: Atlantide Editoriale.

European Commission. (2017). The 2018 Ageing Report, Underlying Assumptions and Projection Methodologies. Institutional Paper 065. https://ec.europa.eu/info/sites/info/files/economy-finance/ip065_en.pdf.

Färber, K. (2017). Mitterrand and the great European design—From the cold war to the European Union. *Baltic Journal of European Studies, 7*(2), 132–147.

Fejérdy, A. (2016). *The Vatican Ospolitik 1958–1978*. Roma: Viella.

Göle, N. (2014). *Islam and public controversy in Europe*. London: Routledge.

Habermas, J., Ratzinger, J., & Schuller, F. (2005). Dialektik der Säkularisierung: Über Vernunft und Religion. Herder, Freiburg im Breisgau, Basel und Wien.

Hämmerli, M., & Mayer, J.-F. (2014). *Orthodox identities in Western Europe: Migration, settlement and innovation*. Farnham: Ashgate.

Hayes, C. J. H. (1926). Nationalism as a religion. In *Essays on nationalism*. New York: Macmillan.

Hayes, C. J. H. (1960). *Nationalism. A religion*. New York: Macmillan.

Helas, P., & Woodhead, L. (2006). *The spiritual revolution*. Oxford: Oxford University Press.

Heyller, H. A. (2010). *Muslims of Europe: The "other" Europeans*. Edimburg: Edimburgh University Press.

Hill, P. C., & Hood, R. W. (Eds.). (1999). *Measures of religiosity*. Birmingham: Religious Education Press.

Horn, G.-R. (2015). *The spirit of Vatican II: Western European progressive Catholicism in the Long Sixties*. Oxford: Oxford University Press.

Iner, D., & Yucel, S. (Eds.). (2015). *Muslim identity formation in religiously diverse societies*. Cambridge: Cambridge Scholars Publishing.

Kay, W., & Dyer, A. (2011). *European pentecostalism*. Leiden: Brill.

Kerikmäe, T., Troitiño, D. R., & Shumilo, O. (2019). An Idol or an Ideal? A case study of Estonian e-Governance: Public perceptions, myths and misbeliefs. *Acta Baltica Historiae et Philosophiae scientiarum, 7*(1).

Leustean, L. (Ed.). (2010). *Eastern Christianity and the cold war, 1945–91*. London: Routledge.

Leustean, L. (2013) Representing religion in the European Union. Does god matter?. London and New York: Routledge.

Leustean, L. (2014). *The ecumenical movement and the making of the European community*. Oxford: Oxford University Press.

Leustean, L., & Madeley, J. (2009). *Religion, politics and law in the European Union*. London: Routledge.

Liedhegener, A., & Odermatt, A. (2018). Religious affiliation as a baseline for religious diversity in contemporary Europe. Making sense of numbers, wordings, and cultural meanings. Zentrum für Religion, Wirtschaft und Politik (ZRWP), Swiss Metadatabase of Religious Affiliation in Europe (SMRE), Universität Luzern.
Lynch, A. (2018). *Global catholicism in the twenty-first century*. Singapore: Springer.
Maioli, E. (2011). Discriminación religiosa y procesos de integración regional: El caso de la Unión Europea. Editorial Académica Española.
McLeod, H. (2007). *The religious crisis of the 1960s*. Oxford: Oxford University Press.
Melloni, A. (2016). *Il Concilio e la grazia. Saggi di storia sul Vaticano II*. Milano: Jaca Book.
Menozzi, D. (2009). Concilio e post-concilio: tra svolta e continuità. In G. Filoramo, D. Menozzi (Eds.), *Storia del cristianesimo. L'Età contemporanea* (pp. 230–251). Bari: Laterza.
Mojzes, P. (2018). *North American churches and the cold war*. Grand Rapids: Eerdmans.
Pace, E. (2019). The changing Soul of Europe: The challenge to the secular state. In F. Cadeddu (Ed.), *EUARE Lectures. Ex nihilo and 1. Annual Conference 2017–2018* (pp. 71-86). Bologna: European Academy of Religion.
Perkins, M. A. (2004). *Christendom and European Identity. The Legacy of Grand narrative since 1789*. Berlin-New York: De Gruyter.
Pollard, J. (2014). *The papacy in the age of totalitarianism, 1914–1958*. Oxford: Oxford University Press.
Poulat, E. (2010). Il caso francese. In R. Morozzo della Rocca (Ed.), *La modernità e i mondi cristiani* (pp. 113–129). Bologna: Il Mulino.
Ramiro Troitino, D., & Pando Ballesteros, M. D. L. P. (2017). Churchill's European integration model. *Revista de Occidente, 433*, 57–71.
Rosati, M. (2015). *The making of a post-secular society*. London: Routledege.
Sachar, H. (2000). *Israel and Europe. An appraisal in history*. New York: Random House.
Spohn, W., Koening, M., & Knöbl, W. (Eds.). (2015). *Religion and national identities in an enlarged Europe*. Basingstoke: Palgrave Macmillan.
Stolz, J., et al. (2016). *(Un)believing in a modern society*. London: Routledge.
Troitiño, D. R., Kerikmäe, T., & Chochia, A. (Eds.). (2018). *Brexit: History, reasoning and perspectives*. Berlin: Springer.
Verhelst, I., & Frederiksen, Y. (2017). *The European court of Justice rules for the first time on discrimination based on religion*. Belgium: Ius Laboris, Global HR Lawyers.
Vilaça, H., Pace, E., & Peterson, P. (Eds.). (2014). *The changing soul of Europe. Religions, and migrations in Northern and Sothtern Europe*. London: Routledge.
Voegelin, E. (1938). *Die politischen Religionen*. Viena: Bermann-Fischer.
Warren, H. A. (1997). *Theologians of a new world order. Reinhold Niebuhr and the Christian Realists (1920–1948)*. New York: Oxford University Press.

Migration to Europe: A Threat or an Opportunity?

Lara Sansus, David Ramiro Troitiño and Tanel Kerikmäe

Abstract The EU has been highly shaken by a deep political crisis revealed through the migration crisis. Indeed, this migration issue qualified as a "crisis" is the consequence of a continuous arrival of economic and political migrants coming from conflicting zones (Syria, Afghanistan) or from poor economic zones (sub-Saharan Africa, Horn of Africa). They are seeking asylum in Europe, perceived as a model in human protection. This wave of migration became widely intensified during the last decade with a peak in the year 2015, mainly coming from the blockage to solve the Syrian conflict. The opened political positions of some Member States, such as Germany at the time of the crisis, widely incited the migrants to join the old continent. It is an opportunity or a threat is still under debate. How the European Union should address such a vital issue for its own citizens and the organization? The majority of the European states and people require decisions, but the model now to be implemented will define Europe in the current century.

Keywords Migration · European population · European Union migration policy

1 Introduction

The EU has been highly shaken by a deep political crisis revealed through the migration crisis. Indeed, this migration issue qualified as a "crisis" is the consequence of a continuous arrival of economic and political migrants coming from conflicting zones (Syria, Afghanistan) or from poor economic zones (sub-Saharan Africa, Horn of Africa). They are seeking asylum in Europe, perceived as a model in human protection. This wave of migration became widely intensified during the last decade with a peak in the year 2015, mainly coming from the blockage to solve the Syrian conflict. The opened political positions of some Member States, such as Germany at the time of the crisis, widely incited the migrants to join the old continent.

L. Sansus (✉) · D. Ramiro Troitiño · T. Kerikmäe
Tallinn University of Technology, Tallinn, Estonia
e-mail: larasansus@gmail.com

D. Ramiro Troitiño et al. (eds.), *The EU in the 21st Century*,
https://doi.org/10.1007/978-3-030-38399-2_5

Nevertheless, even if a legal framework existed at the European level completing the national one, the arriving migrants have been confronted with a deficient management of asylum regimes. The fundamental human rights and those specific for the refugee protection were not fully respected by the EU and its Member States. In addition, the slowness of the political decisions added to their insufficient joint applications created a distrust of the populations in the capacity of Brussels to resolve this migratory question. Moreover, the Member States have been confronted with a nationalist and sovereigntist fall back in view of the last national elections (Lewis et al., The Guardian, Nov 2018). Some countries such as Italy, Hungary, Poland or even the UK chose to elect governments hostile to a further European integration particularly when it came to migratory decisions. The hostile populist wave to the immigration which is growing almost everywhere in Europe testifies that European people distrust in the institutions of Brussels and more widely, in the Union. The 2016 vote of Brexit vote in 2016 illustrated clearly, as well as the formation of nationalist governments everywhere in Europe. Those Eurosceptic movements are denouncing several points through the subject of immigration.

This migratory question appeared as being the most significant challenge that Brussels has to overcome to continue to exist just some years after the severe 2008 economic crisis. Indeed, different visions of the European construction have been exposed: some support a return to fully sovereign states in decision-making and other's request the opposite, i.e. a deeper cooperation or even integration. Furthermore, the Eurosceptic wants to sanction Europe for its non-democratic management of the migratory question, because of the exclusion of any popular consultation and of the absence of solution created by very strict rules. In addition, it appears in Europe, a difference concerning the shared European values, the sense of identity and the social integration of the foreigners. Indeed, some people perceive in immigration a danger for the Christian European identity, perhaps threatened by the fear of the massive arrival of the Arab-Muslim religious culture in particular.

This chapter aims at underlining to what extent the crisis became simultaneously a challenge and an opportunity for the EU's construction. Indeed, this migratory problem is firstly showing the incapacity of the EU to take fast and effective common decisions, because of outdated or non-adapted treaties, for example. In other words, it shows how the migration crisis became a political issue, damaging the cooperation in the EU until threatening the survival of the EU in itself. It is even considered as a test of resistance for the EU as a whole (see. Merkel's speech).[1] However, it also highlights that the migratory consequences of the crisis on the EU integration process can be considered as an opportunity: one of the proposed solutions has been evidently to save the political disputes through more integration. Effectively, for some scholars, any crisis met by the EU is supposed to push the supranational entity towards more integration and a harmonization of its asylum and migration policies among its Member States. Indeed, because of the last crisis: "*the process of European integration is at a crossroads*" (Schultze 2015).[2]

---

[1] Foster (2018).

[2] Schultze (2015).

The chapter does not focus on the migration crisis and its factors. It will be based on the explanation of how Brussels considered the crisis in order to solve it, but it will mainly focus on the actual political crisis known by the Union. It will try to answer the questions: ***To what extent the migratory issue created a political crisis inside the European Union? Can the crisis be resolved with more integration?***

Part I: An existing legal framework in asylum and migration for the EU during the crisis.

2 International Obligations to Protect Migrants

Through some international commitments, the international community is trying to ensure the protection of migrants and asylum seekers (Langford 2013).

Firstly, the Convention for the Protection of Human Rights and Fundamental Freedoms also known as the "European Convention on Human Rights" (ECHR) is protecting refugees since November 1950. In total, 47 European parties are generally committed to the protection of human rights and political freedoms. The convention creates also the European Court of Human rights that protect individual people against governments. It allows anyone (and therefore also the refugees) who feels their rights violated to sue committed state (in the framework of the convention). The Court can force the state concerned by the violation to execute correctly the convention. Article 3 is prohibiting any torture or inhuman or degrading treatment or punishment.[3] It is often applied in the case of migrants.

Also, the United Nations Convention relating to the status of refugees has been the main framework in the field of the refugees' protection. The multilateral treaty commonly called the 1951 Refugee Convention has been signed with the global objective of ensuring the protection of those considered as European refugees. The document principally defines the term "refugee" in its first article, showing the importance of the qualification of the migrants.[4] Moreover, the parties committed themselves to the "*Principle of non-refoulement*" which implies that all the people considered as refugees cannot be sent back to their own countries if the person is in real danger for its freedom or for its life (Article 33). In 1967, the Protocol removed the geographic limitations previously planned by broadening the protection to all the refugees. By April 2015, 146 parties were committed to protect people who are seeking asylum

[3] Article 3. Available at: https://www.echr.coe.int/Documents/Convention_ENG.pdf.

[4] "[…] *owing to well-founded fear of being persecuted for reasons of race, religion, nationality, membership of a particular social group or political opinion, is outside the country of his nationality and is unable or, owing to such fear, is unwilling to avail himself of the protection of that country; or who, not having a nationality and being outside the country of his former habitual residence as a result of such events, is unable or, owing to such fear, is unwilling to return to it*". (Article 1 of the 1951 Refugee Convention).

in tierce countries, including all the EU Member States.[5] Nevertheless, even if the Union is not directly party, the commitments are applied to all its bodies specialized in asylum and migration.

The Convention is nowadays quite criticized: some are asking to modernize it by adapting it to the new context of environmental migrants, for example.

3 The European Union Framework in Refugee Protection

Before the refugee crisis started in the EU, thc supranational entity launched the creation of a common European framework in asylum and migration policies. This process was the beginning of the harmonization of the individual's Member States' policies in this area.

3.1 A General Framework for the EU

In December 2000, the EU Member States and its institutions ratified the Charter of Fundamental Rights (CFR) which acquired nine years after the full legal effect thanks to the Treaty of Lisbon. It created an important legal framework for political, social and economic rights for EU citizens and residents until being qualified as "*the foundational source of human rights guarantees under EU law, and all national*" by Langford (2013).

Moreover, some directives have been taken by the European Council between 2003 and 2005 to harmonize asylum understanding and proceedings among Member States. Indeed, European leaders recognized the divergent interpretations of the asylum right by the states and the necessity to create baseline standards to get an effective human protection and respect asylum seekers' rights.

3.2 Shared Competencies in the European Union on Migration and Asylum?

The asylum and migration policies have been institutionalized through the Treaty of Amsterdam in 1997. It planned, however, that the EU is not the main actor in this area because the Member States have retained the main competency in the management of borders. Therefore, shared competencies do really exist in terms of asylum and migration.

[5]https://www.unhcr.org/protection/basic/3b73b0d63/states-parties-1951-convention-its-1967-protocol.html.

3.2.1 The EU as Harmonizer in Asylum and Migration Policies

Since the Treaty of Rome (1957), the European Community at that time has the mission to "*develop a common immigration policy*". The EU had therefore to harmonize the Member States' distinct policies in this area in order to ensure an effective protection of the refugees and the good management of the asylum processing. Brussels became competent for the control and the protection of the external borders according to the Schengen Agreement of 1985. However, the EU competencies to act depend on the two basics principles of subsidiarity and proportionality.

3.2.2 The Member States, Main Actors in Asylum and Migration

The EU members remain the main actors in the asylum and migration policies (as seen during the crisis). First, it is important to remember that the Council of the EU is composed of the government of each state who can decide to adopt or to block some decisions. In addition, even if all the decisions are taken according to the principles of subsidiarity and proportionality, none of the EU's actions can impinge on the Member States' competencies. Indeed, the states themselves are allowed to manage the flows of migration according to their own history and their economic needs. Also, Article 79 (5) TFEU ensures the right for the states to "*determine volumes of admission of third-country nationals coming from third countries to their territory in order to seek work, whether employed or self-employed*".[6] It means that the quotas decided at the EU's level can be rejected according to the right for states to fix the volume of refugees accepted.

In other words, as shown by the political blocking of the EU during the migration crisis, the states remain indirectly the main actors in asylum and migration policy even if the EU endorsed the mission of harmonization.

3.3 The Existing Common Standards in Asylum and Migration in the European Legal Framework: An Immediate but Insufficient Response

Some common policies and institutions had been launched in this area even before the beginning of the refugee crisis.

---

[6]Article 79 TFUE. Available at: https://eur-lex.europa.eu/legal-content/EN/TXT/PDF/?uri=CELEX:12012E/TXT.

3.3.1 The Schengen Regulation: A First Step Towards an European Harmonization

The creation of the Europe's Schengen area was one of the main steps in the pooling of the European Member States. Indeed, the "Agreement on the gradual abolition of checks at their common borders" signed in 1985 for only few members marked an important step in the process of integration in the European Community (EC). By removing internal borders, Article 17 established the free movement of the people and prepared the basis for a harmonization of the states in the understanding and the management of immigration.[7]

However, even if common standards have been established, the management remained in the signatories' hands. Also, the regulation allows states to reintroduce temporary border checks at their internal borders in case of real threat (Article 25 of the Schengen Borders Code).

This regulation remains considered as the cornerstone of the new shared system based on the EU. Also, the Treaty of Amsterdam (1997) tried to deepen the European management in asylum and migration area by creating minimum standards through directives. By this treaty, the Schengen Agreement entered into the primary law of the EU and has been included in the first pillar, following a supranational logic. As mentioned by Filipec et al. (2018), it revealed the early consciousness of a required unified approach in the management of borders.

3.3.2 Frontex: The Non-effective Prominence of the Member States

By following the Council decided the establishment of "Frontex" considered as an expert body specialized in the border management.[8] It was constructed based on three basic missions of patrolling to secure EU's borders, target migrants smugglers and rescue migrants at risk; the goal of the new agency is remained based on the sense of an effective cooperation, the establishment of common standards and the harmonization of the European external border management.

It was implemented based on a double logic of assistance of the Member States because it action remains limited by the states' willingness but also had independent missions such as the coordination of ad hoc centres, the task to increase the research in common European standards to protect and manage the common external borders (Article 2 Council regulation No 2007/2004) or even the possibility to launch common projects in this area (Article 3). The European Agency for the Management of Operational cooperation at external borders of the Member States of the EU was not

---

[7] Article 17 on the movement of people: "*[the Parties] shall endeavour first to harmonise, where necessary, the laws, regulations and administrative provisions concerning the prohibitions and restrictions on which the checks are based and to take complementary measures to safeguard internal security and prevent illegal immigration by nationals of States that are not members of the European Communities.*".

[8] See. Council regulation No 2007/2004.

effective enough because of the strict submission to its mandate of intervention to the states' consent.

3.3.3 The European Asylum Support Office (EASO) and Its Controversial Dublin Regulation

The EASO established common set of rules and procedures for the EU Members, trying to ensure a better coordination and effectiveness when it comes to migration and asylum. The EU's institutions sought a better management of the asylum requests and an equal treatment of the asylum seekers following their international commitments in the protection of migrants. It created come institutions specialized in asylum and migration such as the EURODAC which collects and shares information about asylum seekers or even the Common European Asylum System or CEAS qualified to support the Member States undergoing migration pressure. However, as mentioned by Mitsilegas (2014) "*the basis of the Common European Asylum System remains the determination of asylum claims at the national level*".

Included, the so-called Dublin Regulation (the last called Dublin III)[9] supposedly implemented to strengthen the EU management of the migrants and "safeguard the constitutional pillar of its asylum policy" became highly criticized during the crisis (Trauner 2016). Indeed, its main goal was to organize the migrants' flows by ensuring their relocation in the state where they first arrived, in order to know rapidly which country is responsible for the examination of the asylum application.[10]

However, the regulation was considered as not fair and not effective: the disproportionate responsibility of the states of arrival such as Italy and Greece generated an incapacity to manage effectively the asylum process and aggravate the pressure on the external borders. Internal political tensions appeared between the South and Central Europe, the latter refusing the amendment of the regulation and its enlargement which planned a larger solidarity to relieve Greece or even Italy.

4 The Early Unexpected Return to Crisis

As seen, even if some policies were established for more cooperation in asylum and migration, Brussels could not be prepared enough regarding its weakness and the volume of arrivals at European borders.

Indeed, the Union just faced the 2008 severe economic crisis which ravaged socially and economically some of its Member States (PIGS*) and millions of their

[9]Regulation EU No 604/2013. Available at: https://eur-lex.europa.eu/legal-content/EN/TXT/PDF/?uri=CELEX:32013R0604&from=EN.

[10]See. Court of Justice which in the case of Abdullahi (Case C-394/12, judgement of 10 December 2013).

*Portugal, Ireland, Greece, Spain

citizens. Consequently, the European Bank decided austerity measures to the very impacted states in order to balance their very high public debt. Greeks and Italians already knew a traumatic period through the economic crisis and its negative consequences. This context participated also to damage the trust of the Europeans in their institutions and in Europe's capacity to solve any crisis. In the end, the European Member States and the EU in itself were far from being prepared enough to manage properly the new crisis, namely the refugee crisis.

In addition, the amount of arriving migrants was not really expected. With a culminant point reached in 2015 with more than 1 million migrants according to the United Nations, the EU had to find fast and effective solution to both ease the first arrival states and respect their international commitments regarding refugee protection.

As mentioned above, the EU was not totally unarmed faced the arriving waves of migrants. But, an incomplete legal framework was implemented at the European level only based on inter-governmentalism. The incompleteness of the process created the political crisis: the management of such event was not fully planned and not adapted to this amount of arrivals. Therefore, first, ad hoc solutions have been taken to appease the crisis before establishing a real plan of action in a long-term view.

Part II. Steps towards an European answer to the refugee crisis

In front of the large influx of migrants and the call of the first arrival states for an Europe a help, the European institutions reacted in time to address the crisis. Rapidly before the peak of the crisis, some the internal changes have been realized, placing the management of migration influx in the top priority of the political agenda.

5 Migration as the New "Top Priority" in the European Institutions

5.1 Changes in the European Leaders

In November 2014, some changes have been done in the leaders of the EU for a better consideration of the refugee situation. The most notable changeover was the modification in the designation of the commissioner dedicated for the home affairs. From this moment, the mission has been broadened to the migration: the commissioner Dimitris Avramopoulos has been nominated as the "European Commissioner for Migration, Home affairs and Citizens". By the way, he ensured through a statement that improving cooperation among member states and find effective solutions in this area would be "*[his] top priority*".[11]

---

[11] Statement of the European commissioner for migration, home affairs and citizenship. Available at http://europa.eu/rapid/press-release_STATEMENT-14-1340_en.htm.

In addition, Federica Mogherini, both High Representative for the external action service and Vice President of the commission targeted migration in its missions and decided additional measures to manage it along the central Mediterranean route.

5.2 Changes in the European Agenda

5.2.1 The Determination of the Priorities in the Crisis

The refugee crisis became rapidly the top priority of the European Agenda. In April 2015, the Member States agreed on a 10-point plan establishing a list of 10 specific solutions for immediate action. The main goal was to address immediately the critical situation through a changeover in the structural asylum and migration policy. Among the proposals, the Foreign and Home Affairs Council proposed jointly a systematic cooperation and meeting between the main European institutions specialized in migration (Europol, Eurojust, EASO, Frontex) or even to consider an alternative solution to the emergency relocation mechanism.[12] The European institutions and the states who committed themselves in further and concrete actions, mainly to prevent the number of deaths among the migrants, unconditionally supported the plan.

Moreover, a month after, the European Agenda on Migration (EAM) was decided, offering solutions for an urgent and medium-term view, but also for long-term perspective to address the issue in a long and sustainable manner.[13] The main goals in a short perspective were the proposal of better help for states in the need and to advert further deaths in the Mediterranean Sea mainly. However, in the long-term view, the document states that "*European cooperation in the area of migration needs to go further*" (p. 17). The Agenda proposes therefore some improvements permitting a common management of the crisis towards a European answer, within the scope of the existing treaties.

5.2.2 The Deployment of Urgent and Ad Hoc Solutions

In the face of the rejection of the Dublin Regulation by some states, some proposals have been done by the Commission under Article 78 (3) of the TFEU to relocate urgently the migrants to ease the first arrival states such as Italy, Malta, Hungary or Greece.

Based on the key principle of solidarity provided by Article 80 of TFEU, a temporary relocation plan for asylum seekers has been triggered based on distribution keys, i.e. on "*objective, quantifiable and verifiable criteria*" showing the real hosting

[12]The 10 point plan. Available at: http://europa.eu/rapid/press-release_IP-15-4813_en.htm.

[13]The European Agenda on Migration (EAM). Available at: http://ec.europa.eu/dgs/home-affairs/what-we-do/policies/european-agenda-migration/background-information/docs/communication_on_the_european_agenda_on_migration_en.pdf.

capacity of each Member State (see. Annex of the EAM). In September 2015, in the context of the EAM, two consecutive relocation plans have been launched through EU Decision. Firstly, the Commission called for the sharing of 40,000 refugees across the continent, and 120,000 for the second.[14] However, in December 2016 only 5% of the targeted volume of refugees has been really relocated from Greece and Italy (Rankin, The Guardian, 2016).

Moreover, the European institutions and the Member States announced some budgetary measures dedicated to the urgent cause. In April 2015, EASO decided an increase of the budget dedicated to Frontex which tripled by €9 million per month and released from the EU budget to the Triton border patrol. In addition, in August, the European Commission accepted a €2.4 billion emergency aid package with around €560 million allocated for Italy and €473 million for Greece to ease them in their migrant rescue efforts. Then, the EU's leaders, for example, proposed to allocate €1.7 billion in EU funding.

6 Towards an External Management of the Refugee Crisis

The EU implemented also towards the strengthening of the management of the crisis outside the territory with the objective of reducing the volume of migrants arriving at the borders and, therefore, to avoid them the perilous journey across the Mediterranean.

6.1 Broadening the Frontex Mandate: The European Border Coast Guard Agency

One of the main measures taken by the EU was the replacement of Frontex by the European Border Coast Guard Agency (EBCG) through the regulation of EU 2016/1624. The spirit of this European Agency remained similar but its mandate has been expanded for a real EU integrated border policy. Indeed, in the state of the Union speech, the President of the Commission Juncker underlined the will to reinforce significantly Frontex's competencies and to "*develop it into a fully operational European border and coast guard system*".[15] Consequently, more power and resources were dedicated to this European body for the protection of the borders and the assistance to the Member States. Among them, the ECBG received more financial resources but also, its own human resources and technical equipment increased for a faster intervention during its missions at hotspots (Ferraro and De Capitani 2016).

---

[14]EU Decision 1523/2015 and EU Decision 1601/2015.

[15]Speech on the State of the Union. Available at http://ec.europa.eu/priorities/soteu/docs/state_of_the_union_2015_en.pdf.

The body was therefore able to deploy those resources during the operations that it could have launched in the highly pressured arriving points.

The EBCG had shown its effectiveness: 375,201 lives have been saved since 2015. The result is evidently not only the fact of the EBCG but it contributed to save them. However, the body remains an alternative to help states: it was designated to assist them but not act above them. Its intervention remains under the government's approbation but the states had to cooperate; otherwise, they could have been rejected temporarily from the Schengen area. Nevertheless, generally speaking, the body has been well welcomed as a helper to manage the unceasing flows of migrants. Nevertheless, as an assistant, the body does not have enough powers and independence to be fully effective. Also, as underlined by Filipec et al. (2018), its intervention blurred the responsibility between the Member States and the body.

6.2 External and Diplomatic Partnership

For decision's taken, the EU launched an external and diplomatic policy aiming at establishing some asylum centres outside Europe to manage the flow of migrants before their arrival on European territory.

6.2.1 (A Way to Assist Greece): The EU-Turkey Refugee Statement

With 885,000 arrivals in 2015 alone, Greece asylum and reception process were exceeded by the volume of arrivals and could not be effective enough to register and provide protection to the persons arriving. Considering the situation, the EU leaders accepted a joint action plan on migration with Turkey. Finally signed in March 2016, it was based on the deal that each irregular migrant crossing Turkish border towards Greek island is sent back to Turkey. The cooperation with the Turkish authorities is not a one-way street according to J. C. Juncker because for each return in Turkey, one Syrian has been resettled to the EU (1:1 mechanism). However, the number of Syrian resettled was almost quadrupled compared to the number of Syrians returned to Turkey (916). In addition, this agreement implies some European commitment in return: a financial support of almost 3 billion has been sent to Turkey to help the country hosting the Syrian refugees for the 2016–2017 periods.

Finally, the objectives of stopping the bleeding in the arrival of migrants from Turkey and to replace it with organized and protected channels were reached. The immediate effectiveness of the Joint Plan was rapidly perceived because the irregular arrivals dropped by 97% and the number of lives lost at sea decreased significantly as well according to the balance sheet of the European Commission published one year after the signature.[16]

6.2.2 (A Way to Support Italy): Partnerships in Northern Africa

In the comprehensive approach of migration by the EU, other's partnership has been established or reinforced with some African states. The main goals are both to support Italy, which is welcoming millions of migrants coming from Africa and to tackle the roots of migration.

Firstly, certain already existing partnership with some African states has been renewed in 2016 to reinforce the EU-African cooperation on migration. The main priority at this moment was to tackle the irregular migration coming from Africa to Italy (144,000 people have already reached Italy only until this period and over 3,600 people died in the Mediterranean). As underlined by Nielsen in the EUobserver (2016), this objective could not have been reached without reinforcing two existing partnership established in 2014: the Khartoum Process and the Sudan's Rapid Support Force. The EU states have set up those cooperation with numerous Northern and Eastern African states (such as South Sudan, Eritrea, Somalia or Egypt) to curb irregular migration. Technical, military and financial supports have been sending and will be reinforced according to A. Merkel's speech in October 2016.

Northern African Partnership

The Northern African partnership was valuable in this critical period. Firstly, the EU was attached to maintain and perhaps reinforce them to reduce the volume of arrivals at EU borders and to avoid migrants to cross the sea.

Firstly, after years of rejection of the EU proposal, Tunisia and Morocco agreed finally in 2013 and 2014 on the Mobility Partnership on migration aiming at sending back the irregular migrants and to cooperate in the influx management. As mentioned by Limam and Del Sarto in 2015, those agreements are part of the EU strategy to create partnership with the states of Middle East and Northern African (MENA) on migration. Also, more recently in October 2016, the European Commission started negotiating bilaterally with Tunisia to implement a visa facilitation and readmission of irregular migrants' procedure.[17]

In addition, in the continuation of a long-term partnership decided back to 2008 called "Treaty of friendship, partnership and cooperation", the Memorandum of understanding was signed between the Italian government and the new UN-backed

[16] EU-Turkey Refugee statement. Available at: https://ec.europa.eu/home-affairs/sites/homeaffairs/files/what-we-do/policies/european-agenda-migration/background-information/eu_turkey_statement_17032017_en.pdf.

[17] The EU and Tunisia start negotiations on visa facilitation and readmission. Available at: http://europa.eu/rapid/press-release_IP-16-3394_en.htm.

Libyan government in 2017.[18] The new Italy–Libya cooperation endorsed by the EU in its Malta's declaration aimed at firstly establishing asylum-processing centres (also called hotspots) to manage the asylum seekers' requests outside of Europe, which means that the migrants could only enter in EU after a positive response in the asylum process (Nakache and Losier 2017). The goal of the partnership was to combat human trafficking in the politically destabilized Libya. Therefore, a help projected to $240 million funds (against $30 million in 2008) has been sent to Libya to ensure the reinforcement of the Libyan coastguard and the navy to catch more effectively the migrants boats (Merelli 2017). Also, it led to the creation of immigration detention centres (Crépeau 2013).

The effectiveness of this partnership is, however, questionable. Indeed, even if it helped reducing the number of arrivals by managing the asylum process outside from the EU, many problems arose. Crépeau (2013) underlined that corruption, misappropriation of the funds and bad treatments of migrants increased a lot. The situation became so dangerous that it pushed even more migrants to leave Libya for Europe through the Mediterranean Sea, considered as being the most dangerous border crossing of the world by the International Organization for Migration. The partnership became controversial: the EU reinforced a collaboration with a country without domestic or international commitment on the protection of migrants. Indirectly, the EU is violating its commitments over the migrants through this partnership (Giuffre 2013).

6.2.3 Strengthening the Balkan's Partnership

The EU can find its principle allies in the states composing the Western Balkans. Effectively, as being geographically direct neighbours, many Balkans states developed close political ties with the EU: some are already in the EU (Croatia in 2013, Slovenia in 2004) and others such as the Republic of North Macedonia, Montenegro and Albania became official candidates for EU membership (respectively in 2005, 2010 and 2014).

For proximity reasons, this region became a route taken by the migrants coming from Greece or Turkey mainly (the "Balkans route") to enter the EU. Therefore, many arrangements can be jointly found to organize the migration routes or to improve the management of the borders. According to Michael Roth, the Germany's deputy minister for foreign affairs, "*a migration policy that is developed without involving the Western Balkans can neither be successful nor sustainable*" (Feilcke 2018, DW). The EU tries to work closely with those states to create a common partnership to strengthen the security policy, in this idea; the Western Balkan Summit took place in London as a signal of close partnership. In addition, after financial commitments, the EU can have a real impact on this region by "*supporting economic and administrative modernization and infrastructure projects*" (Fischer 2015, Social Europe).

[18]Memorandum of understanding. Available at http://www.asgi.it/wp-content/uploads/2017/02/ITALY-LIBYA-MEMORANDUM-02.02.2017.pdf.

In total, almost €18 billion from the EU budget were dedicated to the migration crisis for the 2015–2017 periods. Institutional binding efforts have been quickly done at internal and external levels to address the emergency at EU borders. However, to face an important volume of arrivals, Brussels could not be effective enough to solve effectively the crisis. Therefore, the trust in its capacity to solve the crisis has been challenged, conducting the supranational entity in a political crisis.

Part III. The aftermath faced by the Union after the crisis: towards a deep political crisis

Even after a certain appeasement in the refugee crisis, the EU has emerged internally weakened. Indeed, lots of discrepancies appeared among the Member States and the EU and between states themselves, creating a real European political crisis. The EU's unity has been challenged both by a reconsideration of the political construction of the EU and by a conflict on the European values.

7 Conflict on the Political Construction of the EU: A Reconsideration of the European Sovereignty

The refugee crisis brought also divisions into the Union. Some citizens and therefore their governments, not satisfied by the European management of the crisis, did some steps back in the acceptance of the EU, towards a national fold. A deep "political crisis of Europe" emerged, questioning the political legitimacy of the EU to take decisions and solve issues.

7.1 A Divided Public Opinion on the Refugee Crisis

Faced with the arrival of migrants in some countries and of the media cover of the crisis, an anti-immigration sentiment appeared among lots of citizens, explaining the re-emergence of some sovereigntist political parties all around the EU. Seeing the ineffectiveness in the management of the crisis, some European citizens opted politically for a national response and therefore a rejection of any European solution.

The fear of migrants must be understood in a certain context of insecurity that the Europeans have faced of: after the economic crisis and a high rate of unemployment in some states, the fear was firstly situated in the lack of opportunities in the labour market. By the way, according, Business Insider in 2015, to the statement "*Immigrants today are a burden for our country because they take away our jobs and social benefits*", 52% of the polled in France agreed, 52% in Poland, 69% in Italy and 70% in Greece.[19] Also, the fear has been nurtured mostly by the far-right parties in the context of the Events of the New Year Eve of 2016 in Koln, Germany and of

[19] Also, Germany (29%), the UK (37%), Spain (46%).

the terrorist attacks of Copenhagen and Paris in 2015 (Filipec et al. 2018, p. 103). Indeed, the far-right parties are largely using the argument that terrorists are entering the EU through the migration flow (see Viktor Orban).[20] Based on those fears, in April 2015 an opinion survey showed, for example, that 46% of polled Hungarians supported that asylum seekers should not be allowed to enter Hungary.[21]

This widespread fear and the national fold were concretized in the national elections results with the emergence or the strengthening of many populist and nationalist parties: the far-right coalition in Italy and the emergence of M. Salvini as an informal leader, the strengthening of V. Orban in Hungary, the re-emergence of a far-right and sovereign party in Germany (AfD), etc. They underlined that a part of the public opinion is opposed to the Brussels governance. The political commitments of the newly elected Eurosceptic governments put in trouble the intergovernmental cooperation expected in the EU.

Those results were quite confirmed with the recent European Parliament elections held at the end of May 2019.[22] The last results of the European elections highlighted as well an increasing fragmentation of the European citizens, divided between the pro-Europeans and the sovereigntists, reluctant to a European approach (Erlanger 2019, NYTimes).

7.2 *The Questioning of the Exclusivity of Sovereignty Over Migration Issues: Towards Internal Divisions*

The political crisis of the EU was concretized both by the deterioration of solidarity in the refugee crisis and by a lack of cooperation among member states, but also by the erosion of the EU's authority and its legitimacy to act as the solution for the EU. Indeed, some dissensions appeared in the Member States' asylum practices creating an important disorder in the European political organization based on cooperation. Some leaders and European people are supporting an unilateralist vision of the decision-making and are hostile to the management of Brussels.

Therefore, the issue of the exclusivity of the sovereignty concerning the migratory question always seems questioned. On the one hand, the new Eurosceptic governments accused Europe of imposing them a migratory policy (and, in particular, the respect of the quotas of redistribution of the migrants) which is supposed to be a shared competency between the EU and the Member States. However, on the other hand, states such as France and Germany (which are not countries of the first arrival) wished a communitarization of the migratory policy towards a harmonization in the

---

[20]"*If somebody takes masses of non-registered immigrants from the Middle East into a country, this also means importing terrorism, criminalism, anti-Semitism, and homophobia*". Viktor Orban. Available at: https://www.budapesttimes.hu/2016/03/03/i-maintain-basic-values-europe.

[21]Available at: https://ec.europa.eu/migrant-integration/index.cfm?action=furl.go&go=/news/hungary-xenophobia-at-its-peak&pdf=1).

[22]European Parliament elections results of May 2019. Available at: https://www.election-results.eu/.

asylum practices among Member States. In this way, the French President Emmanuel Macron argued against the states that benefit from the solidarity at the financial level and are egoist in terms of migration subjects. In other words, it is the contents between those who opted for a "*burden sharing*" and those who prefer "*a burden shifting*" putting their national interests above those of the community (Dijkstra et al. 2001).

Reproaching the apparent ineffectiveness of the migration policies and feeling that the crisis was out of control, the distrust of the public opinion over the EU in the Visegrad Group and in Italy rose significantly. Their elected governments wanted therefore to manage themselves the migration policies rather than waiting Brussels decisions. In this way, they both opted for a unilateralist management of the crisis, resisting to the European politics of harmonization and cooperation in this area in order to stop what is considered as an invasion by some (cf. V. Orban).[23] For example, while the firsts rejected all the plans of redistribution of refugees, Italy's leaders were determined to close their ports to non-Italian rescue vessels, challenging the principle of non-refoulement. Those resistant and unilateralist behaviour were also concretized by the construction of fences or walls at the national borders as opposed to the free movement of people implemented through the Schengen regulation.

By that anti-authority behaviour from some Member States, the EU's legitimacy has been highly challenged. Slovakia went until questioning the European Union Court of Justice (EUCJ) on the Brussels right to impose relocated refugees to Member States (Rettman 2015, EU observer).

Those dissensions among Member States on the political competencies of the EU and the unilateralist's behaviour blocked the process of harmonization of the asylum and migration. About this topic, Angela Merkel reminded during a speech at the Bundestag on the eve of an European summit of June 2018 that the EU is an organization where "[we] *advocate the multilateralism and not the unilateralism and this one is essential to continue to appear as a real political organization, in the eyes of the world*". She reaffirmed the principle of multilateralism and of cooperation, basis of the EU construction. In addition, the President of the Commission Juncker condemned the return to national borders by saying that "*walls and fences have no place in EU Member States*".[24] The pro-European leaders tried to condemn those reluctant behaviour by reminded the importance of a multilateral approach to solve this European crisis.

Those divisions have been translated at the European level by a blockage in solving commonly the situation, but also reopened the existing debate on the European values.

---

[23] See. V. Orban.

[24] Speech delivered in 2015. Available at: http://europa.eu/rapid/press-release_SPEECH-15-5614_en.htm.

8 Conflict on the European Values: The Humanitarian Value of the EU Shared Between Multiculturalism or Social Integration

The EU is generally perceived as a model of multiculturalism, understood as the preservation of different cultures or cultural identities through a robust framework on human rights within an unified society by encouraging the distinctiveness (Emerson 2013). Indeed, according to Article 2 of the TEU, "[the] *respect for human dignity, freedom, democracy, equality, the rule of law and respect for human rights, including the rights of persons belonging to minorities*" are imposed. Nevertheless, Chancellor Merkel started talking about the failure of multiculturalism in Europe (Cameron agreed also). With the migration waves, many people brought their own language, culture, religion and ethnicities creating a "super-diversity" in the words of Vertovec (2007). But the EU behaved somehow as a nation-state and legitimized during the crisis the rejection of migrants for the protection of the nationals and their culture (Dijkstra et al. 2001).

The social integration and cohesion policies are normally defined by the Member States individually, following the EU's broadened framework on the prohibition of discriminations and the protections of migrants. Nevertheless, some states adopted unilateralist policies. For example, the leaders from the Visegrad Group rejected migrants based on the fear of a disappearing of the historical Christian identity of Europe and replacement by the culture brought by the refugees. In this idea, the Former Slovak Prime Minister Roberto Fico and Viktor Orban declared their refusal to welcome Muslim migrants because they will try to change the nature, the culture and the values of the European countries. In addition, Poland and Slovakia maintained that they would only accept Christian refugees from Syria. In addition, the "Stop-Soros" policy adopted by the Hungarian parliament allowed to sanction the NGOs dedicated to help migrants. At the end, foreigners are considered as threat if they do not fulfil some cultural preconditions, increasing xenophobia and tacking the image of the EU a welcoming and non-discriminant area (Lentin and Titley 2012, European Journal of cultural studies). This xenophobic behaviour from a part of the EU citizens and their leaders creates problems now in the acceptance of the refugees who obtained a positive asylum answer.

In this context, Rieff (2005) is talking about a "*multicultural fantasy in Europe*", that it could be understood as the conflict in the EU between the lack of multiculturalism policies of almost all of the Member States, and its defence of the universalist value of the EU (protected by its international commitments and the European treaties). And the Member States took different positions on integration: Germany, for instance, encouraged multiculturalism and protected the distinctiveness while France is applying more assimilated policies (Kenan 2015, Foreign Affairs). In this topic, the Hungarian official in France Georg Karolyi declared that the values that the EU wants to defend do not correspond anymore with the Hungarians' ones; showing that this conflict on the European values represents another challenge in the refugee crisis for the supranational entity.

The Member States were divided both on the political organization of the EU and on its values challenging, therefore, its authority. De facto, the Union was completely blocked in its decision-making and could not really force Member States to cooperate and "share the burden" during the refugee crisis. Therefore, a solution appears evidently to solve the EU's crisis: the spillover or a deeper integration in asylum and migration policies, giving more strength to the EU.

Part IV. A strengthen Union to solve the migration crisis: towards a common answer to European issues?

Because the asylum and migration policies are mainly into the divided and somehow reluctant Member States' hands, the solutions found by the EU to save the crisis did not have a full effect. In addition, "*The scales and intensity of migration flows in 2014–2016 have shown the limitedness of national approaches to solving the problem*" (Filipec et al. 2018, p. 114). Therefore, some claim that the EU is the solution as E. Macron did by stating that the EU with a real European asylum right will be the answer to the migration crisis (Bet 2019, Express).

9 Perceiving the EU as the Most Relevant Level: Regaining the EU's Legitimacy and Authority

The EU must regain the trust of the people and their elected leaders. Indeed, the Europeans by over expecting actions from the EU were disappointed on the management of the refugee crisis, undermining its legitimacy. Therefore, this misconception must be corrected to ensure the authority of Brussels and a better effectiveness of its decisions.

9.1 Misunderstanding and Over Expectations by the Citizens on the Role of the EU

Seeing the uninterrupted arrivals of migrants over the months and the difficulties met by some states, the citizens (and therefore their elected leaders) highly criticized and blamed the EU for what it was perceived as its inaction or ineffectiveness of its decisions. Indeed, Brussels was considered responsible for the refugee crisis and as unable to solve it. However, as supported by Filipec et al. (2018) this shared perception is based on a citizens' misunderstanding and over expectations of the EU competencies and responsibilities in the border management. Indeed, the citizens are not fully aware of what the EU really did to solve the migration crisis and the effects of its decisions implemented.

Also, a lot of citizens of the Union believe that Brussels did a "poor job" when it came to the management of the refugee crisis. Indeed, a towering 94% of Greeks disapproved of the way the EU deals with the refugee crisis, almost 90% for Sweden or even 77% for Italy.[25] However, lots also over expected the role of the Union in the crisis. Indeed, the EU is quite often perceived as a magic supranational entity, supposed to solve all the problems faced by the Member States' individually. Effectively, numerous Europeans want the EU to do more about immigration in May 2018 (72% according to the Eurobarometer poll).[26] However, as mentioned earlier, in terms of asylum and migration policies, even if some harmonized policies have been established by Brussels (after the acceptance by all the Member States), the states remain the main actors and their cooperation is required to the well effectiveness of each decision.

Finally, the misunderstanding of the EU role comes also from the lack of cooperation of some states during the refugee crisis. Indeed, the Union can only be effective if the states are cooperating. Nevertheless, through anti-authority government's attitudes from some Member States, the EU authority has been highly defied. On the one hand, this challenge was, for example, concretized by the unilateralist policies established and also by the low record of implementation in the migratory field (Carrera et al. 2015). But also, on the other hand, through the speeches of their Eurosceptic leaders or parties such as V. Orban who said "*Europe can't take in huge masses of foreign people in an unlimited, uncontrolled manner*".[27] Therefore, obviously closer to their national representatives, the citizens were more likely to trust in the incompetence of the EU.

9.2 *Regain the Brussels' Legitimacy and Authority on the Member States and Citizens*

To deal correctly with the migration crisis at an European level, Brussels must win back its legitimacy through regaining trust and support from the European citizens. Indeed, the people must be aware of the decisions taken by at the European level and their real effects on the crisis. Therefore, a better communication from the Brussels can be one solution showing what the EU did and the legal framework in which it was realized.

In addition, as mentioned, this false perception of the EU competencies was also the fact of the reluctant states' behaviours. Lots did not implement the Brussels rules, challenging its authority. However, as reminded by J. C. Juncker "*The rule of law is*

[25] Spring 2016 Global Attitudes Survey, in Pew Research Center. Available at: https://www.pewresearch.org/fact-tank/2016/09/16/european-opinions-of-the-refugee-crisis-in-5-charts/.

[26] 72% of the polled europeans want the EU to do more when it comes to asylum and migration. "EU migrant crisis: facts and figures", 30 June 2017, European Parliament. Available at: http://www.europarl.europa.eu/news/en/headlines/society/20170629STO78630/eu-migrant-crisis-facts-and-figures.

[27] Available at: https://www.sacbee.com/news/nation-world/world/article56017690.html.

not optional in the EU. It is a must".[28] Therefore, to ensure the respect of the Member States' European commitments, some proposed to reinforce or create sanctions.

For example, according to Article 7 of the TEU procedures of penalty can be opened against one reluctant state, as it was voted in September 2018 against the Hungarian government or Poland in 2017.[29] However, those procedures, which require unanimity in the European Council, do not have lots of chances to be finalized, considering the alliances in the EU. Also, against the states who did not apply the Dublin Regulation, sanctions have been decided.[30] Additionally, E. Macron and others proposed that financial penalties should be imposed on states that defy the authority of Brussels to force indirectly reluctant states to enforce approved decisions.

In other words, as stated by Lehne (2019), "*stronger EU rules and institution remain the key solution to control the external borders and establish effective policies and asylum on migration*". Without effective tools to pressure dissenting states, the EU will not be able to regain its legitimacy.

10 A Deeper Integration of the EU After the Crisis

10.1 The Incompleteness of the EU's Framework, Basics of the Spillover Effect

Based on Marco Scipioni's thesis (2018), the political crisis of the EU created on the refugee crisis was obvious. Indeed, the asylum and migration policies shared between the national and the European levels were doomed to failure because of their incompleteness (Castres 2004). In addition, as reminded by Scipioni (2018), those policies were inclined to create a crisis because it combined "*bad factors such as the insufficient harmonization, the lack of solidarity and the nonexistence of central institutions*".

However, the failure of the asylum and migration policies sometimes considered as part of the process of integration, one-step of the spillover effect is described by the neo-functionalists. It is the direct consequence of an incomplete policy at the European level (Jones et al. 2016). It induces that more integration, and therefore a deeper harmonization of those policies at an European level, is the solution to solve the current political crisis. According to Ben (2000), those policies require both an "*expansion of Community competencies and the centralization within EU institutions*", and also the regain of its legitimacy is crucial. Those solutions cannot be done without the modification of the treaties to ensure the respect of those harmonized

---

[28] Jean-Claude Juncker Quotes. BrainyQuote.com, BrainyMedia Inc, 2019. Available at: https://www.brainyquote.com/quotes/jeanclaude_juncker_887348, accessed 15 June 2019.

[29] Article 7 TEU. Available at. https://eur-lex.europa.eu/legal-content/EN/TXT/?uri=celex:12012M007.

[30] ECHR Grand chamber judgement 21 January 2011 in the case of M.S.S. v. BELGIUM AND GREECE, (Application no. 30696/09).

policies that should be given to the EU. In other words, a more integrated EU seems to be the best solution to tackle this crisis and the potential others (Carrera et al. 2015).

10.2 The "Soft" Role of the EU to Solve the Crisis

The EU is based on the cooperation of its members who accepted to share their sovereignty and apply its treaties. Therefore, it cannot effectively work without the goodwill of the Member States. To regain its legitimacy and push the states to support it, Brussels must prefer acting through a flexible and comprehensive perception to avoid a strong opposition of its Member States in times of political and human crisis.

One of the complaints against the EU in the management of the refugee crisis was its ineffectiveness and the slowness of the solution provided. More flexibility for Brussels in the decision-making would be the same as reducing the power of the states towards an increased reactivity according to the urgencies. It seems to be the only way to homogenize those very different European states and find an harmonized asylum and migration policies. In addition, more flexibility in the policies would probably encourage states to accept migrants. For example, the strengthening of a voluntary service financially rewarded could unfreeze some reluctant states to accept to help migrants. The absence of mandatory nature could reduce the reluctance of the states and the public opinion over the EU.

Through a comprehensive approach, the Union would show it as capable of being aware of lots of fields by taking into account the interests of all. This comprehensive approach was established through the "Migration Agenda" which has set up pillars to guide the new common European policy. In addition, the President of the European Council D. Tusk stated, "*Europe is taking its responsibility—saving lives, welcoming refugees and those entitled to international protection, offering more organised routes for legal migration, and dismantling criminal organisations*".[31]

This perspective adopted must be deepened to tend towards a "Flexible solidarity", defined by Filipec et al. (2018) as "[an EU] *that takes into account the interests of the Community, its individual states, the migrants, and the accepting societies*". Indeed, in the migration field, some scholars are reproaching the EU to be security-centred. It must broaden its concerns to propose a better approach of the issues provided by the refugee crisis, for example. A is required to suggest a multi-sector policy to take into account the economic, social and foreign affairs priorities. At the end, the EU must become flexible, broadened itself to survive the next crisis.

[31] See www.consilium.europa.eu/en/meetings/european-council/2015/10/15-16/ and Opening Speech at Valetta Conference. Available at: www.consilium.europa.eu/en/press/press-releases/2015/11-tuskopening-statement-valletta-summit/.

10.3 Conclusion

Finally, even if now the migratory crisis seems to be partially solved (cf. reduction of arriving migrants in European borders), it revealed a deep internal political crisis in the European Union. Indeed, Brussels has to face simultaneously the fear of its citizens and the conflicts between Member States and reopening debates on the basis of the EU construction: sovereignty and values. Furthermore, the hegemony of the Western countries, led by Germany and France, was questioned by the appearance of anti-authority groups in the East, in particular. Indeed, the important mediatisation of the Visegrad Group grants it an important weight to rebalance the debates within the EU. Faced with those conflicts, Brussels' authority has been damaged, and its legitimacy decreased a lot.

Therefore, now, the EU must appear as a powerful and united front to ensure the survival of the supranational entity. Some scholars perceived the crisis as one of the normal consequences of the spillover effect resulting, therefore, to a deeper integration process. Scipioni (2018) supports that the crisis has broken out based on the lack of communautarization of the asylum and migration policies. Therefore, the crisis is supposed to push the Union towards a deeper harmonization. Brussels must endorse the role of mediator and authoritarian guide of the Member States, trying to solve commonly their issues.

Effectively, it is necessary for the EU to become credible again in its capacity to solve the problems faced through a multilateral and cooperative way rather than through an unilateralist manner. In other words, the history taught us that the individual initiatives of the European member states allow rarely resolving problems and sometimes instigating new conflicts. That is why Metcalfe-Hough (2016) insists, "*The EU urgently needs to put in place a coherent, long-term and comprehensive strategy that maximises the benefits of migration and minimises its human and economic costs, including as part of a wider international effort to manage global migration*". To conclude, the European Union must continue to build and transform itself in order to overcome numerous crises.

Primarily References

Convention for the Protection of Human Rights and Fundamental Freedoms.

- Article 3: prohibiting any torture or inhuman or degrading treatment or punishment.

Convention relating to the status of refugees, 1951.

- Article 1 on the Definition of refugee.
- Article 33 on the "Principle of non-refoulement".

Treaty on the Functioning of the European Union, 2007.

- Article 78 (3) of the TFUE on the urgent relocation.

- Article 79 (5) of the TFEU on the competencies in the establishment of the common immigration policy.
- Article 80 of the TFUE on the principle of solidarity.

Convention implementing the Schengen Agreement of 14 June 1985 between the Governments of the States of the Benelux Economic Union, the Federal Republic of Germany and the French Republic on the gradual abolition of checks at their common borders.

- Article 17 of the Schengen Borders Code
- Article 25 of the Schengen Borders Code

Treaty of the European Union, 1992.

- Article 2 TEU.
- Article 7 TEU.

Council Regulation (EC) No 2007/2004 establishing a European Agency for the Management of Operational Cooperation at the External Borders of the Member States of the European Union.

- Article 2 on the competencies of Frontex.
- Article 3 on the launching of common projects. 1

European Commission (2015) Communication from the Commission to the European Parliament and Council. A European Border and Coast Guard and effective management of Europe's external borders. Available at: goo.gl/ipJMy5 (7. 3. 2018).

EU Decision 1523/2015 and EU Decision 1601/2015 on the relocation plans.

EU-Turkey Refugee statement. Available at: https://ec.europa.eu/home-affairs/sites/homeaffairs/files/what-we-do/policies/european-agenda-migration/background-information/eu_turkey_statement_17032017_en.pdf.

Memorandum of understanding. Available at http://www.asgi.it/wp-content/uploads/2017/02/ITALY-LIBYA-MEMORANDUM-02.02.2017.pdf.

Regulation (EU) No 604/2013 of the European Parliament and of the Council of 26 June 2013 establishing the criteria and mechanisms for determining the Member State responsible for examining an application for international protection lodged in one of the Member States by a third-country national or a stateless person (recast).

Regulation (EU) No 1168/2011 of the European Parliament and of the Council of 25 October 2011 amending Council Regulation (EC) No 2007/2004 establishing a European Agency for the Management of Operational Cooperation at the External Borders of the Member States of the European Union.

Regulation (EU) No 2016/1624 of the European Parliament and of the Council of 14 September 2016 on the European Border and Coast Guard and amending Regulation (EU) 2016/399 of the European Parliament and of the Council and repealing Regulation (EC) No 863/2007 of the European Parliament and of the Council, Council Regulation (EC) No 2007/2004 and Council Decision 2005/267/EC.

Secondary References

BET, M. (2019, March). Emmanuel Macron claims European integration will be 'answer to migrant crisis. *Express*. Available at: https://www.express.co.uk/news/world/1097041/eu-news-emmanuel-macron-immigration-crisis-migration-italy-france-fazio-spt.

Carrera, S., et al. (2015). The EU's response to the refugee crisis: Taking stock and setting policy priorities. *Ceps Essay*, (20/16).

Castres, S. (2004). Why migration policies fail. *Ethnic and Racial Studies, 27*(2), 205–227.

Castro, L. D., & Lago, J. R. R. (2018). Educación y diplomacia cultural en la primavera de Europa (1948–1954) = Education and cultural diplomacy in the spring of Europe (1948–1954). *Revista de Educación, 383*, 63–84.

Crépeau, F. (2013). Report of the special rapporteur on the human rights of migrants, Regional study: Management of the external borders of the European Union and its impact on the human rights of migrants. *Human Rights Council*, April 24, 2013. Available at: http://www.ohchr.org/EN/HRBodies/HRC/RegularSessions/Session29/Documents/A_HR.

Dijkstra, S., et al. (2001). Multiculturalism and social integration in Europe. *International Political Science Review, 22*(1), 55–84.

Emerson, M. (2013). Interculturalism: Europe and its Muslims in search of sound societal models. In *A micro-level perspective on the dynamics of conflict, violence, and development*, (p. 126). Available at: http://aei.pitt.edu/32656/1/79._Interculturalism.pdf.

Erlanger, S. (2019, May). European election results show a growing split over Union's future. *NYTimes*. Available at: https://www.nytimes.com/2019/05/26/world/europe/european-elections-results.html?module=inline.

Färber, K. (2017). Mitterrand and the Great European design—From the cold war to the European Union. *Baltic Journal of European Studies, 7*(2), 132–147.

Ferraro, F., & De Capitani, E. (2016). The new European border and coast guard: Yet another "half way" EU reform? *ERA Forum, 17*(3).

Feilcke, A. (2018, July). Western Balkans are vital to curb migration and fight terrorism in Europe. *DW*. Available at https://www.dw.com/en/western-balkans-are-vital-to-curb-migration-and-fight-terrorism-in-europe/a-44589217.

Filipec, O., et al. (2018). Europe and the migration crisis: The response of the EU Member states. Available at: https://s3.amazonaws.com/academia.edu.documents/58443942/EU_Response_to_Migration.pdf?response-content-disposition=inline%3B%20filename%3DEurope_and_the_Migration_Crisis_the_Resp.pdf&X-Amz-Algorithm=AWS4-HMAC-SHA256&X-Amz-Credential=AKIAIWOWYYGZ2Y53UL3A%2F20190701%2Fus-east-1%2Fs3%2Faws4_request&X-Amz-Date=20190701T090812Z&X-Amz-Expires=3600&X-Amz-SignedHeaders=host&X-Amz-Signature=c32bd9fcb3e15458c8b855d4a480b51fe1fbd27cbd264ab7c989705d13163f72.

Fischer, J. (2015, August). Breaking Europe's migration paralysis. *Social Europe*. Available at: https://www.socialeurope.eu/breaking-europes-migration-paralysis.

Foster. P. (2018, June). Angela Merkel warns migration challenge could 'determine Europe's' destiny. *The Telegraph*. Available at: https://www.telegraph.co.uk/news/2018/06/28/angela-merkel-warns-migration-challenge-could-determine-europes/.

Giuffre, M. (2013). State responsibility beyond borders: What legal basis for Italy's Push-backs to Libya? *International Journal of Refugee: Oxford University Press, 24*(4), 692–734.

Hamulák, O. (2018). La carta de los derechos fundamentales de la union europea y los derechos sociales. *Estudios Constitucionales, 16*(1), 167–186.

Jones, E., et al. (2016). Failing forward? The Euro crisis and the incomplete nature of European integration. *Comparative Political Studies, 49*(7), 1010–1034.

Kenan, M. (2015, March). The failure of multiculturalism. *Foreign Affairs*. Available at: https://www.foreignaffairs.com/articles/western-europe/2019–02-18/failure-multiculturalism.

Kerikmäe, T. (Ed.). (2013). *Protecting human rights in the EU: Controversies and challenges of the Charter of Fundamental Rights*. Springer Science & Business Media.

Kerikmäe, T., Troitiño, D. R., & Shumilo, O. (2019). An idol or an ideal? A case study of Estonian e-Governance: public perceptions, myths and misbeliefs. *Acta Baltica Historiae et Philosophiae Scientiarum, 7*(1).

Langford, L. M. (2013). The other Euro crisis: Rights violations under the Common European Asylum system and the unraveling of EU solidarity. *Harvard Human Rights Journal, 26*, 217–259.

Lehne, S. (2019, April). The EU remains unprepared for the next migration crisis. *Carnegie Europe*. Available at: https://carnegieeurope.eu/2018/04/03/eu-remains-unprepared-for-next-migration-crisis-pub-75965.

Lentin, A., & Titley, G. (2012). The crisis of 'multiculturalism' in Europe: Mediated minarets, intolerable subjects. *European Journal of Cultural Studies, 15*(2), 123–138.

Lewil, P., Clarke, S., et al. (2018, November). Revealed: One in four Europeans vote populist. *The Guardian*. Available at. https://www.theguardian.com/world/ng-interactive/2018/nov/20/revealed-one-in-four-europeans-vote-populist.

Limam, M., & Del Sarto, R. (2015). Periphery under pressure: Morocco, Tunisia and the European Union's Mobility Partnership on migration. In *European University Institute: Robert Shuman Centre for Advanced Studies* (p. 27). Available at: http://cadmus.eui.eu/handle/1814/37521.

Martín de la Guardia, R. M., & Pérez Sánchez, G. A. (2001). Historia de la integración europea. *Ariel, Barcelona.*

Merelli, A. (2017). Like Trump in the US, Europe is finding new ways to keep refugees out. *Quartz*. Available at: https://qz.com/904026/europe-has-a-genius-new-strategy-to-deal-with-migrants-pay-war-torn-libya-to-detain-them/.

Metcalfe-Hough, V. (2016). The migration crisis? Facts, challenges and possible solutions. Available at: https://www.odi.org/sites/odi.org.uk/files/odi-assets/publicationsopinion-files/9913.pdf on, 14, 2016.

Mitsilegas, V. (2014). Solidarity and trust in the common European asylum system. *Comparative Migration Studies* 2.2, 181–202. Available at https://link.springer.com/content/pdf/10.5117/CMS2014.2.MITS.pdf.

Nakache, D., & Losier, J. (2017). The European Union immigration agreement with Libya: Out of sight, out of mind?. *E-International Relations, 25*. Available at: https://www.e-ir.info/2017/07/25/the-european-union-immigration-agreement-with-libya-out-of-sight-out-of-mind/.

Nielsen, N. (2016, October). EU seeks migration deal with African states. *EUobserver*. Available at: https://euobserver.com/migration/135486; OIM, 2014.

Outeda, C. C. (2001). *El proceso de constitucionalización de la Unión Europea: de Roma a Niza* (No. 3). Univ Santiago de Compostela.

Pawlas, I. (2015, September). The Visegrad Countries and European Union membership-selected issues. In *Proceedings of International Academic Conferences* (No. 2704866). International Institute of Social and Economic Sciences.

Ramiro Troitino, D., & Pando Ballesteros, M. D. L. P. (2017). Churchill's European integration model. *Revista de Occidente, 433*, 57–71.

Rankin, J. (2016, December). EU met only 5% of target for relocating refugees from Greece and Italy. *The Guardian*. Available at: https://www.theguardian.com/world/2016/dec/08/eu-met-only-5-of-target-for-relocating-refugees-from-greece-and-ital.

Rettman, A. (2015, September). Slovakia filing case against EU migrant relocation. *EUobserver*. Available at: https://euobserver.com/justice/130499.

Rieff, D. (2005). The dream of multiculturalism is over. *International Herald Tribune, 23*.

Rosamond, B. (2000). *Theories of European integration*. Basingstoke: Palgrav.

Schultze, P. (2015). Rethinking Russia. In F. Ondrej, W. Aaron (Eds.), *Europe and the Migration crisis: The response of the EU Member States* (p. 106).

Scipioni, M. (2018). Failing forward in EU migration policy? EU integration after the 2015 asylum and migration crisis. *Journal of European Public Policy, 25*(9), 1357–1375.

Trauner, F. (2016). Asylum policy: The EU's 'crises' and the looming policy regime failure. *Journal of European Integration, 38*(3), 311–325.

Troitiño, D. R. (2017). Jean Monnet before the first European community: A historical perspective and critic. *Trames, 21*(3), 193–213.
Troitiño, D. R., Kerikmäe, T., & Chochia, A. (Eds.). (2018). *Brexit: History, reasoning and perspectives*. Berlin: Springer.
Troitino, D. R., & Faerber, K. (2019). Historical errors in the initial conception of the euro and its subsequent development. *Brazilian Journal of Political Economy, 39*(2), 328–343.
Vertosec, S. (2007). Super-diversity and its implications. *Ethnic and Racial Studies, 30,* 1024–1054.

Decision Justice

Court of Justice which in the case of Abdullahi (Case C-394/12, judgment of 10 December 2013).
ECHR Grand chamber judgement 21 January 2011 in the case of M.S.S. v. BELGIUM AND GREECE, (Application no. 30696/09).

Internal Security: Terrorism and Criminality Fostering Integration in the EU

Nataliia Oliievska, David Ramiro Troitiño and Tanel Kerikmäe

Abstract In 2015, the capital of France saw several terrorist attacks, which left hundreds of people injured and almost 150 people dead. Following terrorist attacks in Belgium, Germany, the UK, Sweden, Spain, and Finland were a cause why the EU has to strengthen its counter-terrorism, police and judicial cooperation. Unfortunately, exactly such tragic events as terrorist attacks from last 4 years showed that terrorist threat is a reality for the European Union citizens. The necessities in this field, and possible solutions, are explored in this research.

Keywords Terrorism · Security · European integration · European criminality

1 Introduction

In 2015, the capital of France saw several terrorist attacks, which left hundreds of people injured and almost 150 people dead. Following terrorist attacks in Belgium, Germany, the UK, Sweden, Spain, and Finland were a cause why the EU has to strengthen its counter-terrorism, police and judicial cooperation. Unfortunately, exactly such tragic events as terrorist attacks from last 4 years showed that terrorist threat is a reality for the European Union citizens.

In 2016, the European Parliament started a survey range on main policies for the EU citizens. It came out that terrorism was on the first place with a result of 77%, followed by unemployment (76%), the protection of the environment (75%), the fight against tax fraud (74%), promotion of peace and democracy (73%), and migration (72%). As results have shown, these topics require a call for more EU intervention in the future.[1]

[1] News European Parliament (2018a).

N. Oliievska (✉) · D. R. Troitiño · T. Kerikmäe
19 Charkivske Shose Street, Apartment 566, 02090 Kyiv, Ukraine

D. R. Troitiño
e-mail: david.troitino@ttu.ee

T. Kerikmäe
e-mail: tanel.kerikmae@taltech.ee

D. Ramiro Troitiño et al. (eds.), *The EU in the 21st Century*,
https://doi.org/10.1007/978-3-030-38399-2_6

Our world is becoming even more and more connected. The existence of the Internet, visa-free traveling is making our life easier, but as well it gives rise to terrorism and criminality. Therefore, we can say that the EU and each member state separately have faced complex security threats, which do not have a simple and fast solution.[2]

The main aim of this chapter is to show how the EU as an entity is dealing with terrorism and criminality, the legal structure of its functioning as a part of the Area of Freedom, Security, and Justice, which was established by the Treaty of Amsterdam in 1999. Also, we would look at the transformation of the cooperation on terrorism and criminality with all mistakes mention: from TREVI group to nowadays the Area of Freedom, Security, and Justice.[3]

2 Evolution of the Area of Freedom, Security, and Justice

The first step in fighting terrorism in the European Union was taken in the 1970s with the creation of the so-called TREVI group. It was established with the aim of creating a cross-border cooperation in the fight against organized crime and terrorism. After that, with next EU enlargements, a need for widening the scope of cooperation has emerged. With establishing of the Schengen Area, changes have started. In 1993, the Maastricht Treaty established the area of cooperation and home affairs as a part of the so-called pillar structure under the jurisdiction of the third pillar. But the power of the Union organs was significantly limited since it was an intergovernmental element. After 6 years, the Amsterdam Treaty transferred some parts of the third pillar to the first pillar, and JHA was renamed to police and judicial cooperation in criminal matters.[4] It was a step of departure from pure intergovernmentalism toward community method. The Amsterdam Treaty transferred the fields of asylum, immigration, civil law matters, and external border controls to the first pillar, but left terrorism in the third one.[5]

Therefore, in 1999 the Area of Freedom, Security, and Justice was formally created. It includes border controls, judicial cooperation in criminal and civil matters, asylum, policing, justice and home affairs ministries of member states and immigration, but they were divided between the first and the third pillar.[6] But finally, in 2009, the Lisbon Treaty put to end the pillar structure of the EU and reunited divided area: the Area of Freedom, Security, and Justice.[7]

---

[2] European Commission (2019).

[3] European Parliamentary Research service blog (2019a).

[4] European values (2014a).

[5] Trauner and Ripoll (2016).

[6] Guild et al. (2010).

[7] Trauner and Ripoll (2016).

In addition, a number of agencies have been set up to help oversee policies in a number of important areas of the AFSJ: Europol, the European Police College, Eurojust, the EU Fundamental Rights Agency, the European Monitoring Centre for Drugs and Drug Addiction, the European Border and Coast Guard (Frontex), the EU Agency for the management of large-scale IT systems in the AFSJ (eu-LISA), and the European Asylum Support Office.[8]

3 Changes After the Lisbon Treaty

With the Lisbon Treaty, the Area of Justice and Home Affairs (JHA) was renamed and reduced to the police and judicial cooperation in criminal matters. Policies of immigration, judicial cooperation in civil matters, and asylum in civil matters were transferred to the European Community (the first pillar). Until that the supranational institutions did not have an authority to make decisions and the policies were decided by the member states as a part intergovernmental cooperation. Therefore, the Lisbon Treaty let the supranational institutions to make decisions in the united area.[9]

3.1 Comparison of Programs

Already before the Lisbon Treaty, namely in 1999, governments of the member states adopted the first program with targets in the aforementioned areas: the Finnish Tampere program, the following Haag program (2004), and Stockholm program (2009).[10] Finnish presidency with its Tampere program has endorsed an ambitious plan which related to possibilities offered by the Amsterdam Treaty, but the program overall was more directed into future issues related to the enlargements. But after the events of 9/11 in the USA and March 11, 2004, in Madrid have provoked some changes in security initiatives. The next program was more focusing on the so-called fight against terrorism. Following the Stockholm program was created in 2009.[11] It was expected that the next 5-year program would be known as the Rome program since it should be adopted during the Italian presidency in 2014. Nevertheless, it did not happen. The Stockholm program was succeeded by a short set of guidelines, not a fully fledged and detailed program like the previous 15 years. Here, it would be logical to compare with the Stockholm program about which we did not mention much before. First, the document from 2009 was 81-pages long. The House of Lords in the UK compared the program with a 'shopping list.'[12] Therefore, the Stockholm

[8]Kristiina Milt (2019).

[9]Trauner and Ripoll (2016).

[10]Trauner and Ripoll (2016).

[11]Guild et al. (2010).

[12]Troitiño et al. (2018).

program was blamed for failing to identify key priorities since too many initiatives were mentioned. This problem was removed in the AFSJ strategic guidelines which took only five pages and were more general.[13] Probably, there was also no need for a new long document since all the programs were linked with a Treaty change: the Amsterdam Treaty, the Constitutional Treaty, and the Lisbon Treaty. [14]The second difference between the 2009 and the 2014 document is that the first one was focusing on expansion and the second one on consolidation in the Area of Freedom, Security, and Justice.[15] It feels like all mistakes were removed but now the AFSJ is blamed for not having new ideas, except the EU Passenger Name Record System. In sum, in comparison with the previous programs, the AFSJ guidelines look like vague, short, and very general document.[16]

Nevertheless, since the AFSJ was created there has been a great development of information technology. Systems of the EU are becoming more and more connected each day, and access to the Internet is providing a way for ordinary people to be aware of current events. Now, it is a reality but just a few years ago it was a dream which was available for a small number of people. Despite all benefits, of course, there are issues with the protection of privacy, but the EU is working on that problem to be sure that the rights of Europeans are not abused.[17] The Area of Freedom, Security, and Justice is a sensitive question, and regarding its nature, some member states decided not to take their full part on the decisions in the area: The UK, Denmark, and Ireland have negotiated exceptions. They could be absent from the legislative processes, and following decisions would not affect them. Also, there are two options of the exceptions—opt-in or opt-out clauses. With opt-in, the states can adopt individual decisions; in turn, opt-out is the situation of not adopting an adopted adjustment at all.[18]

To sum up, we can say that the Lisbon Treaty could be marked as a 'before and after' point in the making of the AFSJ. The Treaty has provided an excellent basis for ambitious ways of how European policy would be structuring next years. Probably, the major deficit of the EU cooperation on AFSJ during those ten years was the first/third pillar structure. It resulted in less clear outputs especially in questions of police and judicial cooperation in criminal matters. Also, the Treaty of Lisbon has widened competences of the ECJ to all freedom, security, and justice issues.[19] Moreover, the Lisbon Treaty gave the ECJ a right to press member states to implement adopted measures. Before that it is the Achilles' heel of EU counter-terrorism measures. So, after the Lisbon Treaty, the EU plays a greater role in the internal security, and the decision-making process became more simple and flexible since

[13]Léonard and Kaunert (2016).
[14]Pascouau (2014).
[15]Färber (2017).
[16]Léonard and Kaunert (2016).
[17]Guild et al. (2010).
[18]European values (2014a).
[19]Guild et al. (2010).

decisions are now taken by the community method[20] (i.e., qualified majority vote among the member states). Moreover, the European Parliament got a greater role in the Area of Freedom, Security, and Justice (full co-decisional powers). In addition, there should be no fear of losing independence since the matters of national security stay in the competence of the member states.[21]

3.2 The Overall Evolution of Cooperation on Counter-Terrorism and Changes in Citizens Expectations

As we have mentioned before, issues of terrorism and criminality are part of the Area of Freedom, Security, and Justice. The general information of how it was developing and changing was provided, and now we can turn to a separate case of terrorism and criminality: the evolution of cooperation in those fields, why changes were done, which agencies are helping to reach the aim of cooperation and what could be improved in the future.[22]

Basically, the ground for the AFSJ is the cooperation to fight terrorism and organized crime. As we have already mentioned, the so-called TREVI group was established exactly for that goal in 1976.[23] TREVI stands for Terrorisme, Radicalisme, Extrémisme et Violence international. It was an intergovernmental network of justice and home ministries representatives. With eliminating borders due to the Schengen system, the Maastricht Treaty has established the pillar system. Terrorism was included in the third pillar, which means that it was intergovernmental cooperation. In 1999, some parts of the third pillar were relocated to the first, but terrorism stayed at the third one. In addition, in the same year, the European Police Office (Europol) started its full activities to enhance police cooperation in Europe. Also, in March 2001, Eurojust has started its functioning, which aim is judicial cooperation in criminal matters. Till 2001, the framework of counter-terrorism was not developing further, but after 9/11 the EU has adopted its first action plan. Moreover, in 2002 the EU adopted a Framework Decision on Combating Terrorism and has provided a joint definition of terrorist offenses, a decision on freezing of assets which have a link to suspected people, and to establish the European Arrest Warrant, which means an automatic transfer of suspected persons from one EU-member to another. Also, the Council has urged better coordination between Europol, Eurojust, judicial authorities, and police corps. Moreover, anti-terrorism cooperation even intensified after the March 11, 2004, Madrid's attack and 2005 terrorist attack in London.[24] On May 27, 2005, Germany, Spain, France, Luxembourg, the Netherlands, Austria, and Belgium

[20] Troitino and Faerber (2019).

[21] Renard (2012).

[22] Guild et al. (2010).

[23] Guild et al. (2010).

[24] European Parliament (2019a, b, c).

signed the Prüm Convention for enhancing collective capabilities to combat terrorism. Moreover, the EU adopted a comprehensive counter-terrorism strategy which was based on four pillars: pursuit, protection, prevention, and response. Last time, the strategy was updated in 2014.[25]

The next terrorist threats that lead to changes were 2015 terrorist attacks in Paris.[26] The 2015 terrorist attacks in Paris showed the reality of terrorism threat for Europe. This year more than 150 people were killed. Next assaults in Brussels, Berlin, London, and Barcelona have just enhanced the pressure and created an atmosphere of danger and fear.[27] That is why the EU has decided to reinforce its counter-terrorism measures to ensure the security of its citizens, prevents radicalization, and more cooperate with partners.

Terrorism was and it still is a real threat to democracy, the enjoyment of human rights, and the rule of law. Therefore, the EU and member states should prevent and suppress terrorism to protect its citizens. And we need to understand that poorly implemented or Draconian counter-terrorism measures would not be effective and productive.[28]

Before we would provide information on what was done by the EU since 2015, let us look on surveys about that topic. Here, the situation seems to have changed. The number of terrorist attacks in 2018 is down over 60% since its peak in 2017. However, it is too early to say that the fight against terrorism is over and a threat does not exist anymore. To understand the situation, we should measure the level of terrorist threat not just by the number of successful attacks, but also by failed efforts. For example, in 2018, there were 12 well-documented terrorist plots and half of them have resulted in attacks. In addition, 11 plots were poorly documented. For sure, this decrease is a result of better counter-terrorism cooperation among member states. In comparison with 2017, the number is 50% smaller, but we still cannot say that the threat of terrorism is low. If we would compare this number to the results of any year before 2015, it is still high.[29]

As we know, terrorism is not a brand-new phenomenon. Some of the EU countries have a long history of fighting terrorist groups,[30] but some events underline the dangerous nature of terrorism and spread fear among citizens. Between 2000 and 2018, approximately 753 people were killed due to terrorist attacks in the European Union, and 1115 Europeans more feel victim in terror outside the EU. In 2015, the enormous wave of terrorist attacks began. The number of attacks has decreased, but as we have already mentioned, it is still higher than before 2015. What is interesting is that most terrorists in the EU were European citizens, who were born in Europe and radicalized without leaving the continent.[31] It is not a surprise. Thanks to digital

[25] European values (2014a).

[26] European Council (2019).

[27] European Commission (2019a, b, c).

[28] European Parliament (2018a).

[29] European Parliament (2019a, b, c).

[30] Ramiro Troitino and Pando Ballesteros (2017).

[31] Outeda (2001).

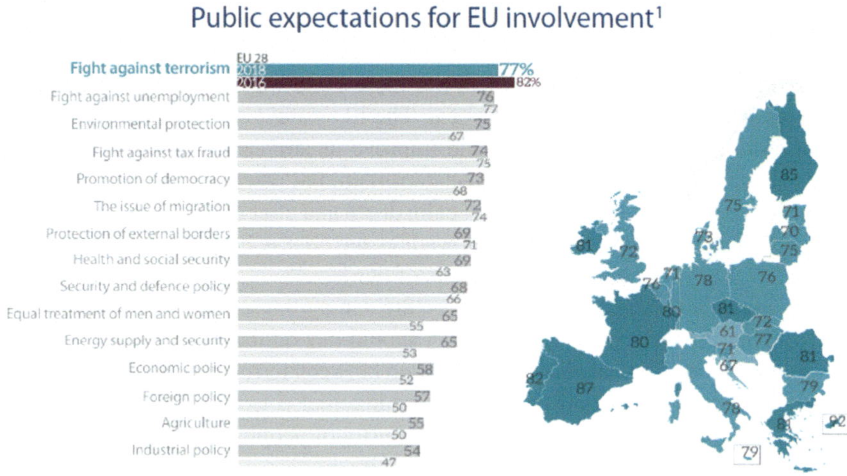

Fig. 1 Percentage of respondents who would like the EU to intervene more than at present. *Source* 85.1.2016; 89.2.2018

evolution which is offering simple ways how to radicalize, you even do not need to go abroad: The Internet, the darknet, encrypted communication channels in Telegram for the aim of propaganda, recruitment purposes, and training make it possible. The European Parliament has carried out a series of Eurobarometer surveys on perceptions and expectations about terrorism. According to this data, EU citizens' support for a stronger involvement in counter-terrorism in 2018 decreased to 77% in comparison with 82% in 2016. Nevertheless, this policy area is still with the highest level of peoples' expectations for more involvement. Also, the decrease in expectations is not presenting in every EU-country. In Spain, we can see an increase of 3%, Ireland and Poland—2%, and Finland—1%. The highest expectations are in Finland (85%), Spain (87%), and Cyprus (92%) (Fig. 1).[32]

Also, satisfaction with EU involvement has changed. In 2016, just 23% of European citizens were satisfied with what the EU is doing to fight terrorism, but in 2018 the percentage has increased to 32%. There was another survey about dissatisfaction in that area. In 2018, just 57% of Europeans evaluate EU's involvement as dissatisfied in comparison with 69% in 2016. Obviously, the positive change is due to significant improvement in people's perception of what the EU is doing in the area of fighting terrorism. Of course, we can see dramatical changes in the counter-terrorism. The EU actions here are based on Title V of the TFEU on the Area of Freedom, Security, and Justice. But even considering this fact, the competence of the EU is limited. Article 4(2) of the TEU states that internal security stays in responsibility of each member state.[33]

[32]European Parliament (2019a, b, c).

[33]European Parliament (2019a, b, c).

The European Union has made one huge mistake. It has lost attention to terrorism when the number of terrorist attacks reduced after 2005. Terrorists have caught the Union when nobody has expected. So, there is no way in the near future that the terrorist threat would totally disappear. The EU should constantly pay attention to that issue and always modernize and improve its strategy and policy. Now, the EU is increasing its spending on counter-terrorism, but when the number would be minimum the history can repeat itself—calm down and after dozens of people would be killed. We should not forget that nowadays terrorist is better connected among themselves than ever before with no limits of borders.[34]

Moreover, there is another issue that is threatening the security of European citizens—cyber-threats and enough attention should pay on that problem as well. But what is even more interesting is the connection between terrorism and cyber-attacks, where the second one could be used for conducting a terrorist attack.[35] So, the only solution here is always to ensure the security of people. Therefore, we cannot prioritize fighting with one or another type of attacks.[36]

To combat terrorism and crime efficiently, the authorities of criminal justice need to work collectively. The only option how those problems could be solved is to create a realm of trust and reliance among the member states. We have already mentioned the importance of counter-terrorism measures itself, but also judicial cooperation has a great matter. There is no common criminal law in the EU, but the existing police and judicial cooperation on criminal matters are increasing the confidence of citizens in the fairness of proceedings, and people would know that they are protected even if they are not in a home country.[37]

Nowadays, people have more access to travel, live, or study abroad, and therefore European citizens could become potential victims of crime. Since 2012, the European Union has established minimum standards on the rights, protection, and support of victims of crime. So, the aim of the EU is to continuously ensure that people would receive support and protection the time when they need in any country of the Union.[38] Mutual recognition in this area is necessary.[39]

3.3 *Combating Terrorism 2015–2019: What Was Done and What Needs to Be Improved in the Future*

Since 2015, the EU spending for counter-terrorism has radically increased, and it is still growing in 2019. Here, we can see the increasing of financing not just for EU agencies, but for cooperation with third countries. Also, many new instruments

[34]Hamulák (2018).

[35]European Commission (2019a, b, c).

[36]Council of Europe (2019).

[37]Nesser (2018a).

[38]European Commission (2019a, b, c).

[39]European Commission (2019a, b, c).

and rules have been adopted since that time: harmonization of definitions related to the topic of terrorist offenses and sanctions, share of data and information, better protection of borders and measures to stop terrorist financing, and regulation of firearms.[40]

Also, we can see changes in the Internal Security Fund (ISF). This multiannual financial framework is aimed to support security-enhancing initiatives in the Union. For a period of 2014–2020, the total budget for ISF amounts at 3.8 billion euro. The ISF has a structure which is directly related to counter-terrorism—the ISF Police. This body was designed to combat serious and organized crime, to ensure a high level of security in the Union, and it has a budget of more than 1 billion euro.[41]

In general, the ISF's funding is using to support the involvement of EU bodies in counter-terrorism. For example, European Counter-Terrorism Center which was created within Europol, in 2016 received 2 million euro. Also, the Radicalization Awareness Network Center of Excellence which was established in 2015 got 25 million euro until 2020. Therefore, we can see that the overall funding for security has raised. More than 1 billion euro were allocated for the period of 2018–2020 to innovation and research to improve security under Horizon 2020. Out of that, 135 million euro are received for projects directed to terrorism threats and crime.[42]

In 2015, the European Commission adopted the European agenda on security. Therefore, it is the major policy instruments which define the responses of the Union to security challenges in 2015–2020. The document is focusing on three threats: terrorism and radicalization, organized crime, and cybercrime. In general, it was covering such issues like information exchange between EU agencies and law enforcement authorities, EU co-funding for security and operational police cooperation. Now, we can see the result of that agenda on the example of action plans which were adopted in the period of 2015–2018: stricter control and limits on explosives and firearms in 2015, more pressure and attention on the fight against terrorist financing in 2016, increasing the level of the European response to a fraud of travel document also in 2016, and strengthening of the protection of public spaces in 2017. Also in 2017, the EU took initiatives about preparedness against biological, chemical, nuclear, and radiological security risks, and in 2018 enlarged those to maritime security.[43]

There is some other legislation which was adopted with the aim to end up the wave of terrorist attacks in the EU. For better understanding of what was done, we will divide all adopted legislation into five types: harmonization of criminal laws, assistance to victims of terrorism, combat funding of terrorism, regulation of weapons and the protection of the EU borders. So, let us start with the first one.[44] In 2017, the Council and European Parliament adopted the Directive on Combating Terrorism which implemented new international standards like criminalization of traveling for terroristic purposes, receiving of terrorist training, or the addition of cyber-attacks

[40]European Parliament (2019a, b, c).

[41]European Parliament (2019a, b, c).

[42]European Parliament (2019a, b, c).

[43]European Parliament (2019a, b, c).

[44]Kerikmäe et al. (2019).

to the definition of a terrorist offense. Moreover, the rights of victims of terrorist attacks received new provisions to improve assistance to be equally provided in any EU-country. Third, combating with terrorism financing was strengthened. The EU has adopted the Fifth Anti-Money-Laundering Directive. It is aimed for increasing transparency and identification. Other three pieces of legislation update or harmonize already existing rules: a regulation on controls on cash entering, a directive on countering money laundering by the establishment of common minimum sanctions in criminal law, and a regulation on the mutual recognition of freezing and confiscation orders. New rules entered in force in 2018 and will apply since 2020.[45] Fourth changes are related to the regulation of weapons. Lately, two legislative acts were adopted: a regulation on deactivation standards for ensuring that deactivated firearms are rendered irreversibly inoperable and a directive on the control of the possession and acquisition of weapons. Both laws started to apply in the previous year, 2018. What about the borders, the Union has sought to optimize using already existing databases and with the help of creating new ones to close information gaps. Recently, two information systems were adopted: a European Travel Information and Authorisation System (ETIAS) for bolstering security checks on visa-exempt non-EU nationals, and an entry/exit system (EES) for registration of an entry and exit data and refusal for non-EU citizens crossing EU borders.[46] In plans, those systems should start its functioning from 2020 in case of EES and 2021—ETIAS. Here, we can smoothly move to the last part—exchange of information. It is very important for the fight against terrorism that law enforcement authorities are sharing information without limitation of borders at least within the EU. Lately, the EU has established a system to collect flight passenger data for detection of suspicious travelers (2016). Two years after that, new rules for strengthening the Schengen information system were adopted. According to the new rules, police and border guards can enter and consult alerts on missing or wanted persons and stolen or lost property. Also, in December 2018, the co-legislators agreed on a new centralized system for the aim of exchanging criminal records of the non-EU citizens in the European Union (ECRIS-TCN). Moreover, the Commission has proposed interoperability between EU information systems. In February 2019, such initiative was agreed by the co-legislators, and it should start its functioning after 2023. It means that it will provide law enforcement authorities and border guards with a common interface for their search and biometric matching service to facilitate identification.[47]

Also, there is a need to mention measures to respect the rights and freedoms of EU citizens. In 2018, two laws entered into the application: the Data Protection Police Directive and the General Data Protection Regulation (GDPR). They are setting standards for protecting citizens in the processing of their data in relation to a criminal offense.[48]

---

[45] Pawlas (2015).

[46] Castro and Lago (2018).

[47] European Parliament (2019a, b, c).

[48] European Parliament (2019a, b, c).

Of course, the problem with terrorism cannot be solved just on the internal level without global influence. For that reason, the EU is cooperating with international bodies and organizations like the United Nations, the Council of Europe, the Global Counterterrorism Forum, the Financial Action Task Force, and the Global Coalition against Da'esh. For example, the EU has implemented the 2006 UN global counter-terrorism strategy and acceded to the 19 UN conventions which were related to terrorism since 1963. Moreover, the European Union ratifies the Council of Europe Convention on the Prevention of Terrorism and Additional protocol.[49]

As we can see, there is huge progress, but also we should consider the fact that the EU legislation on counter-terrorism often presented in a form of directives which after should be transposed into national law. And the problem is that the implementation of the EU rules in member states was always a challenge, and it suffers delays. A Commission report of December 2018 says that some important measures still have not been transposed by all EU-members. In this list, we can find the directives on the EU PNR system, on cybersecurity, the Fourth Anti-money Laundering Directive, the directive on combating terrorism, on the protection of personal data by law enforcement, on the control of acquisition and possession of weapons.[50]

To sum up, considering all the information above, recommendations of a special committee on terrorism seem to make sense. First, the EU should strengthen its agencies dealing with counter-terrorism and security. Also, the powers of the European Public Prosecutor's Office should be expanded to cover terrorism and organized crime. Second, a European Commission-based EU center of excellence for prevention of radicalization should be set up for the prevention and countering of radicalization. Next, as it was already mentioned, the Union needs to have interoperability of information systems for information exchange and enhancing cooperation. Also, the mandate of the European Border and Coast Guard Agency should be reinforced, and the access to all relevant databases needs to be provided. To add, for stepping up the fight against the financing of terrorism, the recently adopted EU legislation should be fully implemented. In addition, considering the scope of the problem, international cooperation should be intensified as well.[51]

Fortunately, some developments are already happening: a proposal on terrorist content online to be removed by Internet providers within the period of one hour after receiving of a notification from law enforcement authorities; a proposal imposing stricter rules for marketing and use of explosive precursors; a proposal to enhance the security of ID cards and residence permits by setting common security standards, and also to make biometric data mandatory for EU countries where ID cards are using; a proposal on improving law enforcement access to financial information which is necessary for investigations of serious crime; proposals to facilitate access by law enforcement to electronic evidence in criminal matters.[52]

[49] European Parliament (2019a, b, c).

[50] European Parliament (2019a, b, c).

[51] European Parliament (2019a, b, c).

[52] European Parliament (2019a, b, c).

Despite the fact that it seems unrealistic for the nearest future that European Intelligence Unit would be established, the EU leaders have that a joint EU intelligence school will be created for a goal of promotion of a common intelligence culture and benefit of European security. Also, we must underline that the budget of the agencies has increased. For example, Europol's budget in 2002 amounted 53 million euro, in 2008—68 million euro, whereas in 2018—135 million euro. Moreover, the Commission intends to give 461 million euro to implement the interoperability of EU databases, including €261 million for eu-LISA, for the period of 2019–2027. In addition, the High Representative for the Union for Foreign Affairs and Security Policy has proposed to set up a European peace facility to help the Union build strengthen and peace international security.[53]

3.4 Cooperation on Police and Judicial Cooperation

As we have already mentioned at the beginning, the elimination of borders and border controls within the Union has made the movement in Europe as simple as it was never before,[54] but it also made the easier movement for criminals as well and gave them a chance to operate transnationally. Therefore, the EU has established judicial cooperation in criminal matters and police cooperation as well.[55]

Under Articles 82 to 86 of the TFEU, judicial cooperation in criminal matters in the European Union should be based on the principle of mutual recognition in some areas: trafficking in human beings and sexual exploitation of women and children, terrorism, illicit arms trafficking, money laundering, illicit drug trafficking, corruption, computer crime, counterfeiting of means of payment and organized crime.[56] Nevertheless, judicial cooperation in criminal matters (including police cooperation) was not entirely integrated into the EU framework. The Commission shares its initiatives power with each member state.[57]

Here, we can see a significant work of agencies as well. Since 1999, EU agencies are helping to more build more strong the Area of Freedom, Security, and Justice. Some of Justice and Home Affairs (JHA) agencies, namely nine, are operating as a network since 2006: Frontex, EASO, eu-LISA, EMCDDA, CEPOL, EIGE, Europol, Eurojust, and FRA. Europol, Eurojust, and CEPOL are working to enhance police and judicial cooperation, thus contribute to security in Europe. More concretely, the functioning of Eurojust is aimed at strengthening of judicial cooperation, coordination to fight terrorism, and cross-border crime by supporting the coordination of investigations and prosecutions.[58] Another agency which is combating international

[53]European Parliament (2019a, b, c).

[54]Troitiño (2017).

[55]Milt (2018).

[56]Martín de la Guardia and Pérez Sánchez (2001).

[57]European Parliament (2019a, b, c).

[58]Kerikmäe (2014).

and organized crime, terrorism is Europol. It serves as a support center for all law enforcement authorities of EU-members and also as a criminal information hub. Moreover, Europol has established the European Counter-Terrorism Center, which provides operational and analytical support to the EU-members' investigation (ESPR BRI) Therefore, the main two agencies in the area of police and judicial cooperation in criminal matters are Europol and Eurojust. The European Police Office (Europol) is the main instrument for police cooperation, which officially begun to work on July 1, 1999. Its role is to help national police in each EU-country and other similar authorities to act more effectively and facilitate cooperation among them. The focus is on combating and preventing terrorism, drug trafficking, cybercrime, and some other forms of serious cross-border crime. Despite the fact that Europol cannot conduct searches or make arrests since it does not have coercive powers, its operational powers have increased. Also, the European Police Office has enhanced its analytical capabilities because of establishing of European Cybercrime Centre (EC3). Moreover, after the terrorist attacks in Copenhagen and Paris in 2015, Europol was mandated by the Justice and Home Affairs Council for establishing an Internet Referral Unit with the aim to combat online terrorist propaganda and some other extremist activities.[59] Eurojust is aimed at judicial cooperation in criminal matters among agencies of the member states. It helps to combat serious organized crime by helping national authorities work together.

As we can see, the Area of Freedom, Security, and Justice is based on mutual recognition and mutual trust.[60] That is the main characteristic of judicial and police cooperation in criminal matters.

With time, EU agencies are getting more and more power in combating crime. One of the latest changes is related to the access the electronic evidence. With the evolution of technology, it is obvious that more than half of all criminal investigations nowadays include a cross-border request to access texts, messaging apps, or e-mails. It was a reason why in February 2019 the Commission proposed new rules which would make it faster and easier for judicial authorities and police to access the electronic evidence they need.[61]

4 What Could Be Improved and Done in the Future

To sum up, the main problem in dealing with terrorism in the past was the fact that terrorism stayed a part of intergovernmental cooperation. It was a challenge to implement regulation and directives through that type of cooperation. The second mistake is not paying enough attention and initiatives before. The European Union is 'relaxing' each time when the number of terrorist attacks is decreasing, and it seems like terrorists are using that moment. As it was already mentioned, the security of

[59] European Parliament (2019a, b, c).

[60] European Commission (2019a, b, c).

[61] European Commission (2019a, b, c).

citizens in any of the forms (protection from cyber-attacks, terrorism, criminality, etc.) always should be in priority. Third, the Area of Freedom, Security, and Justice should be improved and updated, but not complicated. Before 2014, the programs were not concentrated and focusing on crucial problems. In addition, more focus should be paid on implementation of EU legislation by the member states since the effectiveness of combating terrorism and criminality depend on that. Finally, terrorism and criminality should be connected to cyberspace. Every day more than 6 million data are stolen ar lost worldwide and over 4000 cyber-attacks are launched.[62]

Last but not least, considering all the facts provided above, we can summarize that there is progress in the area of fighting with terrorism and criminality. EU is doing a great job now, but it should not give the same mistakes happen again. Nevertheless, now the main responsibility for issues with terrorism is on the hands of member states, but the EU definitely should play a supportive and initiative role for help to respond to the threat more effectively.[63]

References

Bassot, E. (2019). Ten issues to watch in 2019. European Parliamentary Research Service, January, http://www.europarl.europa.eu/RegData/etudes/IDAN/2019/630352/EPRS_IDA(2019)630352_EN.pdf. Accessed April 8, 2019.

Castro, L. D., & Lago, J. R. R. (2018). Educación y diplomacia cultural en la primavera de Europa (1948–1954) = education and cultural diplomacy in the spring of Europe (1948–1954). *Revista de educación, 383,* 63–84.

Council of Europe (2019). Counter-terrorism. https://www.coe.int/en/web/counter-terrorism. Accessed April 12, 2019.

European Commission (2019a). EU strategy on criminal justice. https://ec.europa.eu/info/policies/justice-and-fundamental-rights/criminal-justice/eu-strategy-criminal-justice_en. Accessed 4 April, 2019.

European Commission (2019b). European agenda on security. 27 June, https://ec.europa.eu/home-affairs/what-we-do/policies/european-agenda-security_en. Accessed 1 April, 2019.

European Commission (2019c). Rights of suspects and accused. https://ec.europa.eu/info/policies/justice-and-fundamental-rights/criminal-justice/rights-suspects-and-accused_en. Accessed 16 April, 2019.

European Council (2019). Response to the terrorist threat and recent terrorist attacks in Europe. https://www.consilium.europa.eu/en/policies/fight-against-terrorism/foreign-fighters/. Accessed 1 April, 2019.

European Parliament (2018a). How to stop terrorism: EU measures explained (infographic). 22 March, http://www.europarl.europa.eu/news/en/headlines/security/20180316STO99922/how-to-stop-terrorism-eu-measures-explained-infographic. Accessed 6 April, 2019.

European Parliament (2018b). How to stop terrorism: EU measures explained (infographic). http://www.europarl.europa.eu/news/en/headlines/security/20180316STO99922/how-to-stop-terrorism-eu-measures-explained-infographic. Accessed 6 April, 2019.

[62] Bassot (2019).

[63] European values (2014a).

European Parliament (2019a). Judicial cooperation in criminal matters achievements during the legislative term 2014–2019: the role of the European Parliament. May, http://www.europarl.europa.eu/RegData/etudes/BRIE/2019/621913/IPOL_BRI(2019)621913_EN.pdf. Accessed 12 April, 2019.

European Parliament (2019b). Police cooperation. May, http://www.europarl.europa.eu/factsheets/en/sheet/156/police-cooperation. Accessed 7 April, 2019.

European Parliament (2019c). The fight against terrorism. www.europarl.europa.eu/…/EPRS_BRI(2019)635561_EN.pdf. Accessed 5 April, 2019.

European Parliamentary Research service blog (2019a). Area of freedom, security, and justice: Cost of non-Europe. 14 May, https://epthinktank.eu/2019/05/14/area-of-freedom-security-and-justice-cost-of-non-europe/. Accessed 9 April, 2019.

European Parliamentary Research service blog (2019b). Area of freedom, security, and justice: Cost of non-Europe. https://epthinktank.eu/2019/05/14/area-of-freedom-security-and-justice-cost-of-non-europe/. Accessed 15 April, 2019.

European values (2014a). The area of freedom, security, and justice. 31 July, https://www.europeanvalues.net/vyzkum/the-area-of-freedom-security-and-justice/. Accessed 17 April.

European values (2014b). The area of freedom, security, and justice. https://www.europeanvalues.net/vyzkum/the-area-of-freedom-security-and-justice/. Accessed 17 April, 2019.

Färber, K. (2017). Mitterrand and the great European design—From the cold war to the European union. *Baltic Journal of European Studies, 7*(2), 132–147.

Guild, E., Carrera, S., Eggenschwiler, A. (2010). The area of freedom, security, and justice: Ten years on successes and future challenges under the Stockholm program, (p. 112). ISBN 978-94-6138-034-0.

Hamulák, O. (2018). La carta de los derechos fundamentales de la union europea y los derechos sociales. *Estudios constitucionales, 16*(1), 167–186.

Kerikmäe, T. (2014). Protecting Human Rights in the EU. *Controversies and challenges of the charter of fundamental rights*.

Kerikmäe, T., Troitiño, D. R., Shumilo, O. (2019). An idol or an ideal? A case study of Estonian e-governance: Public perceptions, myths and misbeliefs1. *Acta Baltica Historiae et Philosophiae scientiarum, 7*(1).

Léonard, S., Kaunert, C. (2016). Beyond Stockholm: In search of a strategy for the European Union's area of freedom, security, and justice. *European politics and society, 17*(2), 143–149. https://doi.org/10.1080/23745118.2016.1160636.

Martín de la Guardia, R. M., Pérez Sánchez, G. A. (2001). Historia de la integración europea. *Ariel, Barcelona*.

Milt, K. (2018). Judicial cooperation in criminal matters. European Parliament, October, http://www.europarl.europa.eu/factsheets/en/sheet/155/judicial-cooperation-in-criminal-matters. Accessed 4 April, 2019.

Milt, K. (2019). An area of freedom, security, and justice: General aspects. European Parliament, May, http://www.europarl.europa.eu/factsheets/en/sheet/150/an-area-of-freedom-security-and-justice-general-aspects. Accessed 15 June, 2019.

Nesser, P. (2018a). Europe hasn't won the war on terror. Politico, 12 May, https://www.politico.eu/article/europe-hasnt-won-the-war-on-terror/. Accessed 2 April, 2019.

Nesser, P. (2018b). Europe hasn't won the war on terror. https://www.politico.eu/article/europe-hasnt-won-the-war-on-terror/. Accessed 2 April, 2019.

News European Parliament (2018a). A Europe that delivers: EU citizens expect more EU level action in future 18 September, http://www.europarl.europa.eu/news/en/press-room/20180918IPR13718/a-europe-that-delivers-eu-citizens-expect-more-eu-level-action-in-future. Accessed 15 April, 2019.

News European Parliament (2018b). A Europe that delivers: EU citizens expect more EU level action in the future. http://www.europarl.europa.eu/news/en/press-room/20180918IPR13718/a-europe-that-delivers-eu-citizens-expect-more-eu-level-action-in-future. Accessed 15 April, 2019.

Outeda, C. C. (2001). *El proceso de constitucionalización de la Unión Europea: de Roma a Niza* (No. 3). Univ Santiago de Compostela.
Pascouau, Y. (2014). The future of the area of freedom, security and justice. European Policy Center, 23 January, https://www.epc.eu/.../pub_4092_discussion_paper.pdf. Accessed 15 May, 2019.
Pawlas, I. (2015, September). The Visegrad countries and European union membership-selected issues. In *Proceedings of International Academic Conferences* (No. 2704866). International Institute of Social and Economic Sciences.
Ramiro Troitino, D., & Pando Ballesteros, M. D. L. P. (2017). Churchill's European integration model. *Revista De Occidente, 433*, 57–71.
Renard, T. (2012). EU counterterrorism policies and institutions after the lisbon treaty. Center of global counter-terrorism cooperation, September, https://www.files.ethz.ch/isn/.../Renard_policybrief_1216.pdf. Accessed 15 April, 2019.
Trauner, F., Ripoll, A. (2016). The communitarization of thc arca of freedom, security and justice: Why institutional change does not translate into policy change, *54*(6), 1417–1432. https://doi.org/10.1111/jcms.12397.
Troitiño, D. R. (2017). Jean Monnet before the first European community: A historical perspective and critic. *Trames, 21*(3), 193–213.
Troitiño, D. R., Kerikmäe, T., Chochia, A. (Eds.), (2018). *Brexit: History, reasoning and perspectives*. Springer.
Troitino, D. R., & Faerber, K. (2019). Historical errors in the initial conception of the euro and its subsequent development. *Brazilian Journal of Political Economy, 39*(2), 328–343.

Internal Development of the Union

European Union and Great Britain: After Brexit, Who Wins the Break-Up?

Essi Laitinen, David Ramiro Troitiño and Tanel Kerikmäe

Abstract Although a member state's decision to leave the European Union is a new phenomenon, the implications are not a separate event. Rather than speculating what the exact outcomes of Brexit will be on European integration, this chapter portrays the core reasons behind Brexit in order to reveal how the history of the relations between the UK and the European Union has impacted the integration process so far and to assess what the European Union should learn from Brexit. Furthermore, the authors claim that Brexit ought to be viewed as a rational outcome of a long historical process, where Britain's opposition towards further integration anywhere other than the single market, its strong national identity characterized by exceptionalism, and the backlash of globalization, have shaped European integration since Churchill. Ironically, the leave campaign slogan 'take back control' reveals the key lesson for the European Union to learn.

Keywords Brexit · UK-EU relations · European integration

1 Introduction

The decision of the UK to leave the European Union (a phenomenon hereby referred to as *Brexit*) arguably poses a fundamental challenge to the European peace project—the implications of which are nowhere near clear. For the first time in over 60 years of its existence, the European Union (EU) faces a situation where instead of enlarging or integrating, one of its member states (MS) has decided to leave the union. Since Brexit is a new phenomenon, there exists no precedence to assist in explaining what the exact implications of the break-up will be. Consequently, the

E. Laitinen (✉)
Faculty of Social Sciences, Tampere University, Tampere, Finland
e-mail: essi.a.laitinen@gmail.com

D. R. Troitiño · T. Kerikmäe
Tallinn Law School, Tallinn University of Technology, Tallinn, Estonia
e-mail: david.troitino@taltech.ee

T. Kerikmäe
e-mail: tanel.kerikmae@taltech.ee

D. Ramiro Troitiño et al. (eds.), *The EU in the 21st Century*,
https://doi.org/10.1007/978-3-030-38399-2_7

possible outcomes of Brexit have become an object of intense debate and speculation within academia and policy-makers, as well as international media. For example, the implications of Brexit have been speculated in terms of its effects on the rights of the citizens of UK,[1] the future of the European Union,[2] and the role of British media in the decision to leave the union.[3]

Rather than speculating the exact implications of Brexit on the EU, the aim of chapter is firstly to detect how Brexit has so far affected the European integration process towards an 'ever closer union' and secondly to analyse what the EU should learn from Brexit to come out as the winner of the regrettable break-up.[4] In order to find the answer to both of these questions, it is necessary to detect what exactly are the core reasons behind the decision to leave the world's largest trade block, particularly by a state that has managed to negotiate the most flexible terms amongst all EU MS when it comes to following through with further integration. Rather than assessing Brexit as an irrational and radical state of events, the authors attempt to portray it as a rational outcome of a historical process as old as the EU itself. Moreover, the core reasons behind Brexit and the lessons to be learned here are the determining factors visible in the *history of Brexit*—the history of the relationship between the UK and the EU, where the UK has had a significant impact on the course of European integration process since Winston Churchill. Furthermore, this chapter portrays Brexit as an outcome of several factors visible in the history of Brexit that are irreversibly linked with the Brexit campaign slogan 'take back control'.

2 Three Interpretations of Taking Back Control

The concepts 'an awkward partner', 'British exceptionalism', and 'Europe à la carte' are often present when discussing the relationship between the UK and European integration—a relationship that has been rocky since the establishment of the predecessor of the European Union in 1957, the European Economic Community (EEC). Rather than embracing the newly established European peace project based on economic and political cooperation, the UK has merely been interested in the economic benefits and free trade of Europeanism. Dating back to the creation of the European Coal and Steel Community, the UK has pursued '[alternative models] of cooperation based exclusively on industrial free trade [such as] the European Free Trade Association'.[5] Consequently, when it came to the establishment of the EEC, the UK was not amongst the founding members and did not intend to join the project.[6] Thus when the UK ultimately showed its aspirations of joining the European communities and

[1] Mindus (2017).

[2] Oliver (2018).

[3] Jackson et al. (2016).

[4] Kerikmäe (2014).

[5] Ramiro Troitino et al. (2018).

[6] Chochia et al. (2018).

submitted its first application for membership to the EEC in 1963, its true intentions were questioned. Perhaps the most prominent opponent of the British accession to the EEC was the French President of the time, Charles de Gaulle. In fact, President de Gaulle vetoed two times to prevent the British accession to the EEC in 1963 and 1967, declaring that Britain is 'incompatible' with Europe.[7] It was only after de Gaulle's presidency ended in 1969 that Britain applied for its third time, finally receiving a green light. After accepting most of the *acquis communautaire*,[8] the UK became a full member of the EEC on 1 January 1973.[9] However, only two years after acceding to the EEC, a referendum on whether to stay or leave the European communities was held in the UK.[10] Although similar to the one held in 2016, the referendum in 1975 ended in a decision to stay with a support percentage of 67. However, the occurrence itself set the tone for the future of UK-EU relations.

The following three subsections will present the core reasons behind the British decision to leave the EU through a historical process, where these exact reasons have already shaped European integration for decades. Furthermore, the notion of Brexiteers, 'take back control' is interpreted in terms of (2.1) the battle between cooperation and integration, (2.2) British exceptionalism national identity, and (2.3) the backlash of globalization.

2.1 The Battle Between Cooperation and Integration

The battle between cooperation and integration is one of the most prominent factors in the UK-EU relations and has both shaped European integration and contributed to the decision of the UK to leave the union. While the UK has clearly been more prone to economic rather than political cooperation, the crucial asymmetries between the perceptions of UK and EU on European integration have been how decisions are made on an EU level and the role that the EU plays in them. The UK has in the hands of its leaders beginning from Winston Churchill and Margaret Thatcher, openly opposed any other decision-making method than intergovernmental and any attempts to share more sovereignty amongst the MS or as much as grant the EU more competences. Thus, 'taking back control' in this subsection entails taking back or maintaining 'democratic sovereignty'.[11]

Churchill is amongst the Founding fathers of the European Union.[12] In his famous speech in Zurich in 1946, still referred to today, he called for a 'United States of Europe'[13] built around a Franco–German association. Meanwhile, Churchill was a

---

[7]BBC (1967).

[8]Ramiro Troitino et al. (2018), p. 116.

[9]BBC (1967).

[10]Tekin (2016), p. 6.

[11]Outhwaite (2017), p. 42.

[12]EU Pioneers (2019).

[13]Churchill (1946).

strong advocator of the European peace project, and he never imagined Britain to be part of it, but rather a 'friend and sponsor' of the project alongside the USA.[14] Churchill could not see Britain and the Commonwealth sharing sovereignty and submitting their policies under federal or supranational rule.[15] Additionally, Churchill relentlessly promoted good relations with the USA, which according to him was the 'priority of the British government in foreign affairs'.[16] Furthermore, rather than prioritizing Europe, Churchill took a rather global approach in accordance with the British Empire concerning foreign policy.

Due to his criticism towards majority voting instead of unanimity, and opposition towards the accession of UK in the EEC, prominent Eurosceptic forces to justify their perceptions on the EU have quoted Churchill. For example, Nigel Farage has criticized the commission of painting Churchill as a supporter of Europe, for according to Farage, Churchill was a Eurosceptic. He referred to a speech given by Churchill where he stated: 'If Britain must choose between Europe and the open sea, she must always choose the open sea'.[17] Consequently, Farage has been criticized for misleading quotation of Churchill, for despite his criticism towards the communities, Churchill was a 'Europeanist at his time', when there were more than the two options existing today, in or out of EU.[18]

Where Churchill was still for further European economic and political integration (excluding Britain, of course), Margaret Thatcher was openly against it. Thatcher's premiership from 1979 to 1990 was characterized by the very determining factors behind British accession to the European communities: commitment to global free trade, and opposition towards supranational institutions and the establishment of a European federation.[19] Moreover, while Churchill thought there is a need for a United States of Europe, Thatcher viewed the goal as 'utopic'.[20] In her perspective, the EEC should be understood as a means to achieve the best possible solutions to its members, rather than as an end itself. However, at the same time Thatcher was a strong advocate of the single market and contributed to the completion of Europe's common market in goods, services, capital, and labour—the establishment of the Single European Act in 1987.[21] Thus, Thatcher's support for integration when it came to the single market, and opposition towards integration in other policy fields, seems 'self-contradictory and surprising',[22] since she partially traded British sovereignty for merely economic compensation. Nevertheless, both Churchill and Thatcher laid the ground for what the future perceptions of Britain and its leaders would be concerning European integration. The UK has ever since clearly focused on

[14] Ibid.

[15] Ramiro Troitino et al. (2018), p. 49.

[16] Ibid, p. 41.

[17] Danzig (2013).

[18] Ramiro Troitino et al. (2018), p. 54.

[19] Vollaard (2018), p. 19.

[20] Weiss (2018).

[21] Ramiro Troitino et al. (2018), p. 150.

[22] Ibid.

the economic benefits of integration and pushed for EU enlargement instead of 'an ever closer union', in order to manufacture a wide organization based on cooperation, rather than supranationalism.[23] Ultimately, also Thatcherism re-emerged in British nationalism prior to the EU referendum.[24]

Arguably, the British position has played a significant role in altering the course of European integration. In other words, due to its attempts to either 'keep' or 'take back control', UK has led European integration towards a 'multi-speed Europe'. Britain is often referred to as 'an awkward partner' or 'the awkward partner', due to its opposition towards further integration and demands for special treatment to avoid participating in certain policy areas.[25] In fact, the UK has repeatedly promoted the concept of 'Europe à la carte'[26]: a method of integration where the EU countries would be allowed to select policy areas they wish to be involved in from a 'menu', although the EU would still have some common goals.[27] The outcome has been differentiated integration: instead of applying the principle of 'single set of policies and obligations that would more or less apply in the same way to all Member States at the same time'.[28] The aim is paving the way for 'different paths of integration for different Member States, allowing those that want to deeper integration to move ahead, whilst respecting the rights of those that do not want to take such a course'.[29] In practice, opt-outs represent a popular form of differentiated integration. The UK has negotiated opt-outs from the Schengen Agreement, the Economic and Monetary Union, the Charter of Fundamental Rights of the European Union, and the Area of Freedom, Security and Justice. With altogether four opt-outs, UK is the front runner in opt-outs from the treaties of the EU, with Denmark with three, Ireland with two, and Poland with one opt-out.

Opt-outs have concretized the different levels and 'speeds' of integration that exists in the EU, perhaps the most clear-cut example being the Eurozone, where 19 out of 28 (27) MS have established a monetary union and adopted a common currency. In a complex setting of negotiating with 28 (27) MS with the purpose of reaching a consensus, integration has been achieved due to the possibility of opting-out and vetoing against the 'next integration step'.[30] Although UK has been against further integration, by opting out from certain policy areas it has enabled other MS to proceed with integration. For example, by excluding itself from the Eurozone, UK's opposition towards further integration has not impacted the policy area and further integration can be expected to take place with no notable immediate impact after Brexit.[31] However, the UK has voiced the concerns of the 'euro opt-outs', such as

[23]Tekin (2016), p. 7.

[24]Taylor (2017), p. 19.

[25]Oliver et al. (2018).

[26]Sacco (2019), p. 6.

[27]Weiss (2018).

[28]Tekin (2016), p. 4.

[29]Ibid.

[30]Sacco (2019), p. 6.

[31]Oliver et al. (2018), p. 24.

Sweden and Denmark—the 'voice' of which can potentially be diminished because of Brexit. Similar to Eurozone, integration in the field of Freedom, Security and Justice has not been prevented by UK due to its absence in the policy framework. Rather, Britain has allowed other MS to pursue deeper integration in matters concerning the Schengen Area and immigration, as long as it were to retain its opt-out.[32]

On the other hand, when it comes to the internal market of the EU, the UK has followed the Thatcherism perception on integration. This is one of the key policy areas in the EU, and it has been actively promoted and developed by the UK. The UK has not only benefited substantially from the internal market of the EU economy-wise, but also been able to promote its liberal-oriented form of policy-making through internal market.[33] Thus, the UK's decision to leave the union will in all likeliness alter the direction integration in this policy area, since the EU is losing one of its 'fervent supporters for the completion of the single market and particular in services'.[34]

Whereas the UK's opt-outs have enabled other countries to pursue further integration in those policy areas without the UK, the areas where the UK is involved, integration has mostly been stalled in order for the UK to 'maintain' and 'take back control'. While Britain is a notable European military power and has traditionally been a strong advocate of transatlantic security cooperation, it has also been the 'leading obstacle'[35] to integration in the area of Common Foreign and Security Policy, which has been considered one of the remaining hopes of neo-functionalists after the euro crisis in 2008. Although most of EU MS have relied on NATO for their defence, and the EU has not traditionally been viewed as a potential military alliance, the recent changes in the security environment and inside NATO have prompted more action. However, Britain has chosen to promote bilateral cooperation rather than EU cooperation in this field, and any reduction of the intergovernmental essence of the policy field, as well as any proposals that could undermine NATO, has been blocked and disputed by the UK.[36]

Since UK is not the only MS that has opted out from certain policy areas, it would be hasty to say that it has only been the UK altering the course of European integration. However, UK, as the third largest country in the EU with the second largest economy, has definitely had a significant impact on the courses of action. Thus, needless to say, Brexit has the potential to turn the course of European integration in various policy areas for better or worse. While the future implications of Brexit remain open to speculation, the road closer to the decision to exit for Britain arguably began by opting out from four policy areas the UK distanced itself from the 'core' Europe. Although a multi-speed Europe allows different MS to integrate according to their own pace and willingness, it has the potential to distance some members and create '"first" and "second class" members of the community',[37] where Eurozone represents

[32]Oliver et al. (2018), p. 21.

[33]Oliver et al. (2018), p. 10.

[34]Oliver et al. (2018), p. 8.

[35]Oliver et al. (2018), p. 29.

[36]Ibid.

[37]Ramiro Troitino et al. (2018), p. 193.

the 'first class members that will drive integration forward'.[38] Furthermore, when it comes to the development of differentiated integration, the process is now in the hands of the remaining awkward partners.[39]

2.2 *The Island Nation*

The EU has strived to develop a common European identity amongst its MS. By adopting a common flag and a national anthem, by granting European citizenship to the people of EU MS, and by establishing the Erasmus exchange programme in 1987 as well as grants and prizes, such as the Charlemagne Prize, the EU has pursued a feeling of European unification. Judging by the Eurobarometer survey on European identity in 2018,[40] where in 20 MS over half of the respondents felt attached to the EU, the efforts of the EU have not gone to waste since a good fraction of Europeans actually feel the European. However, in 2016, the British people were asked how they felt about the EU, and almost 52% felt unattached.

Although having been part of the EEC and the EU for over 50 years, the British still identify themselves as separate from the continental Europe and are often described as 'reluctant Europeans'.[41] Starting from the beginning of the European integration process, the UK has rather fostered transatlantic relations and global stance on foreign policy. As the British are physically isolated from mainland Europe, they have traditionally perceived themselves as being between the EU and the USA and as the 'balancer in the European political landscape',[42] rather than actually being inside Europe. Whereas the goal of the EU is arguably to create of notion of Europeans as *us* and countries outside Europe as *others*, the 'island nation' perceives itself in contrast to the continental Europe, where *us* is considered as the British and *others* as mainland Europeans. Moreover, the British do not *feel* European unlike most of the population in 20 other MS.[43]

A notable factor in British identity and British Euroscepticism is their exceptionalism ideology.[44] Stemming from the memory politics of the British Empire, the British view themselves as separate and different from other states, and thus they feel they ought to be treated differently.[45] The rejection towards European integration ultimately is linked with the legacy of the British Empire. Jeremey Black[46] elaborated the British Empire dilemma as follows: 'In 1945, Britain was a world power able to

[38]Tekin (2016), p. 7.
[39]Oliver (2018).
[40]EC (2018).
[41]Taylor (2017), p. 15.
[42]Ramiro Troitino et al. (2018), p. 154.
[43]Castro and Lago (2018).
[44]Taylor (2017), p. 16.
[45]Ramiro Troitino et al. (2018), p. 155.
[46]Black (2017), p. 198.

support Western European unity but not to see its destiny in those terms. By 2016, there were overseas possessions, including the Falkland Islands, Ascension Island, and Saint Helena, but there was no empire'. Despite the declining status of UK as an imperial power, the British have rejected European integration, for it has the potential to diminish the 'greatness that underpinned the self-belief of British elites'.[47] In other words, the British manifested in the Brexit vote in order to 'take back control' of their identity rather than absorb a European one. The rise of Euroscepticism in the UK has also been explained as a 'cultural backlash against cosmopolitan liberalism'.[48] Indeed, as Thatcher[49] put it:

> Europe will be stronger precisely because it has France as France, Spain as Spain, Britain as Britain, each with its own customs, traditions and identity. It would be folly to try to fit them into some sort of identikit European personality.

British exceptionalism has not only shaped European integration process but also contributed to the culmination of Brexit. According to Mölder,[50] Brexit is in fact a logical outcome of a discourse, where British political elites supported the feeling of otherness, which has ultimately emphasized Euroscepticism and negative perceptions towards mainland Europe—and Brussels in particular. The argument is also supported by Tekin,[51] who concludes that although political elites in Britain are aware of the benefits of the common market and EU foreign policy opportunities, simultaneously they are not prepared to 'give control' by participating in European integration. Naturally, when the British people expressed their feelings towards the EU, it was considered as the victory and breakthrough of Euroscepticism and nationalism. The EU was prophesied to come to its end and an ever closer union to remain utopic.[52] However, the effects have been rather the opposite. Although Eurosceptic parties did gain support in the latest European Parliament elections, their perceptions have changed when it comes to leaving the union. Moreover, Eurosceptic politicians, such as Marine Le Pen and Matteo Salvini, have stated that they are no longer aiming to leave the EU. Their current vision is to change the EU from within and make it better than it is, rather than leaving.[53] A newly elected Finnish MEP from the True Finns Eurosceptic party also justified their decision to alter their perception on leaving with the fear of the upcoming 'revenge' of the EU that has been visible in the Brexit case.[54] Furthermore, the past three years have changed the course of the nationalist and Eurosceptic agenda from wanting to break down the EU, to wanting to change it from within.

---

[47] Taylor (2017), p. 17.

[48] Taylor (2017), p. 56.

[49] Weiss (2018).

[50] Ramiro Troitino et al. (2018), p. 171.

[51] Tekin (2016), p. 7.

[52] Bickerton (2019).

[53] TRT World (2019), and Albanese and Totaro (2019).

[54] Huhtasaari (2019).

The EU has been able to remain united and in control of the Brexit negotiations and to pursue integration in the Eurozone and CFSP.[55] Additionally, a Eurobarometer survey[56] measured the highest level of support for the EU amongst EU citizens in 35 years. On the one hand, it seems safe to say that the dissolution of the EU remains an unlikely scenario. However, since Brexit is a long-term and ongoing process, the risk remains that the UK ultimately becomes an appealing 'non-EU alternative',[57] especially since the implications of a new Eurosceptic coalition in the EP wanting to change the union from within still remain to be seen.

2.3 Winners and Losers

The analysis on why exactly Brexit took place often circles around the notion of 'winners' and 'losers' of globalization, where (ironically) winners were the ones in favour of remaining and the losers in favour of leaving. 'Winners' in the highly globalized contemporary society have been categorized as the highly educated and highly paid, as well as the youth living in large, multicultural cities such as London.[58] Moreover, the winners are the ones that have most benefited from the EU's educational, career, and leisure opportunities. On the other hand, 'losers' are considered to be the ones existing in the lower-paid ends of work opportunities, the ones not in the beneficiary end of the EU's arrangement of free movement of workers, and the ones living in more rural areas of Britain.[59] Ironically, the losers in this case turned out as the winners of the Brexit vote, for they were able to deliver their message and 'take back control'. Consequently, the rationality of the Brexit vote winners has been put under question and their voting preference described in terms of 'misleading campaigns and foreign backers'.[60] However, in this subsection, Brexit phenomenon is discussed in a global context where the decision to leave was a rational outcome of globalization.[61]

The slogan 'take back control' suggests the feeling of relevance and powerlessness in a highly globalized society. While the emergence of global economy, free trade, and spread of democracy have marked the victory of liberal values, they have also created 'spillback' effects in the form of social and economic inequality that translate to rising nationalism. According to Pastor and Veronesi,[62] the extent of nationalism is interrelated with Gini coefficient: the more unequal a country is, the more there exists nationalism, and the more there are 'losers' of globalization. However, an important

---

[55]Oliver et al. (2018), p. 6.

[56]EP News (2018).

[57]Oliver (2018).

[58]Taylor (2017), p. 45 and Outhwaite (2017), p. 23.

[59]Ibid.

[60]Pastor and Veronesi (2018).

[61]Martín de la Guardia and Pérez Sánchez (2001).

[62]Ibid.

distinction is that generally Brexiteers are not willing to throw away liberal ideology, only the global aspect of it.[63] Furthermore, the British majority decision to leave the union and retain what they once had is a part of a global phenomenon, where people find themselves alienated and detached from the decision-making process concerning their lives and excluded from the benefits of globalization. As Harari[64] put it, the reaction of nationalism is to go back, take back, or make back again. Just as the Brexiteers wanted to take back the control that once was them before acceding to the EU, Americans wanted to 'Make America Great Again' by electing Donald Trump as their president in 2016, and Vladimir Putin wants to return to the tsarist times of Russia.[65] Moreover, the British decision to leave the EU can be understood in terms of a global phenomenon, where discontent towards the inequalities of power and wealth as well as 'false promises made by liberalism'[66] is expressed now that it is still possible.[67] Thus, rather than Brexit being a result of irrational behaviour, Brexiteers in fact did make a rational decision based on 'real anger and alienation [...] linked to real inequalities and injustices', as Taylor[68] put it. Moreover, the 51.89% that voted in favour of leaving did so to ensure that their life will be 'better 30 years from now'.[69] However, the Brexit vote did not only manifest against globalization in terms of global capitalism, but also with European integration.[70] Furthermore, globalization and European integration have together generated a sense of 'belonging beyond the nation state' that has given an impetus to the defence of British identity and 'exceptionalism', translated as Euroscepticism.[71] In addition, as Outhwaite[72] put it, the EU is easier to pinpoint than global capitalism.

The Brexit result is logical also due to the reality of nation states and territories becoming more and more irrelevant. In the presence of a global economy and multiple global and regional problems, such as climate change and mass immigration, a distinct need exists for global and regional solutions. The existing national political systems are ineffective, for them or nationalist ideology, and do not have the capacity to tackle global-scale problems.[73] As Joseph Weiler[74] quite aptly put it, the time 'to protect national sovereignty is passé'. The EU is now between a battle of a clear need for closer integration on one side and a backlash in the form of nationalism created by globalization and integration on the other.[75]

---

[63] Harari (2018), p. 27.

[64] Harari (2017).

[65] Ibid.

[66] Harari (2018).

[67] Outhwaite (2017), p. 26.

[68] Taylor (2017), p. 46.

[69] Outhwaite (2017), p. 23.

[70] Outhwaite (2017), p. 22.

[71] Taylor (2017), p. 50.

[72] Outhwaite (2017), p. 22.

[73] Harari (2017).

[74] Outhwaite (2017), p. 42.

[75] Ramiro Troitino et al. (2018), p. ix.

3 Lessons Learned

Brexit has involved around three elements that are irreversibly linked with the Brexit campaign slogan: 'take back control'. Firstly, the history of the relations between UK and EU reveals a consistent battle between British aspirations for cooperation rather than further integration. Starting from Winston Churchill, the UK has rather perceived itself as a global power, promoted transatlantic relations, and viewed the EU through its economic benefits, rather than the EU as an outcome itself. Thus, the Brexit vote can be understood in terms of the British people protesting against loss of democratic sovereignty during the European integration process and wanting to 'take back control' or their sovereignty. Secondly, the decision to leave the EU can be explained in terms of conflicts of identity. Due to a strong legacy as the British Empire, and their physical isolation from mainland Europe, the British people feel 'separated' and 'exceptional' compared to continental Europeans. With the emergence of European identity and further integration, the Brexit vote can be interpreted to symbolize 'taking back control' as the people of a powerful and 'exceptional' nation, rather than submitting to a European identity. Finally, 'take back control' refers to a global phenomenon, where inequality creates a backlash for globalization. Brexiteers were mostly considered to be the 'losers' of globalization with low socio-economic statuses, who protested against unequal distribution of wealth and the feeling of irrelevance. Thus, although often described as irrational and idiotic, Brexiteers acted rationally in order to protest against globalization and attempt to 'take back control' of their livelihoods.[76]

Whereas Brexit was an outcome of the battle between cooperation and integration, British exceptionalism identity, and the counter effects of globalization, the three have also shaped the European integration process. British critical stance on integration has given an impetus on the development of differentiated integration, where different MS can move at different levels and speeds of integration because of which further integration has prevailed in the EU despite British unwillingness to join it. Additionally, British Thatcherism and exceptionalism identity have inspired Euroscepticism in an outside Britain. Finally, the inequalities in wealth, opportunities, and between areas created by globalization have resulted in dissatisfaction towards the EU. Thus, the core reasons behind Brexit have actually shaped the EU already for decades. However, what should the European Union learn from this arguably multifaceted phenomenon, in order to continue the road towards an 'ever closer union'?

Since the current issues—state of economy, immigration, climate change, security, and defence—that Britain is facing are in essence global, or by the least regional, they require global and regional solutions. Neither Britain nor any other European state is not able to tackle these issues alone for, as Harari[77] put it 'We have a global ecology, we have a global economy, but we have national politics. In addition, this does not work together. This makes the political system ineffective because it has no

[76]Outeda (2001).

[77]Harari (2017).

control over the forces that shape our life'. Thus, the EU remains particularly relevant to its MS.[78] When it comes to the matter of identity, the EU has already promoted European identity from student exchange to culture and sports and managed to score the best approval in 35 years.[79] In addition, geographically wise, Brexiteers mostly inhabit rural areas of Britain—areas that are constant recipients of EU aid.[80] Thus, it appears that it is not the essence of EU per se that has sparked Euroscepticism in the UK, but rather how the role of EU has been perceived.[81]

Problems that affect all need solutions from a united front of all. Brexiteers have so far been able to promote their agenda more effectively than the 'stronger together' discourse of the pro-Europeans. However, now it is time for 'global patriotism'.[82] Although the British have not necessarily 'gotten' the EU, the Eurobarometer survey revealed that feeling European does not need to shut out feeling German, French, or Spanish. Loyalty on an EU level is exactly what is needed, and thus, the ultimate lesson learned of Brexit remains: How can the European Union deliver its message persuasively for all? Ironically, the leave campaign slogan 'take back control' delivers the key for the EU to learn from the unfortunate break-up and allows it to proceed towards an 'ever closer union'.

References

Albanese, C., Totaro, L. (2019). Italy's Salvini Says Country Won't Leave EU, Just Wants Changes, Bloomberg, 15 February 2019, https://www.bloomberg.com/news/articles/2019-02-15/league-s-borghi-voices-fresh-threat-of-italy-quitting-the-eu.

BBC. (1967). De Gaulle says 'non' to Britain—Again, BBC, 27 November 1967, http://news.bbc.co.uk/onthisday/hi/dates/stories/November/27/newsid_4187000/4187714.stm.

Betts, A. (2016). Why Brexit happened—What to do next. Ted Talks. Accessible at: https://www.ted.com/talks/alexander_betts_why_brexit_happened_and_what_to_do_next.

Bickerton, C. (2019). The EU will still be here in five years—But it will be ruined by far-right politics, The Independent, 7 May 2019, https://www.independent.co.uk/voices/brexit-eu-italy-france-far-right-populism-salvini-politics-extremism-a8902861.html.

Bickerton, C., Irondelle, B., Menon, A. (2010). Security Co-operation beyond the Nation-State: The EU's Common Security and Defence Policy. *Journal of Common Market Studies*, *49*(1), 1–21.

Black, J. (2017). *A history of Britain: 1945 to Brexit*. Indiana University Press. Accessible at ProQuest Ebook Central.

Castro, L. D., & Lago, J. R. R. (2018). Educación y diplomacia cultural en la primavera de Europa (1948–1954) = education and cultural diplomacy in the spring of Europe (1948–1954). *Revista de educación, 383*, 63–84.

Chochia, A., Troitiño, D. R., Kerikmäe, T., Shumilo, O. (2018). Enlargement to the UK, the Referendum of 1975 and Position of Margaret Thatcher. In *Brexit* (pp. 115–139). Cham: Springer.

[78] Pawlas (2015).

[79] EC (2018).

[80] Betts (2016).

[81] Kerikmäe et al. (2019).

[82] Harari (2017).

Churchill, W. (1946). Churchill speaking on 19 September 1946 in Zurich. Accessible at: https://rm.coe.int/16806981f3.

Danzig, J. (2013). Winston Churchill: A founder of the European Union, Ideas on Europe, November 10, 2013. https://eu-rope.ideasoneurope.eu/2013/11/10/winston-churchill-a-founder-of-the-european-union/.

EC. (2018). Standard Eurobarometer 89, Report on European Citizenship, European Commission. Accessible at: http://webcache.googleusercontent.com/search?q=cache:SK3WQrvLeQQJ:ec.europa.eu/commfrontoffice/publicopinion/index.cfm/ResultDoc/download/DocumentKy/83538+&cd=1&hl=fi&ct=clnk&gl=fi&client=safari.

EP News. (2018). Eurobarometer survey shows highest support for the EU in 35 years, European Parliament News, May 25, 2018. http://www.europarl.europa.eu/news/en/headlines/eu-affairs/20180522STO04020/eurobarometer-survey-highest-support-for-the-eu-in-35-years.

EU Pioneers. (2019). European Union. Accessible at: https://europa.eu/european-union/about-eu/history/eu-pioneers_fi.

EUR-Lex. Glossary of summaries. https://eur-lex.europa.eu/homepage.html.

Haagendoorn, S. (2017). The historical evolution of EU-UK relations. Council of the European Union, June 2, 2017. https://www.consilium.europa.eu/sv/documents-publications/library/library-blog/posts/the-historical-evolution-of-eu-uk-relations/.

Harari, Y. N. (2017). Nationalism versus globalism: The new political divide. Ted Dialogues with Yuval Noah Harari. Accessible: https://www.ted.com/talks/yuval_noah_harari_nationalism_vs_globalism_the_new_political_divide/details?language=fi.

Harari, Y. N. (2018). 21 Lessons for the 21st Century. United States, United Kingdom: Spiegel & Grau, Jonathan Cape.

Huhtasaari, L. (2019). The future and the European Union, Yle Areena, May 9, 2019. Accessible at: https://areena.yle.fi/1-50089999 (Language: Finnish).

Jackson, D., Thorsen, E., Wring, D. (2016). EU Referendum Analysis 2016: Media, Voters and the Campaign. The Centre for the Study of Journalism, Culture and Community, Bournemouth University, Poole. Accessible at: http://irep.ntu.ac.uk/id/eprint/28759/1/PubSub6174_Henn.pdf.

Kerikmäe, T. (2014). Protecting Human Rights in the EU. Controversies and Challenges of the Charter of Fundamental Rights.

Kerikmäe, T., Troitiño, D. R., Shumilo, O. (2019). An Idol or an Ideal? A Case Study of Estonian e-Governance: Public Perceptions, myths and misbeliefs1. *Acta Baltica Historiae et Philosophiae scientiarum*, *7*(1).

Martín de la Guardia, R. M., & Pérez Sánchez, G. A. (2001). *Historia de la integración europea*. Barcelona: Ariel.

Mindus, P. (2017). *European Citizenship after Brexit: Freedom of Movement and Rights of Residence*. Palgrave and Pivot, Palgrave Studies in European Union. Accessible at: https://link.springer.com/content/pdf/10.1007%2F978-3-319-51774-2.pdf.

Nugee, J. (2013). British Exceptionalism and the European Union, The Globalist, February 7, 2013. https://www.theglobalist.com/british-exceptionalism-and-the-european-union/.

Oliver, T. (2018). Does Brexit spell boom or doom for European integration? The London School of Economics and Policial Science Blogs, August 3, 2018. https://blogs.lse.ac.uk/brexit/2018/08/03/does-brexit-spell-boom-or-doom-for-european-integration/.

Oliver, T., Walshe, G., Barnard, C., Hantrais, L., Matthius, M., Peers, S. (2018). The impact of the UK's withdrawal on EU integration. European Parliament's Policy Department for Citizens' Rights and Constitutional Affairs. European Union 2018. http://www.europarl.europa.eu/RegData/etudes/STUD/2018/604973/IPOL_STU(2018)604973_EN.pdf.

Outeda, C. C. (2001). *El proceso de constitucionalización de la Unión Europea: de Roma a Niza* (No. 3). Univ Santiago de Compostela.

Outhwaite, W. (2017). *Brexit: Sociological Responses*. London: Wimbledon Publishing Company. Accessible at: https://books.google.fi/books?id=fUE2DgAAQBAJ&pg=PA22&dq=globalization+brexit&hl=fi&sa=X&ved=

0ahUKEwipz4632LTjAhXNo4sKHZFdBd0Q6AEIJjAA#v=onepage&q=globalization%20brexit&f=false.
Pastor, L., Veronesi, P. (2018). A rational backlash against globalisation, The London School of Economics and Political Science Blogs, October 5, 2018. https://blogs.lse.ac.uk/brexit/2018/10/05/a-rational-backlash-against-globalisation/.
Pawlas, I. (2015, September). The Visegrad Countries and European Union Membership-Selected Issues. In *Proceedings of International Academic Conferences* (No. 2704866). International Institute of Social and Economic Sciences.
Ramiro Troitino, D., Kerikmäe, T., Chochia, A. (2018). *Brexit: History, reasoning and perspectives*. Springer International Publishing AG 2018.
Sacco, M. (2019). *Brexit: A way forward*. Vernon Press Series in Law. https://books.google.fi/books?id=K3OSDwAAQBAJ.
Taylor, G. (2017). Understanding Brexit: Why Britain voted to leave the European Union. United Kingdom: Emerald Publishing Limited. Accessible at EBSCOhost eBook Collection.
Tekin, F. (2016). Brexit or No Brexit? political and institutional implications of an EU without the UK. Institutional Affari Internazionali (IAI). https://www.iai.it/sites/default/files/iaiwp1607.pdf.
Troitiño, D. R. (2017). Jean Monnet before the first European community: A historical perspective and critic. *Trames, 21*(3), 193–213.
Troitino, D. R., & Faerber, K. (2019). Historical errors in the initial conception of the euro and its subsequent development. *Brazilian Journal of Political Economy, 39*(2), 328–343.
TRT World. (2019). Le Pen drops 'Frexit' in favour of an 'EU of the far-right', TRT World, April 15, 2019. https://www.trtworld.com/europe/le-pen-drops-frexit-in-favour-of-an-eu-of-the-far-right-25868.
Tuck, R., Bickerton, R. (2017). A Brexit proposal by Christopher Bickerton and Richard Tuck, briefings for Brexit, August 17, 2018. https://briefingsforbrexit.com/a-brexit-proposal-by-christopher-bickerton-and-richard-tuck/.
Vollaard, H. (2018). European disintegration: A search for Explanations. Palgrave Macmillan Limited. Accessible at ProQuest Ebook Central.
Weiss, K. (2018). 30 years after Bruges: Margaret Thatcher's Vision for Europe Revisited. Austrian Economics Center. https://www.austriancenter.com/wp-content/uploads/2018/09/Thatcher_Bruges.pdf.

The Post-crisis European Union Before the Political Union: Coordinates and Keys of the Future Institutional Architecture

Celso Cancela-Outeda

Abstract Historically, the European integration is a relatively recent process and in permanent evolution. Over time, the EU has moved from what is international towards what is political-constitutional. This last dimension has been stressed during the Euro crisis (bank union, fiscal…), in addition to becoming obvious to the citizens. The management of political conflicts requires political legitimacy and, consequently, the adjustment of institutional architecture. Apparently, now is the time to formalize the European political union. But, what type of union? It is mandatory to reflect on the basic political elements and on the institutional architecture such as federalism, distribution of competences, separation of powers or democracy. Moreover, the post-crisis European reality is characterized by the politicization and the constitutionalization of the EU. These elements constrain the institutional adaptation of the EU. Specifically, one of the keys is the establishment of guarantees for the articulation of multiple governments and institutions within the EU.

Keywords Institutional reform · Political union · Functionalism · Federalism · Democracy

1 Introduction[1]

In the last decade, the EU has gone through a hectic phase, at times, tumultuous and confusing. The ingredients of this situation are, among others, the Euro crisis (2008–2012), the Greek crisis (2015), the refugee crisis (2015) and the British referendum result on Brexit in June 2016. Retrospectively, there is not much that is new or unusual in this situation. It could be said that it is the usual scenario, normal in the EU since the late eighties (fall of the Berlin Wall, negotiations in Maastricht, the former Yugoslavia conflict, the failure of the constitutional treaty, etc.). What is

[1] Partially, the following ideas and questions can be seen *in extenso* in Pereira-Menaut and Cancela-Outeda (2012).

C. Cancela-Outeda (✉)
University of Vigo, Vigo, Spain
e-mail: ccancela@uvigo.gal

D. Ramiro Troitiño et al. (eds.), *The EU in the 21st Century*,
https://doi.org/10.1007/978-3-030-38399-2_8

new in the current post-crisis context lies in the impact on state institutions (governments, parliaments, constitutions…), on public policies, on public opinion (political disaffection, Euro-scepticism, populism…) and on European institutions (European Council, EC, EP, ECB…). After having channelled the Euro crisis (bank union, fiscal union…), the removal of (political) competences that the state members have experienced is clear, as well as the created interdependencies, particularly in the Eurozone. Today, the divisions among states (north south regarding Euro or east west regarding immigration) are evident, generating political differences. After the crisis, it is explicit that the EU has adopted a redistributive profile that coexists with the regulatory profile, creating winners and losers. The reform of the European institutions should take into account the politicization (and constitutionalization) experienced by the EU. It also has to consider the attribution of new state competences to Brussels (taxation, budget…) to proceed with a new institutional reform (institutions and decision-making). At first sight, the EU is at a crucial juncture. In fact, the current European narrative points towards the political union. This way, there are many and complex questions in the European agenda: What type of union will be implemented, how and when it will be carried out, and which institutional design will be adopted?

It is not necessary to insist that European integration is a successful experience. It has generated peace, prosperity, growth, better living standards… However, alone, these outcomes cannot justify (results legitimacy) the orientation of the post-crisis EU towards the political union. It is no longer possible to tiptoe around political terms with the citizens. These understand clearly that the adopted measures (bank union, fiscal union, financial rescues and memorandums…) have an impact on everyday life (public services) and that winners and losers have emerged among states and citizens. Despite the effort against some political forces, it seems that they have understood that national sovereignty is not the remedy. The EU is already a politicized and constitutionalized space (in part) that needs an institutional architecture in line with certain principles, values or basic elements.

In parallel to this crisis period, a reformist scenario was configured. It was created with some degree of optimism (supported by the general economic growth and increasing confidence in the EU) thanks to the increase of EU reform initiatives. There are numerous initiatives and with different profiles. The initiatives are different regarding ambition and objectives (reform, re-foundation), origin (some are an output of the EU institutions, others are an output of leaders or national political representatives), scope (institutional reform of the Eurozone or the EU itself), some have a institutional profile confronting others that are more personal, some are articulated and detailed (technocratic) and others are more general (political). Nevertheless, they create a context of institutional reform. Among the institutional ones, in 2015 *The Five President's Report: Completing Europe's Economic and Monetary Union* was presented. In 2016, the *Report on possible evolutions of and adjustments to the current institutional set-up of the European Union*[2] was passed. In March 2017, the

---

[2] *Report on possible evolutions of and adjustments to the current institutional set-up of the European Union (2014/2248(INI) Committee on Constitutional Affairs*. Rapporteur: Guy Verhofstadt.

European Commission launched the *White Paper on the Future of Europe.*[3] Later on, in September, Emmanuel Macron publicly presented *Initiative pour l'Europe. Une Europe souveraine, une Europe unie, une Europe démocratique.*[4] At the end of the same year, Martin Schulz, leader of the German SPD, proposed the constitution of the United States of Europe in 2025 through a constitutional treaty.[5] In 2018, the *Manifiesto para la democratización de Europa*[6] was presented.

These help to identify political-institutional deficiencies and challenges faced by the EU (institutions, democratization, European competences and federalism, European public policies…). Once these elements have been identified, it will be the time to perform EU institutional reform, to a more or less broad extent. As a previous step to this task, it is compulsory to review certain political structural questions regarding the integration process (principles, values, method, orientation…) that affect the institutional architecture of the EU. This should be able to give an answer to the question that the political community has to address: What type of society do we want to build?

This chapter is structured around three main sections. The first is to position the current EU configuration in the political and constitutional arena. If the EU decides to advance towards political union, it will not be starting from scratch because in a significant number of fields it is already behaving as a political-constitutional system. The second section reviews a series of basic elements that should guide the movement towards political union: federalism, the distribution of competences, the separation of powers and democracy. To conclude, the third section gathers some notes on the EU institutional architecture towards the political union.

Available in http://www.europarl.europa.eu/doceo/document/A-8-2016-0390_EN.pdf (last access: 6th July 2019).

[3] *White paper on the future of Europe*, https://ec.europa.eu/commission/sites/beta-political/files/white_paper_on_the_future_of_europe_en.pdf (last access: 15th July 2017).

[4] It started by stating that "Faced with the great challenges of our times, such as defence and security, great migrations, development, climate change, the digital revolution and regulation of a globalized economy, have European countries found means to defend their interests and values, and to guarantee and adapt their democratic and social model that is unique worldwide? Can they address each of these challenges alone? We cannot afford to keep the same policies, the same habits, the same procedures and the same budget. No more can we choose to turn inwards within national borders. The only way to ensure our future, is the rebuilding of a sovereign, united and democratic Europe". Available at https://es.ambafrance.org/Initiative-pour-l-Europe-intervention-du-President-de-la-Republique. In 2019, just before the elections to the European Parliament, Emmanuel Macron published a letter called "A European Renaissance" (4th of March, 2019). In it, he mentions a variety of challenges and proposes the implementation of a set of institutions (common border policy, an Asylum European Office, a Home Security European Council, a European Security Council, European Climate Bank…). This document can be consulted at https://es.ambafrance.org/Pour-une-Renaissance-europeenne.

[5] This document can be consulted at https://euobserver.com/political/140200.

[6] Proposes the creation of a federal budget, under real democratic control and with the capacity to invest on a European level. Available at http://tdem.eu/en/manifesto/.

2 The Post-crisis EU: Political and Constitutional Coordinates

The scenario after the above-mentioned crisis, in particular, the Euro crisis, placed the EU in a political (and constitutional) arena, particularly the states of the Eurozone. The European measures that have been adopted generated winners and losers among the member states and the citizens.[7] This leads to the justification of the EU politicization. Now it is obvious; it is sufficient to review the measures adopted and the reactions provoked among the different political agents (member states, constitutional courts or political parties). However, politicization is not only the result of the recent anti-crisis measures (Eurozone governance). Before, the single market and the Euro had already provoked divergences and economic, financial and monetary (structural) imbalances in the Eurozone with the consequent political differences (emergence of internal centrifugal forces, attitudes of no support or cooperation among the member states, coalitions or groups of member states).[8] Thus, it was possible to identify beneficiaries/winners and disadvantaged/losers in the single market and the Euro (concentration of wealth and deindustrialization). Now, the domestic decisions taken after the European political decisions to resolve the Euro crisis are undeniable. In technical terms, these were the result of the intervention of experts (ECB, Troika…). First lesson: inspiration and technocratic attitudes are not sustainable. That place must be occupied by political perspective. The current institutional architecture must be oriented towards the improvement of political legitimacy and to mitigate the structural divergences (e.g. European budget nurtured with broad investment capacity). Also, it is important to provide it with European political leadership that supports and gives credibility to the European measures.

Certainly, European integration evolved from the functional-technocratic to the political-constitutional. With the founding of the European Coal and Steel Community, the integration was developed in an accelerated and asymmetric manner, inspired by the functionalist method. It advanced towards political integration in certain areas (single market, common currency, foreign trade, etc.), areas where the member states gave the capacity of sovereign actions (supranationalism/federalism) in benefit of the European institutions. Meanwhile, other fields such as foreign policy, defence and security, taxation, etc., remained in the area of agreements among state governments (intergovernmentalism). In the nineties, approximately, the European integration showed a manifest political and constitutional dimension (partial and fragmentary). Until that time, the orientation and inspiration of the European institutional reforms had answered to specific needs, according to the functionalist approach (technocratic inspiration). From this time, the principles and values, the rights and liberties (European citizenship), the distribution of competences and democracy confirmed the agenda and the European political debate. The successive reforms of the constitutive treaties were oriented, partially, towards that political

[7] Torreblanca (2014).

[8] Delaume and Cayla (2017).

dimension. The EU conversion to a compound political community progressively altered the interstate and interinstitutional interaction patterns.[9] Academically, the EU started to be examined as a political system with the capacity to influence its member states and its citizens through public policies.[10]

During the nineties, the integration sped up. In barely a decade, three modifications of the treaties (Maastricht in 1992, Amsterdam in 1997 and Nice in 2001) inspired by the political and constitutional aspects (European citizenship, Economic and Monetary Union, distribution of competences and the principle of subsidiarity, improvement of the democratic legitimacy…) came into force.[11] Of course, the Convention on the future of Europe (2002) profoundly treated questions such as the distribution of competences, the rights and freedoms, the institutional powers, etc. After the constitutional crisis of 2005, the work was included almost completely in the Treaty of Lisbon. This intended to be a stop to European integration, but the Euro crisis forced new singular institutional reforms, even outside the reform procedure established in the treaties and the assumption of new state competences by the EU. At the same time, it has created a political dynamic (winners and losers) that stressed the mentioned politicization.

Moreover, a process of constitutionalization of the European integration occurred, that is to say, the progressive development of elements of a constitutional nature that were detectable from a material perspective and that affected the interactions among the EU institutions and between the EU and its member states.[12] Thus, it is safe to say that "after the first decisions of the European Court of Justice (Van Gend and Loos 1962, Costa/ENEL 1964),[13] the then Common Market started to develop

---

[9]Hix and Hoyland (2012).

[10]At an academic level, this transformation influenced the emergence of new theoretical approaches. Thus, Hix writes that "the recognition of the EU as 'just another polity' enabled a new generation of scholars to approach the EU from the fields of comparative politics and comparative public policy. This new generation brought a new set of research questions. Until the early 1990 s, the main focus had been to explain bargaining between the member states, power relations between member states and the supranational institutions, and the general long-run process of economic and political integration in Europe, mainly from the field of international relations" (Hix, 2007).

[11]The EU Charter of Fundamental Rights (2000), the Declaration 23 of the Treaty of Nice, the Laeken Declaration (2001) or the Lamassoure Report on the division of competences between the EU and the member states (2002) have political-institutional inspiration.

[12]Pereira-Menaut and Cancela-Outeda (2012).

[13]The Court of Justice has supported a political-constitutional vision of European integration. Thus, the decisions of the Court are understood. Decisions such as Van Gend and Loos (1962) where the principle of the direct effect was established in the constitutive treaties or the decision Costa/ENEL (1964), that established the principle of primacy of European Law over the state Law. In 1969, the protection line started with the fundamental rights and freedoms regarding the act of European institutions on the base of general principles, common constitutional traditions and the European Convention on Human Rights and Fundamental Freedoms (1950). Another remarkable legal contribution is that referred to as the consideration of the European Communities (today the EU) as a Legal community (the European institutions act subject to the rule of Law), to the safeguard of a certain separation of powers among the main European institutions, based on the principle of institutional balance. In this respect, the Court of Justice has acted somehow as a federal court, particularly when referring to the delimitation of the competences among the member states and

a material, non-codified sort of a constitution. Over time, the European Court of Justice, the national constitutional courts, and the reformed Treaties have put on more touches to the portrait after a constructivist fashion, thus adding increasingly more elements of a constitutional nature (direct elections, fundamental rights, rule of law)". Thereby, European integration has been the most powerful agent of constitutional changes in their member states. Over decades it was a case of what has been termed a "creeping constitutionalisation", but after Maastricht its pace accelerated and the process became clearer and more "official". Every important European modification has implicitly resulted in a reform or mutation of national constitutions.[14] Proof of this is the conflicts arisen from the state constitutions (and the reaction of some constitutional courts) and, in some cases, the reforms in constitutional texts (and constitutional mutations). Consequently, the constitutional identity of the state members started to be affected by the European integration.

Nowadays, it is possible to support the existence of a non-formalized material European constitution (un-coded), disperse, fragmented and asymmetric, composed of mixed parts, overlapping and interdependent (even inconsistent). It consists of constitutional parts from the TEU, TFEU and the Charter of Rights. Moreover, some protocols and declarations should be added: the Convention of Rome, jurisprudence from the Luxembourg and Strasbourg Court, some state constitutional courts, some articles from state constitutions, principles and values from the treaties, common European traditions and certain parts from the *acquis communautaire*. This scheme relates to the constitutionalism of the postmodern political communities.

As these coordinates (politicization and constitutionalization) define the EU, its institutional architecture should allow the debate and definition of a European public interest and democratically legitimize the consequent public policies. Furthermore, they should guarantee the rights and freedoms, act in accordance with the *rule of law*, and respect the distribution of competences… In short, the politicization and the constitutionalization of the EU are key conditions for future institutional reforms. The EU has already started the reforms in both dimensions, so it will need institutional adjustments but it will not be necessary to completely rebuild the institutional architecture. However, there are some key elements to guide the institutional reform operation.

3 Political-Constitutional Bases of the EU Institutional Architecture

The development achieved by the European integration process demands that the EU adapts to and satisfies certain political and constitutional demands that are specific

---

the EU. The political significance of these decisions is unquestionable, in practice, moving the EU towards a federal style political system. Regarding EU constitutionalization, see Cancela (2001).

[14]Ibid.

to a political community (e.g. integration in a common political project and participation in making binding decisions). In part, it is already doing this, even though its current institutional architecture has political (and constitutional) weaknesses that were probably aggravated during the last decade. Actually, there is a mismatch between the political and the economical. Before outlining the institutional reform of the EU, a set of basic political-constitutional elements should be considered.

4 Federalism

It is common to point out that the EU lacks historical precedents or that it constitutes an "Unidentified Political Object". It would be a singular, unique and original process. The truth is that history offers diverse political integration experiences (Roman Empire, USA, Germany, UK, France or Spain…). However, it does not offer a unique political integration model. The EU is a case of partial and imperfect federalism that has originated a political community composed of political communities whose self-governance must be guaranteed. Instead of the federal formula, the functionalist method was followed for the first decades of integration (when it scarcely presented any political-constitutional dimension). Functionalism involved an elitist and technocratic attitude oriented towards the achievement of results (peace, prosperity and economic growth). Its successes and achievements are obvious. Nevertheless, the posterior development of the political-constitutional dimension did not imply the abandonment of functionalism. From the nineties onwards, this method started to show its limitations facing the background problems and political challenges connected with the political union. It was unable to add a joint sense to the integration process, to face and eliminate its ambiguity and its political indeterminacy. The institutional reforms guided by a functional vision resulted partial and insufficient in order to advance towards the political union. Only from a federal perspective is possible openly raising fundamental questions: Which political objects should the EU seek? Which principles and values should orient its political-institutional architecture?

At this time, Brexit demonstrates the constitutional and political dimension of the EU and the limits of the functionalist approach.[15] It is not a simple retreat from an international organization (in practice it is similar to a negotiated secession process), it is not about the simple activation of a formal procedure (art. 50 TEU) supervised by technicians (jurists and economists), nor making financial calculations, whether more or less complex. This implies a dose of realism on the political nature of integration. From an integration point of view, this episode, yet unresolved, acts as an EU adhesive rather than a diluent.

At this point in European integration, the needs are how to govern a political community composed of political communities (with their respective constitutions and constitutional identities), for which purpose the functionalist method is not the most adequate. As long as the EU did not develop this political and constitutional

[15] Troitiño et al. (2018).

dimension, it did not threaten the political and constitutional identity of the rest of member states. Nevertheless, currently the state members do not deserve the condition of sovereign (they are in the sense of original holders of sovereignty). Justifiably, Colomer says, "in fact, 'national sovereignty' [...] has become one of the most obsolete political concepts nowadays. Currently, the EU is characterized by having a governance structure with multiple levels where nobody is sovereign: not the traditional states, 'member' states of the Union, prevented from competences in important political questions and subject to strong restrictions and controls by the EU institutions, not a single local or regional government could claim that ambition. The EU member states have transferred or shared powers derived from their previous sovereignties but so far, they have not created a new European sovereignty. Each level of government has exclusive powers in some fields, shares powers in other fields, each has to be specifically financed to cover the costs of their services and no one can impose their will over others in everything, as would be implied by sovereignty. The European population lives under various jurisdictions of different fields and scopes that usually overlap".[16] As a matter of principle, this multilevel scenario, characterized by the absence of sovereignty, is ideal for federalism.

Now, the EU has quickly advanced towards centralization and standardization.[17] The facts demonstrate that "it is not necessary to promote them [centralization and standardization], they come alone, and that is why the objective is to counter them with constitutional mechanisms".[18] For four decades, approximately, these constitutional limitations were not necessary, nor democratizing measures of a political power in formation. Now, in a composed political community, these mechanisms are needed, including federalism. Its implementation should be accompanied by the abandonment of the functionalist attitude (characterized by technocratic approach and efficiency) in favour of the federal attitude, which is more appropriate for the creation of the United States of Europe. From the political-constitutional perspective, the key is the articulation of the different political and constitutional levels. The preservation of political capacities on these government levels (state, regional and local) is an inexorable condition. Avoiding its transformation into delegate agents of the EU, mere administrative or planning units are a characteristic of federalism. In order to achieve this, it is necessary to follow articulation criteria for government levels (and constitutionality levels to protect the constitutional identity of member

---

[16]Colomer (2018).

[17]On uniformization, MacLaren wrote: "In attempting to achieve the internal market through the approximation of laws in the 1970s and early 80s, lengthy bargaining produced excessively detailed EC rules. Rather than secure total regulatory harmonization, the Commission has had to resort to mutual recognition of national regulations and a limited number of essential safety and technical requirements" (MacLaren 2001). Regarding centralization, Hix points out the following: "for example, consider the evolution of competences in the EU and the US. Both polities started with a low level of policy centralization. However, policy centralization occurred remarkably quickly in the EU compared to the US, and in some area faster than others" (Hix 2007).

[18]Pereira-Menaut (2017).

states) such as subsidiarity, the restrictive interpreting of implicit powers or the distribution of competences among the EU and member states (and regional entities). Dual or Anglo-American federalism can offer relatively satisfying solutions.[19]

Lastly, the key idea of centralism is the existence of a certain territorial balance among the federate states, characterized by equality among them and the preservation of an effective state political space. In the European case, the successive anti-crisis measures (accumulation and overlapping of measures, occasionally, with scarce rationality) have undermined that balance. Two examples illustrate this position. On one side, the passing of the European Stability Mechanism (ESM) and Fiscal Compact through international treaties, that allowed avoiding the needed agreement of all the member states and on the other side, the voting rights in the ESM reflect the respective financial contributions more than the condition of equal sovereign states.[20]

5 Distribution of Competences

The distribution of competences among the EU and the rest of government levels is closely linked to federalism. This issue was tackled by the successive reforms of the treaties (in 2001, Laeken Declaration specifically insisted on the need to clarify the distribution of competences). In which fields can the EU act? In formal-legal terms, the answer involves the principle of attribution of competences (art. 1 and 5 TEU) and the three competence categories (exclusive, shared, supportive, coordination and complement), contained in the Lisbon Treaty (art. 2 and 3, TEU, mainly). We should also mention the presumption clause of general competence of the state ("Competences not conferred upon the Union in the Treaties remain with the Member States" art. 4.1 and 5.2 TEU) and the prevision of competences or implicit powers (art. 352 TFEU).

From a political point of view, generically, experience shows that the competences distribution is not fixed. In the long term, it tends towards centralization, to strengthening the federal institutions. The Lisbon Treaty does not establish a clear competence delimitation (inspired in dual federalism) nor establish limits to the competence expansion of Brussels. Secondly, the EU has great powers in certain fields (in addition to other implicit powers), but presents an imbalance, weakness and lack of cohesion in other fields. In practice, the EU is weak where it should be strong (defence, foreign policy or immigration) and strong (excessively controlling and interventionist) where it should be weak.[21] Thus, it is possible to explain that it has been unable to maintain certain coherence regarding immigration but was able to

[19]But which federal version should inspire this process? The answer is not simple because there is no unique concept or meaning. Thus, "the term 'federalism' evokes different models of government in the large states. Roughly speaking, to the Germans it describes a division of powers; to the French an association of nation states; to the British a super-state" (MacLaren 2001).

[20]Dawson and de Witte (2016).

[21]Pereira-Menaut (2017).

impose restrictions and limits on Greece and Portugal that eliminate its sovereignty and constitutional identity.

Thirdly, the EU is going through continuous expansion of its competences. This is explained by the existence of horizontal or transversal competences based on the pursuit of goals with the effect of dilution of state competences.[22] In addition, there is also generous use of the implicit powers clause and the jurisprudence of the TJEU. Thus, it is not surprising that important state competences are undermined, emptied or turned into mere delegated powers.[23] This is also the result of the method and the functional-technocratic attitude of the integration process. It is understandable and natural that the EU regulates, standardizes and centralizes certain material fields. Nevertheless, the intense micromanagement coexists with the lack, or the lack of exercise, of competences in central issues. In other cases, European competition exists but it was practiced with notorious political disorientation. This cannot be amended with greater competence shares for Brussels but rather deciding how we want the political community and its constitution to be. Thus, the attribution of more competences is not useful if it is not possible to define the political approach and will for its effective exercise or activation. Institutional reform should meet the defect that generates, in the medium and long term, important political consequences for the EU.

Lastly, the competence distribution is affected by the functionalist attitude and thinking that subsists in the EU. As Pereira points out, "the functionalist method, specialized in what is specific and ordinary, detects every possible mistake, it does not matter how hidden it is in the different social activities. As it is an alternative from technocracy, focused on regulating specific things being as efficient as possible, it tends not questioning the constitutional aspects. Each regulated thing, relevant or not to the great objective of the European Integration, tends to be centralized and standardized. As in each technocracy, this makes it difficult to tackle the great political problems, but it worked so well during the first decades that it grew roots. This way, Brussels is comfortable with the routine and the technical administration but before the great problems, its natural reaction is to absorb a new competence or to give it another opportunity".

From the dual federalism approach, the EU should count with relatively few and important competences and arrange institutional capacities to make them effective. In this regard, it needs to assume its political and constitutional dimension and disregard the functional-technocratic approaches. In this way, regarding the distribution of competences, the effective preservation of the state and regional governments is

[22]The treaties inspire planning, uniformity and regulation (and also soft policy tools). At this point, the French influence is remarkable. Thus, as MacLaren points out: "The French political class have also largely determined the nature of post-war European integration. The edifice in Brussels reflects above all their habits, interests and vision of Europe. (For example, the European Union is run by a bureaucratic elite like France itself.)" (MacLaren 2001).

[23]Hix warns that "for example, the states can be protected against policy drift to the center via a clear catalog of competences and independent judicial review of competence disputes. Nevertheless, under all constitutional designs, the division of competences is never completely fixed, and the long-term trend in most multi-level polities has been policy centralization" (Hix 2007).

important, to avoid emptying. After all, a real multilevel governance system means levels of government endowed with original and effective political capacities. During the last years (at the same time of the management of the Euro crisis), through the facts and without a reform of the Lisbon Treaty, the EU took measures that implied a great centralization of power and an assumption of important competences.[24] It turns out that the context is not beneficial for the restraint of centralization and the clarification of competences. The remedy would be the adoption of institutional measures.

6 Separation of Powers

This is a classic constitutional mechanism to prevent power and to guarantee citizen freedom. It presents a political-constitutional objective: limiting power through power (prevention of tyranny). Generally, at a constitutional level, this is translated as the attribution of the main political functions (legislative, executive and judicial) to various institutions (parliament, government and courts). In a strict sense, the separation of powers is not specified in the political-constitutional systems. There is always some type of interaction configured among these institutions (presidential system, semi-presidential system and parliament system). The concept of "checks and balances" gathers the functioning logic of this mechanism that, moreover, presents connections with democracy and the rule of law.

With the current evolution state of the EU (political community), its integration to the institutional architecture is impossible. In part, it already has acknowledgement through the principle of institutional balance where each institution exercises the competences conferred by the treaties (art. 13.2 TEU). However, the EU political process is characterized by the growth of diverse agents and stakeholders (governance). This generates a high institutional complexity that affects the institutional legitimacy when diluting the attribution of political responsibility and distances the citizens from the EU.[25] An average European citizen should be able to answer the following question: Who runs the EU? Today, from a democratic point of view, this question does not have a clear and useful answer.

Firstly, the clarification of the functions carried out by the different institutions to favour the separation of powers, the demand for political responsibility and the increase of formal legitimacy is an urgent task. Thus, the Council, which holds executive functions, should be limited to adopting decisions by ordinary legislative procedure. Secondly, the future reform should aim towards the strengthening of a political leadership within the EU. Specifically, the coexistence of the five presidencies does not seem feasible (for several reasons, the EP and the ECB do not raise problems), that has a negative impact in the field of political responsibility and

[24]Torreblanca (2014) and Kreuder-Sonnen (2016).

[25]Conway (2011).

transparency. Politically, the situation of the European Commission, the European Council and the Euro group is compromising.

Thirdly, in general, decision-making in the EU is oriented towards avoiding conflict and reaching decisions by consensus. The presence of various institutions with the power to initiate the elaboration of public policies (agenda-setting power) or veto capacity (veto-players) during the legislative procedure slows down or blocks the decision-making. To gain in dynamism and in speed of response is an essential objective because the vote rules are important (unanimity and qualified majority). Regarding this, during the management of the Euro crisis, the EP and the European Commission were marginalized in the search for agility, efficiency and speed. This implied an alteration of the power balance (succession of formal and informal meetings of the European Council and the Euro group, use of international treaties), and it implied a minoritization of the democratic legitimacy in favour of the technocratic component. Dawson and De Witte highlight this political-institutional impact when they write the following: "Since the start of the euro-crisis, we have seen a drastic change in the EU institutional structure towards executive dominance. Agenda-setting has shifted from the Commission to the European Council—with the Commission increasingly playing an enforcement role in monitoring compliance with its political choices, while the European Parliament (and national parliaments) has been all but side lined from the new structures for economic and monetary governance. These changes, we argued, further decrease the stability and legitimacy of the Union by removing choices over binding norms away from representative institutions, which serve to mediate between different conceptions of the 'good' in society and as such, help to legitimize the policy choices they make".[26]

After the crisis, the EU intervened in redistributive issues that generated political and social conflicts. Thus, institutional reform should point towards internalization or integration within the EU (representation of different interests by the institutions) so that these issues receive political treatment and create legitimate political measures. In essence, it is necessary to overcome the institutional balance in favour of the separation of powers in such a way that the EU institutional reforms are aimed towards increasing legitimacy, representativeness and efficiency.

7 Democracy

In institutional terms, politicization demands institutions that process demands and offer answers (collective decisions oriented towards the European common interest). For its part, the democratic component is composed of participation, control (limits) and responsibility from the rulers before the citizens. From the nineties, specifically from the Maastricht Treaty onwards, there is frequent referral to the "democratic deficit" of the EU. For several decades, European integration rested on the so-called permissive consensus, so that the (positive) results were legitimating its measures and it barely paid attention to the formal democratic legitimacy. To amend

[26]Dawson and de Witte (2016).

this situation, measures were adopted such as election by direct universal suffrage of the EP, the investment of the EC President and the College of Commissioners, the implementation of a co-decision procedure or ordinary legislative, or the citizen initiative…

With the Euro crisis, the critics of the EU democratic legitimacy have increased, creating a democracy discomfort.[27] The anti-crisis measures, guided by efficiency, reduced the state's decision capacity and weakened the state democracy. The EU has penetrated the field of redistributive policies that presuppose agreements of a higher density. These policies have an impact on politically sensitive fields: taxation, budget, labour market, liberalization of public services, pensions, privatization, etc. Consequently, the state's capacity for taking autonomous decisions decreases in favour of the EU. Thus, the political conflict should be structured around a cleavage (conflict among citizens) that overcomes the national (conflict among states). From an institutional point of view, the existence of institutions that gather, channel and express the different preferences, needs and desires of different social group on a European level, are necessary. At this point, it is unnecessary to refer to the role to be played by political parties, trade unions, NGOs, mass media or social movements. We again find the functionalist inertia of the EU, since the competence delimitation prevents an open debate on the political orientation of the decisions. Moreover, another obstacle comes from the treaties, because they establish fixed political preferences in certain fields (inflation, budget stability).

Lastly, the institutional architecture of the EU should consider the two dimensions offered by responsibility, that is to say, ex ante responsibility (responsiveness) and ex post responsibility (accountability). Thus, the democratic legitimacy will win at European level.

8 The Institutional Architecture of the EU Facing the Political Union

For some, the European political unit could and should be a reality in a brief period of time, for others, it is a type of painkiller for the current political situation (Euro-scepticism, disaffection, low confidence) Be as it may, it is essential to reflect on the institutional machinery that the EU should adopt. In these last years, Euro-scepticism has advanced, together with populism and nationalism. The EU, because of action, not omission, has fed it with the adoption of unpopular measures due to the Euro crisis (bank union, fiscal union, economical union) and the implementation of the economical governance. These measures have favoured detachment from the EU institutions because the citizens have held them accountable for the responsibility of that technocratic, opaque management without accountability. Before the Euro crisis, the EU adopted an authoritarian behaviour that does not benefit stability and legitimacy.[28]

[27] Torreblanca (2014).

[28] Dawson and de Witte (2016) and Pereira-Menaut (2019).

The correction of the deficiencies of the institutional design of the Economic and Monetary Union has oriented the decision-making process towards Intergovernmentalism (relevance of the state governments) represented by the European Council and the Euro group (and the signature of international treaties).[29] They were times of primacy of efficiency, speed, dynamism and boldness. The European Commission has shown its weaknesses before this crisis. It lacks any political capacity to raise its voice defending the common interest and to take the lead generating credibility and foreseeability. The European Commission is an essential piece but the crisis has revealed that the advance without an institution that acts as a political leader (assumption of political responsibility) and bestowed of the capacity of taking critical decisions (without any condition from the states) is not possible. From a leadership point of view, the Commission should look to the European Central Bank. Within the framework of economic governance, it is necessary to strengthen the representative institutions, instead of the governments, with the capacity to control and to demand accountability.

It is undeniable that the EU needs to be reformed to guarantee a greater political integration as well as to counteract the democratic deficit induced by the exceptional and fast competence transfer in the economic, fiscal or budget field to the Commission and the Euro group, without widening the political control capacity of the European Parliament to them. The state governments have lost the capacity to carry out differentiated economic policies. In fact, there is an economical federation, but it lacks a political system capable of sustaining and legitimating it.[30] As a political community, the EU acts in the field of redistributive policies where it is possible to identify winners and losers. Thus, the arguing and the management of redistributive conflicts should be upon the social groups or sectors, not in attention of the state interests. The political process should channel and integrate the interests and preferences of the citizens (electorate), based on majorities, not based on consensus within different institutions in such a way that the political argument (common good) is fostered. Debate, control and legitimacy will be benefited. Thus, according to Dawson and de Witte (2016), "we need a radical overhaul of the Union's decision-making process. Rather than bracketing social and political conflict (as the Union has done so far) and channelling it to the narrative that pits Member States against each other, the EU will need to foster and channel new forms of social and political conflict, so as to allow for common control of citizens over the conditions of life and so as to mediate between different conceptions of the 'common good'".

From a political point of view, the institutional reform should consider, as Hix and Hoyland think, that the "EU has gradually approached a 'constitutional balance'. The basic EU political architecture now has certain logic and coherence".[31] The EU institutional system has evolved permanently.[32] Nevertheless, it shows a tendency towards stability in such a way that it is not possible to predict drastic changes that

[29] Cancela (2014).

[30] Torreblanca (2014).

[31] Hix and Hoyland (2012).

[32] Chryssochoou et al. (2003).

affect the relationships between EU member states or interinstitutional relationships. Therefore, it will not consist of a demolition and reconstruction operation. However, it is necessary to take into account that the EU has increased its institutional complexity and enjoys power and a high capacity to influence the European population.[33] Simplification of the institutional architecture is advisable, in such a way that makes it easy to assign political responsibility and to define of key institutions so that the citizens understand them as such and increase its legitimacy. Moreover, it should be oriented in such a way that the European institutions internalize the conflicts arisen from the differences between interest and preferences.

Note that the tension between the intergovernmental vision and the federal integration vision still exist. In the institutional field, this means that strengthening the role of institutions (federal dimension) such as the European Commission, the European Parliament or the European Central Bank undermines the European Council and the Council (intergovernmental dimension). On the other hand, this also affects the reform method that will be carried out. For intergovernmentalism, the possible institutional adjustments must be carried out regarding the establishments of the treaties (executive level negotiations, unanimity and ratification). For the federal vision, the formula would be a constitutional convention or similar to reform the treaties and add transparency, a democratic control and accountability.

The EU needs to reinforce its political legitimacy and its effectiveness, but at the heart of it there is an institutional fight for power. In connection with legitimacy, there is an agreement on the unfeasibility of the election formula for the high institutional positions (Commission, EP President, European Council, High Representative in Foreign Policy, ECB President). In July 2019, the designation of these positions has become the symbol of the dark, anti-democratic market (closed-door marathon negotiation sessions) of the head of States and the Union Government. The geographical and political criteria from the intergovernmental field are more important than the polls.

To finish, some brief notes on the specific institutions. Regarding the EU presidency, some prefer the election of a president for both the Commission and the European Council (unification) while others defend the election of the president of the European Council. The achievement is the exterior visualization and strengthening of the democratic legitimacy of the EU. There are some key elements to determine (functions or the election formula, direct or indirect). Regarding the European Commission, the proposals move towards conversion in a real European government.[34] For some, this implies the increase of its faculties and direct election, according to the presidential formula. Others prefer the parliamentary model, where the European Parliament would be the one investing the President of the Commission and their government.[35] Consequently, the first would be enabled to demand political

---

[33]Troitiño (2017).

[34]De Areilza (2016).

[35]The *Spitzenkandidaten* formula consists of binding the winner of the elections to the European Parliament with the presidency of the European Commission. To elaborate on this formula and expand it for future, European commissioners would contribute to the democratization and the

responsibility through a motion of censure. In any case, any of the formulas should guarantee efficient operation (size) and the establishment of government-opposition dialogue that involves the competence among different options and political visions.

Regarding the EU Council, designed as the representation body of state interests, it would be composed of state representatives, similar to a House of territorial representation, following the Bundesrat model. In order to act efficiently, the general rule for decision-making would be the qualified majority, not unanimity. It would share this task with the parliament. This is designed as a House of population representation. The reform proposals are aimed to reinforce the political role through the generalization of the ordinary legislative procedure and, considering legitimacy, to modify the election mode.[36] Because of Brexit, using the seats released by the UK, a transnational list has been created.[37]

9 Conclusions

As a reaction to the situation of the Euro crisis, the Bratislava Declaration (2016) pointed out that the EU should show unity and capacity to guarantee political control of events. With this desideratum and the historical (progressive politicization and constitutionalization) and recent (transference of substantive competences and development of redistributive policies) transformations, the political union seems, a priori, the most adequate path for the EU. This implies not only the execution of specific institutional reforms but, previously, reflecting and defining the political code, the basic elements (federalism, distribution of competences, separation of powers and democracy). The above is an invitation for the EU to abandon the inertia derived from the functionalist method (technocracy, interventionism…), the political effects of which are profound and broad ranging (centralization).[38]

As the EU already acts on a reality that creates political conflicts (political and social cleavages), the European representative institutions should treat this. Its reform must be oriented in such a way that politicians adopt decisions that channel these conflicts and allow for the configuration of alternative politics. Moreover, the institutional simplification is basic if the citizens understand the political process (who decides) and can assign political responsibilities (who is the political authority). Finally, the articulation of the government effective levels and the constitutional identities is essential. In a multilevel government, the results do not only depend on the higher level but also on the inferior levels. This requires the adoption of a federal and plural approach and a concept of multilevel constitution (multilevel constitutionalism) in

---

transparency of the European executive designation process. But this path has been revoked by the member estates in 2019.

[36] Colomina (2018).

[37] This is one of the formulas included in the French president's Initiative for Europe. Specifically, he defended the need to have transnational lists for the European elections of 2019.

[38] Kerikmäe et al. (2019).

such a way that the articulation of several governments and constitutions within the EU can be articulated.[39]

References

Cancela, C. (2001). *El proceso de constitucionalización de la Unión Europa. De Roma a Niza.* Santiago de Compostela: USC.

Cancela, C. (2014). A nova xeira da Unión Europea. *Informe Nós no Mundo 2014/We in the World 2014-IGADI* (pp. 38–40). Available in http://www.igadi.org/web/sites/all/arquivos/igadi_weintheworld_2014.pdf.

Chryssochoou, N., et al. (2003). Debating the future of Europe. In: N. C. Dimitris, J. T. Michael, S. Stelios, I. Kostas (Eds.), *Theory and reform in the European Union* (196–223). New York: Manchester University Press.

Colomer, J. (2018). *España: la historia de una frustración*. Barcelona: Anagrama.

Colomina, C. (2018). Reformar la Unión Europea en 2018: cinco propuestas, cinco voluntades políticas. *Notes internacionals CIDOB, 187.*

Conway, G. (2011). Recovering a separation of powers in the European Union. *European Law Journal, 17*(3), 304–322.

Dawson, M., & de Witte, F. (2016). From balance to conflict: A new constitution for the EU. *European Law Journal, 22*(2), 204–224.

De Areilza, J. M. (2016). Retos institucionales en el desarrollo de una unión política. *Revista Española de Derecho Constitucional Europeo, 26.*

Delaume, C., & Cayla, D. (2017). *La fin de l'Union européenne*. Michalon.

Färber, K., et al. (2017). Mitterrand and the great European design—From the Cold War to the European Union. *Baltic Journal of European Studies, 7*(2), 132–147.

Hix, S. (2007) The European Union as a polity (I). In K. E. Jorgensen, M. A. Pollack, & B. Rosamond (Eds.), *Handbook of European Union Politics* (141–158). London: Sage.

Hix, S., & Hoyland, B. (2012). *Sistema político de la Unión Europea*. Madrid: McGraw-Hill.

Kerikmäe, T., Troitiño, D. R., & Shumilo, O. (2019). An idol or an ideal? A case study of estonian e-governance: Public perceptions, myths and misbeliefs. *Acta Baltica Historiae et Philosophiae scientiarum, 7*(1), 71–80.

Kreuder-Sonnen, C. (2016). Beyond integration theory: The (Anti-)constitutional dimension of European crisis governance. *Journal of Common Market Studies, 54,* 1350–1366.

MacLaren, M. (2001) *European integration in context: Lessons in political organization? German Law Journal.* Available at http://www.germanlawjournal.com/index.php?pageID=11&artID=90.

Pereira-Menaut, A. C. (2017). Aniversarios con luces y sombras: Constitución española, integración europea y "defectos estructurales" de la UE. *Revista de Derecho Político, 100,* 1140–1168.

Pereira-Menaut, A. C. (2019). Europeísmo ayer y hoy: En diálogo con el profesor Argimiro Rojo. In A. X. En López Mira, E. J. Varela Álvarez (Eds.), *Argimiro Rojo Salgado, o home smiling through. Libro homenaxe a un politólogo cosmopolita* (pp. 339–348). Andavira-Servizo Publicacións, Universidade de Vigo.

Pereira-Menaut, A. C., & Cancela-Outeda, C. (2012). *Resetting the European Union constitutional engine*. Regensburg: Universitätsverlag Regensburg.

Pereira-Menaut, A. C., & Cancela-Outeda, C. (2016). *Reconsidering integration after the Brexit. EU à la carte?* (pp. 122–127). Comisión Europea: Bruselas.

Torreblanca, J. I. (2014). *¿Quién gobierna en Europa? Reconstruir la democracia, recuperar a la ciudadanía*. Madrid: Catarata/Fundación Alternativas.

Troitiño, D. (2017). The European Union: The building of a nation. *MEST Journal, 5,* 119–134.

Troitiño, D. R., Kerikmäe, T., & Chochia, A. (Eds.). (2018). *Brexit: History, reasoning and perspectives*. Berlin: Springer.

[39]Pereira-Menaut and Cancela-Outeda (2012) and Pereira-Menaut (2017).

Trustworthy AI as a Future Driver for Competitiveness and Social Change in the EU

Alexander Antonov and Tanel Kerikmäe

The way we approach AI will define the world we live in.
European Commission—AI Strategy—April 2018.

Abstract Artificial intelligence has become a frequent subject of discussion at different international forums in recent years. Classified by the European Union as one of the "most strategic technologies in the 21st century", in 2018 the EU Commission mandated a 52-member strong High-Level Expert Group on AI to discuss the ethical, legal, economic and social impact of this promising technology. Providing a holistic view on the main ethical and legal questions surrounding AI-powered systems, this chapter intends to explore the latest EU initiatives on AI governance with a view to identifying the main challenges ahead for the EU to become a "leader in cutting-edge AI that can be trusted throughout the world".

Keywords European Union · Artificial intelligence · High-Level Expert Group on AI · Trustworthy AI · AI race

1 Introduction

Having stood at a crossroads for years, in April 2018 the Juncker Commission finally devised a European strategy on Artificial intelligence (hereafter AI) paving its own,

---

This chapter makes reference to three reports on autonomous intelligent technologies to which the authors had contributed as part of the project "Lep18096 'Elaborating legal Solutions related to autonomous intelligent technologies (15.12.2018–30.04.2019)'", coordinated by Prof. Kerikmäe and financed by the Estonian government (EV Riigikantselei). Special thanks are due to Prof. Hoffmann (TalTech University, Department of Law) for his helpful comments on the manuscript.

A. Antonov (✉) · T. Kerikmäe
Tallinn University of Technology, Ehitajate Tee 5, 19086 Tallinn, Estonia
e-mail: alanto@taltech.ee

D. Ramiro Troitiño et al. (eds.), *The EU in the 21st Century*,
https://doi.org/10.1007/978-3-030-38399-2_9

European way, guided by a coordinated, proportionate and human-centric approach towards a future regulatory regime for "trustworthy AI".[1] The EU Commission put forward incentives that allow the 27 post-Brexit Member States to join forces to govern the development of "trustworthy AI".

In the context of a global competition on AI, which is also often labelled an "AI race"[2] among the three AI global players,[3] the USA, China and the EU, the EU strategy aims to preserve the fundamental rights of its 500 million citizens in the digital era while giving its around 5000 top AI researchers,[4] 800 AI companies[5] and European public institutions enough leeway to leverage the potential of AI-powered systems.[6]

Likened to the invention of the steam engine or electricity, AI has been characterised by the EU as one of the "most strategic technologies in the 21st century".[7] It is not without reason why the latest OECD figures suggest a rise in global AI equity investment in the European Union. Over a period of 6 years, the share has increased from 1% in 2013 to 8% in 2017[8] lending credence to a study conducted by McKinsey Global Institute, which estimated that AI applications could potentially generate an additional global GDP growth of around 1.2 per cent annually until 2030.[9] Discussions on the ethical and social implications of AI have dominated the agenda of

---

[1]COM (2018a) 237 final.

[2]Castro et al. (2019); for a critical account on the (term) "AI race", see: Dignum (2019).

[3]The term "AI players" includes research centres, academic institutions and businesses which have taken part in at least one project related to AI (such as R&D processes, industrial production and marketing, specific AI-related services). According to the EU Commission, "the EU is among the geographical zones with the highest number of players active in AI (25%), just behind the United States (26%), and just ahead of China (24%)" European Commission (2019b).

[4]For estimates for the year 2017, consider study by: Castro et al. (2019), p. 5.

[5]This number may be overestimated, as during the current hyperbole around AI, some tech businesses want to be identified as an AI company for economic reasons, see: Castro et al. (2019), pp. 27, 84.

[6]European Commission (2019a) and Craglia (2018), pp. 12–13.

[7]COM (2018a) 237 final, p. 2.

[8]OECD (2019), pp. 40–41.

[9]McKinsey Global Institute (2018), p. 3.

different international forums in recent years, ranging from the OECD[10] to G7 and G20 Summits.[11]

Having chosen the "ethical by design" approach, which implies that AI-powered products have to be regulated already at the early stage of their development,[12] European policymakers have been reflecting on the fundamental question as to how this technology can be "designed to augment, complement and empower human cognitive, social and cultural skills" rather than "unjustifiably subordinate, coerce, deceive, manipulate, condition or herd humans".[13] AI is therefore not only considered a general purpose but also a disruptive technology.[14]

While there is no internationally agreed definition of AI, the European Commission's Communication on AI refers to it as "systems that display intelligent behaviour by analysing their environment and taking actions—with some degree of autonomy—to achieve specific goals".[15]

1.1 Methodology: Purpose and Scope

Predicated on the assumption that the EU's competitiveness as regards the development of AI-powered systems by the private sector and research talent by the public sector depends on the unity among the post-Brexit 27 Member States, this chapter intends to explore the latest EU initiatives on AI governance.

Taking a holistic view on the ethical risks and legal questions related to AI-powered systems, the authors consult pertinent EU Communications, EU regulations and directives, specifically the GDRP, and the latest reports by the Joint Research Centre (JRC) of the European Commission on Artificial Intelligence (2018) and by the High-Level Expert Group on Artificial Intelligence (hereafter AI HLEG) (2019).

---

[10]See OECD principles on AI:

"1. AI should benefit people and the planet by driving inclusive growth, sustainable development and well-being.

2. AI systems should be designed in a way that respects the rule of law, human rights, democratic values and diversity, and they should include appropriate safeguards—for example, enabling human intervention where necessary—to ensure a fair and just society.

3. There should be transparency and responsible disclosure around AI systems to ensure that people understand AI-based outcomes and can challenge them.

4. AI systems must function in a robust, secure and safe way throughout their life cycles and potential risks should be continually assessed and managed.

5. Organisations and individuals developing, deploying or operating AI systems should be held accountable for their proper functioning in line with the above principles" OECD (2019).

[11]OECD (2019), p. 3.

[12]Craglia (2018), p. 10.

[13]High-Level Expert Group on AI (2019a), p. 12.

[14]Craglia (2018), pp. 8, 63.

[15]COM (2018a) 237 final, p. 1.

Since AI can be applied both for civil and military purposes, it is also called a dual-use technology. Lethal autonomous weapon systems would fall within the latter category. This chapter deals solely with the former.

Most estimates, e.g., on investments into AI research or on the availability of venture capital are taken directly from studies mainly conducted by McKinsey Global Institute and the Centre for Data Innovation.

While the figures should be taken with caution as most statistics on AI remain weak or speculative in nature,[16] we consult them mainly for two reasons. Whereas the EU Commission also referred to figures published by McKinsey Global Institute, the methodology of the latest report by the Centre for Data Innovation, a non-partisan research institute, affiliated with the Information Technology and Innovation Foundation proved to be most evidence-based among the studies conducted on AI. The comparative analysis, which relies upon, *i.e.,* statistical data used by the OECD, or crunch base, applies both quantitative and qualitative methods and analyses the performance of China, the European Union and the USA looking on the dimensions of AI "talent, research, enterprise development, adoption, data, and hardware" and employing absolute metrics.[17]

Additional inspiration on the legal debate on AI regulation was drawn from expert opinions of (legal) scholars mainly from Western Europe such as Easterbrook (1995), Lessig (1999; 2006), Buiten (2018), Franke (2019) and Floridi (2019).

Prior to mapping the EU's approach to trustworthy AI, it is worthwhile looking at the features and the associated ethical risks ensuring from employing this technology, which no matter of the amount of attention devoted by the media to AI remains to be intangible. Interestingly enough, the most acclaimed AI researchers have even struggled to define intelligence.[18]

2 What Is AI?

2.1 From Desktop Computers to AI-Powered Systems

The pace of technological changes and breakthroughs over the recent decades is unparalleled in history, and we are only witnessing the beginning of this transformative process longing from desktop computers to 3D printers and from voice-controlled Internet of Things devices to AI-powered machines. The progress in the development of Information and Communication Technologies (hereafter ICTs) seems to be

[16]European Commission (2019a): "AI is rapidly applying to almost all economic sectors. However, {...} no official statistics are available yet, so AI is escaping traditional industrial and product classifications". the OECD's estimates on global private equity investment into AI remain one of the few official statistics on one specific aspect of AI, even though they are also based on figures by Crunchbase (July 2018).

[17]For a detailed account on the methodology of the study, see: Castro et al. (2019), pp. 13–15.

[18]Tegmark (2017), p. 49.

unlimited with influential AI researchers already pondering the bleak scenario that we might see super-intelligent machines overtaking us in all dimensions of human intelligence in the future, alluding to the concept of artificial general intelligence (hereafter AGI).[19]

Computers (based on input, storage, processing and output of data) have become indispensable to our contemporary way of life, to how policymakers and managers organise economies and societies and make predictions of the future. They have transformed the global economic landscape and brought societies closer together spurring the development of previously inconceivable products and making information accessible to billions of people via the Internet.[20]

With the advent of a rapid increase in computational power and data, catalysed by the commercialisation of the Internet, one specific field in the application of computer programmes has recently grown to prominence: AI. The generic term refers to an emerging research field and technology, which allows for machines to replicate human-like reasoning, the ability to learn and solve complex tasks.[21]

Bearing great potentials reaching from making cost-effective predictions to detecting cancer cells, AI-powered systems have experienced an increasing uptake by different sectors.[22] The following non-exhaustive list provides an overview of the sectors, in which AI-powered systems have already been deployed:

- Transport sector
- Agriculture
- Financial sector
- Marketing and advertising
- Science
- Health care
- Criminal justice/law enforcement
- Securing the public sector
- Augmented and virtual reality.[23]

2.2 *Birth of the Discipline of AI*

It is a widely held view that the computer scientist, John McCarthy, coined the generic term AI in the 1950s, defining the discipline as a "science and engineering of making intelligent machines".[24] In summer 1956, he invited a selected group of leading

[19] See, e.g., Tegmark (2016); for a lucid overview of the different views on AGI among acclaimed AI researchers, see: Vincent (2018).
[20] Craglia (2018), p. 16.
[21] Russell and Norvig (2016), pp. 4–8.
[22] OECD (2019), p. 47.
[23] Ibid.
[24] Solomonoff (1956) and Pearl (2017).

researchers from the same field, there under Marvin Minsky and Ray Solomonoff, to Dartmouth, New Hampshire, to test the assumption of whether "every aspect of learning or any feature of intelligence can in principle be so precisely described that a machine can be made to simulate it".[25] What was then called the "Dartmouth Summer Research Project on Artificial Intelligence" is today considered the birth of AI as an academic discipline.[26]

From then on, the field of AI has gone through various cycles of successes ("AI Summer") and failures ("AI Winter").[27] A beneficial combination of a recent breakthrough in computation power and a rapidly growing data pool has catalysed an AI "renaissance".[28] Specifically a sub-field of AI, "machine-learning (hereafter ML)", has given the discipline new impetus.[29] This approach is grounded on the technical ability of a programmed machine to learn optimising its own processes and improving its own decisions (output) mainly based on large data sets (input).[30]

2.3 *The Promising Sub-field of AI—Main Approaches to Machine Learning*

ML revolutionised computing. Whereas classical programming is deductive in nature, implying that a machine processes data following a pre-defined algorithmic logic to answer (a) question/s posed to it, ML reverses this logic by creating its own rules mainly based on a vast amount of data and pre-given answers to the machine.[31]

The cognitive abilities of a human being, captured by reasoning and learning, are replicated by the machine either through *supervised learning* (e.g. used for picture recognition: feeding the machine with thousands of photographs so that it can later on identify persons and objects based on other pictures it has never seen before), *unsupervised learning* (e.g. applied for marketing purposes: AI-powered algorithms target customers with tailor-made advertisements after the computer categorised large data sets) and *reinforcement learning* (e.g. AlphaGo: giving the machine for each decision a signal that it made either a good or bad decision, independent of the size of the data it was tasked with processing).[32]

The most successful among the various methods associated with machine learning relates to *deep learning*, which, put in simplified terms, is an approach that is built upon different hidden layers between the input and output data. Deep learning systems

[25] McCarthy et al. (1955).

[26] Russell and Norvig (2016), pp. 3, 17.

[27] Russell and Norvig (2016) pp. 16–27 and Boulanin (2019) pp. 14–15.

[28] COM (2018a) 237 final, p. 2 and Boulanin (2019), p. 3.

[29] Färber (2017).

[30] Surden (2014), pp. 87–88.

[31] Craglia (2018), p. 20.

[32] European Commission (2019c), p. 4.

replicate a neural network, which allows the computer, for example, to recognise in several mathematical steps an image or a voice. The algorithmic logic is hierarchical, which also implies that deep learning renders it possible for the computer to learn complex concepts such as pictures by creating a simpler version of them in successive steps.[33]

These rule-based systems are supposed to decrease the error rate or, e.g., in terms of image or facial recognition its *bias*. Nevertheless, independent of the amount of data, a certain error rate always remains.[34] Potential flaws in data can have serious consequences for the end consumer of a product, especially in automated decision-makings. Achieving a high degree of accuracy should therefore take centre stage in AI research.[35]

Even though it has been demonstrated that ML techniques can outperform human beings in certain tasks such as pattern recognition or games as chess or Go, as of today, these systems fall short of the promises enunciated by the Dartmouth participants. Neither do they embody a "common sense reasoning, {nor} self-awareness {nor} the ability {…} to define its own purpose".[36] It is for this reason, why the current systems fall within the category of so-called narrow/weak AI.[37] In other words, the algorithms for now are unable to think out of the box.[38] Despite its great potential, AI is neither magic nor a panacea.[39]

3 Ethical and Legal Aspects of AI

3.1 Ethical Risks of AI

It is a shared view among scientists and policymakers that those taking the lead in developing AI will not only harness the technology but also influence its further ethical trajectory.[40] The director of OpenAI, Jack Clark, aptly set the context of the great challenge ahead for policymakers to keep pace in developing and regulating the use of AI:

> AI let us encode values into systems that have been scaled against sometimes entire populations. If we fail here {to lead}, then the values that our society lives under are partially determined by whichever society wins in AI so that the values of that society encodes become the values of what we experience. So I think the stakes here are societal in nature and we

[33] Goodfellow et al. (2016), pp. 1, 5, 8 and Boulanin (2019), p. 16.

[34] Wirtz et al. (2018), p. 9.

[35] Ramiro Troitino and Pando Ballesteros (2017).

[36] European Commission (2019c), p. 5, see also: Kerikmäe and Särav (2017), p. 219.

[37] Ibid.

[38] As also discussed in the context of AI applications in the field of Legal Tech: Kerikmäe et al. (2018), p. 92.

[39] Buchanan and Miller (2017), pp. 26, 46 and Coglianese and Lehr (2017), p. 1155.

[40] O'Meara (2019).

> should not think about this as a technological challenge but as how we as a society want to become better and the success here will be the ability to articulate values for the rest of the world.[41]

While the use of AI-powered systems comes along with various social and economic opportunities, examples of the abuse of this technology have demonstrated the need to evaluate the possible ethical, legal and technical challenges ensuing from deploying a technology that is conceived as a "black-box".[42] In this vein, the future regulation of AI-powered systems is compounded by the fact that even its designers or programmers struggle to fully understand the decision-making process of this opaque technology.[43]

Apart from projections about large-scale job losses from automation,[44] cases of documented bias,[45] nudging,[46] cyber-security risks[47] or deep-fakes,[48] large-scale applications of facial recognition technologies by law enforcement units,[49] some of which even intentionally deployed to identify individuals from a minority group,[50] undergird the argument that AI is a double-edge sword-bearing great economic potential but if not ethically governed can cause grave if not irreversible harm to the rights of human beings subjected to a potentially abusive use of this technology. Additionally, the fact that AI-powered systems can create legally binding decisions based on automated processing and profiling of a vast amount of personal data makes it a compelling case for a future regulatory regime.[51]

A unique approach to AI governance illustrating this ethical dilemma has been taken by Estonia, which created a special metaphor for AI, the so-called Kratt.[52] Drawing on an old Estonian mythological creature, Kratt symbolises AI, a technology that "is devoted to serving its master, but can become bad if left idle".[53]

---

[41] US House of Representatives Committee on Science, Space, & Technology (2019).

[42] Scherer (2016) and Thierer et al. (2017), p. 31.

[43] Mittelstadt et al (2016), p. 3 and Buiten (2018), p. 56.

[44] For a lucid overview, consider: Press (2019).

[45] Buchanan and Miller (2017), pp. 32–36.

[46] Mittelstadt et al (2016), p. 9.

[47] Craglia (2018), pp. 89–90 and Buchanan and Miller (2017), pp. 39–40.

[48] Knight (2019).

[49] Outeda (2001).

[50] Mozur (2019).

[51] For cases of automated decision making in the European Union, see report by AlgorithmWatch: Spielkamp (2019), p. 35 *ff*.

[52] Kerikmäe et al. (2019), p. 1 and Kratid (2019).

[53] Kerikmäe (2019) and e-Estonia (2019).

3.2 Scholarly Debate and Regulatory Fields of AI

The commercialisation of the ever more converging ICTs has required policymakers to rethink traditional approaches to governance and regulations. While policymakers intend to limit the unpredictable effects of new technologies by creating regulatory frameworks that allow different actors, be it private citizens, public officials or companies to thrive on and harness advanced technological systems, the intangible nature of ICTs complicates the lawmaking process.

With the advent of the introduction of the Internet, a debate on the regulation of cyberspace between two Western legal scholars from the USA provided the starting point for a discussion on the question of how to regulate ICTs or in the case of this chapter, AI-powered systems. It is also illustrative for the current discussions at the EU level as which approach might be the most applicable one in regulating AI-powered systems.[54]

Judge Easterbrook (1996) compared the regulation of algorithm-based computing systems with legal problems related to horses making the argument that cyberspace ought to be studied through the lenses of traditional fields of law, be it administrative law, criminal law or property law.[55] More importantly, before creating new legislation for cyberspace, *de lege ferenda*, he advocated improving and clarifying *de lege lata*, the law as it stands now.[56]

Lessig (1999) took issue with this view, contending that there was "something when we think about the regulation of cyberspace that other areas would not show us", alluding to the unique architecture of cyberspace.[57] Contrary to the physical space, the novelty of cyberspace was due to its malleable code, which is written by a plethora of programmers.[58] In this regard, the changeable nature of code makes it impossible to apply the law of the horse to cyberspace.[59]

He therefore proposed a four-dimensional model, the "Four Modalities of Regulation in Real Space and Cyberspace", (1) law, (2) social norms, (3) market and (4) architecture, and suggested regulators to study the novel characteristics of cyberspace by means of his multidimensional model, the "net regulation".[60]

In other words, while Easterbrook believed that the technological evolution would not necessitate a new regulatory field, captured by the term cyberlaw, Lessig refuted

---

[54]Troitiño (2017).

[55]Easterbrook (1996), p. 207: "{T}he best way to learn the law applicable to specialized endeavors is to study general rules. Lots of cases deal with sales of horses; others deal with people kicked by horses; still more deal with the licensing and racing of horses, or with the care veterinarians give to horses, or with prizes at horse shows. Any effort to collect these strands into a course on "The Law of the Horse" is doomed to be shallow and to miss unifying principles".

[56]Ibid.

[57]Lessig (1999), p. 502.

[58]Lessig (1999), p. 506.

[59]Ibid.

[60]Lessig (1999), p. 507.

this argumentation positing that given the changing nature of the architecture of code, legal norms alone could not help achieve the goal of creating legal values that guide a society through times of rapid technological changes.[61]

Another approach to regulating AI-powered systems can be drawn from the value-sensitive design framework espoused by, e.g., Van den Hoven (2017). In line with the view that the architecture of advanced technologies beard considerable impacts on the values of the society by whom the technology is employed, van den Hoven's approach would suggest that policymakers should create a regulatory framework that allowed ethical issues to be taken into account at the design process of the technology, "when value considerations can still make a difference".[62]

Hence, the main focus of regulations should be placed on the work of the programmer or code writer. The conclusion is especially valid when considering Lessig's assumption that "code {was} law".[63] Applying this logic to the regulation of AI-powered systems would imply that policymakers are well advised to "open the black-box of AI"[64] and identify the conceivable challenges this technology poses to the society. As argued by Buiten (2018), this goal could be best attained if the causes of the risks were addressed and regulatory mechanisms were established with a view to increasing the societal capacity to absorb or even control those identified risks.[65] Even prior to that, the point of departure in regulating AI-powered systems should be questioning *by whom* and *for which purpose* this technology will be designed and related to that *by whom* they are owned and deployed and *in which contexts* they will be applied.[66]

Nevertheless, rather than "inventing the wheel" as regards future AI regulations, it is helpful to map the current applicable regulatory framework for ICTs (e.g. Product Liability Directive: Council Directive 85/374/EEC; Machinery Directive 2006/42/EC) at the European level and avoid national solo-efforts or silo thinking.[67] Legal initiatives on AI should therefore be coordinated by the EU Commission. The "Coordinated plan on Artificial Intelligence" which *i.a.* requests EU Member States to draft their own national AI strategies by mid-2019 constitutes a good starting point for a comprehensive and structured approach towards a future EU regulatory regime for trustworthy AI-powered systems.[68]

Apart from only reflecting upon regulating AI-powered systems, a second relevant regulatory field pertains to its raw material, namely data. A recent study by the International Data Corporation has found that the world has been seeing an annual increase of 61% in data volume and projected that by 2025 four times more data will

[61] Lessig (1999), p. 546.

[62] Van den Hoven (2017), p. 70.

[63] Lessig (2006), p. 5.

[64] Buiten (2018), p. 49.

[65] Ibid.

[66] Pawlas, (2015).

[67] Kerikmäe et al. (2019), p. 10.

[68] COM (2018b) 795 final, p. 9.

exist than today.[69] Since Europe lags behind the USA and China in accumulating data,[70] European policymakers are well advised to boost initiatives that facilitate data sharing, its reuse and storage of both personal and non-personal data within the bounds of EU law.[71]

While sharing non-personal data is less problematic from the point of privacy laws, some researchers have already criticised the EU's GDPR framework, specifically taking issue with Art. 5(1)(c), which they contend "created an artificial scarcity of data by making it more difficult for organizations to collect and share data" and put European companies and public agencies from the European Union at a disadvantage in developing and using AI-powered systems in comparison with the USA and China, where the processing of data, be it of personal or non-personal nature, is less strictly regulated.[72]

4 Trustworthy Artificial Intelligence

4.1 Europe's AI Strategy in the Context of a Global Competition on AI

The EU's comprehensive AI strategy was released one year after the publication of China's *New Generation Artificial Intelligence Development Plan* in which Beijing announced to "become the world's premier artificial intelligence innovation center" by 2030 and projected the value of its AI industry to reach US$150 billion in the next decade.[73]

What makes the European approach unique not only in comparison with the Chinese strategy but also the American AI Initiative, launched in February 2019 on an executive order by the US president,[74] is that the European debate on AI is primarily value-orientated and neither solely driven by business nor national security interests.[75] Most importantly, the European Union strives to regulate the use of AI-powered systems with a purpose similar to the creation of the GDPR framework.[76]

---

[69]Reinsel et al. (2018).

[70]Castro et al. (2019), p. 42.

[71]Hamulák (2018).

[72]Ibid; Franke (2019), pp. 3–5; for a study on the negative effects of the GDPR on investments in European technology companies, see: Jia, Zhe Jin and Wagman (2018); for Art. 5(1)(c) of the GDPR (Principles relating to processing of personal data), see: Regulation (EU) 2016/679: "Personal data shall be adequate, relevant and limited to what is necessary in relation to the purposes for which they are processed ('data minimisation')".

[73]Future of Life Institute (2019) and Mozur (2017).

[74]The White House (2019).

[75]Martín de la Guardia and Pérez Sánchez (2001).

[76]Kayali (2019).

Respect for and protection of the rights of the individual in the digital age takes centre stage for EU policymakers. As stated in the EU's AI strategy, the goal is threefold:

1. "1. Boost the EU's technological and industrial capacity and AI uptake across the economy
2. Prepare for socio-economic changes and
3. Ensure an appropriate ethical and legal framework".[77]

Whereas the latest American AI Initiative focuses on similar goals as those mentioned in points 1 and 2 in the European AI strategy, the current US administration considers regulations to place "obstacles" for AI businesses and researchers because regulatory barriers might "cede the competitive edge to authoritarian governments who do not share {the American} values".[78] The American debate is therefore geared towards incentivising businesses and AI researchers to accelerate the development of AI by having less strict data protection rules in place, making considerably more investments into AI R&D programmes and American companies having more venture capital at their disposal than in the EU and China.[79] A study by McKinsey Global Institute (2018) estimated that both North America (EUR 12.1–18.6 billion) and Asia (EUR 6.5–9.7 billion) have surpassed the EU (EUR 2.4–3.2 billion) in private investments in AI R&D programmes already in 2016.[80]

Estimates also indicate that China has been made up considerable leeway on AI research, a field where the USA still remains in the leading position with home to above 10,000 top AI researchers.[81] For the EU to attract AI researchers or to at least entice its talented IT experts to stay in the EU,[82] the EU Commission intends to help establish AI research excellence centres in Europe and support Master and PhD programmes in AI willing to devote in total EUR 20 billion per year in the next decade to these goals.[83] First steps into this direction have been taken by increasing the funding scheme Horizon 2020 for research and innovation by 70%.[84] Until the end of next year, around EUR 1.5 billion are reserved for AI-related projects.[85]

Against this background, testing and experimentation facilities are considered to be especially effective in developing trustworthy AI for the transport, agriculture, manufacturing or healthcare sector.[86] Questions, however, remain as to how the

---

[77]COM (2018a) 237 final, p. 4.

[78]Kratsios (2019).

[79]Castro et al. (2019), pp. 2–3, 10, 18, 25.

[80]McKinsey Global Institute (2018) (as cited in COM (2018a) 237 final, p. 5).

[81]Castro et al. (2019), p. 5.

[82]According to the "2018 Silicon Valley Index" by Joint Venture Silicon Valley, only in Silicon Valley around 240,000 Europeans worked for tech businesses in 2018 (as cited in COM (2018b) 795 final, p. 5).

[83]COM (2018b) 795 final, pp. 5–6 and COM (2018a) 237 final, p. 10.

[84]COM (2019) 168, p. 1.

[85]Ibid.

[86]Ibid.

operation of these testing centres can be squared with the strict data protection rules in the EU without preventing researchers and businesses from innovating with AI-powered technology.

Data has been described as the "raw-material" of AI-powered systems.[87] Kai-Fu Lee, a prominent Chinese venture capitalist and head of Google's subsidiary in China in the previous decade, believes that data will play a significant role for AI innovation and the development of AI-powered systems as a whole.[88]

The main competitive advantage of the USA and China to the EU is the amount of data American private businesses such as Google, Facebook or Amazon, control, and the Chinese State possess. As stated by German Chancellor Angela Merkel: "In the US, control over personal data is privatised to a large extent. In China the opposite is true: the state has mounted a takeover".[89] For the EU to succeed in the development of AI, German Chancellor Angela Merkel likes to see Brussels finding a middle course between these two approaches.[90]

The findings of an online consumer survey conducted by Northstar Research Partners (2017) with around 4000 participants from the USA, Europe and China give a first understanding to the question of why the EU is well advised to seek this middle ground and regulate the use of data by AI-powered systems in the future: "Asian respondents were the most bullish about the positive effect of AI in the future, while Europeans were the least optimistic".[91] While additional studies should be carried out to shed more light on the still unexplored field of European citizens' perceptions towards AI, the report's conclusions indicate a general tendency of Europeans being more sceptical of the latest developments in the use of AI. In this regard, Franke (2019) cites one specific example, namely the coverage of the Cambridge Analytica scandal, which falls in line with other misuses of ICTs.[92]

Additionally, the fact that the EU has taken a firm stand against Google's and Facebook's dominance levying fines in the millions of dollars,[93] undergirds the argument that the EU Commission's actions not only raise awareness of data breaches among European citizens but also of large-tech companies responsibility for protecting European citizens data. This awareness of the potential for abuse of new technologies for economic purposes could additionally reflect in a rather more sceptical view among European citizens making it even more necessary to take regulatory initiatives that could increase trust in AI-powered systems.

---

[87] COM (2018a) 237 final, p. 3.

[88] Lee (2018).

[89] The Economist (2018).

[90] Ibid.

[91] Northstar (2017), p. 12.

[92] Franke (2019), p. 5.

[93] Satariano (2019).

4.2 *Trustworthy AI—Reports by the EU High-Level Expert Group on AI*

The EU's human-centric approach is reflected in two latest reports by the AI HLEG. Mandated by the EU Commission as part of its AI strategy to scrutinise the ethical, legal and societal implications of AI, a 52-member strong independent group comprising computer scientists, experts from industry and civil society and researchers with interdisciplinary background elaborated ethics guidelines[94] and developed a series of policy recommendations for "trustworthy AI".[95]

The underlying tenet of both documents is that "trustworthy AI" systems should be "lawful, ethical and robust, and fully aligned with fundamental rights" as enshrined in the EU Charter.[96] Both documents emphasise that "trustworthy AI" designed the EU ought to respect the human dignity in the digital age which can only be achieved if these systems are developed under the following principles:

(i) respect for human autonomy;
(ii) prevention of harm;
(iii) fairness; and
(iv) explicability.[97]

Having set a distant goal to become "a leader in cutting-edge AI", the EU Commission aims to align social trust with economic competitiveness.[98] Establishing a unique trademark for "trustworthy AI", AI-powered technology made in Europe could then not only be trusted among EU citizens but in countries around the world.[99]

In the light of the EU's goal to facilitate the development of trustworthy AI, it is commendable to see the EU establishing a "European AI Alliance", which allows a broad spectrum of actors to voice their opinions and shape the legal discourse on AI in the European Union.[100] As a complimentary initiative to the AI HLEG, ideas of around 500 participants have been incorporated in the work of the expert group.[101] The goal of developing AI for good and remaining competitive on the international plane requires taking the European citizens perceptions towards AI into account and evaluating them over a long time period. The proposed idea by the expert group to envisage a holistic 10-year plan to continuously assess the "opportunities and challenges of AI" and to monitor and "adapt {...} impactful actions on a short-term rolling basis" can be considered as a wise approach, since the "future of AI is full of unknown unknowns".[102]

---

[94] Castro and Lago (2018).

[95] High-Level Expert Group on (2019a) and High-Level Expert Group on AI (2019b).

[96] High-Level Expert Group on AI (2019a), p. 49.

[97] High-Level Expert Group on AI (2019a), p. 12.

[98] COM (2019) 168, pp. 9–10.

[99] Ibid.

[100] European Commission (2019e).

[101] Ibid.

[102] High-Level Expert Group on AI (2019b), p. 49 and Floridi (2019), p. 13.

4.3 Regulating AI's Raw Material—Data

AI-powered systems run on a myriad of both personal and non-personal data, which are for the time being only partially governed by a European regulatory framework initiated during the 5 years term of the Juncker Commission.[103]

While the GDPR laid the foundation for the protection of personal data controlled and processed by businesses and most public agencies servicing customers and citizens of the European Union, the Commission maintained its pace towards the creation of a Digital Single Market and recently complemented the GDPR with a regulation on the free flow of non-personal data.[104]

Projecting that the data economy will make up 5.4% of the EU's annual GDP in 2025, these legislative measures have been agreed upon with a view to removing national barriers and to enabling the private and public sector to "make the most out of data and its opportunities".[105] The latest regulation is aimed at facilitating EU wide data storage and processing within the bounds of EU law.[106] In this regard, it is also worthwhile highlighting the goal of the EU to create common data spaces as part of the Digital Single Market strategy. This initiative bears special importance for the collection of new data, which is necessary to train AI-powered systems and allows for the creation of innovate goods.[107]

5 The Way Forward—Concluding Remarks

Briefly before the presentation of the newly appointed EU Commissioners, information has surfaced about the EU's resolve to restrict any potential "indiscriminate use of facial recognition technology" not only by businesses but also by public authorities.[108] Granting the European citizens, the right to "know when {facial recognition} data is used" testifies to the fact that the EU continues to build on the principles of the GDPR.[109] Finding a prudent balance between business-friendly legislation, legitimate national security interests and the protection of EU citizens' fundamental rights as to privacy remains a delicate task in the digital era.

Whereas the Juncker Commission avoided legislating on AI-powered systems directly and instead brought forward legislation on data protection, cyber-security and telecommunication, the next president of the EU Commission, Ursula von der Leyen, did not shy away from making the bold promise for "put[ting] forward legislation for

---

[103]Troitiño et al. (2018).

[104]Regulation (EU) 2018/1807.

[105]Vice-President for the Digital Single Market Andrus Ansip quoted in: European Commission (2019d).

[106]Ibid.

[107]Ibid.

[108]Khan (2019).

[109]Ibid.

a coordinated European approach on the human and ethical implications of artificial intelligence drafting" after taking office in the beginning of November this year.[110]

von der Leyen's goal falls in line with previous statements made by the French president Macron and German chancellor Merkel, who both advocate regulating the use of AI-powered systems on the European level, to "recreate a European sovereignty in AI" and to elucidate that AI "serves humanity".[111]

The European Union has deliberately chosen the path towards regulating AI-powered systems and remains resolved to shape the future of the Digital Single Market. While the AI High-Level Experts has created the architecture for a future regulatory regime of trustworthy AI, fundamental questions remain as to how the ambitious goal of becoming the "leader in cutting-edge AI that can be trusted throughout the world"[112] can be attained within the next decade.

Whereas tailored investments into the digital infrastructure of EU Member States such as Germany are of utmost importance to remain competitive at world level, the European Union is well advised not to succumb to the temptation of believing that it should run an AI race together with the USA and China. It should rather use the current AI momentum at the European level and invest in AI research that will be the key to translate or encode the EU ethical and legal guidelines into AI-powered machines. Whether this core, technical question can be answered at all, remains a "black-box" that can only be opened if the programmers or designers of these systems find a common language with all relevant stakeholders, and most importantly, with the policymakers.

In the words of the AI HLEG: "In a competition amongst different economic entities, the single most important element is the capability to apply and learn fast and consistently over a long period of time".[113]

Bibliography

Books, Journal Articles and Reports

Boulanin, V. (Ed.). (2019). *The Impact of artifical intelligence on stategic stability and nuclear risk* (Vol. 1). SIPRI: Euro-Atlantic Perspectives.

Buchanan, B., & Miller, T. (2017). *Machine learning for policymakers: What it is and why it matters.* Harvard Kennedy School—The Cyber Security Project.

Buiten, M. (2018). Towards intelligent regulation of artificial intelligence. *European Journal of Risk Regulation, 10*(1), 41–59.

Castro, L. D., & Lago, J. R. R. (2018). Educación y diplomacia cultural en la primavera de Europa (1948–1954) = Education and cultural diplomacy in the spring of Europe (1948–1954). *Revista de Educación, 383,* 63–84.

[110] von der Leyen (2019).

[111] Franke (2019), p. 6 and Kayali (2019).

[112] COM (2019) 168, p. 9.

[113] High-Level Expert Group on AI (2019b), p. 49.

Castro, D., McLaughlin, M., & Chivot, E. (2019) Who is winning the AI Race: China, the EU or the United States? Available at: https://www.datainnovation.org/2019/08/who-is-winning-the-ai-race-china-the-eu-or-the-united-states/. Accessed: September 6, 2019.

Coglianese, C., & Lehr, D. (2017). Regulating by Robot: Administrative decision making in the machine-learning era. *The Georgetown Law Journal, 105,* 1147–1223.

Craglia, M. (Ed.). (2018). Artificial intelligence—A European perspective. Publications Office of the European Union. EUR 29425 EN.

Färber, K. (2017). Mitterrand and the great European design—From the cold war to the European union. *Baltic Journal of European Studies, 7*(2), 132–147.

Floridi, L. (2019). What the near future of artificial intelligence could be. *Philosophy & Technology, 32,* 1–15.

Franke, U. (2019). Harnessing artificial intelligence. *European Council on Foreign Relations, 289,* 1–9.

Goodfellow, I., Bengio, Y., & Courville, A. (2016). *Deep learning*. Cambridge: The MIT Press.

Hamulák, O. (2018). La carta de los derechos fundamentales de la union europea y los derechos sociales. *Estudios constitucionales, 16*(1), 167–186.

High-Level Expert Group on AI. (2019a). *Ethics guidelines for trustworthy AI.* European Commission.

High-Level Expert Group on AI. (2019b). *Policy and investment recommendations for trustworthy AI.* European Commission.

Jia, J., Zhe Jin, G., & Wagman, L. (2018). *The short-run effects of GDPR on technology venture investment* (pp. 1–42). NBER Working Paper No. 25248.

Kerikmäe, T., & Särav, S. (2017). Paradigms for automatization of logic and legal reasoning. In: D. Krimphove, G. M. Lentner (Eds.). *Law and logic: Contemporary issues* (205–222). Duncker & Humblot.

Kerikmäe, T., Troitiño, D. R., & Shumilo, O. (2019). An idol or an ideal? A case study of Estonian e-governance: Public perceptions, myths and misbeliefs1. *Acta Baltica Historiae et Philosophiae scientiarum, 7*(1).

Kerikmäe, T. (2019) *Autonoomsed intelligentsed tehnoloogiad ja õigusruum. Eesti Krati tegevuskava koostamise lõpuseminar, TalTech.* Tallinn: Majandus- ja Kommunikatsiooniministeerium, Riigikantselei. May 28, 2019

Lee, K. F. (2018). *AI superpowers*. Boston: Houghton Mifflin Harcourt.

Lessig, L. (1999). The law of the horse: What cyberlaw might teach. *Harvard Law Review, 113*(2), 501–549.

Lessig, L. (2006). *Code: Version 2.0* (2nd ed.). New York: Basic Books.

Martín de la Guardia, R. M., & Pérez Sánchez, G. A. (2001). *Historia de la integración europea.* Barcelona: Ariel.

McCarthy, J., et al. (1955). A proposal for the Dartmouth summer research project on artificial intelligence. Available at: http://www-formal.stanford.edu/jmc/history/dartmouth.pdf. Accessed: September 16, 2019.

McKinsey Global Institute. (2018). *Notes from the AI Frontier: Modeling the impact of AI on the world economy.* New York: McKinsey & Company. Available at: https://www.mckinsey.com/~/media/McKinsey/Featured-Insights/Artificial-Intelligence/Notes-from-the-frontier-Modeling-the-impact-of-AI-on-the-world-economy/MGI-Notes-from-the-AI-frontier-Modeling-the-impact-of-AI-on-the-world-ec. Accessed: September 15, 2019.

Mittelstadt, B. D., Allo, P., Taddeo, M., Wachter, S., & Floridi, L. (2016). The ethics of algorithms: Mapping the debate. *Big Data & Society*, 1–21

Northstar. (2017) *AI today, AI tomorrow: Awareness, acceptance and anticipation of AI: A global consumer perspective*. Available at: https://www.arm.com/solutions/artificial-intelligence/survey. Accessed: September 6, 2019.

OECD. (2019). *Artificial intelligence in society*. Paris: OECD Publishing.

Outeda, C. C. (2001). *El proceso de constitucionalización de la Unión Europea: de Roma a Niza* (No. 3). Univ Santiago de Compostela.

Pawlas, I. (2015, September). The Visegrad Countries and European Union membership-selected issues. In *Proceedings of International Academic Conferences* (No. 2704866). International Institute of Social and Economic Sciences.
Ramiro Troitino, D., & Pando Ballesteros, M. D. L. P. (2017). Churchill's European integration model. *REVISTA DE OCCIDENTE, 433,* 57–71.
Reinsel, D., Gantz, J., & Rydning, J. (2018). The digitization of the world: From edge to core. *An IDC White Paper*. Available at: https://www.seagate.com/files/www-content/our-story/trends/files/idc-seagate-dataage-whitepaper.pdf. Accessed: September 17, 2019.
Russell, S. J., & Norvig, P. (Eds.). (2016). *Artificial intelligence: A modern approach* (3rd ed.). Essex: Pearson education.
Scherer, M. (2016). Regulating artificial intelligence systems: Risks, challenges, competencies and strategies. *Harvard Journal of Law & Technology, 29*(2), 353–400.
Solomonoff, G. (1956). *Ray Solomonoff and the Dartmouth summer research project in artificial intelligence*. Available at http://raysolomonoff.com/dartmouth/dartray.pdf. Accessed: September 16, 2019.
Spielkamp, M. (Ed.) (2019). *Automating society: Taking stock of automated decision-making in the EU. AlgorithmWatch*. Available at: https://algorithmwatch.org/wp-content/uploads/2019/01/Automating_Society_Report_2019.pdf. Accessed: September 17, 2019.
Surden, H. (2014). Machine learning and law. *Washington Law Review, 89,* 87–115.
Tegmark, M. (2016). *Life 3.0: Being human in the age of artificial intelligence*. London: Penguin Books.
Troitiño, D. R. (2017). Jean Monnet before the first European Community: A historical perspective and critic. *Trames, 21*(3), 193–213.
Troitiño, D. R., Kerikmäe, T., & Chochia, A. (Eds.). (2018). *Brexit: history, reasoning and perspectives*. Berlin: Springer.
Van den Hoven, J. (2017) Ethics for the digital age: Where are the moral specs?—Value sensitive design and responsible innovation. In: H. Werthner, & F. van Harmelen (Eds.). *Informatics in the future* (pp. 65–76).
Von der Leyen, U. (2019) *A union that strives for more—My agenda for Europe—By candidate for President of the European Commission*. Political Guidelines for the Next European Commission 2019–2024.
Wirtz, B. W., Weyerer, J. C., & Geyer, C. (2018). Artificial intelligence and the public sector—Applications and challenges. *International Journal of Public Administration* 1–20.

Others

COM. (2018a). Communication from the Commission to the European Parliament, the European Council, the Council, the European Economic and Social Committee and the Committee of the Regions, Artificial Intelligence for Europe. 237 final
COM. (2018b). Coordinated Plan on Artificial Intelligence. 795 final
COM. (2019). Communication from the Commission to the European Parliament, the Council, the European Economic and Social Committee and the Committee of the Regions—Building Trust in Human Centric Artificial Intelligence, 168
Dignum, V. (2019). *There is no AI—race and if there is, it's the wrong one to run*. Alliance on Artificial Intelligence. Available at: https://allai.nl/there-is-no-ai-race/. Accessed: 6 September 2019)
e-Estonia. (2019). Estonia accelerates artificial intelligence *development*. Available at: https://e-estonia.com/estonia-accelerates-artificial-intelligence/. Accessed: September 18, 2019.

European Commission. (2019a). *AI landscape and indicators—AI players*. Available at: https://ec.europa.eu/knowledge4policy/ai-watch/topic/ai-landscape-indicators_en. Accessed: September 6, 2019.

European Commission. (2019b). *AI players in Europe*. Available at: https://ec.europa.eu/knowledge4policy/visualisation/ai-players-europe_en. Accessed: September 6, 2019.

European Commission. (2019c). *A definition of AI: Main capabilities and scientific disciplines High-Level Expert Group on artificial intelligence*. 8 April. Available at: https://ec.europa.eu/digital-single-market/en/news/definition-artificial-intelligence-main-capabilities-and-scientific-disciplines. Accessed: September 18, 2019.

European Commission. (2019d). *Digital single market: Commission publishes guidance on free flow of non-personal data*. Brussels, 29 May. Available at: https://europa.eu/rapid/press-release_IP-19–2749_en.htm. Accessed: September 18, 2019.

European Commission. (2019e). *The European AI alliance*. Available at: https://ec.europa.eu/digital-single-market/en/european-ai-alliance. Accessed: September 18, 2019.

Future of Life Institute. (2019). *AI Policy—China*. Available at https://futureoflife.org/ai-policy-china/. Accessed: September 6, 2019.

Kayali, L. (2019, 18 July). Next European Commission takes aim at AI Artificial intelligence will be the next GDPR. *Politico*. Available at https://www.politico.eu/article/ai-data-regulator-rules-next-european-commission-takes-aim/. Accessed: September 18, 2019.

Khan, M. (2019, 22 August). EU plans sweeping regulation of facial recognition. *Financial Times*. Available at: https://www.ft.com/content/90ce2dce-c413–11e9-a8e9-296ca66511c9. Accessed: September 14, 2019.

Knight, W. (2019). Facebook is making its own AI deepfakes to head off a disinformation disaster. *MIT Technology Review*. Available at: https://www.technologyreview.com/s/614269/facebook-is-making-ai-deepfakes-to-head-off-a-disinformation-disaster/. Accessed: September 17, 2019.

Kratid. (2019). *Estonia will have an artificial intelligence, or so-called Kratt strategy*. Available at: https://www.kratid.ee/in-english. Accessed: September 18, 2019.

Kratsios, M. (2019, 22 May). Artificial intelligence: Next steps. *The Forum—Network*. Available at: https://www.oecd-forum.org/users/262053-michael-kratsios/posts/49175-artificial-intelligence-next-steps. Accessed: September, 18 2019.

Mozur, P. (2017, 20 July). Beijing wants A.I. to be made in China by 2030. *The New York Times*. Available at: https://www.nytimes.com/2017/07/20/business/china-artificial-intelligence.html. Accessed: September 6, 2019.

Mozur, P. (2019, 14 April). One month, 500,000 face scans: How China is using A.I. to profile a minority. *The New York Times*. Available at: https://www.nytimes.com/2019/04/14/technology/china-surveillance-artificial-intelligence-racial-profiling.html). Accessed: September 17, 2019.

O'Meara, S. (2019, 21 August). Will China lead the world in AI by 2030? *Nature*. Available at: https://www.nature.com/articles/d41586-019-02360-7. Accessed: September 16, 2019.

Pearl, A. (2017, 2 June). Homage to John McCarthy, the father of artificial intelligence (AI). *Artificial Solutions*. Available at: https://www.artificial-solutions.com/blog/homage-to-john-mccarthy-the-father-of-artificial-intelligence. Accessed: September 16, 2019.

Regulation (EU) 2016/679 of the European Parliament and of the Council of 27 April 2016 on the protection of natural persons with regard to the processing of personal data and on the free movement of such data, and repealing Directive 95/46/EC (General Data Protection Regulation) L118, 4 May 2016, pp. 1–88

Regulation (EU) 2018/1807 of the European Parliament and of the Council of 14 November 2018 on a framework for the free flow of non-personal data in the European Union. PE/53/2018/REV/1.

Satariano, A. (2019, 21 January). Google is fined $57 million under Europe's data privacy law. *The New York Times*. Available at: https://www.nytimes.com/2019/03/20/business/google-fine-advertising.html. Accessed: September 18, 2019.

The Economist. (2018, 20 September). Big data, small politics: Can the EU become another AI superpower? *The Economist*. Available at https://www.economist.com/business/2018/09/20/can-the-eu-become-another-ai-superpower. Accessed: September 18, 2019.

The White House. (2019). Accelerating American Leadership in Artificial Intelligence. 11 February. Available at: https://www.whitehouse.gov/articles/accelerating-americas-leadership-in-artificial-intelligence/). Accessed: September 18, 2019.

Thierer, A, O'Sullivan, A., & Russel, R. (2017). *Artificial intelligence and public policy*. Mercatus Center—George Mason University. Available at https://www.mercatus.org/publications/technology-and-innovation/artificial-intelligence-and-public-policy. Accessed September 16, 2019.

U.S. House of Representatives Committee on Science, Space, & Technology. (2019). *Artificial Intelligence: Societal and Ethical Implications*. 26 June. Statement by Clark, J. Between minute 1:00:30 and 1:01:30. Available at https://science.house.gov/hearings/artificial-intelligence-societal-and-ethical-implications. Accessed: September 16, 2019.

Vincent, J. (2018, 27 November). This is when AI's top researchers think artificial general intelligence will be achieved. *The Verge*. Available at: https://www.theverge.com/2018/11/27/18114362/ai-artificial-general-intelligence-when-achieved-martin-ford-book. Accessed: September 16, 2019.

Challenges and Possibilities of Enforcing the Rule of Law within the EU Constitutional Edifice—The Need for Increased Role of Court of Justice, EU Charter and Diagonality in Perception

Ondrej Hamuľák and Andrea Circolo

Abstract This chapter deals with the phenomena of rule of law within the constitutional edifice of European Union. The aim is to determine its content and scope and to elaborate its promotion and enforcement in practice. A traditional approach sees this principle mostly as one-way-street focused only on Member States and as political requirement enforceable by the political procedures (Article 7 TEU). This chapter covers the rule of law as two-way proviso addressed to the EU itself and the Member States and discusses alternatives of its promotion. The key hypothesis is that operability of the rule of law concept requires its diagonal application, depoliticisation and judicialisation and concretisation via visible list of contents (in our proposal the EU Charter).

Keywords EU · Rule of law · Enforcement · Remedies · Diagonal application · Materialisation · EU charter · Member States

1 Introduction

The question of the protection of the rule of law is one of the most discussed topics in contemporary European discourse. It certainly deserves attention as one of the building pillars on which the European Union stands. Moreover, it is attracting the

O. Hamuľák (✉)
Faculty of Law, Palacký University Olomouc, Olomouc, Czech Republic
e-mail: ondrej.hamulak@upol.cz

TelTech Law School, Tallinn, Estonia

Comenius University, Bratislava, Slovakia

A. Circolo
Department of Economic and Legal Studies, Parthenope University of Naples, Naples, Italy
e-mail: andrea.circolo@uniparthenope.it

D. Ramiro Troitiño et al. (eds.), *The EU in the 21st Century*,
https://doi.org/10.1007/978-3-030-38399-2_10

interest of politicians,[1] scientists and academics.[2] It is being discussed in the context of the crisis of liberal democracy, the future of the European Union and the reforms, which are ahead of it; it is the subject of critical reflections and the subject of detailed studies.[3] The main theme of most of the works devoted to this topic is the existence, effectiveness and functioning of the mechanisms for protecting and strengthening the rule of law within the Union, in particular the analysis of the operability of the suspensive clause mechanism under Article 7 TEU in relation to Member States.[4] Minor part of the texts also deals with the content and origin of this principle.[5] The presented text is a follow-up to the existing research, but its aim is primarily to address the question of the functionality of the rule of law in general. In an ideal world, the rule of law could be deliberated as a category of constitutional metaphysics. In the real world, however, it is necessary to identify functional tools that ensure its acceptance and enforcement. In the following paper, we discuss and determine three key problems related to the rule of law functionality in the Union.

The first problem we want to point out is that the rule of law enforcement is currently understood very unilaterally and is directed almost exclusively towards the Member States or at the level of the EU's external relations towards third countries. Such a strategy (albeit pursuing a noble ideal) may eventually have a counterproductive effect and significantly damage the ideal itself. As regards the understanding and enforcement of the rule of law within the Union, it is necessary to introduce certain equilibrium in the form of reciprocal application—towards Member States as well as Union itself—in certain type of diagonal matrix.[6]

The next problem is the materialisation of the rule of law. Within the scientific discourse, there is a controversy over what concrete content (what values and principles) is hidden behind the concept of the rule of law[7]; whether this concept should be understood as universal one; or, on the contrary, it may have different content and contours within the individual systems (global international law, EU law, national law).[8] Here we propose the thesis of simplified embodiment of the concept of rule of law with using of most available tool—the EU Charter of Fundamental Rights.[9]

The last issue to be addressed in our paper is the problem of the operability of the rule of law concept. It is indisputable that Union is building its future and vision of its functioning on respect of the principles of rule of law. At the same

[1] It is worth to mention that upholding of rule of law plays a key role in political agenda of newly elected President of the European Commission Mrs. Ursula von der Leyen. See: "A Union that strives for more—My agenda for Europe" available at https://ec.europa.eu/commission/sites/beta-political/files/political-guidelines-next-commission_en.pdf.

[2] Konstadinides (2017).

[3] Schroeder ed. (2019).

[4] Sehnálek (2016).

[5] Müller-Graff (2014).

[6] Nagy (2018).

[7] Šišková (2018).

[8] Elbert (2015).

[9] Jakab (2016).

time, however, Europe is facing the biggest crisis of liberal democracy that touches upon these principles, as well as a crisis of legitimacy and confidence in the Union's governance system. EU is clearly trying to address the visible problem by a plethora of instruments and proposals for the rule of law enforcement. Many suggestions, debates and promises[10] give the impression that the Union does not currently have sufficient apparatus to ensure respect for the rule of law. Our goal is to prove that this impression is erroneous and that there are available instruments that can produce effective results. The prerequisite, however, is the depoliticisation of this subject and its practical judicialisation.

2 Diagonalisation of Rule of Law

The concept of the rule of law was inserted into the Treaties (by Treaty of Amsterdam in 1999) as a manifestation of a common European consensus. It was essentially a textual expression of the fact which Union has in its genetic code as a child of Western democracies. Since its introduction, the concept itself has been perceived (rightly) as one of the philosophical starting points (along with the concept of supranationality, division of competences or the principle of mutual trust and recognition) rather than an enforceable rule of conduct. However, past but mostly present threats to this concept confirm the fact that in its perception we must change our attitude and descend from metaphysical heights to the practical level. It is necessary to understand it as a standard commitment, as a legal obligation. Since its inception, the community, today the Union, has placed as a *leitmotiv* at the heart of the process of European integration the respect for those values without which its own *ratio existendi* is lacking. These values form its 'spiritual and moral heritage'[11] and permeate its entire legal and institutional structure, including its policies. Article 2 TEU, which contains the list, begins with the expression the Union is founded on the 'values [...]'. It is therefore clear from the outset that they do not constitute 'mere ideal and political statements'[12], but they are an essential condition for the survival of a 'Union [based on the rule] of law' as the European Union has sought to be since the *Les Verts* case law.[13] Moreover, the privileged position within the Treaties, as the second provision

---

[10]See in detail section 4.1 enforcing rule of law requirements in relation to Member States—call for judicialisation, further in this chapter.

[11]Preamble to the Charter of Fundamental Rights of the European Union.

[12]Adam and Tizzano (2017).

[13]294/83 *Les Verts v. Parlament*, ECLI:EU:C:1986:166., para 23: 'It must first be emphasized in this regard that the European Economic Community is a community based on the rule of law, inasmuch as neither its Member states nor its institutions can avoid a review of the question whether the measures adopted by them are in conformity with the basic constitutional charter, the Treaty'. The expression, which has now replaced that of 'community based on the rule of law' can be traced back to the judgement of the Court of Justice of 27th February 2018, C-64/16, Associação Sindical dos Juízes Portugueses, ECLI:EU:C:2018:117, para 31.

only after the affirmation of legal equality between the TEU and the TFEU, is enough to recall its fundamental importance.

In this regard, the Court of Justice has pointed out that '[...] each Member State shares with all the other Member States, and recognises that they share with it, a set of common values on which the EU is founded [...]. That premise implies and justifies the existence of mutual trust between the Member States that those values will be recognised and, therefore, that the law of the EU that implements them will be respected'.[14]

It is therefore a necessary presence for a constitutional order of liberal-democratic inspiration such as the Union. This justifies why failures to comply with them have even more serious legal consequences than the violation of any other obligation laid down.[15]

In view of the above, one of the values on which the Union is founded is properly the 'rule of law'. The rule of law is in fact the 'backbone' of every modern constitutional democracy. It imposes the effective observance of (Union) law on all those subject to its shadow cone, namely institutions and bodies, Member States and individuals—natural and legal persons.[16]

Understanding the rule of law in the proposed diagonal perception would bring many benefits. A practical understanding and enforcement of the rule of law, not only against the Member States, but also towards the Union itself, will lead to some conceptual absolutisation, which is inherent in Article 2 TEU and follows both from its text and from its purpose. Respect for the rule of law as a constitutional principle and the commitment of the Union itself is one of the tools for enhancing the legitimacy of EU governance in terms of strengthening the so-called output democracy.[17] This strengthens the bond and trust between the Union and individuals, what is unquestionably in a line with the Jean Monnet's programming statement (presented in Washington, 30 April 1952[18]): *'Nous ne coalisons pas des États, nous unissons des hommes'*. Moreover, the introduction of equilibrium can also have a positive impact on Member States' reactions and attitudes. States and the Union, as bearers of the same commitments, will be able to respect each other in more precise manner, what is necessary precondition for alleviation of the tensions, competence creep and sovereignty games in European constitutional edifice. Diagonal approach to rule of law would help to maintain the federal balance in the EU.[19] In essence, unidirectional enforcement of the rule of law commitments opens and returns the so-called Solange

[14]Opinion of the Court of Justice of 18th December 2014, 2/13, *Accession of the European Union to the European Convention for the Protection of Human Rights and Fundamental Freedoms*, ECLI:EU:C:2014:2454.

[15]Fumagalli (2014).

[16]Kerikmäe et al. (2019).

[17]Lenaerts and Cambien (2009).

[18]Troitiño (2017).

[19]von Bogdandy and Spieker (2019).

reservation[20] on the scene. At the heart of this reservation was the requirement to introduce a comparable approach/level of respect for human rights at supranational and national level. Achieving equilibrium then promoted the acceptance and full effect of EU law in the application practice in the Member States. In our opinion, a similar logic should be applied in relation to the fundamental values defined in Article 2 of the TEU and above all in the approach to rule of law.

3 Materialisation of Rule of Law

The concept of the rule of law is an abstract quality and is generally associated with certain elementary elements ensuring good governance. There is a broad consensus on the basic elements of the concept, but its precise definition still lies at the level of abstraction rather than the form of sum of specific enforceable obligations and duties. In an ideal world, it is sufficient to know what is and what is not in accordance with the concept of the rule of law. In the real world—or rather in the reality of contemporary Europe (with the rise of populism, the strengthening of non-systemic parties, the boom of illiberal democracy and authoritarian tendencies)—the concept of the rule of law needs to be as tangible as possible, linked to a concrete commitment that is identifiable and applicable in law enforcement processes. Here we start from understanding the rule of law as a guarantee that any public power interference into specific individual rights will be controllable and enforceable. We base our thesis on opinion of Francis Jacobs, who regards the judicial reviewability of decisions of public authorities as the cornerstone of the functioning of the rule of law.[21] In the other words, we may say that availability of tools securing that wrongs will be remedied stands as backbone of the rule of law.

We therefore propose to draw attention to the EU Charter of Fundamental Rights. Its general recognition and wide application should serve as the best guarantee for achieving and maintaining the desired quality of the rule of law across the Union.[22] The Charter itself refers to the rule of law in the preamble and its content is a factual materialisation of the basic elements of the rule of law. These elements are protected by the Charter, inter alia, by emphasising human dignity (Article 1), protecting liberty and personal security (Article 6) by guaranteeing political rights (Articles 10, 11, 12), ensuring the equality before the law (Article 20), emphasising the good governance (Article 41) and access to documents (Article 42) and, in particular, by a broad understanding of the right to an effective remedy and a fair trial (Article 47). Last but not least, the functioning of the rule of law in the European Union is also linked to the proportionality of human rights interventions (Article 52 para 1). In spite of all

[20]The so-called Solange reservation was formulated decades ago by the German Constitutional Court in connection with the deficits in protection of fundamental rights at European Community level.

[21]Jacobs (2008).

[22]Kerikmäe (2014).

its gaps and shortcomings,[23] the Charter has become a prominent and powerful tool for promoting elements of the rule of law—the Charter as a hard law.[24] Of course, we are not claiming that the Charter has and can be the only carrier of the rule of law principles in the Union. But we see its potential in being the most effective and affordable tool to promote these values. The materialisation of the rule of law in the form of the Charter shifts the question of the protection of these principles from the level of legal idealism[25] to the level of practical enforceability. The number of guardians (individuals) is increasing and so is the pressure on public institutions to respect the given principles in their activities.

The fact that the Charter represents a genuine materialisation of the rule of law is confirmed also by the recent case law of the Court of Justice, in which the functionality of an independent judicial system and the availability of legal protection instruments are underlined as a key factor for the rule of law in the Union.[26] In case *Associação Sindical dos Juízes Portugueses*[27] CJEU endorsed that: "The very existence of effective judicial review designed to ensure compliance with EU law is of the essence of the rule of law..." This position was reaffirmed also in key case Minister for Justice and Equality (LM)[28] where Court of Justice underlined that: "judicial independence forms part of the essence of the fundamental right to a fair trial. It is a right which is of cardinal importance as a guarantee ... that the values common to the Member States set out in Article 2 TEU, in particular the value of the rule of law will be safeguarded".

4 Operability and Enforcement of Rule of Law[29]

The most fundamental challenge for the rule of law concept within the European Union is its enforceability. Especially in connection with the Member States, the question of the malfunctioning of the system is one of the most discussed in contemporary discourse.[30] Contrary to endless discussion and the search for new tools of enforcement, we base our opinion on the thesis of the existence of a sufficient spectrum of tools, which, however, must be practically used. The following text is

[23]The most discussed are these five: 1. Limited application in relation to Member States (art. 51/1); 2. Charter of different speed? (Protocol No. 30); 3. National torpedoes and mines! (art. 52/4, art. 53 and national conditionality clauses); 4. Provisions of different weight or the rationale for the inclusion of toothless "principles" (art. 52/5); 5. No special procedural mechanisms.

[24]de Búrca (2013).

[25]So from the Platonic legal heaven to reality, as pointed out by the AG Mazák Opinion in case C-411/05 *Palacios de la Villa*, ECLI:EU:C:2007:106.

[26]von Bogdandy et al. (2016).

[27]C-64/16, Associação Sindical dos Juízes Portugueses, ECLI:EU:C:2018:117, para 36.

[28]C-216/18 PPU, Minister for Justice and Equality, ECLI:EU:C:2018:586, para 48.

[29]This section is based on our previous research published in special issue of European Journal of Transformation Studies, see Hamuľák and Circolo (2019).

[30]Closa and Kochenov eds. (2018).

divided into two parts. In the first, we look at the question of moving from purely political to judicial enforcement of the values of the rule of law in relation to the Member States. The second part contains an overview on the applicability of the rule of law in relation to the Union itself. Both parts are linked by thesis on the need for judicialisation of the enforcement of the values of the rule of law in the Union.

4.1 Enforcing Rule of Law Requirements in Relation to Member States—Call for Judicialisation

Recent concerns about the state of health of the rule of law in the certain Member States[31] of the EU have required the intervention of the European institutions that monitor the correct application of EU law.[32] It was therefore necessary to activate the specific procedure that the Treaties allocate to safeguard the founding values of the Union, listed in Article 2 TEU and which include the rule of law (*id est*, the Article 7 TEU).

The so-called suspension clause establishes that the Council may suspend certain rights (including voting rights within the Council itself) of the offending State, without this ceasing to be bound by the obligations deriving from the Treaties, after the violation of the values referred to in Article 2 TEU has been ascertained several times—and this is where the 'drama' begins.[33]

The mere reading of the provision immediately makes it clear that we are faced with a procedure where the intergovernmental method prevails. The Council and the European Council are in fact the only bodies delegated to ascertain the existence of the violation and to decide on the suspension of the rights to the detriment of the non-complying State. However, the European Parliament has a decidedly marginal role. Indeed, it intervenes: (a) in the activation of the procedure (it is one of the subjects entitled to request the intervention of the Council through a motivated proposal); (b) in taking the determination, but only through prior approval of the decision of the Council first and then of the European Council. On the other hand, it does not play a role in the definition of the rights of the Member State to be suspended.

The use of a procedure very different from the co-decision procedure, in terms of the relationship between Parliament and the Council, is justified in the light of what has been defined as the 'sensitivity to sovereignty'.[34] Since condemning a Member State immediately is a very delicate operation recalled as nuclear option,[35]

---

[31] Hegedüs (2019).

[32] The reference is to the incidents that have involved and continue to involve mainly two EU Member States, Poland and Hungary. In addition, there are recent concerns about violations in Slovakia and Malta: on this point, it is permitted to recall to Circolo (2019).

[33] Casolari (2016), Sanna (2014).

[34] Kumm (2013).

[35] Šišková (2018).

given its possible political repercussions, the use of the intergovernmental method is more appropriate because of the considerable room for manoeuvre left to individual sovereignties.

However, at the time of its first and real application, this mechanism proved to be ineffective in substance. The procedural complexities and voting thresholds made its use impractical.[36] In particular, the unanimity within the European Council required by Article 7 TEU to certify the actual existence of the infringement favours, in substance, the emergence of alliances between States. The substantial failures of the current mechanisms for protecting the rule of law have called for a redefinition of the framework of safeguards by all EU institutions involved in the supervision of the correct application of EU law.

To deal with the critical issues inherent in the system established by Article 7 TEU, various instruments have been proposed and/or prepared: the communication of the Commission of 2014,[37] the modification of the deliberative *quorum,*[38] the 'Copenhagen Commission',[39] the expulsion from the Union,[40] the 'Systemic Deficiency Committee',[41] the outsourcing of the protection,[42] the DRF mechanism (democracy, rule of law, fundamental rights),[43] the regulation on EU's budget.[44] These can be summarised into three major macro-categories: instruments that require revision of the

[36]Mori (2016).

[37]European Commission, Communication from the Commission to the European Parliament and the Council—a new EU Framework to strengthen the Rule of Law, COM (2014) 158, 11th April 2014.

[38]For example, moving from unanimity to qualified majority voting.

[39]It would be an independent body responsible only for supervising respect for the values referred to in Article 2 TEU, a sort of small Commission formed by eminent political figures, such as former Heads of State, former Presidents of Parliaments, etc., and endowed with various sanctioning powers.

[40]There are many doubts about its possible contrast with the 'hard core' of the Treaties, which is considered unchangeable even with Article 48 TEU.

[41]It is conceived as a part of the Commission (but administratively and economically independent, in the wake of OLAF). This is a fascinating thesis, since it goes beyond the impediment of the revision procedure—needed for the Copenaghen Commission—through the use of the flexibility clause of Article 352 TFEU, considering that the protection of the values of Article 2 TEU falls within the scope of application of the competences of the Union. Nevertheless, it is not acceptable, since it would be a question of establishing not a simple committee, but a supervisory body with several powers over the *status* of a Member State, a change that could only be made during the revision (von Bogdandy et al. 2016).

[42]Entrusted, for example, to the Venice Commission. If this scenario silences the risk of instrumental political persecution against certain Member States in alleged violations of the principle of the equality of States (Article 4(2) TEU), it is not clear how an authority outside the Union can impose its conclusions on the parties concerned in a binding manner.

[43]See the European Parliament Resolution of 13 December 2016 on the situation of fundamental rights in the European Union in 2015 [2016/2009(INI)]. It is a proposal to conclude an interinstitutional agreement, under Article 295 TFEU, between the Parliament, the Council and the Commission for the launch of monitoring procedures to defend these values, including the publication of an annual report on the state of the art of compliance with these rights.

[44]European Commission, Proposal for a regulation of the European Parliament and of the Council on the protection of the Union's budget in case of generalised deficiencies as regards the rule of law in the Member States, COM(2018) 324 final 2018/0136 (COD), 2nd May 2018. The proposal, which

Treaties in order to be implemented (the lowering of the *quorum*, the Copenhagen Commission, the outsourcing of the protection, the expulsion); valid instruments that are, in substance, ineffective (the Commission's 2014 communication; the DRF mechanism); instruments that 'circumvent' the letter of the Treaties in order to offer alternative protection (Systemic Deficiency Committee, regulation on EU's budget).

Nonetheless, none of them has proved to be the decisive one for the above-mentioned critical issues. The impression is that it is no longer justifiable for Member States to be unwilling to refer such situations to the Court of Justice. However, this must always be done in accordance with the 'rules of the game' that the Member States have set themselves. What is called the 'Copenhagen dilemma', that is the paradox whereby the candidate countries for accession are required to respect the founding values of the Union, the violation of which is not effectively censurable after accession, cannot legitimise the forcing of the procedures that the Treaties allocate for the modification of the letter of the same. All that remains, therefore, is to continue to promote a constructive dialogue between the Union and 'rogue' States and to wait until and if there is a moment of community of purposes within the Union that can enable the players on the European scene to seise the ideas drawn from practice, such as modifying the Treaties.

It is true that the possible jurisdiction of the Court of Justice over respect for the founding values, values which are common to the constitutional traditions of the Member States,[45] risks creating further conflicts of jurisdiction between the Union's courts and the national courts, '*traditionellement jalouses de leur rôle de gardien des valeurs fondamentales dans les systèmes internes*'.[46] However, often, it is precisely the internal courts that are the addressees of the measures in breach of Article 2 TEU, thus incapable of protecting those values. The institutional role of the Court, on the contrary, remains undisputed. From the outset of the Community, that role

was recently adopted at first reading in the EP (P8_TA(2019)0349, 4th April 2019), would allow the Commission, assisted by a group of independent experts, to identify 'generalised deficiencies regarding the rule of law' and to decide on the most appropriate financial measures to be implemented (i.e. suspension of payments for EU programmes). These sanctions can only be applied after approval by the Council. If it is true that this mechanism seems to be effective from the point of view of safeguards, it also raises more than a few doubts as to its compatibility with the Treaties. The connection to the legal basis is indeed indirect and forced. Even from a mere reading of the rule, it emerges that Article 322 TFEU only allows to establish financial rules on the modalities of implementation of the budget; certainly not, on the contrary, to protect the expenditure of the Union against the generalised deficiencies of the rule of law. Bending the legal basis in this direction would lead to the violation of another fundamental principle of EU law, namely the prohibition of abuse of rights, which prevents the exploitation of a benefit resulting from formal compliance with a rule, since its use goes beyond the objectives of the rule itself. This regulation would in fact censure: the same violations (systemic violations and not one-off); of the same principle (the rule of law); in the same way (the suspension of payments is nothing more than a suspension of a right deriving from the Treaties, the same rights that the Council may suspend according to Article 7 TEU). It is therefore not clear how and when one mechanism should be preferred to the other. In the end, it seems to be an *escamotage* to circumvent the revision of the Treaties and the unanimity needed to reform the existing protection mechanism.

[45] Ramiro Troitino and Pando Ballesteros (2017).

[46] Porchia (2018).

constitutes an added value for its consecration to a community based on the rule of law and for the achievement of increasingly advanced legal, economic, social and political integration.[47]

Waiting for this, the supervision on the respect for the rule of law can and must still be left to the Commission and the Court, but through the mechanism that the Treaties already reserve, as far as we can see, for the defence of Union law and its values, that is to say, the infringement procedure. Contrary to what was assumed in the proposal for a regulation, Article 7 TEU and Articles 258 *et seq.* TFEU, both of which are in the primary legislation, do not explicitly conflict with each other. The interpretation of those provisions as cumulative and non-alternative means of protection does not appear to be subject to express legal obstacles. It is not possible to find in the Treaties the postulate on which one of their assumed ontological differences is based, that is the circumstance that the former only takes into account the systemic violations of these rights and that the latter is limited to 'one-off' non-compliance. Article 258 para 1 TFEU just states: 'If the Commission considers that a Member State has failed to fulfil an obligation under the Treaties [...]'. How can compliance with the founding values not be considered as failure to fulfil an obligation under the Treaties? Furthermore, the thesis of the alleged generic nature of the obligation to respect the founding values cannot be considered acceptable.[48] Indeed, as initially envisaged, they are not programmatic rules, but the essential premise of the existence of the EU, whose specific violations must be irreparably censored.

The Court has not yet expressly ruled on the possibility that the fundamental values may serve as a parameter between the infringement and the opening of an infringement procedure[49]; however, as part of the doctrine has already shown, such an intervention is highly desirable.[50]

However, problems may arise with regard to the application of the *ne bis in idem* principle. First of all, it has to be marked the breadth of these principles, borrowed from national legal systems, once they have been incorporated in the Union's legal order. Once these legal categories have been acquired, they take on a new meaning in relation to the specific features of the European legal system, even if they continue to maintain the same label. In this sense, the application of *ne bis in idem* must always be balanced with the effectiveness of these other principles on which the entire Union is based. The exceptional nature of the case could well justify the joint application of the intergovernmental procedure and the action for failure to fulfil obligations. Moreover, by failing to recognise the cumulative effect of remedies, the infringement could well be brought whenever the Member States are unable to activate the Article 7 TEU procedure, or, conversely, the latter could no longer be used if the non-compliant State has already been punished under Articles 258 TFEU and 260 TFEU.

[47] Hamuľák (2016).

[48] Compare with the judgement of the Court of Justice of 16th December 2004, case C-293/03, *Gregorio My/Office national des pensions*, ECLI:EU:C:2004:821, para 29 (Gormley 2017).

[49] Miglio (2018).

[50] Hillion (2016).

However, if such an interpretation seems to be able, at least potentially, to go beyond the 'quantitative' argument, it is not equally capable of extending to the 'qualitative' argument, that is to say, to the hypothesis that the infringement cannot be traced back to the cone of shadow of EU law but refers to purely internal situations. In this sense, however, some recent landings of the Court's case law seem to show openings. The reference is to the judgement of the Court *Associação Sindical dos Juízes Portugueses*.[51] The expansion of the value of Article 19(1) TEU, operated by the Court in conjunction with Article 2 TEU, allows to activate infringement procedures that could be able to tackle violations of the principle of effective judicial protection, and so of the rule of law too.[52] In *ASJP*, the CJEU affirmed that Article 19(1) TEU 'gives concrete expression to the value of the rule of law stated in Article 2 TEU' (para 32). Therefore, in providing effective judicial protection of the rights deriving from EU law to individuals within their respective jurisdictional systems, national courts also ensure respect for the rule of law.[53]

Entrusting the protection of the values referred to in Article 2 TEU to the exclusive jurisdiction of the Court of Justice probably constitutes a Copernican Revolution to which the Member States have shown that they are not yet ready. But it would achieve 'the most perfect design of contemporary constitutionalism, which gives the Supreme Court the power to arbitrate, on the basis of law, political conflicts between the constitutional actors of the legal order'.[54]

4.2 *Enforcing the Rule of Law Requirements Vis-Á-Vis Union—Note on Open Approach to Available Judicial Tools*

Our thesis is that existing procedural framework and EU remedies serve as sufficient set of instruments to enforce rule of law—especially as materialised in the provisions of the EU Charter.[55] There is no need for elevation of any new remedies or instruments of judicial enforceability of such fundamental values within the EU legal system.[56]

---

[51] *Supra*, footnote 3. It was pointed out that: 'The Court took advantage of this case to emphasise the potential of EU law to consolidate and defend the rule of law structures in the Member States. The Court discovered a justiciable rule of law clause in Art. 19, para. 1, TEU, which enshrines the principle of effective judicial protection before national courts. This provision makes the enforcement of rule of law standards vis-à-vis the Member States more straightforward as compared to the enforcement of Art. 47 of the Charter of Fundamental Rights of the EU. In the future, Art. 19, para. 1, TEU could be enforced by means of infringement proceedings under Art. 258 TFEU to counteract the undermining of judicial independence at the national level' (Krajewski 2018).

[52] Krajewski (2018), Coli (2018).

[53] Parodi (2018).

[54] Cannizzaro (2018).

[55] Hamuľák (2018).

[56] Ward (2017).

The existing system of procedural tools offers us a wide variety of instruments thinkable (and already being used) as means of enforcement of core EU values vis-á-vis Union institutions and bodies. Those are applicable in wide sense, even in situations when institutions 'act outside the EU legal framework'.[57] In following text, we will try to summarise the potential instruments available for judicial enforcement of principal EU values in relation to EU bodies. We are speaking about incidental remedies here, i.e. actions brought before the courts by individual seeking the protection of its concrete individual right(s) interconnected with the rule of law values (e.g. access to impartial court, personal freedom, proportionality of public encroachments into individual rights, etc.). The logic and importance of this kind of enforcement are the protection of individual against the encroachments into conferred rights for which public (EU) bodies are responsible.

There is no space for evaluation of all available tools and to determine the practical impact of those remedies. Our goal is to point on those remedies which are practically available and open a further discussion on their applicability and accuracy as the instruments of enforcement of rule of law. The prominent instrument is definitely the legality/validity review of EU acts before Union courts. It could be commenced via direct action for annulment under Article 263 TFEU[58] or as preliminary reference from the national courts under Article 267 TFEU.[59] Both paths were already used as the tools for enforcement of fundamental EU values and offer a wide space for further development of rule of law standards. Partially and indirectly, we could think also about application of other tools such as action for failure to act under Article 265 TFEU or action for damages under Article 268 TFEU. The latter one was already confirmed as the tool of promotion of very basic aspect of rule of law—the right to judicial decisions of individual matter in a reasonable time.[60]

[57]See C-8/15 P *Ledra Advertising v Commission and ECB*, ECLI:EU:C:2016:701, p. 67.

[58]The most prominent example is the so-called Kadi saga: C-402/05 P and C-415/05 P, Kadi and Al Barakaat International Foundation v Council and Commission, ECLI:EU:C:2008:461; Joined cases C-584/10 P, C-593/10 P and C-595/10 P, European Commission and Others v Yassin Abdullah Kadi, ECLI:EU:C:2013:518. For a brief commentary on the Kadi jurisprudence see eg: Lentner (2013). And succeeding case law (T-208/11 *Liberation Tigers of Tamil Eelam (LTTE) v Council of the European Union*, ECLI:EU:T:2014:885; T-384/11 *Safa Nicu Sepahan v Council*, ECLI:EU:T:2014:986; T-316/14 *Kurdistan Workers' Party v Council of the European Union*, ECLI:EU:T:2018:788; T-240/16 *Klyuyev v Council*, ECLI:EU:T:2018:433; C-530/17 P *Azarov v Council*, ECLI:EU:C:2018:1031; AG Opinion in case C-225/17 P *Islamic Republic of Iran Shipping Lines and Others v Council*, ECLI:EU:C:2018:720.).

[59]To mention the most significant, we could refer to the cases: C-236/09 *Test-Achats*, ECLI:EU:C:2011:100; C-293/12 *Digital Rights Ireland*, ECLI:EU:C:2014:238; C-362/14 *Maximillian Schrems v Data Protection Commissioner*, ECLI:EU:C:2015:650.

[60]C-411/15 P *Timab Industries a CFPR v. Komise*, ECLI:EU:C:2017:11; C-603/13 P, *Galp Energía España a další v. Komise*, ECLI:EU:C:2016:38.

5 Conclusion

In contemporary scholarly discussions and expert analyses, the principles of the rule of law have been turning into a very sophisticated system, which reaches to the certain level of abstraction and thus moves away from practical enforceability. Of course, it is necessary to determine the content of the rule of law. But in our view, in order to give the concept of the rule of law concrete contours, it is necessary to identify its content by a simple medium, which we believe may be the EU Charter of Fundamental Rights, as the codification of fundamental values on which EU and Member States are based.

Opting for EU Charter as the path of materialisation of EU law is interconnected also with other two problems related to the smooth operation of rule of law requirements within the Union. The first is misbalanced application of rule of law enforcement, which is mostly focused only in relation to the Member States and omitting its general scope. That is to say, that Article 2 TEU does not contain a mere obligation on the part of Member States. On the contrary, it is a standard defining the fundamental values of the Union as a whole, so the question of enforcement of its principles must be addressed also in relation to the EU institutions. In this context, we are talking about the absolutisation of the concept of the rule of law. Acceptance, tolerance and a serious approach to the values of the rule of law within the European Union require the introduction of a so-called diagonal approach. The principles of the rule of law must be respected and their violations effectively addressed both in terms of units (Member States) and in relation to the Union and its institutions. Second advantage resulting from the materialisation of rule of law via EU Charter is the availability of remedies. Today enforcement of rule of law is mostly discussed in connection to Article 7 TEU procedures and other political paths, which are being discussed. Our proposal brings the benefit of judicialisation by usage of broad spectrum of already existing tools of Charter enforcement.[61]

References

Adam, R., & Tizzano, A. (2017). *Manuale di diritto dell'Unione europea*. Turin: Giappichelli.

Cannizzaro, E. (2018). Il ruolo della Corte di giustizia nella tutela dei valori dell'Unione europea. In *Liber Amicorum Antonio Tizzano. De la Cour CECA à la Cour de l'Union: le long parcours de la justice européenne*, Turin: Giappichelli.

Casolari, F. (2016). Il rispetto della rule of law nell'ordinamento giuridico dell'Unione europea: un dramma in due atti. *DPCE* online.

Circolo, A. (2019). Il rispetto dei valori fondanti dell'Unione e l'attivazione della procedura di controllo alla luce delle recenti vicende di Polonia e Ungheria. In *DPCE online*, *35*(1).

Closa, C., & Kochenov, D. (Eds.). (2018). *Reinforcing rule of law oversight in the european union*. Cambridge: Cambridge University Press.

Coli, M. (2018) The Associação Sindical dos Juízes Portugueses judgment: what role for the Court of Justice in the protection of EU values? diritticomparati.it.

[61] Ward (2017).

De Búrca, G. (2013). After the EU charter of fundamental rights: The court of justice as a human rights adjudicator? *Maastricht Journal of European and Comparative Law, 20*(2), 168–184.

Elbert, Ľ. (2015). Regionalism and the rule of law. In: J. Klučka & Ľ. Elbert (Eds.), *Regionalism and its contribution to general international law* (pp. 117–152). Košice: UPJŠ in Košice.

Fumagalli, L. (2014) *Commento all'art. 2 TUE*. In A. Tizzano (Ed.), *Trattati dell'Unione europea*, II ed., Milan: Giuffre.

Gormley, L. W. (2017). Infringement proceedings. In A. Jakab & D. Kochenov (Eds.), *The enforcement of EU law and values: Ensuring member states' compliance*. Oxford: Oxford University Press.

Hamuľák, O. (2016). Coven of layers and its child—emancipated and dominant EU law. *National sovereignty in the european union-view from the czech perspective* (pp. 13–28). Springer International: Cham.

Hamuľák, O. (2018). The variations of judicial enforcement of EU charter of fundamental rights vis-á-vis union institutions and bodies. *European Studies—The Review of European Law, Economics and Politics, 5*(1), 98–112.

Hegedüs, D. (2019). What role for EU institutions in confronting Europe's democracy and rule of law crisis? In *GMF Policy Paper, No. 4/2019*.

Hillion, C. (2016). Overseeing the rule of law in the EU. In C. Closa & D. Kochenov (Eds.), *Reinforcing rule of law oversight in the European Union* (pp. 59–81). Cambridge: Cambridge University Press.

Jacobs, F. (2008). The state of international economic law. Rethinking Sovereignty in Europe. *Journal of International Economic Law, 11*(1), 5–41.

Jakab, A. (2016). The EU charter of fundamental rights as the most promising way of enforcing the rule of law against EU member states. In C. Closa & D. Kochenov (Eds.), *Reinforcing rule of law oversight in the European Union* (pp. 187–205). Cambridge: Cambridge University Press.

Kerikmäe. T. (2014). EU charter: Its nature, innovative character, and horizontal effect. In T. Kerikmäe (Ed.), *Protecting human rights in the EU. Controversies and challenges of the charter of fundamental rights* (pp. 5–19). Berlin, Heidelberg: Springer.

Kerikmäe, T., Troitiño, D. R., & Shumilo, O. (2019). An idol or an ideal? A case study of estonian e-governance: public perceptions, myths and misbeliefs1. *Acta Baltica Historiae et Philosophiae scientiarum, 7*(1).

Konstadinides, T. (2017). *The rule of law in the european union—the internal dimension*. Oxford: Hart Publishing.

Krajewski, M. (2018). Associação Sindical dos Juízes Portugueses: The court of justice and Athena's Dilemma. *European Papers, 3*(1), 395–407.

Kumm, M. (2013). Discussion in J.-W. Müller, Safeguarding democracy inside the EU Brussels and the future of liberal order. In *Transatlantic Academy Paper Series, No. 3/2013*.

Lenaerts, K., & Cambien, N. (2009). The democratic legitimacy of the EU after the treaty of Lisbon. In J. Wouters (Ed.), *European constitutionalism beyond Lisbon* (pp. 185–207). Antverps: Intersentia.

Lentner, G. (2013) M. Kadi II before the ECJ—UN targeted sanctions and the European legal order. In *European Law Reporter* (pp. 202–205).

Miglio, A. (2018). Indipendenza del giudice, crisi dello stato di diritto e tutela giurisdizionale effettiva negli Stati membri dell'Unione europea. *Diritti umani e diritto internazionale, 12*(2), 421–431.

Mori, P. (2016). Verso i 60 anni dai Trattati di Roma, stato e prospettive dell'Unione europea. In A. Tizzano (Ed.), *Quaderni della rivista, Diritto dell'Unione europea*. Turin: Giappichelli.

Müller-Graff, P-Ch. (2014). The idea and rule of law as foundation of the EU-Acquis. In N. Šišková (Ed.), *From eastern partnership to the association—a legal and political analysis* (pp. 164–172). Newcastle upon Tyne: Cambridge Scholarship Publishing.

Nagy, C. I. (2018). *The EU bill of rights' diagonal application to member states*. The Hague: Eleven Publishers.

Parodi, M. (2018). Il controllo della Corte di giustizia sul rispetto del principio dello Stato di diritto da parte degli Stati membri: alcune riflessioni in margine alla sentenza Associação Sindical dos Juízes Portugueses. *European Papers, 3*(2), 985–992.
Porchia, O. (2018). Le respect de l'État de droit dans les états membres: la complémentarité des initiatives politiques et le rôle de la Cour de justice. In *Liber Amicorum Antonio Tizzano. De la Cour CECA à la Cour de l'Union: le long parcours de la justice européenne*, Turin: Giappichelli.
Ramiro Troitino, D. R., & Pando Ballesteros, M. D. L. P. (2017). Churchill's European integration model. *Revista de Occidente, 433,* 57–71.
Sanna, C. (2014) *Commento all'art. 7 TUE*. In A. Tizzano (Ed.), *Trattati dell'Unione europea*, II ed., Milan: Giuffre.
Schroeder, W. (2019). *Strengthening the rule of law in Europe. From a common concept to mechanisms of implementation*. Oxford: Hart Publishing.
Sehnálek, D. (2016). Nový postup EU pro posílení právního státu. *Časopis pro právní vědu a praxi, 24*(2), 191–201.
Šišková, N. (2018). European Union's legal instruments to strengthen the rule of law, their actual reflections and future prospects. In N. Šišková (Ed.), *The European Union—what is next? A Legal analysis and the political visions on the future of the union* (pp. 136–162). Köln: Wolters Kluwer Deutschland GmbH.
Troitiño, D. R. (2017). Jean monnet before the first european community: A historical perspective and critic. *Trames, 21*(3), 193–213.
von Bogdandy, A., Antpöhler, C., & Ioannidis, M. (2016). Protecting EU values: Reverse solange and the rule of law framework. In A. Jakab & D. Kochenov (Eds.), *The enforcement of EU law and values: Ensuring member states' compliance*. Oxford: Oxford University Press.
von Bogdandy, A., Spieker, L. (2019). Countering the judicial silencing of critics—article 2 TEU values, criminal liability and reverse Solange. In *MPIL Research Paper No. 8/2019.*
Ward, A. (2017). Remedies under the EU charter of fundamental rights. In S. Douglas-Scott & N. Hatzis (Eds.), *Research handbook on EU law and human rights* (pp. 162–185). Cheltenham: Edward Elgar.

Ondrej Hamuľák is a Senior Lecturer at the Faculty of Law, Palacký University Olomouc (Czech Republic), Adjunct Professor in EU Strategic Legal Affairs, TelTech Law School (Estonia), and researcher at the Faculty of Law, Comenius University in Bratislava (Slovakia). He participated in the work on this paper on behalf of project no. 17-22322S 'The Influence of the Charter of Fundamental Rights of the EU on the Constitutional Law of the Visegrad Group Countries' funded by the Czech Science Foundations (GAČR).

Economic Development: A Pillar for the European Union Integration

Iwona Pawlas

Abstract Pawlas focuses on economic development as a target of integration processes developed by the EU. Pawlas explores the Treaties concerning economic development and follows with the identification of the scale of disparities among and within the EU Member States in terms of economic development. The chapter provides insight into the Lisbon Strategy and the Europe 2020 Strategy as the EU answers to developmental challenges of the twenty-first century and their correlation with New Cohesion Policy 2007–2013 and EU Policy of Economic, Social and Territorial Cohesion 2014–2020. Pawlas concludes with some remarks regarding a new strategic agenda 2019–2024. Pawlas stresses the need for higher inclusiveness and sustainability of economic development, which can be achieved only if structural reforms and systemic institutional changes are implemented.

Keywords European economic integration · European Union · European development

1 Introduction

The European Union is an example of deep, multidimensional, and multilayered integration. It includes economic, social, and political elements. The integration process evolved over time both geographically, and concerning its scope and complexity. As a result, the first communities that were established by six West European countries transformed gradually into twenty-eight EU Member States since mid-2013.[1] As far as the depth of integration is concerned, the initial customs union changed through single market into economic and monetary union with some elements of political union.[2] Economic development was put in the center of integration processes in the

[1] Moussis (2007).

[2] Borowiec (2011), pp. 55–57.

I. Pawlas (✉)
University of Economics in Katowice, Katowice, Poland
e-mail: iwona.pawlas@ue.katowice.pl

D. Ramiro Troitiño et al. (eds.), *The EU in the 21st Century*,
https://doi.org/10.1007/978-3-030-38399-2_11

1950s already.[3] Later, its significance even was strengthened because both Southern enlargements (1981, 1986) and Eastern enlargements (2004, 2007, and 2013) resulted in widening the gap between the rich Member States and the poor ones.[4] Moreover, the integration process itself also caused the rise of disparities in economic development. Therefore, the European Communities and—later—the European Union had to respond to the challenges and introduce new policies, instruments, and actions devoted to the promotion of economic development.[5] The promotion of regionally balanced economic development lied in the center of common regional policy (introduced in 1988), which was later transformed into EU Policy of Economic, Social and Territorial Cohesion.[6] Structural funds served as financial instruments used mostly for stimulating socioeconomic development in convergence regions of the EU and—to some extent—in other more developed regions (European Regional Development Fund). It also promoted employment in those EU regions that were characterized by higher unemployment rates (European Social Fund), while Cohesion Fund (introduced in mid 1990s) focused on huge and costly investment projects in the area of transport infrastructure and environmental protection in poor EU Member States.[7] Additionally, the pace and direction of the world economy evolutions brought further challenges relating to economic development which the EU also had to face. Because of the process of tightening the relations between and among nations in the global economy, it is obvious that the situation and development opportunities of less-developed economies depend on the economic phenomena and processes in the leading economies. But also the situation of the wealthiest economies is—to some extent—dependent to the changes and economic condition of the least developed countries.

2 Economic Development—Theoretical Background

Economic categories of economic growth and economic development are connected with each other. Economic development, however, is much broader a category than economic growth. Economic growth focuses on quantitative changes, while economic development entails both quantitative changes and qualitative ones.[8] Economic growth is considered a single-dimensional category, while economic development is seen as a multidimensional one. Moreover, economic growth can be viewed both in short term and in long term, while the perspective of economic development is rather long term. Economic growth is defined as an increase in goods and services produced by an economy or a nation within a specific period of time (usually a year).

[3]Moussis (2007), pp. 24–25.

[4]Pawlas (2018), pp. 1162–1171.

[5]Troitiño (2017).

[6]Pietrzyk (2007).

[7]Dziembała (2013).

[8]Schiller (1991), p. 383.

Economic growth is reflected in real GDP rise. Economic growth is due to growth in inputs, such as labor and capital, and to improvements in technology. Economic growth results from the accumulation of factors of production, particularly capital, and from increased productivity.[9] Economic development can be defined as "the movement of an economy from agricultural activities using simple technology to the production of industrial products and a range of services using modern technology" or "the cumulative growth of per capita income, accompanied by structural and institutional changes."[10] According to Encyclopedia Britannica's definition, economic development is "the process whereby simple, low-income national economies are transformed into modern industrial economies."[11] Economic development includes socioeconomic transformations and changes aiming at economic welfare increase and higher standard of living of a population.[12] Increased income per capita and reduced poverty constitute crucial objectives of economic development. Furthermore, economic development should bring increased protection of natural environment, rise in life expectancy, increase of literacy and educational attainment of current and the future generations, better health, as well as more political freedom and civil liberties. Balcerowicz considered economic development as a key concept of contemporary economic policy and political economy and indicated that economic development should bring long-term, large-scale improvement of living standard.[13] According to the Princeton Encyclopedia of the World Economy, economic development involves three areas (not just increase in per capita income alone):

- Development of the economic system of the country—economic development is facilitated by structural changes, including urbanization, increase in the size of companies, relative decline in the importance of agricultural sector (both in employment and in GDP), rising significance of processing industry and service sector, geographical expansion of markets, and increased diversity of produced and traded products;
- Distribution of benefits resulting from economic growth, which should bring considerable reduction of poverty;
- Sustainable development, i.e., development that allows meeting the needs of current generations at a level that does not limit the possibility to meet the needs of the future generations.[14]

A number of forces—both economic factors and non-economic ones, including, determine economic development: population growth and demographic changes, investment and accumulation of physical capital, changes in human capital, as well as technical and technological advancement. Moreover, economic policy may stimulate the process of economic development, or it may create significant obstacles for

---

[9]Dornbusch et al. (2011), pp. 52–54.

[10]Little (1982), pp. 118–119. Compare: Swadźba (2013), pp. 146–150.

[11]Encyclopedia Britannica.

[12]Martín de la Guardia and Pérez Sánchez (2001).

[13]Balcerowicz (1995), p. 51.

[14]Reinert and Rajan (2009), pp. 277–280.

economic development.[15] As far as the role of economic policy in economic development process is concerned, one should underline wise monetary and fiscal policy, trade liberalization, financial liberalization, and foreign assistance.[16] Openness of a national economy constitutes another essential determinant of economic development: participation in international trade, inflow of capital in the form of foreign direct investment, engagement in the processes of regional economic integration, and involvement in the processes of globalization should be stressed here. Many experts underline that economic development should be characterized by durability, attention to social cohesion, and respect for natural environment.[17]

The concept of sustainable development entails three crucial dimensions, i.e., environmental sustainability, economic sustainability, and social sustainability. As far as environmental sustainability is concerned, development processes are supposed to be conducted along with the protection of natural environment and promotion of rational use of natural resources; therefore, environmentally sustainable development falls in line with preventing excessive use of nature rather than treating nature as an inexhaustible source of resources. Environmental sustainability of economic development can be achieved though the promotion of renewable sources of energy, increased effectiveness of raw materials' use, responsible use of water, as well as support for sustainable mobility. Economic sustainability of development constitutes the second dimension of sustainability concept. It is related to equal economic growth, based on responsible investment and equal distribution of economic resources, generating wealth for all (including future generations). The third dimension of sustainable development is social sustainability. The social dimension of sustainability relates to the development of societies, communities, and individuals; fair distribution of income, education and healthcare, as well as promotion of gender equality lie in the center of social sustainability of development.[18] The need for sustainable development was stressed by the UN in *Agenda 21* and adopted in 1992. Later, the UN repeatedly underlined the necessity for stronger actions toward sustainability of development. The UN Millennium Development Summit in 2000 adopted *The Millennium Development Goals,*[19] United Nations Conference on Sustainable Development in 2012 in Rio de Janeiro (Rio+20) resulted in the adoption of document *The Future We Want*[20] and UN Sustainable Development Summit in 2015 in New York ended up with the adoption of *Transforming Our World: the 2030 Agenda for Sustainable Development.*[21]

Global crisis 2008+ brought enormous increase of income and wealth inequalities both concerning international dimension of disparities and to internal disparities observed within national economies. This has led to an increase of popularity and

---

[15] Kerikmäe (2014).

[16] Rugman and Hodgetts (2003), p. 439.

[17] Piasecki (2003), Sachs (2013), Stiglitz (2004).

[18] Giddings et al. (2002).

[19] United Nations (2000).

[20] United Nations (2012).

[21] United Nations (2015).

further development of a concept of inclusive development. Inclusive development is multidimensional in its character. It includes the issues relating to basic needs and basic rights (How to define them? How to meet them? How to provide them?), allocation of resources, responsibilities and risks in a non-discriminatory way (According to what rules and principles should they be guided?), as well as wealth and well-being (How to promote wealth and wellbeing?). Inclusive development can also be described as a multidisciplinary concept, because economists, environmentalists, sociologists, lawyers, political scientists, anthropologists and engineers, develop it. Moreover, inclusive development concerns gender studies, as well. Pouw and Gupta[22] define inclusive development as "focusing on social wellbeing and protecting the ecosystem services of nature through redefining political priorities." World Economic Forum relates the dynamic development of inclusive growth and development model to common feeling of inadequate progress in standard of living combined with widened inequalities which contributed to polarization of societies after the global crisis 2008+ observed both in advanced economies and in emerging economies. Therefore, World Economic Forum experts indicate the need for strong involvement of structural economic policy actions accompanied with stronger institutions in order to achieve higher economic growth and wider social participation in the process of growth and in benefits resulting from economic growth. According to World Economic Forum, measuring inclusive growth and development should embrace a number of indices, and in particular: GDP per capita, labor employment, productivity, healthy life expectancy (i.e., economic and growth pillar of inclusive growth and development), median household income, poverty rate, income Gini, wealth Gini (i.e., inclusion pillar), and adjusted net savings, public debt as share of GDP, dependency ratio, and carbon intensity of GDP (i.e., intergenerational equity and sustainability pillar of inclusive growth and development).[23] Pouw and Gupta stress that social inequality results in the reduction of opportunities for enhancing human well-being, limiting resource base, and rising climate vulnerability of the excluded. They also indicate relationally as an important feature of inclusive development.[24] Corrado and Corrado point out to the significance inclusive financial markets (e.g., microfinance) for reducing poverty and enhancing inclusive socioeconomic development.[25] Pansera and Owen analyzed the specificity of inclusive innovation.[26] Grover indicated possible positive impact of corporate social responsibility on inclusive development.[27] Arts focused on human rights aspects of inclusive development.[28] Likoko and Kini concentrated on inclusiveness concerning business activity.[29] Correlation

[22]Pouw and Gupta (2017a), pp. 104–108. See also: Gupta et al. (2015), pp. 541–559.

[23]World Economic Forum (2018).

[24]Pouw and Gupta (2017b), pp. 96–103.

[25]Corrado and Corrado (2017), pp. 19–23.

[26]Pansera and Owen (2018), pp. 23–34.

[27]Grover (2014), pp. 103–108.

[28]Arts (2017), pp. 58–62.

[29]Likoko and Kini (2017), pp. 84–88.

between aging population and inclusive wealth lied in the center of research conducted by Yamaguchi.[30] Karar and Jacobs-Mata studied the barriers for and possible impact of inclusive governance.[31]

3 Economic Development as an Objective of the EU Integration—What Was Put in the Treaties?

Economic development has been considered one of the most essential objectives of integration processes from the very beginning. Therefore, statements regarding economic development have been included in the Treaties. Article 2 of the Treaty of Rome establishing European Economic Community stated: "... The Community shall have as its task ... to promote throughout the Community a harmonious development of economic activities, a continuous and balanced expansion, an increase in stability, an accelerated raising of the standard of living ...."[32]

Single European Act of 1986 focused on the problem of considerable disparities in socioeconomic development observed in mid 1980s.[33] In Title V Economic and Social Cohesion, in Article 130 A we could read: "In order to promote its overall harmonious development, the Community shall develop and pursue its actions leading to the strengthening of its economic and social cohesion. In particular the Community shall aim at reducing disparities between the various regions and the backwardness of the least-favored regions." Moreover, in Article 130 B they added: "The Community shall support the achievement of these objectives by the action it takes through the structural Funds (European Agricultural Guidance and Guarantee Fund, Guidance Section, European Social Fund, European Regional Development Fund), the European Investment Bank and the other existing financial instruments", while in Article 130 C the importance of the European Regional development Fund in the process of disparities reduction was stressed: "... The European Regional Development fund is intended to help redress the principal regional imbalances in the Community through participating in the development and structural adjustment of regions whose development is lagging behind and in the conversion of declining industrial regions." The significance of "... the economic and social development of the Community as a whole and the balanced development of its regions ..." was underlined once again in Article 130 Q.[34]

Treaty on European Union concluded in Maastricht in 1992 introduced a new version of Article 2, in which stronger accent was put on economic development. We could read here: "The Community shall have as its task, by establishing a common market and an economic and monetary union and by implementing the common

[30] Yamaguchi (2014), pp. 21–25.

[31] Karar and Jacobs-Mata (2016), pp. 15–22.

[32] The Treaty of Rome (1957), Article 2.

[33] Färber (2017).

[34] Single European Act (1987).

policies or activities referred to in Articles 3 and 3a, to promote throughout the Community a harmonious and balanced development of economic activities, sustainable and non-inflationary growth respecting the environment, a high degree of convergence of economic performance, a high level of employment and of social protection, the raising of the standard of living and quality of life, and economic and social cohesion and solidarity among Member States ....”[35] Moreover, in Article 103 they added: “In order to ensure sustained convergence of the economic performances of the Member States, the Council shall, on the basis of reports submitted by the Commission, monitor economic developments in each of the Member States and in the Community as well as the consistency of economic policies with the broad guidelines ... and regularly carry out an overall assessment.”[36]

In Amsterdam Treaty of 1997, in Part 1 Substantive Amendments, the Article 1 point 2 related to the following amendment of the Treaty on European Union, regarding the issue of development as an overall objective of the EU: “Determined to promote economic and social progress for their peoples, taking into account the principle of sustainable development and within the context of the accomplishment of the internal market and of reinforced cohesion and environmental protection, and to implement policies ensuring that advances in economic integration are accompanied by parallel progress in other fields ...”; moreover, in point 5 they added: the following construction of an objective of the EU: “... to promote economic and social progress and a high level of employment and to achieve balanced and sustainable development, in particular through the creation of an area without internal frontiers, through the strengthening of economic and social cohesion and through the establishment of economic and monetary union, ultimately including a single currency ....”[37]

According to the Treaty of Lisbon, in Article 2 of Treaty on the European Union should take the following form: “The EU ... shall work for the sustainable development of Europe based on balanced economic growth and price stability, a highly competitive social market economy, aiming at full employment and social progress, and a high level of protection and improvement of the quality of the environment. It shall promote scientific and technological advance. It shall combat social exclusion and discrimination ... It shall promote economic, social and territorial cohesion ....”[38] Moreover, Treaty of Lisbon added the amendment to article 163; according to the aforementioned amendment Article 163 took the following form: “The Union shall have the objective of strengthening its scientific and technological bases by achieving a European research area in which researchers, scientific knowledge and technology circulate freely, and encouraging it to become more competitive, including in its industry, while promoting all the research activities deemed necessary virtue of other Chapters of the Treaties.”[39]

---

[35]Treaty on European Union (1992).

[36]Ibidem.

[37]Treaty of Amsterdam Amending the Treaty on European Union, the Treaties Establishing the European Communities and Certain Related Acts (1997).

[38]The Treaty of Lisbon (2007).

[39]Ibidem.

4 Disparities in Economic Development as a Challenge for the EU in the Twenty-First Century

Disparities in economic development remain a challenge for the European Union in the twenty-first century. Figure one presents GDP per capita for EU28 according to purchasing parity standard (PPS) from 2004 to 2017, while Fig. 2 presents relative GDP per capita according to PPS with EU28 average amounting to 100 for the same period: maximum, minimum, median, as well as first quartile and third quartile have been shown on both figures. Moreover, Table 1 entails the information regarding the EU economics with the highest and lowest values of GDP per capita, as well as the average GDP per capita for the EU28 in each year in the analyzed period (Fig. 1).

The persistence of huge disparities is easily visible. The average GDP per capita PPS for EU28 increased from 22,500 in 2004 to 26,100 in 2007–2008, then—as a result of the global crisis it fell down to 24,500 in 2009. The next years brought gradual increase of GDP per capita PPS for the EU28 up to 30,000 in 2017. Unfortunately, disparities remained more or less the same. Luxembourg kept the position of the wealthiest EU Member State with GDP per capita PPS amounting to 54,200 in 2007 and to around 76,000 in 2016–2017, which represented 240% of the EU28 average in 2007 and 253% in 2017 (relative GDP per capita PPS for Luxembourg was the highest in 2014 when it represented 269% of the EU28 average). Romania was the poorest of all EU28 economies in 2004–2005, with GPD per capita PPS amounting to 7700 (2004) and 8300 (2005), which stood for 34–35% of the EU28 average only. From 2005 to 2017, Bulgaria's GDP per capita PPS was the lowest (it amounted to 9200 in 2006 and increased gradually to 14,800 in 2017). Despite this increase, however, in relative terms GDP per capita PPS in Bulgaria did not reach 50% of the EU28 average in the analyzed period of time (in 2017, it represented 49% of the EU28 average GDP per capita).

Regional disparities in economic development constitute another dimension of inequalities in the EU. Regional dispersion of regional GDP per capita PPS within the EU grew substantially with the entry of ten economies in 2004, followed by the accession of further two countries in 2007 and yet another one in 2013. The aforementioned regional disparities were not reduced despite the implementation of Common Regional Policy/EU Policy of Economic, Social and Territorial Cohesion (the financial instruments of which were directed mostly to the poor regions and poor countries). The list of wealthiest and poorest EU regions in 2017 is presented in Table 2. Regional GDP per capita PPS of North-West region in Bulgaria represented just 31% of EU28 average in 2017, while regional GDP per capita of the British region Inner London West stood for 626% of the EU28 average, i.e., over 20 times more.

Many experts stress the need for a more inclusive development. Therefore, it is important to diagnose and identify not only the disparities among EU economies on national and regional level, but also within the EU countries. Table 3 presents GINI index for EU28 economies.

Table 1 GDP per capita PPS

Specification	2004	2005	2006	2007	2008	2009	2010	2011	2012	2013	2014	2015	2016	2017
EU28	22,500	23,400	24,700	26,100	26,100	24,500	25,500	26,200	26,600	26,800	27,700	29,100	29,300	30,000
Maximum	54,200 (LU)	57,900 (LU)	64,500 (LU)	69,100 (LU)	68,400 (LU)	62,500 (LU)	65,400 (LU)	69,300 (LU)	69,200 (LU)	70,000 (LU)	74,400 (LU)	77,300 (LU)	76,200 (LU)	75,900 (LU)
Minimum	7700 (RO)	8300 (RO)	9200 (BU)	10,400 (BU)	11,100 (BU)	10,600 (BU)	11,200 (BU)	11,800 (BU)	12,200 (BU)	12,200 (BU)	12,900 (BU)	13,700 (BU)	14,200 (BU)	14,800 (BU)
EU28	100	100	100	100	100	100	100	100	100	100	100	100	100	100
Maximum	240 (LU)	247 (LU)	261 (LU)	265 (LU)	262 (LU)	255 (LU)	257 (LU)	265 (LU)	260 (LU)	261 (LU)	269 (LU)	266 (LU)	260 (LU)	253 (LU)
Minimum	34 (RO)	35 (RO)	37 (BU)	40 (BU)	43 (BU)	43 (BU)	44 (BU)	45 (BU)	46 (BU)	45 (BU)	47 (BU)	47 (BU)	48 (BU)	49 (BU)

Source EUROSTAT database

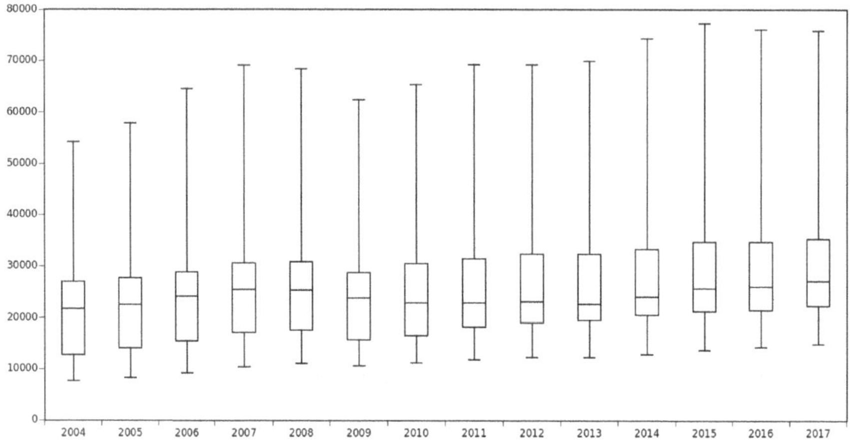

Fig. 1 GDP per capita (PPS). *Source* Own elaboration based on statistical information taken from EUROSTAT database

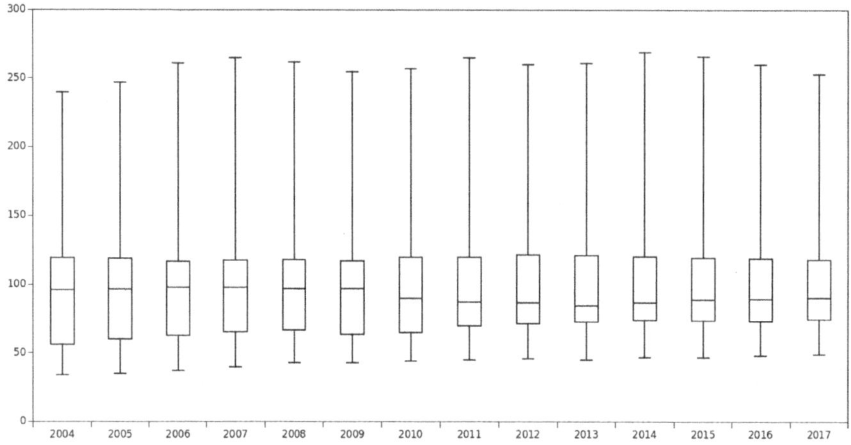

Fig. 2 GDP per capita PPS (EU28 = 100). *Source* Own elaboration based on statistical information taken from EUROSTAT database

Significant internal disparities can be noted for EU28 economies, though GINI index for every EU member economy was much lower than, e.g., for the USA (GINI for the US amounted to 41.5 in 2016).[40] Czech, Slovakia, and Slovenia constitute a trio of the EU Member States with the lowest internal GINI index (a bit over 26 in 2015). Moreover, a relatively low level of internal disparities is also characteristic for Denmark, Finland, Sweden, Belgium, and the Netherlands (GINI index amounted to less than 28 in 2015). On the other hand, Bulgaria, Greece, Portugal, and Romania with GINI index over 36 as well as Italy, Latvia, Lithuania, and Spain with GINI

[40]World Bank (2019).

Table 2 Regional GDP per capita in EU—wealthiest and poorest regions in 2017 (PPS, EU28 = 100)

21 wealthiest EU regions		20 poorest EU regions	
Region	Regional GDP per capita (PPS)	Region	Regional GDP per capita (PPS)
Inner London—West (UK)	626	North-West (BG)	31
Luxembourg (LU)	253	North-Central (BG)	34
Southern (IE)	220	Mayotte (FR)	34
Hamburg (DE)	202	South-Central (BG)	35
Brussels region (BE)	196	North-East (BG)	39
Eastern and Midland (IE)	189	North-East (RO)	39
Prague (CZ)	187	South-East (BG)	43
Bratislava (SK)	179	North Great Plain (HU)	43
Upper Bavaria (DE)	177	South Transdanubia (HU)	45
Ile-de-France (FR)	177	South-West Oltenia (RO)	45
Inner London—East (UK)	168	East Macedonia, Thrace (GR)	46
North Holland (NL)	167	North Hungary (HU)	46
Capital (region) (DK)	166	Epirus (GR)	48
Stockholm (SE)	166	North Aegean (GR)	48
Stuttgart (DE)	159	South Great Plain (HU)	48
Darmstadt (DE)	157	Lubelskie (PL)	48
Bremen (DE)	155	Western Greece (GR)	49
Utrecht (NL)	155	French Guiana (FR)	49
Warsaw-capital (PL)	152	Warmińsko-Mazurskie (PL)	49
Vienna (AT)	151	Podkarpackie (PL)	49
Salzburg (AT)	151		

Source EUROSTAT Newsrelease (2019)

index amounting to over 35 constituted a group of the EU Member States with a relatively high level of internal disparities.

The promotion of development requires strong long-term real GDP growth. Figure 3 presents real GDP growth in EU28 from 2007 to 2018: maximum, minimum, and median levels of real GDP growth, as well as first quartile and third quartile have been shown. Moreover, in Table 4, the average real GDP growth for the EU28

Table 3 GINI index for EU economies

Economy	2004	2007	2008	2009	2012	Last available year
Austria	29.8	30.6	30.4	31.5	30.5	30.5 (2015)
Belgium	30.5	29.2	28.4	28.5	27.5	27.7 (2015)
Bulgaria	l.d.	36.1	33.6	33.8	36.0	37.4 (2014)
Croatia	l.d.	l.d.	l.d.	32.6	32.5	31.1 (2015)
Cyprus	30.1	31.1	31.7	32.1	34.3	34.0 (2015)
Czechia	27.5	26.0	26.3	26.2	26.1	25.9 (2015)
Denmark	25.2	26.2	25.2	26.7	27.8	28.2 (2015)
Estonia	30.4	31.3	31.2	30.5	l.d.	31.7 (2015)
Finland	27.9	28.3	27.8	27.5	27.1	27.1 (2015)
France	30.6	32.4	33.0	32.7	33.1	32.7 (2015)
Germany	30.1	31.1	31.7	32.1	34.3	34.0 (2015)
Greece	33.6	34.0	33.6	33.6	36.2	36.0 (2015)
Hungary	29.9	27.9	27.5	27.0	30.2	30.4 (2015)
Ireland	33.6	31.9	30.9	32.7	33.2	31.8 (2015)
Italy	34.3	32.9	33.8	33.8	35.2	35.4 (2015)
Latvia	36.4	37.5	37.2	35.9	35.2	34.2 (2015)
Lithuania	37.0	34.8	35.7	37.2	35.1	37.4 (2015)
Luxembourg	30.2	31.1	32.6	31.2	34.3	33.8 (2015)
Malta	l.d.	29.2	29.0	30.2	29.4	29.4 (2015)
Netherlands	29.8	29.6	29.3	27.9	27.7	28.2 (2015)
Poland	35.4	33.5	33.7	33.6	32.4	31.8 (2015)
Portugal	38.9	36.7	36.6	34.9	36.0	35.5 (2015)
Romania	l.d.	37.5	36.4	35.6	36.5	35.9 (2015)
Slovakia	27.1	24.7	26.0	27.2	26.1	26.5 (2015)
Slovenia	24.8	24.4	23.7	24.8	26.2	25.4 (2015)
Spain	32.6	34.1	34.2	34.9	35.4	36.2 (2015)
Sweden	26.1	27.1	28.1	27.3	27.6	29.2 (2015)
United Kingdom	36.0	35.7	34.1	34.3	32.3	33.2 (2015)

Source World Bank (2019)

as well as the EU economies with maximum and minimum real GDP growth were shown.

In the analyzed period, real GDP growth rate for EU28 ranged from minus 4.3% in 2009 (the crisis year) to 2.5% in 2017. In each year, the differences in real GDP growth rates among EU economies were significant, e.g., in the aforementioned crisis year, 2009 real GDP growth rate in Poland amounted to 2.8%, while in Estonia it equaled minus 14.8% and in 2015, real GDP growth rate in Ireland reached 25.1%, while in Greece it amounted to minus 0.4%. The situation of Greece has been most

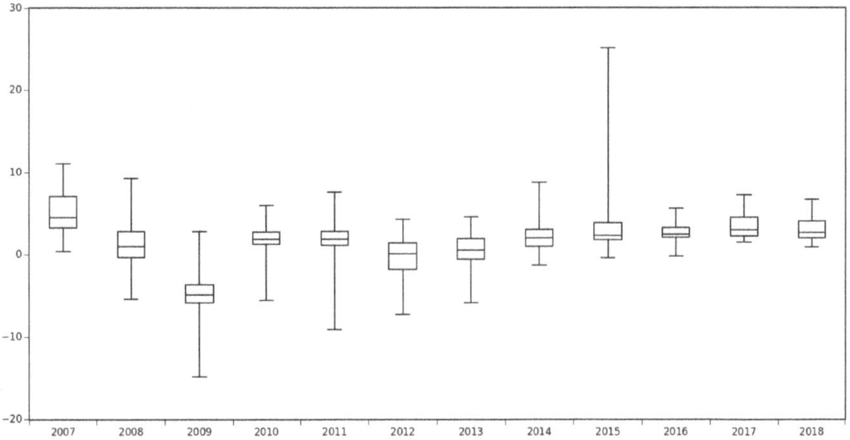

Fig. 3 Real GDP growth in EU—maximum, minimum, median, 1st quartile, and 3rd quartile (%). *Source* Own elaboration based on statistical information taken from EUROSTAT database

problematic (the Greek economy experienced fall in real GDP in seven years out of twelve analyzed years; six times real GDP growth rate for Greece was the lowest of all EU28 economies). When it comes to the Irish economy, its situation was quite complicated. Ireland experienced considerable reduction of real GDP in the crisis years 2008–2009[41] (by 4.4% and 5% respectively). Successive years, however, brought rise in real GDP, especially successful was the period 2013–2017 with real GDP growths amounting on average to 10.56% and ranging from 5% in 2015 to 25.1% in 2014.

5 The Twenty-First Century and EU Attempts to Promote Economic Development

5.1 The Lisbon Strategy

The Lisbon Strategy was adopted in 2000. It was a development plan for the economy of the European Union for the 1st decade of the twenty-first century. The Lisbon Strategy was an attempt of the European Union to address the challenges resulting from globalization and the emergence of a new knowledge-driven economy. M. J. Rodriguez played an important role in the process of the Lisbon Strategy formulation. The main aim of the Lisbon Strategy was to transform the European Union into the most competitive and dynamic knowledge-based economy in the world. The crucial intention of the Lisbon Strategy was to deal with low productivity and stagnation of

[41] Troitiño et al. (2018).

Table 4 Real GDP growth (%)

Specification	2007	2008	2009	2010	2011	2012	2013	2014	2015	2016	2017	2018
EU28	3.1	0.5	−4.3	2.1	1.8	−0.4	0.3	1.8	2.3	2.0	2.5	2.0
Maximum	11.1 (LT)	9.3 (RO)	2.8 (PL)	6.0 (SE)	7.6 (EE)	4.3 (EE)	4.6 (MT)	8.8 (IE)	25.1 (IE)	5.6 (MT)	7.2 (IE)	6.7 (IE)
Median	4.55	1.0	−4.85	1.85	1.85	0.1	0.55	2.05	2.3	2.45	2.95	2.7
Minimum	0.4 (HU)	−5.4 (EE)	−14.8 (EE)	−5.5 (GR)	−9.1 (GR)	−7.3 (GR)	−5.8 (CY)	−1.3 (CY)	−0.4 (GR)	−0.2 (GR)	1.5 (GR)	0.9 (IT)

Source EUROSTAT database. https://ec.europa.eu/eurostat/tgm/table.do?tab=table&init=1&language=en&pcode=tec00115&plugin=1

economic growth in the European Union. The concepts of innovation and knowledge-based economy (in other words, knowledge economy or learning economy) served as the bases for the Lisbon Strategy. At the time of its creation, the Lisbon Strategy was based on two pillars: economic one and social one. In 2001, the decision was made to introduce the third pillar, i.e., the environmental dimension.[42] Unfortunately, the Lisbon Strategy goals were not achieved. The Lisbon Strategy's targets were truly ambitious, but there were no efficient tools created for their achievement.[43] The failure of the Lisbon Strategy was partly due to the global crisis 2008+ and it partly stemmed from Eastern enlargement of the EU (with the access of more than ten relatively poor economies characterized by lower level of socioeconomic development that EU15 countries, it was even more difficult to try to obtain satisfying results).[44]

The stress placed on competitiveness, innovativeness, research and development activity in the Lisbon Strategy, as well as the Eastern enlargement of the EU resulted in changes introduced in the New Cohesion Policy 2007–2013. The following three priorities were realized in the period 2007–2013: I. Convergence, II. Regional Competitiveness and Employment, and III. European Territorial Cooperation. The use of both structural funds (European Regional Development Fund and European Social Fund) and Cohesion Fund had to fall in line with the priorities of the EU included in the Lisbon Strategy, namely the promotion of competitiveness and creation of jobs. At least 60% of the expenditure on the convergence objective and at least 75% of the spending on the regional competitiveness and employment objective had to be assigned to the aforementioned priorities.[45]

5.2 The Europe 2020 Strategy

The Europe 2020 Strategy served as the basis for EU policies for the years 2010–2020.[46] It was created due to the failure of the Lisbon Strategy. Moreover, the EU had to face new challenges caused partly by the implications of the global financial crisis 2008+. It was, therefore, necessary to redirect the activity of the EU and its Member States in order to promote economic development and meet the challenges of the twenty-first century.[47] The Europe 2020 Strategy was much more complex than the Lisbon Strategy. It focused on three priorities: I. Smart growth, II. Sustainable growth, and III. Inclusive growth.[48] Smart growth priority aimed at developing an economy based on knowledge and innovation. Sustainable growth priority stressed

[42] European Council (2000).

[43] Dyduch et al. (2012), p. 8.

[44] European Parliament (2010).

[45] European Commission (2007).

[46] Pawlas (2019), pp. 327–343.

[47] Hamulák (2018).

[48] European Commission 2010.

the need for stronger promotion of sustainable development of the EU economy. The target of the second priority of the Europe 2020 Strategy was to transform the EU economy into green and resource-efficient economy. The third priority of the Europe 2020 Strategy, i.e., inclusive growth, underlined the need for social inclusion, in order to fight poverty and social exclusion through both higher employability and social and territorial cohesion.[49]

The aforementioned three priorities were transmitted into several measurable targets, namely:

- 75% of the population aged 20–64 should be employed;
- 3% of the EU's GDP should be invested in R&D;
- greenhouse gases emissions should be reduced by 20% compared to 1990 level;
- the share of renewable energy should constitute 20% of final energy consumption in the EU;
- energy efficiency should be increased by 20%;
- the share of early school leavers should be reduced below 10%;
- at least 40% of the younger generation (people aged 30–34 in 2020) should have a tertiary degree;
- The number of people at risk of poverty or social exclusion should be reduced by 20 million.[50]

Due to the significance of the Europe 2020 Strategy and its complexity, all EU institutions had to be engaged in the process of its implementation (the European Commission, the European Parliament, the Council of the EU, the European Council, the European Economic and Social Committee, and the Committee of the Regions). Moreover, it was necessary to get real engagement of EU Member States on national, regional, and local levels in its realization process. The implementation of the Europe 2020 Strategy's targets was supported by EU budgetary sources and by the financial means of European Investment Bank (since 2015 especially through European Fund for Strategic Investment).[51] The introduction of seven flagship initiatives was supposed to help in the process of achieving the targets. The following flagship initiatives were introduced: "Innovation Union," "Youth on the move," "A digital agenda for Europe," "Resource efficient Europe," "An industrial policy for the globalization era," "An agenda for new skills and jobs," and "European platform against poverty." The "Innovation Union" flagship initiative aimed at strengthening R&D and innovation activity. The flagship initiative "Youth on the move" concentrated on enhancing the performance of education systems and facilitating the entry of the young to the labor market at the post-crisis time. The crucial objective of the flagship initiative "A digital agenda for Europe" was to broaden access to high-speed Internet and to facilitate the creation of a digital single market. The flagship initiative "Resource efficient Europe" was built in order to support the shift toward a low carbon economy, increase the use of renewable energy sources, modernize transport sector, and promote efficient

[49] Ibidem.

[50] Ibidem.

[51] European Commission (2019).

use of energy.[52] "An industrial policy for the globalization era" aimed at improving the business environment and supporting developing sustainable industrial base. The flagship initiative "An agenda for new skills and jobs" was supposed to promote lifelong education, labor mobility, as well as modernization of labor markets. Finally, yet importantly, the flagship initiative "European platform against poverty" concentrated on ensuring social and territorial cohesion, which should result in the reduction of social exclusion.[53]

Having in mind the recent changes in the world economy and understanding the necessity to respond to them, the European Commission adopted *A new European Consensus on Development* as part of the EU's development policy which plays an important role in the implementation of the *2030 Agenda*. A new *European Consensus on Development* is holistic in its character. It fully reflects the *2030 Agenda*. The European Commission treated the *2030 Agenda* as universal, i.e., applying to all countries, including all EU Member States. The European Commission stressed that the new *European Consensus on Development* was a key element of the EU response to the challenges. Moreover, the European Commission underlined that the EU had to act united (strong cooperation of the EU and all EU Member States is of vital importance[54]) in order to achieve the common objectives and make the biggest contribution to the *2030 Agenda*. Therefore, the development action of the EU and its Member States should be built around the priorities of the *2030 Agenda*, namely: people (human development and dignity), planet (protecting the environment, managing natural resources, and tackling climate change), prosperity (inclusive and sustainable growth and jobs), peace (peaceful and inclusive societies, democracy, effective and accountable institutions, and rule of law and human rights for all), and partnership (fostering stronger, more inclusive multi-stakeholder partnerships, the development partnerships reflecting capacities and needs).[55]

Tables 5, 6, 7, and 8 present the starting point for the implementation of Europe 2020 Strategy, national targets, as well as the so far implementation of the Europe 2020 Strategy regarding the achievement of its targets.

Well-functioning educational system is considered an essential determinant of economic development. Better-educated society was put in the center of the 1st Priority and the 3rd Priority of the Europe 2020 Strategy. The EU Member States aimed at reducing school drop-out rates and to promoting higher education (tertiary education). Because of considerable disparities among the EU Member States, national targets regarding early school drop-out rates differed a lot: from 4% in Croatia and 4.5% in Poland to 16% in Italy and 15% in Spain. From 2010 to 2018, school drop-out rate was reduced by 3.3% points, which means the EU did not manage to achieve the goal though the distance to the target amounted to just 0.6% point in 2018. Fourteen EU Member States achieved the target in 2018. Considerable surpluses over the national targets were noted in Greece (plus 5.1% points), Luxembourg (plus 3.6%), Lithuania

[52] Castro and Lago (2018).

[53] European Parliament (2012).

[54] Kerikmäe et al. (2019).

[55] European Commission (2016).

Table 5 Early school leavers and tertiary education

Economy	Early school leavers						Tertiary education					
	2010	2018	Target	2010–2018 change	Distance to target (−)/surplus over target (+)	Target achieved	2010	2018	Target	2010–2018 change	Distance to target (−)/surplus over target (+)	Target achieved
EU28	13.9	10.6	10.0	−3.3	−0.6		33.8	40.5	40	6.7	0.5	X
Austria	8.3	7.2	9.5↑	−1.1	2.3	X	23.4	40.7	38↓	17.3	2.7	X
Belgium	11.9	8.6	9.5↑	−3.3	0.9	X	44.4	46.9	47↑	2.5	−0.1	
Bulgaria	12.6	12.4	11.0↓	−0.2	−1.4		28.0	33.7	36↓	5.7	−2.3	
Croatia	5.2	3.1	4.0↑	−2.1	0.9	X	24.5	32.5	35↓	8.0	−2.5	
Cyprus	12.7	7.9	10.0	−4.8	2.1	X	45.3	57.1	46↑	11.8	11.1	X
Czechia	4.9	6.4	5.5↑	1.5	−0.9		20.4	33.5	32↓	13.1	1.5	X
Denmark	11.0	9.8	10.0	−1.2	0.2	X	41.2	48.8	40	7.6	8.8	X
Germany	11.8	10.4	10.0	−1.4	−0.4		29.7	34.8	42↑	5.1	−7.2	
Estonia	11.0	11.5	9.5↑	0.5	−2.0		40.2	47.6	40	7.4	7.6	X
Finland	10.3	8.4	8.0↑	−1.9	−0.4		45.7	44.0	42↑	−1.7	2.0	X
France	12.7	9.0	9.5↑	−3.7	0.5	X	43.2	45.5	50↑	2.3	−4.5	
Greece	13.5	4.9	10.0	−8.6	5.1	X	28.6	44.4	32↓	15.8	12.4	X
Hungary	10.8	12.4	10.0	1.6	−2.4		26.1	33.4	34↓	7.3	−0.6	
Ireland	11.9	4.7	8.0↑	−7.2	3.3	X	51.4	55.4	60↑	4.0	−4.6	
Italy	18.6	14.5	16.0↓	−4.1	1.5	X	19.9	27.9	26↓	8.0	1.9	X
Latvia	12.9	8.0	10.0	−4.9	2.0	X	32.6	42.8	34↓	10.2	8.8	X

(continued)

Table 5 (continued)

Economy	Early school leavers						Tertiary education					
	2010	2018	Target	2010–2018 change	Distance to target (−)/surplus over target (+)	Target achieved	2010	2018	Target	2010–2018 change	Distance to target (−)/surplus over target (+)	Target achieved
Lithuania	7.9	4.8	9.0↑	−3.1	4.2	X	43.8	57.6	48.7↑	13.8	8.9	X
Luxembourg	7.1	6.4	10.0	−0.7	3.6	X	46.1	54.7	66↑	8.6	−11.3	
Malta	23.8	17.5	10.0	−6.3	−7.5		22.1	33.9	33↓	11.8	0.9	X
Netherlands	10.1	7.4	8.0↑	−2.7	0.6	X	41.4	49.2	40	7.8	9.2	X
Poland	5.4	4.7	4.5↑	−0.7	−0.2		34.8	45.5	45↑	10.7	0.5	X
Portugal	28.3	12.0	10.0	−16.3	−2.0		24.0	33.1	40	9.1	−6.9	
Romania	19.3	16.9	11.3↓	−2.4	−5.6		18.3	24.9	26.7↓	6.6	−1.8	
Slovakia	4.7	9.1	6.0↑	4.4	−3.1		22.1	36.8	40	14.1	−3.2	
Slovenia	5.0	4.0	5.0↑	−1.0	1.0	X	34.8	43.5	40	8.7	3.5	X
Spain	28.2	18.3	15.0↓	−9.9	−3.3		42.0	41.9	44↑	−0.1	−2.1	
Sweden	6.5	8.7	7.0↑	2.2	−1.7		45.3	52.2	45↑	6.9	7.2	X
United Kingdom	14.8	10.6	l. d.	l. d.	l. d.		43.1	48.9	l. d.	5.8	l. d.	

Source Own elaboration based on information from EUROSTAT database

Table 6 Employment rate and R&D expenditure

Economy	Employment rate age group 20–64 years (%)						R&D expenditure (% GDP)					
	2010	2017	Target	2010–2017 Change	Distance to target (−)/surplus over target (+)	Target achieved	2010	2017	Target	2010–2017 change	Distance to target (−)/surplus over target (+)	Target achieved
EU28	68.6	72.2	75	3.6	−2.8		1.92	2.06	3.0	0.14	−0.94	
Austria	73.9	75.4	77↑	1.5	−1.6		2.73	3.16	3.76↑	0.43	−0.60	
Belgium	67.6	68.5	73.2↓	0.9	−4.7		2.05	2.58	3.0	0.53	−0.42	
Bulgaria	64.7	71.3	76↑	6.6	−8.3		0.56	0.75	1.5↓	0.19	−0.75	
Croatia	62.1	63.6	62.9↓	1.5	0.7	X	0.74	0.86	1.4↓	0.12	−0.54	
Cyprus	75.0	70.8	75	−4.2	−4.2		0.45	0.56	0.5↓	0.11	0.06	
Czechia	70.4	78.5	75	8.1	3.5	X	1.34	1.79	1.0↓	0.45	0.79	X
Denmark	75.8	76.9	80↑	1.1	−3.1		2.92	3.05	3.0	0.13	0.05	X
Germany	75.0	79.2	77↑	4.2	2.2	X	1.58	1.29	3.0	−0.29	−1.71	
Estonia	66.8	78.7	76↑	11.9	2.7	X	3.73	2.76	4.0↑	−0.97	−1.24	
Finland	73.0	74.2	78↑	1.2	−3.8		2.18	2.19	3.0	0.01	−0.81	
France	l. d.	70.6	75	l. d.	−4.4		2.71	3.02	3.0	0.31	0.02	X
Greece	63.8	57.8	70	−6.0	−12.2		0.60	1.13	1.2↓	0.53	−0.07	
Hungary	59.9	73.3	75	13.4	−1.5		1.14	1.35	1.8↓	0.21	−0.45	
Ireland	65.5	73.0	69↓	7.5	4.0	X	1.59	1.05	2.0↓	−0.54	−0.95	
Italy	61.0	62.3	67↓	1.3	−4.7		1.22	1.35	1.53↓	0.13	−0.18	
Latvia	64.3	74.8	73↓	10.5	1.8	X	0.61	0.51	1.5↓	−0.10	−0.99	

(continued)

Table 6 (continued)

Economy	Employment rate age group 20–64 years (%)						R&D expenditure (% GDP)					
	2010	2017	Target	2010–2017 Change	Distance to target (−)/surplus over target (+)	Target achieved	2010	2017	Target	2010–2017 change	Distance to target (−)/surplus over target (+)	Target achieved
Lithuania	64.3	76.0	72.8↓	11.3	3.2	X	0.78	0.89	1.9↓	0.11	−1.01	
Luxembourg	70.7	71.5	73↓	0.8	−1.5		1.50	1.26	2.3↓	−0.24	−1.04	
Malta	60.1	73.0	70↓	12.9	3.0	X	0.61	0.54	2.0↓	−0.07	−1.46	
Netherlands	76.8	78.0	80↑	1.2	−2.0		1.70	1.99	2.5↓	0.29	−0.51	
Poland	64.3	70.9	71↓	6.6	−0.1		0.72	1.03	1.7↓	0.31	−0.67	
Portugal	70.3	73.4	75	3.1	−1.6		1.53	1.33	2.7↓	−0.2	−1.37	
Romania	64.8	68.8	70↓	4.0	−1.2		0.46	0.50	2.0↓	0.04	−1.50	
Slovakia	64.6	71.1	72↓	6.5	−0.9		0.62	0.88	1.2↓	0.26	−0.32	
Slovenia	70.3	73.4	75	3.1	−1.6		2.06	1.86	3.0	−0.20	−1.14	
Spain	62.8	65.5	74↓	2.7	−8.5		1.35	1.20	2.0↓	−0.15	−0.80	
Sweden	78.1	81.8	80↑	3.7	1.8	X	3.21	3.40	4.0↑	0.19	−0.60	
United Kingdom	73.5	78.2	l. d.	l. d.	l. d.		1.66	1.66	l. d.	0.00	l. d.	

Source Own elaboration based on information from EUROSTAT database

Table 7 Renewable energy and greenhouse gas emissions

	Share of renewable energy sources in final energy consumption (%)						Greenhouse gas emissions (1990 = 100)			
Economy	2010	2016	Target	2010–2016 change	Distance to target (−)/surplus over target (+)	Target achieved	2010	2016	2010–2016 change	Target achieved
EU28	12.9	17.0	20	4.1	−3.0		85.83	77.64	−8.19	X
Austria	30.2	33.5	34↑	3.3	−0.5		109.32	103.06	−6.26	
Belgium	5.7	8.7	13↓	3.0	−4.3		91.41	81.53	−9.88	
Bulgaria	14.1	18.8	16↓	4.7	2.8	X	58.31	57.02	−1.29	X
Croatia	25.1	28.3	20	3.2	8.3	X	87.31	76.19	−11.12	X
Cyprus	6.0	9.3	13↓	3.3	−3.7		162.37	152.92	−9.45	
Czechia	10.5	14.9	13↓	4.4	1.9	X	70.71	65.62	−5.09	X
Denmark	22.1	32.2	30↑	10.1	2.2	X	91.15	73.91	−17.24	X
Estonia	24.6	28.8	25↑	4.2	3.8	X	52.45	48.62	−3.83	X
Finland	32.4	38.7	38↑	6.3	0.7	X	106.74	84.03	−22.71	
France	12.7	16.0	23↑	3.3	−7.0		95.08	85.64	−9.44	
Germany	10.5	14.8	18↓	4.3	−3.2		76.52	74.05	−2.47	X
Greece	9.8	15.2	18↓	5.4	−2.8		114.56	89.69	−24.87	
Hungary	12.7	14.2	13↓	1.5	1.2	X	70.06	65.82	−4.24	X
Ireland	5.7	9.5	16↓	3.8	−6.5		112.37	113.42	1.05	
Italy	13.0	17.4	17↓	4.4	0.4	X	98.12	83.85	−14.27	
Latvia	30.4	37.2	40↑	6.8	−2.8		47.77	43.77	−4.00	X
Lithuania	19.6	25.6	23↑	6.0	2.6	X	42.99	42.00	−0.99	X

(continued)

Table 7 (continued)

	Share of renewable energy sources in final energy consumption (%)						Greenhouse gas emissions (1990 = 100)			
Economy	2010	2016	Target	2010–2016 change	Distance to target (−)/surplus over target (+)	Target achieved	2010	2016	2010–2016 change	Target achieved
Luxembourg	2.9	5.4	11↓	2.5	−5.6		101.99	87.53	−14.46	
Malta	1.0	6.0	10↓	5.0	−4.0		142.32	99.42	−42.9	
Netherlands	3.9	6.0	14↓	2.1	−8.0		99.02	91.63	−7.39	
Poland	9.3	11.3	15↓	2.0	−3.7		87.07	85.03	−2.04	
Portugal	24.2	28.5	31↑	4.3	−2.5		118.41	115.77	−2.64	
Romania	23.4	25.0	24↑	1.6	1.0	X	49.56	45.82	−3.74	X
Slovakia	9.1	12.0	14↓	2.9	−2.0		62.65	55.63	−7.02	X
Slovenia	20.4	21.3	25↑	0.9	−3.7		105.68	95.19	−10.49	
Spain	13.8	17.3	20	3.5	−2.7		125.92	116.43	−9.49	
Sweden	47.2	53.8	49↑	6.6	4.8	X	91.32	76.1	−15.22	X
United Kingdom	3.7	9.3	15↓	5.6	−5.7		79.26	63.64	−15.62	X

Source Own elaboration based on information from EUROSTAT database

Table 8 People at risk of poverty or social exclusion (thousand)[a]

Economy	2010	2011	2012	2013	2014	2015	2016	2017	2010–2017 Change
EU28	117,907	120,858	123,774	122,849	122,026	119,049	118,040	112,978	−4929
Belgium	2235	2271	2356	2286	2339	2336	2335	2296	61
Bulgaria	3719	3693	3621	3493	2909	2982	2890	2767	−952
Czechia	1495	1598	1580	1508	1532	1444	1375	1267	−228
Denmark	1007	969	965	1025	1006	999	951	980	−27
Germany	15,962	16,074	15,909	16,212	16,508	16,083	16,035	15,516	−446
Estonia	289	307	311	313	338	315	318	305	16
Ireland	1220	1319	1392	1377	1279	1207	1135	1088	−132
Greece	3031	3403	3795	3904	3885	3829	3789	3702	671
Spain	12,029	12,363	12,628	12,630	13,402	13,175	12,827	12,236	207
France	11,712	11,840	11,760	11,245	11,540	11,048	11,463	10,771	−941
Croatia	1322	1384	1384	1271	1243	1216	1159	1085	−237
Italy	14,891	16,858	17,975	17,229	17,146	17,469	18,137	17,407	2516
Cyprus	202	207	234	240	234	244	234	215	13
Latvia	798	821	731	702	645	606	554	544	−254
Lithuania	1068	1011	975	917	804	857	871	843	−225
Luxembourg	83	84	95	96	96	95	114	126	43
Hungary	2948	3093	3272	3398	3097	2735	2541	2465	−483
Malta	86	90	94	102	101	99	90	87	1
Netherlands	2483	2598	2492	2648	2751	2744	2797	2864	381
Austria	1566	1593	1542	1572	1609	1551	1542	1563	−3

(continued)

Table 8 (continued)

Economy	2010	2011	2012	2013	2014	2015	2016	2017	2010–2017 Change
Poland	10,409	10,196	10,128	9748	9337	8761	8221	7273	−3136
Portugal	2693	2601	2667	2879	2863	2765	2595	2399	−294
Romania	8425	8265	8673	8392	8043	7435	7694	7040	−1385
Slovenia	366	386	392	410	410	385	371	345	−21
Slovakia	1118	1112	1109	1070	960	963	950	856	−262
Finland	890	949	916	854	927	904	896	849	−41
Sweden	1648	1730	1679	1748	1752	1813	1799	1765	117
United Kingdom	14,211	14,044	15,099	15,586	15,271	14,997	14,359	14,325	114

[a]Maximum for a country underlined
Source EUROSTAT database

(plus 4.2% points), and Ireland (plus 3.3% points). In six EU Member States, the school drop-out rate was reduced below 5% level in 2018 (Ireland (4.7%), Greece (4.9%), Lithuania (4.8%), Croatia (3.1%), Slovenia (4.0%), and Poland (4.7%).

Considerable disparities regarding the tertiary education in EU Member States were reflected in targets included in the Europe 2020 Strategy and in the so far implementation process. The tertiary education targets were higher than for the EU as whole in the case of eleven EU Member States, while in the case of ten EU Member States, they were lower than for the EU as a whole. The tertiary education targets ranged from only 26% in Italy and 26.7% in Romania to 66% in Luxemburg and 60% in Ireland. In 2018, the tertiary education targets were achieved by fifteen EU Member States and by the EU as a whole. In 2018, tertiary education attainment levels ranged from just 24.6% in Romania to over 57% were observed in Cyprus and Lithuania. Moreover, it should be underlined here that Austria significantly increased tertiary education attainment level by as much as 17.3% points up to 40.7%: it was the highest advancement regarding the tertiary education target of all EU Member States.

The adopted national targets regarding employment rate ranged from 62.9% for Croatia and 67% for Italy to 80% for Denmark, the Netherlands, and Sweden. In 2017, nine EU member States completed the employment goals only, and in particular by three old EU Member States (Germany, Sweden, and Ireland) and six new EU Member States (Czech Republic, Estonia, Croatia, Latvia, Lithuania, and Malta). Therefore, in the analyzed period, the EU as a whole did not meet the employment objective. The highest distance to the employment target in 2017 was noted in Greece (minus 12.2%), Spain (minus 8.5%), and Bulgaria (minus 8.3%).

National R&D targets ranged significantly, too: from only 0.5% GDP in Malta to as much as 3.76% GDP in Austria) and 4% GDP in the case of Finland and Sweden. In 2017, only three EU Member States (Denmark, Germany, and Czech Republic) completed R&D goals. Therefore, the implementation of the R&D target for the EU in the analyzed period was far from satisfactory: GERD increased from 1.92% GDP to 2.06%, which means that in 2017, there was still a considerable distance to the R&D target amounting to 0.94% GDP. Even though Sweden, Austria, and Finland did not meet the goals then, relatively high levels of GERD in those economies (as compared to other EU Member States) should be underlined here (3.40% GDP, 3.16% GDP, and 2.76% GDP, respectively). Furthermore, it is of vital importance to indicate that because of the fact that the R&D target for the EU amounting to 3% GDP was set already in the Lisbon Strategy with 2010 as the initial deadline for its achievement, the existing level of GERD in the EU in 2017 was even more disappointing. It did express the weakness of the EU and its low potential for creating higher innovativeness and higher competitiveness.

There were significant disparities regarding ecological sustainability of development among EU Member States. National targets relating to the share of renewable energy sources in final energy consumption ranged from 10% in Malta and 11% in Luxembourg to 49% in Sweden and 40% in Latvia. In the case of fifteen EU Member States, national targets regarding renewable energy sources in final energy consumption were set below the EU target, while for eleven EU Member States, the national targets levels were above the EU target. Ten EU Member States achieved the target relating to the share of renewable energy sources in final energy consumption in 2016, while eighteen EU Member States were still far from meeting the challenge regarding renewable energy sources' usage. The biggest advancement between 2010 and 2016 was noted in Denmark (in 2010, renewable energy sources accounted for 22.1% of final energy consumption in Denmark, while in 2016, they stood for 32.2%, i.e., 2.2% points over the target set for Denmark). In 2016, the highest share of renewable energy sources in final energy consumption was observed in Sweden (53.8%) and the lowest one amounting to 6% was noted in Malta and in the Netherlands. On the EU level, an increase of the share of renewable energy sources in final energy consumption from 12.9% in 2010 to 17% in 2016 occurred. Therefore, the distance to the target was reduced to 3.0% points in 2016.

Another element of ecological sustainability is the reduction of greenhouse gases emissions. The EU goal to reduce the level of greenhouse gases emissions by 20% in comparison to the 1990 level adopted in 2010 was completed in 2016. It was possible thanks to the achievement of the target by thirteen EU Member States; unfortunately, the remaining fifteen EU Member States did not reach the goals in the analyzed period. The persistence of extremely big differences among the EU Member States concerning the level of greenhouse gases emissions should be underlined here: In 2016, greenhouse gases emissions ranged from 42% of the 1990 level in Lithuania to almost 153% of the 1990 level in Cyprus.

Promoting inclusiveness of economic development means that the process of economic development of the EU should result in reducing social exclusion and poverty. The EU goal to reduce the number of people at risk of poverty or social exclusion by 20 million was not met between 2020 and 2017, reducing it by 4.93 million people. In 2017, still almost 113 million EU citizens were considered to be endangered with poverty or social exclusion. Moreover, in the case of Belgium, Estonia, Greece, Spain, Italy, Cyprus, Luxembourg, the Netherlands, Sweden, and United Kingdom, the number of people at risk of poverty or social exclusion in 2017 was higher than in 2010 (especially problematic was the situation in Italy, where this number increased by over 2.5 million).

EU Policy of Economic, Social and Territorial Cohesion 2014–2020 fully falls in line with the Europe 2020 Strategy. According to the agreed Multiannual Financial Framework 2014–2020, 33% of total EU funds (EUR 351.8 billion) will be spent on EU Policy of Economic, Social and Territorial Cohesion. According to the concentration principle, the majority of funds will be invested in the lagging behind regions, i.e., the ones with GDP per capita lower than 75% of the EU average. But even more developed regions will also get some financial assistance from the EU budget for further development. Out of almost EUR 352 billion designed for EU Policy of Economic, Social and Territorial Cohesion 2014–2020, over EUR 182 billion (52%) will be invested in less-developed regions. Eleven thematic objectives (fully connected with three priorities of the Europe 2020 Strategy) were developed. The following objectives were adopted: I. Research and development, II. Information and communication technologies, III. Competitiveness of small and medium enterprises, IV. Low carbon economy, V. Combating climate change, VI. Environment and resource efficiency, VII. Sustainable transport, VIII. Employment and mobility, IX. Social inclusion, X. Better education and training, and XII. Better public administration. In order to stronger promote inclusive development, the role of European Social Fund (ESF) was strengthened: ESF is to account for at least 23.1% of Cohesion Policy 2014–2020. Moreover, at least 20% of ESF resources in every EU Member State are to be spent on social inclusion, fight against poverty, and any form of discrimination.[56] Undoubtedly, EU Policy of Economic, Social and Territorial Cohesion should be perceived as an important EU instrument of promoting economic development.

Considerable disparities in socioeconomic development among the EU Member States are reflected in differences in their international competitiveness. Table 9 presents competitive positions of EU economies from 2007 to 2019. In 2007, four EU economies were positioned among the top ten most competitive economies in the world (Luxembourg was classified on the 4th place, Denmark took the 5th position, the Netherlands occupied the 8th place, and Sweden was positioned on the 9th place). In 2019, the Netherlands, Ireland, Denmark, and Sweden were considered the most competitive EU economies with the positions 6th–9th in the ranking. As far as the most spectacular advancement of competitive position within the period 2007–2019 among the EU economies is concerned, Poland is the winner: Poland's 38th position in 2019 was 14 places higher than in 2007 when it occupied the 52nd place. On the other hand, the most dramatic drop of competitive position in the analyzed period was experienced by Greece (by 22 places from 36th position in 2007 down to 58th place in 2019). Moreover, one should also note spectacular worsening of competitive positions of: Slovakia (drop from 34th place in 2007 down to 53rd place in 2019), Hungary (drop from 35th place in 2007 down to 47th place in 2019), and Estonia (drop from 22nd place in 2007 down to 35th place in 2019). The fact that in 2019 the least competitive EU economy, i.e., Croatia was classified as the 60th economy means there was still enormous gap in economic development between the youngest EU member economy and EU leaders in competitiveness like the Netherlands, Ireland, Denmark, or Sweden.[57]

5.3 A New Strategic Agenda 2019–2024

Economic development is positioned in the center of integration proposals, scenarios, and instruments for the coming years. The European Commission and the Council of the European Union took important steps in May 2019, while the European Council did so in June 2019. In May 2019, the European Commission expressed its opinion on the current situation of the EU and on the ways, the EU should respond to global challenges in the document "Europe in May 2019. Preparing for a more united, stronger and more democratic Union in an increasingly uncertain world."

---

[56] European Commission (2014). See also: European Commission (2015).

[57] Pawlas (2014), pp. 71–91.

Table 9 Competitiveness of the EU MSs in the light of competitiveness rankings (positions)

Economy	2019	2018	2017	2016	2015	2014	2013	2012	2011	2010	2009	2008	2007	Change 2007 and 2019
Netherlands	6	4	5	8	15	14	14	11	14	12	10	10	8	+2
Ireland	7	12	6	7	16	15	17	20	24	21	19	12	14	+7
Denmark	8	6	7	6	8	9	12	13	12	13	5	6	5	−3
Sweden	9	9	9	5	9	5	4	5	4	6	6	9	9	0
Luxembourg	12	11	8	11	6	11	13	12	11	11	12	5	4	−8
Finland	15	16	15	20	20	18	20	17	15	19	9	15	17	+2
Germany	17	15	13	12	10	6	9	9	10	16	13	16	16	−1
Austria	19	18	25	24	26	22	23	21	18	14	16	14	11	−8
United Kingdom	23	20	19	18	19	16	18	18	20	22	21	21	20	−3
Belgium	27	26	23	22	23	28	26	25	23	25	22	24	25	−2
Lithuania	29	32	33	30	28	34	31	36	45	43	31	36	31	+2
France	31	28	31	32	32	27	28	29	29	24	28	25	28	−3
Czechia	33	29	28	27	29	33	35	33	30	29	29	28	32	−1
Estonia	35	31	30	31	31	3	36	31	33	34	35	23	22	−13
Spain	36	36	34	34	37	39	45	39	35	36	39	33	30	−6
Slovenia	37	37	43	43	49	55	52	51	51	52	32	32	40	+3
Poland	38	34	38	33	33	36	33	34	34	32	44	44	52	+14
Portugal	39	33	39	39	36	43	46	41	40	37	34	37	39	0
Latvia	40	40	40	37	43	35	41	l.d	l.d.	l.d.	l.d	l.d.	l.d.	l.d.
Cyprus	41	41	37	l.d.	l.d	l.d.	l.d.	l.d	l.d.	l.d.	l.d.	l.d.	l.d.	l.d.
Italy	44	42	44	35	38	46	44	40	42	40	50	46	42	−2

(continued)

Table 9 (continued)

Economy	2019	2018	2017	2016	2015	2014	2013	2012	2011	2010	2009	2008	2007	Change 2007 and 2019
Hungary	47	47	52	46	48	48	50	45	47	42	45	38	35	−12
Bulgaria	48	48	49	50	55	56	57	54	55	53	38	39	41	−7
Romania	49	49	50	49	47	47	55	53	50	54	54	45	44	−5
Slovakia	53	55	51	40	46	45	47	47	48	49	33	30	34	−19
Greece	58	57	57	56	50	57	54	58	56	46	52	42	36	−22
Croatia	60	61	59	58	58	59	l.d.	l.d.	l.d.	l.d.	l.d.	l.d.	l.d.	l.d.

Source IMD (2007, 2008, 2009, 2010, 2011, 2012, 2013, 2014, 2015, 2016, 2017, 2018, 2019)

The European Commission listed four crucial challenges facing the European Union, namely:

- digitalization and new technologies which will revolutionize the way the EU citizens live and work;
- climate and environmental changes which result in growing risks for prosperity, sustained standards of living, and security;
- demographic and societal changes, including aging population and welfare gap risks widening within the EU Member State;
- Rising multi-polarization of the world economy.[58]

The European Commission called for the creation of protective, competitive, fair, sustainable and influential Europe created largely by the European Union. The European Commission included specific and detailed recommendations regarding the development of the European Union in the period 2019–2024 in each aforementioned dimension. The creation of European Security Union and European Defense Union should help achieve protective EU. In order to make EU more competitive, it is necessary to concentrate research and development activity and innovation activity on ecological, social, and economic transitions and related societal challenges, as well as leveraging the strengths and achievements of the EU into leadership in breakthrough and disruptive innovation. Moreover, the European Commission stressed the need for stronger digital transformation, also with the use of artificial intelligence. The European Commission underlined the urgent necessity of upgrading and completing single market, including single digital market and single energy market, and making the Economic and Monetary Union stronger. When it comes to the creation of a more-fair European Union, the European Commission stressed the importance of the European Pillar of Social Rights, higher social inclusion, and equality (including access to health care and housing). Fighting climate change, reversing environmental degradation, and promoting transition toward a more resource-efficient circular European economy constitute crucial elements of sustainability pillar of the European Commission's recommendations.[59]

An informal meeting of the Council of the European Union in Sibiu in May 2019 brought the Sibiu Declaration in which leaders of EU27 Member States stressed fairness, responsibility, sustainability, inclusiveness of the EU current and future activity, as well as protective and safeguarding roles of the EU.[60]

In June 2019, the European Council adopted *A New Strategic Agenda 2019-2024*.[61] Preparing the aforementioned Strategic Agenda, the European Commission made an attempt to get adjusted to the rapid changes, rising unsettledness and complexity of the contemporary world economy of the 2nd decade of the twenty-first century. The Strategic Agenda is meant to direct the EU response to current challenges and to serve as a framework for the response. The European Council listed

[58] European Commission (2019).

[59] Ibidem.

[60] Council of the EU (2019).

[61] European Council (2019).

four priorities, namely: I. Protecting citizens and values, II. Developing a strong and vibrant economic base, III. Building a climate neutral, green, fair, and social Europe, and IV. Promoting European interests and values on the global stage. Mostly, priorities II and III are strongly connected with further economic development,[62] but some elements related to the creation of adequate base for further economic development can be found in the remaining priorities of the Strategic Agenda, as well. A truly strong economic base is of vital importance for increasing competitiveness of EU economies, providing wealth of EU citizens and keeping the position of the EU as a global player. The European Council underlined the importance of technological, security, and sustainability challenges, which reshape the global world economy more and more dynamically and more and more intensely. Therefore, the European Council suggested undertaking actions directed toward long-term sustainability, long-term-inclusiveness, and higher cohesion of the EU. As far as developing the future European economic base is concerned, the list of recommendations of the European Council embraces:

- Deepening the Economic and Monetary Union;
- Completing the Banking and Capital Markets Union;
- Strengthening the euro as an international currency;
- Deepening and strengthening the Single Market and its four freedoms;
- Reforming industrial policy so as to address the current challenges and fit present situation;
- Taking active part in the digital revolution and taking advantages and benefits from the digital revolution;
- Ensuring fair and effective taxation;
- Stimulating investment in education and training;
- Stimulate research and development activity and innovation;
- Promote entrepreneurship.[63]

As far as inclusiveness and sustainability of development are concerned the European Council calls for:

- Treating climate change as existential threat;
- In-depth transformation of the EU economy and society in order to achieve climate-neutrality;
- Treating the green transition as opportunity (not only as expenditure and cost);
- Building strong public–private investment partnership in the area of creating an effective circular economy;
- Accelerating the transition to renewables;
- Increasing energy efficiency;
- Reducing dependence on outside sources;
- Diversifying energy supplies;
- Preventing further generational, territorial, and educational divides;

---

[62] Outeda (2001).

[63] Ibidem.

- Providing equal opportunities for all;
- Adequate social protection, inclusive labor markets, and the promotion of cohesion.[64]

Moreover, the European Council underlined the need for higher assertiveness and effectiveness of the EU, if the EU is to keep its global position and its role in the more and more globalized world economy. To achieve this goal, the EU has to become more united and more determined. Furthermore, it has to better use its limited resources and/or try to collect more resources.

6 Conclusion

From the very beginning of the creation of integration processes by European Communities, economic development was concerned one of crucial objectives. The need for regionally balanced growth, rising employment, reduced unemployment, and increased standard of living was stressed in the Treaty of Rome establishing the EEC already. Moreover, environmental protection and social security were also underlined in the very same Treaty of Rome. Gradual enlargement of the European Communities/the European Union caused further rise in disparities among EU Member States (both internationally, on national level and on regional one). Therefore, the need for strengthening the efforts relating to the reduction of disparities in economic development resulted in the creation of Common Regional Policy, which was later transformed into EU Policy of Economic, Social and Territorial Cohesion. The last two decades brought intensification of EU pro-development programs. One should underline the significance of the Lisbon Strategy (designed for the period 2000–2010), the Europe 2020 Strategy (adopted for the years 2010–2020) and A New Strategic Agenda 2019–2024. Still, disparities among EU Member States and within EU economies are far too big; the overall competitiveness of the EU is not satisfactory. The disparities in economic development ought to be reduced, especially having in mind the current stress given to inclusive development (not only on EU level, but worldwide, e.g., by the United Nations). It seems that the EU does have a sort of unexploited potential that could and should be used to gain higher dynamics of socioeconomic growth and to redirect the development processes to achieve higher inclusiveness and sustainability of economic development. In order to do so, however, structural reforms and systemic institutional changes are necessary both on national level and on EU level. As many experts indicate, inclusive development and sustainable development must be prioritized, while technological progress (especially the 4th Industrial Revolution) and international economic integration should be used to support rising living standards. If increased standard of living is experienced not only by a small fraction of the EU society but by its majority, the EU itself will be perceived as important organization by EU citizens and it' will manage to keep its global position.

[64] Ibidem.

References

Arts, K. (2017). Inclusive sustainable development: A human rights perspective. *Current Opinion in Environmental Sustainability, 24,* 58–62.

Balcerowicz, L. (1995). *Wolność i rozwój*. Znak, Kraków: Ekonomia wolnego rynku. Wyd.

Borowiec, J. (2011). *Ekonomia integracji europejskiej*. Wrocław: Wydawnictwo Uniwersytetu Ekonomicznego we Wrocławiu.

Castro, L. D., & Lago, J. R. R. (2018). Educación y diplomacia cultural en la primavera de Europa (1948–1954) = education and Cultural Diplomacy in the Spring of Europe (1948–1954). *Revista de educación, 383,* 63–84.

Corrado, G., & Corrado, L. (2017). Inclusive finance for inclusive growth and development. *Current Opinion in Environmental Sustainability, 24,* 19–23.

Council of the EU. (2019). The Sibiu Declaration 9 May 2019. https://www.consilium.europa.eu/en/press/press-releases/2019/05/09/the-sibiu-declaration/pdf.

Dornbusch, R., Fischer, S., & Startz, R. (2011). *Macroeconomics* (11th ed.). New York: McGraw Hill.

Dyduch, J., Klimowicz, M., & Michalewska-Pawlak, M. (2012). *Selected policies of the European Union. Evolution in the context of the treaty of Lisbon and the Europe 2020 strategy* (p. 291). APRA, Warsaw: University of Wroclaw. Faculty of Social Sciences.

Dziembała, M. (2013). *Spójność ekonomiczno-społeczna i konkurencyjność regionów w polityce Unii Europejskiej*. Katowice: Wydawnictwo Uniwersytetu Ekonomicznego w Katowicach.

Encyclopedia Britannica, Economic development. Download at: https://www.britannica.com/?EB-checked/topic178361/economic-development.

European Commission. (2007). Cohesion Policy 2007–2013. Commentaries and official texts. Office for official publications of the European communities. Luxembourg, pp. 162.

European Commission. (2010). Europe 2020. A European strategy for smart, sustainable and inclusive growth. Download at: http://ec.europa.eu/eu2020/pdf/COMPLET%20EN%20BARROSO%20%20%20007%20-%20Europe%202020%20-%20EN%20version.pdf.

European Commission. (2014). An Introduction to EU Cohesion Policy 2014–2020. Download at: https://ec.europa.eu/regional_policy/sources/docgener/informat/basic/basic_2014_en.pdf.

European Commission. (2015). European Structural and Investment Funds 2014–2020. Official texts and commentaries. Download at: https://ec.europa.eu/regional_policy/sources/docgener/guides/blue_book/blueguide_en.pdf.

European Commission. (2016). Communication from the commission to the European parliament, the council, the European economic and social committee and the committee of the regions. Proposal for a new European consensus on development. Our world, our dignity, our future. *COM,* 740 final. Strasbourg 22.11.2016

European Commission. (2019). Europe in May 2019. Preparing for a more united, stronger and more democratic Union in an increasingly uncertain world. Download at: https://ec.europa.eu/commission/sites/beta-political/files/euco_sibiu_communication_en.pdf.

European Council. (2000). Lisbon European council 23 and 24 March presidency conclusions. Download at: http://www.europarl.europa.eu/summits/lis1_en.htm.

European Council. (2019). A new strategic agenda 2019–2024. European Council. https://www.consilium.europa.eu/media/39914/a-new-strategic-agenda-2019-2024.pdf.

European Parliament. (2010). The lisbon strategy 2000–2010. An analysis and evaluation of the methods used and results achieved. *Final Report*. Download at: http://www.europarl.europa.eu/document/activities/cont/201107/20110718ATT24270/20110718ATT24270EN.pdf.

European Parliament. (2012). Focus on flagship initiatives and the cohesion policy. REGI November 2012.

EUROSTAT Database. (2019). Download at: https://ec.europa.eu/eurostat/data/database.

EUROSTAT Newsrelease. (2019). GDP per capita in 281 EU regions. 34/2019–26 February 2019. Download at: https://ec.europa.eu/eurostat/documents/2995521/9618249/1-26022019-AP-EN.pdf/f765d183-c3d2-4e2f-9256-cc6665909c80.

Färber, K. (2017). Mitterrand and the great European design—from the cold war to the European Union. *Baltic Journal of European Studies, 7*(2), 132–147.

Giddings, B., Hopwood, B., & O'Brien, G. (2002). Environment, economy and society: Fitting them together into sustainable development. *Sustainable Development, 10*(4), 187–196.

Grover, A. (2014). Importance of CSR in Inclusive development. *Procedia—Social and Behavioral Sciences, 157,* 103–108.

Gupta, J., Pouw, N. R. M., & Ros-Tonen, M. A. F. (2015). Towards an elaborated theory of inclusive development. *The European Journal of Development Research, Palgrave Macmillan; European Association of Development Research and Training Institutes (EADI), 27*(4), 541–559.

Hamulák, O. (2018). La carta de los derechos fundamentals de la union europea y los derechos sociales. *Estudios constitucionales, 16*(1), 167–186.

IMD. (2007). *The world competitiveness yearbook 2019*. Lausanne: IMD.

IMD. (2008). *The world competitiveness yearbook 2019*. Lausanne: IMD.

IMD. (2009). *The world competitiveness yearbook 2019*. Lausanne: IMD.

IMD. (2010). *The world competitiveness yearbook 2019*. Lausanne: IMD.

IMD. (2011). *The world competitiveness yearbook 2019*. Lausanne: IMD.

IMD. (2012). *The world competitiveness yearbook 2019*. Lausanne: IMD.

IMD. (2013). *The world competitiveness yearbook 2019*. Lausanne: IMD.

IMD. (2014). *The world competitiveness yearbook 2019*. Lausanne: IMD.

IMD. (2015). *The world competitiveness yearbook 2019*. Lausanne: IMD.

IMD. (2016). *The world competitiveness yearbook 2019*. Lausanne: IMD.

IMD. (2017). *The world competitiveness yearbook 2019*. Lausanne: IMD.

IMD. (2018). *The world competitiveness yearbook 2019*. Lausanne: IMD.

IMD. (2019). *The world competitiveness yearbook 2019*. Lausanne: IMD.

Karar, E., & Jacobs-Mata, I. (2016). Inclusive governance: The role of knowledge in fulfilling the obligations of citizens, world water week 2015. *Aquatic Procedia, 6*, 15–22.

Kerikmäe, T. (2014). Protecting Human Rights in the EU. *Controversies and Challenges of the Charter of Fundamental Rights*.

Kerikmäe, T., Troitiño, D. R., & Shumilo, O. (2019). An idol or an ideal? A case study of Estonian e-Governance: Public perceptions, myths and misbeliefs1. *Acta Baltica Historiae et Philosophiae scientiarum, 7*(1).

Likoko, E., & Kini, J. (2017). Inclusive business—a business approach to development. *Current Opinion in Environmental Sustainability, 24*, 84–88.

Little, I. M. D. (1982). Economic development: Theory, policy, and international relations. McGraw Hill, New York.

Martín de la Guardia, R. M., & Pérez Sánchez, G. A. (2001). Historia de la integración europea. Ariel, Barcelona.

Moussis, N. (2007). Access to European Union. Law economics, policies 16th revised Edition. Rixensart: European Study Service.

Outeda, C. C. (2001). *El proceso de constitucionalización de la Unión Europea: de Roma a Niza* (No. 3). Univ Santiago de Compostela.

Pansera, M., & Owen, R. (2018). Framing inclusive innovation within the discourse of development: Insights from case studies in India. *Research Policy, 47*, 23–34.

Pawlas, I. (2014). Competitiveness of the Polish economy against the background of other European Union member states. Selected issues. *International Journal of Business and Management, II*(3), 71–91.

Pawlas, I. (2018). Disparities in development based on taxonomic research. A case of Poland in the European Union. In M. Stanickova, L. Melecky, E. Kovarova, K. Dvorokova (Eds.), *Proceedings of the 4th International Conference on European Integration 2018*. ICEI 2018, May 17–18, 2018. Ostrava, Czech Republic: VSB—Technical University of Ostrava.

Pawlas, I. (2019). The implementation of Europe 2020 strategy—attempt of evaluation and recommendations for the future. In A. Lorga da Silva, D. Tomic, & A. Grilec (Eds.), Economic and Social Development (Book of Proceedings), 39th International Scientific Conference on

Economic and Social Development—Sustainability from an Economic and Social Perspective. Varazdin: Varazdin Development and Entrepreneurship Agency, pp. 327–343.
Piasecki, R. (2003). *Rozwój gospodarczy a globalizacja*. Warszawa: PWE.
Pietrzyk, I. (2007). *Polityka regionalna Unii Europejskiej I region w państwach członkowskich*. Warszawa: Wydawnictwo Naukowe PWN.
Pouw, N., & Gupta, J. (2017a). Inclusive development: A multi-disciplinary approach. *Current Opinion in Environmental Sustainability, 24*, 104–108.
Pouw, N., & Gupta, J. (2017b). Towards a trans-disciplinary conceptualization of inclusive development. *Current Opinion in Environmental Sustainability, 24*, 96–103.
Rugman, A. M., & Hodgetts, R. M. (2003). *International business* (3rd ed.). Harlow London New York: Pearson Education.
Reinert, K. A., & Rajan, R. S. (Eds.). (2009). *The Princeton Encyclopedia of the World Economy* (Vol. 1). Princeton University Press, Princeton and Oxford.
Sachs, J. D. (2013). Miasta i zrównoważony rozwój, Project Syndicate. A World of Ideas, 27.11.2013. Download at: http://www.project-syndicate.pl/artykul/miasta-i-zrownowazony-rozwoj,429.html.
Schiller, B. R. (1991). *The economy today*. New York: McGraw-Hill.
Single European Act. (1987). *Official Journal of the European Communities*. No L 169/1, 29.06.1987.
Stiglitz, J. (2004). Zrób to sam, "Polityka" No. 20.
Swadźba, S. (2013). Systemowe uwarunkowania wzrostu i rozwoju gospodarczego. Studia Ekonomiczne. *Prace naukowe Uniwersytetu Ekonomicznego w Katowicach*, 146–150.
The Treaty of Lisbon. (2007). Download at: http://www.europarl.europa.eu/ftu/pdf/en/FTU_1.1.5.pdf.
The Treaty of Rome. (1957). Download at: https://ec.europa.eu/romania/sites/romania/files/tratatul_de_la_roma.pdf.
Treaty of Amsterdam amending the treaty on European Union, the treaties establishing the European communities and certain related acts. (1997). Download at: http://www.europarl.europa.eu/topics/treaty/pdf/amst-en.pdf.
Treaty on European Union. (1992). https://europa.eu/european-union/sites/europaeu/files/docs/body/treaty_on_european_union_en.pdf.
Troitiño, D. R. (2017). Jean Monnet before the first European community: A historical perspective and critic. *Trames, 21*(3), 193–213.
Troitiño, D. R., Kerikmäe, T., & Chochia, A. (Eds.). (2018). *Brexit: History*. Reasoning and Perspectives: Springer.
United Nations. (2000). The millennium development goals. Download at: https://www.un.org/en/mdg/summit2010/pdf/List%20of%20MDGs%20English.pdf.
United Nations. (2012). Rio+20 United Nations conference on sustainable development: The future we want. Download at: https://sustainabledevelopment.un.org/content/documents/733FutureWeWant.pdf.
United Nations. (2015). Transforming our world: The 2030 agenda for sustainable development. Download at: https://sustainabledevelopment.un.org/post2015/transformingourworld.
World Bank. (2019). Gini Index (World Bank Estimate). Download at: https://data.worldbank.org/indicator/si.pov.gini.
World Economic Forum. (2018). *The inclusive development index 2018 summary and data highlights*. Geneva: WEF.
Yamaguchi, R. (2014). Inclusive wealth with a changing but aging population. *Economics Letters, 124*, 21–25.

External Necessities of the European Union

Foreign Affairs of the European Union: How to Become an Independent and Dominant Power in the International Arena

David Ramiro Troitiño, Tanel Kerikmäe and Archil Chochia

Abstract The European Union is facing external challenges of major implications for its success. The European Union cannot become an island of a common market without a strong voice in the world to protect its interest and the interest of the member states of the organization. The EU needs pushing forward the European model of society, as human rights, protection of the environment or any other policy that influences other parts of the world, but also the own Union. Obviously, currently, there is an unbalance situation between the historical and economic international influence of Europe and its power politically, based on the cooperation model of the EU external policy. The necessity of further integration is a must in all the areas implicated in foreign affairs in the EU, from trade to development, a wide political spectrum needs more coherence that can be achieved by speeding up the integration process.

Keywords External relations · European integration · CFSP · Future of Europe

1 Introduction

The European Integration started officially with the Treaty of the European Coal and Steel Community (ECSC). It created a community including France, Germany, Netherlands, Belgium, Luxembourg and Italy to integrate the economical field of steel and coal as the first step to build a united Europe and avoid the nationalistic confrontations.

The ECSC was the first step in the international relations of Europe, establishing the first offices of the High Authority outside the member states in 1954 in Washington and in 1955 in London in order to deal with the international agreements related to this economic field. The High Authority in the ECSC was the predecessor to the current European Commission in the European Union but it was more independent and, what is more important, had more power and more freedom in the decision-making process.

D. Ramiro Troitiño (✉) · T. Kerikmäe · A. Chochia
Ehitajate tee 5, 19086 Tallinn, Estonia
e-mail: david.troitino@ttu.ee

D. Ramiro Troitiño et al. (eds.), *The EU in the 21st Century*,
https://doi.org/10.1007/978-3-030-38399-2_12

The establishment of these offices in USA and UK marked the beginning of the External Service of a common Europe.

During these first steps of the European Integration, the attention of the European Institutions mainly focused in the Western World because these countries were the main commercial partners of the member states of the ECSC. However, there were also political reasons in the context of the Cold War as the defence done by the USA on European soil against the threat of a communism expansion. After the creation of the ECSC and other European Communities, the USSR pictured it as a tool of capitalism against the workers of the world, an organization promoted by USA to fight against the USSR. This situation meant that the international influence of the EU in the communist world was minimal until the fall of the Soviet Union. Hence, the first steps on the external relations of the Union were marked by the confrontation of two superpowers and the alienation of the EU on the American side.

The EU developed its external relations via the Commercial Policy, the Lomé Agreement and the Common Agricultural Policy. After the collapse of the Soviet Union, a new approach was taken and the EU adapted its international role to a new situation, where its international political power did not match its economic power.

The end of the Cold War is the main source of the current problems the EU is facing in the field of foreign policy. Europe is not any more a battlefield between USA and USSR, and the influence of Soviet Union in the world has disappeared even though Russia is still seen as a threat by many members of the Union, and the conflict of Ukraine reflects the ineffectiveness of the EU. Nevertheless, China is trying to fill the empty space left by USSR, without forgetting other new global players, as India. It means that after a bipolar world divided between USA and USSR, the Americans became the sole power of the world, a situation that other States are trying to balance. In this context, the European Union is having a problem of identity, a problem to define its own role in the world affairs, leading to a weak foreign policy, troubles and huge internal disagreements.[1]

2 The EU Global Role

The European Union population is 513 million people, more than USA (327) and Russia (144) together, just behind China (1386) and India (1340). It makes the European Union the third political area of the world in terms of population. Moreover, if we consider that the population of the European Union is highly educated and have higher professional skills, the EU is a giant in terms of population.

On the other hand, in terms of global wealth, the European Union is one of the leaders of the world, generating around one-quarter of global wealth, even when the gap with Asia is closing. It means that the European Union is one of the most developed areas of the world, being a main player in economic terms. In relation with international trade, the EU is the biggest player of the world, by far surpassing

[1] Booker and North (2016), p. 80.

USA or China.[2] It makes Europe a great economic power in the world, a leading area with a great economic power.

The global currency of the world is still the US dollar, even when in meeting of the G8 in January 2010 China, Russia and Brazil were lobbying for an alternative global currency reserve to substitute the dollar.[3] Neither of their currencies, the Yuan, the Ruble or the Real are really a challenge to the supremacy of the dollar. The second international currency of the world currently is the Euro, the European Union currency, and is the only one currently that could substitute the supremacy of the dollar in future. Nevertheless, it is clear that the Euro, just born in 2002, is one of the most important currencies of the world, and it makes the European Union one of the most important financial agents of the world.[4]

The European Union is also the biggest donor of the world; EU and its member states contributed with €74.4 billion in 2018 on assistance projects and other humanitarian actions. The European Union is a main player in the world, and can influence other regions, and hence increase its international role, via the donations for development. The rules of the EU about Human Rights and Environment were designed to make a better world, but are decreasing the international influence of the EU. States as China do not have such scruples, and even with less money spent, are increasing its influence in the world, as in Africa, where the EU is losing influence. The debate is clear, and the EU should define its targets in order to be more efficient.[5]

Finally, the idea of the international influence of the European Union based on the rule of law will spread all over the world the European model.[6] According to this theory, the example of the European Integration will be imitated by other regions of the world, first with similar economical communities, as MERCOSUR, the American Common Market or the African Common Market, and after with deeper integration. The European Union will be like a mirror to the rest of the world, a model of integration and progress to be imitated. Clearly, the international role of the EU in this field is important as the European market has connections with all the planet and countries and companies want to trade with Europe and hence must respect the European legislation. Nevertheless, the idea of the rule of Europe in the XXI century is based in the good faith of human beings who always want the best for them, something unlikely to happen in countries as China, or something very weak in situations as the war of Yugoslavia.

The EU is a leading player in the international world in several fields, and others were stands beside the main powers of the world. It would be logical that the EU is a world power, a world leader, but its position is still behind other major countries.

---

[2]http://stats.oecd.org/index.aspx?datasetcode=MEI_TRD.

[3]http://www.eleconomista.es/empresas-finanzas/noticias/1388273/07/09/Russia-China-to-push-global-currency-at-G8-summit.html.

[4]http://www.wto.org/english/res_e/statis_e/Statis_e.htm.

[5]Ramiro Troitino and Pando Ballesteros (2017).

[6]Leonard (2005).

3 The External Relations Working System in the EU

At the beginning of the European integration, the external relations were based in the Common Trade Policy and it is still the main vehicle of the international relations of Europe. Its importance comes from the economic power of the EU and the predominant role of the European Commission in this policy. A common market with common customs was created by virtue of the EEC. Hence, any good that entered the market through any of its borders could afterwards move without restrictions in the area. The European Commission managed the market, because it was an institution focused on European necessities, instead of national interests. The European market developed an international dimension for the European Commission, because this common institution was in charge of the negotiations of trade agreements.[7]

The rules of the Common Trade Policy are very complex. The Treaty of Rome deals with traditional trade in the articles 131–134, the ECSC Treaty deals with the economic sector, and the Security Policy and Agricultural Policy deal with their respective fields. The main problem here is the article 133 of the Treaty of Rome related to the goods included in the Trade Policy because it includes in this policy just the traditional trade. The European Commission representing this policy was present in the meetings of the World Trade Organization and in different negotiations there were sitting in the same table the European Commission and different member states, the former representing the traditional trade, and the latter other kinds of trade. In 1994, a new directive included more goods in the Trade Policy to avoid these situations, and the Treaty of Amsterdam ruled that if all the member states agree, the European Commission could negotiate in the international organizations about the trade of goods not included in the Treaties. The Treaty of Nice also reformed this article and included many other goods. Once that it is in the European Treaties and the member states share sovereignty, the European Commission will deal with it in the name of the European Union.[8]

The tools of the Trade Policy are under the regulation of the Commission and are mainly imports and trade defence, common customs and regime of imports. The regulations of the European Commission can have a worldwide impact because the companies that want to trade with the European Union should respect European Union laws. The economic importance of the EU makes it impossible for almost any big company in the world to avoid the European legislation, risking their access to the European market.[9] The examples are numerous, as in the case of General Electric and Honeywell, the merge of two North American companies approved by the American government but was not implemented because it was against the monopoly policy of the European Union.[10] It means a great international power for the European Union, a power to decide over companies all over the world, and as has been mentioned before, it is a European power, because it resides in the hands

[7] Moravcsik (2013), p. 144.

[8] http://europa.eu/pol/comm/index_en.htm.

[9] Färber (2017).

[10] http://www.mauricilucena.es/docs/politica_competencia_europa_eeuu.pdf.

of the European Commission and not in the Council, representation of the member states.

The Lomé Agreements are also important for the international influence of the European Union. This policy started in 1975 and works based on cooperation and help from the European Union to countries that were ex-colonies of member states of the EU, the ACP countries, from Caribbean, Africa and the Pacific areas. In terms of international relations, these agreements represent, in the context of the Cold War, the loss of influence of France on its colonies. As Paris could not keep its colonies, and afterwards not even her influence in the new states because the French capabilities could not compete with those of USA or USSR, France included this policy on the European level to use the resources of the member states in order to keep her influence in her ex-colonies. In the European Communities of six members, only France had ex-colonies, and most of them were located in Africa. Nowadays, France is nostalgic about its relations with Francophone Africa, because most of the member states of the EU have no historical ties with the ACP countries.

The character of Lomé and the subsequent treaties are mainly economical,[11] regarding trade of mainly raw materials and farm exports and economic aid, but there are many problems and the agreement is not working properly in order to increase the international influence of the EU. First, there is not a consensus between the ACP countries before the negotiations with Europe, and the EU goes to the meetings as a whole. It means that the negotiation power of the EU is much stronger than other weak institutions involved in the Lomé Agreements.

There is also disparity in many fields. Germany wants to reduce the financial assistance and France wants to increase it, the African countries prefer money and the Caribbean countries prefer access to the European market, there are weak staffs in the ACP countries but strong staff in the EU. Therefore, in the negotiations, the ACP countries present arguments based on philosophical views, as the former trade of slaves, and the EU presents numbers, statistics or analysis. During one meeting between the ACP countries and the European Union, the ACP countries were asking money to Europe because according to them the development of the economy of Europe was a direct consequence of the slave trade based on African people. They presented the idea that the Europeans went to Africa to buy slaves paying for them with European manufactures. Afterwards, the Europeans sailed to America, where they sold the slaves with a huge economic benefit. The money was partly spent on raw materials. Then, they went back to Europe with financial resources and raw materials basic for the development of the European industry, starting again this economic circle. The ACP position of asking money to the European Union because of this theory was rejected by the EU who was more interested in agreements based on current macro-economic data.

Another important problem is the Development Fund, which is included in the Budget of the European Union but is in reality under the power of the member states. There is a rule of no allocation in the European Budget. It means that the money goes to the EU and afterwards the European institutions decide where to spend it

[11] http://ec.europa.eu/development/geographical/lomegen_en.cfm.

through an annual budget. There is an exception with the Development Fund,[12] where the States decide where the money will be allocated. It means the influence of the national States is increased at the expense of EUs influence.

The EU is the largest donor of humanitarian aid, and the lack of results is leading Europe to a donor fatigue.[13] The results of Lomé and the next Treaties were poor. The gap between Europe and the ACP countries is now bigger than before. Many members of the ACP countries have been involved in civil conflicts and political chaos. The European market of raw materials is declining, and the preferential access to the European market is also declining.

Finally, the inclusion of environmental protection and human rights as conditions for the economic aid is leading these countries to look for new partners less invasive. However, the economic aid to third countries is not just conducted by the Lomé agreement; Europe also has other tools, as the European Development Fund. The development assistance is influenced by human rights standards. The problem of the EDF is that it does not follow the EU budget rule of no assignment. It means that the incomes in the budget are not linked with any determine outcome. First, the EU collects its money, and with the whole money accumulated decides where to spend it. There are a few exceptions, and one is the European Development Fund. The member states give the money to the EDF and at the same time, they decide in which project is going to be allocated. The states control all the process and keep intact their influence in other countries of the world. Hence, the influence of the EU is reduced because does not control the process and where the money is going to be allocated.

Also, the European Initiative for Democracy and Human Rights spends 100 million euros on strengthening democracy, support for the worldwide abolition of death penalty, fight against torture and impunity, and fight against racism and xenophobia

The Common Agricultural Policy (CAP) is the third pillar of international influence of the EU in the world. The Common Trade Policy supports the liberalization of markets in other parts of the world for European companies, but the CAP is doing the opposite, closing the European market to other economies. The international influence of the CAP is very negative because of two reasons. First, the domestic system is based on subsidies that promote the local production and block the imports from other parts of the world. It means that many countries based on an agricultural economy which want to have access to the European market will not open their economies to EU companies in other fields unless the EU opens its agricultural market. It creates many problems to the Common Trade Policy, the most effective tool of the EU in the world. On the other hand, the European population cannot consume the huge surplus created in the agricultural market of the EU, so it has to be sold in the international market. As the prices of the international market are lower than in the European market, the European surplus has to be sold cheaper, with the consequence of lowering prices in the international market for other producers.[14] As we

---

[12] http://europa.eu/legislation_summaries/development/overseas_countries_territories/r12102_en.htm.

[13] Booker and North (2016). p. 189.

[14] http://europa.eu/pol/agr/index_en.htm.

can see, this system is harming the international influence of the EU in the world, but the system is currently under a very important reform and the European agricultural market is becoming more open to other producers of the world.

4 EU International Companions

The European Union most intensive relations are with Norway[15], Iceland and Lichtenstein. The three countries were members of the European Free Association, and after most of the members of the EFTA joined the European Union, the three signed a new agreement creating the European Economic Area. It includes four freedoms of the Single Market, the free movement of goods, persons, services, and capital among the EEA and EU countries. Mainly is an economical agreement of free trade that gives mutual access to the markets of both areas. Nevertheless, it is not an equal agreement because the EEA countries have to adopt the European legislation related to the Single Market[16] without participating in its elaboration. These three countries are included in the European Budget, although they contribute financially to it.[17] It means that they contribute financially for being part of the market, but they do not receive any funding from EU policies and development funds, as the member states do. Norway is the main contributor to the EU per capita, €1167 million over the 2004–2009 periods.

Switzerland is another important partner. Previously, a member of the EFTA, the Swiss government applied also to the EEA and even membership to the EU, but an internal referendum rejected the enlargement. Hence, bilateral treaties between the EU and Switzerland were the solution to entail the country into the Single Market. As a result, most of the EU legislation applies in Switzerland.

Other important partners in Europe are Macedonia, Serbia, Montenegro and Albania, because their determination to join the organization. Montenegro already has the Euro as the national currency, even when it is not members of the Eurozone, as the autonomous region of Kosovo also does. Nevertheless, all these States[18] will be eventually members of the European Union. Here, we can also feel the international influence of the EU with the membership that acts as a carrot for the countries willing to join the organization as they reform their countries according to EU standards. These countries have free access to the EU market; obtain EU support for domestic reform programs, plus other advantages.

The case of Turkey is similar, whether it belongs to Europe or not, whether it will join or not, it is a candidate to join the EU. The negotiations started and the Turkish government was pushing the implementation of reforms to adapt the country to the European customary.

---

[15]With the exception of Svalbard, and archipelago in the Arctic Ocean.

[16]It means the biggest part of the EU legislation.

[17]Rifkin (2004), p. 120.

[18]Not Kosovo because is not recognized as a State by many member states of the EU.

Other partners in Europe and in the Mediterranean shore drive their relations with Brussels via the European Neighbourhood Policy.[19] It includes Algeria, Armenia, Azerbaijan, Belarus, Egypt, Georgia, Israel, Jordan, Lebanon, Libya, Moldova, Morocco, Palestine, Syria, Tunisia and Ukraine. The idea of the EU is to bring stability to these countries in order to secure its own borders, as a preventive action to prevent any danger for Europe.

This policy is divided in two areas, Eastern neighbours and Mediterranean neighbours and is based on trade concessions and financial assistance (3 billion euros 2000–2006). On the other hand, these countries have to become more democratic, transform to market economies and achieve a greater respect to human rights. In addition, there is a program to strengthen their borders to block the arrival of illegal immigrants to Europe. The Barcelona process pretended to establish a Free Trade Area with Mediterranean countries (including Israel) by 2010, but now the dateline was too ambitious. The European Neighbourhood Policy invested billions of euros and the results have been demoralizing. Nevertheless, it is another example of the European external relations, based mainly in economic matters.[20]

The relations with Russia are very important for the EU, because it is the third biggest trade partner of the EU, and because of the Russian supplies of oil and gas to the European market and because it acts as a brake for the expansion of the organization eastwards. The relations are based in four areas, economic issues and the environment; freedom, security and justice; external security; and research and education, including cultural aspects.[21]

However, the relation with Russia is also influenced by other factors, as cultural, historical or political. Countries, as the Baltic States or Poland, with a bloody past under the Soviet power, are less friendly towards the politics of Moscow and its interference in their domestic issues. Most Western Countries are more interested in trade and energy, dividing and weakening Europe from inside, because some member states feel more secure with USA than with the own EU, and Europe's position to Russia. The war in South Ossetia, the annexation of Crimea and the war in Ukraine are a violent escalation that is increasing the radical positions of all the actors, as well as a Russian warning about its area of influence and the incapacity of the European Union to expand there.

Outside European continent, the main partner of the EU is, without any doubt, the USA. US goods and services trade with the EU totalled nearly $1.3 trillion in 2018. Exports totalled $575 billion; imports totalled $684 billion. The US goods and services trade deficit with the EU was $109 billion in 2018.

The USA had an $807 billion in total (two ways) goods trade with European Union countries during 2018. Goods exports totalled $319 billion; goods imports totalled $488 billion. The US goods trade deficit with European Union countries was $169 billion in 2018.

---

[19] http://ec.europa.eu/world/enp/index_en.htm.

[20] Troitino and Faerber (2019).

[21] http://ec.europa.eu/external_relations/russia/index_en.htm.

Trade in services with the EU (exports and imports) totalled an estimated $452 billion in 2018. Services exports were $256 billion; services imports were $196 billion. The US services trade surplus with the EU was $60 billion in 2018.

According to the Department of Commerce, US exports of goods and services to the EU supported an estimated 2.6 million in jobs in 2015 (latest data available) (1.2 million supported by goods exports and 1.4 million supported by services).

The economic ties between these two areas are very important, being both economical giants in the world.

However, the States is the main power in the international relations and the EU cannot compete in political terms in the international arena with the Americans. The CFSP of the European Union tries to solve this problem, because USA works with a single voice in the world and the EU works in different levels with different voices. The EU should increase the cooperation in external affairs in order to achieve an important role in the world, even more, should go from cooperation to integration.

The non-operant system of the EU during the war of Yugoslavia was a trigger. Several member states took different positions and the lack of military muscle ended up the European actions with mere economic sanctions that could not stop the war in Europe. It was USA that finished the war, the killings and the ethnical clean ship, showing the lack of effectiveness of the EU. After the war, the main efforts to rebuild the new countries emerged after was, and is still, done by the EU. It reflects the words of Ronald Rumsfeld about the relations between USA and the EU as the relation between a cook and a dishwasher. USA does, is the cook, and the EU fixes, is the washdisher.[22]

The situation in other areas of the world back this opinion, like in Israel and Palestine. USA is the main player for both, the Palestinian government and the Israeli government, both look to USA to try signing agreements, both look to USA to support their positions, but the EU is the bigger economical donor of the Palestinians, and the EU is the bigger commercial partner of Israel.[23] Without the European economic aid, the Palestinian government could not survive, and Israel could not afford a blockade from the European market to their products. Again Europe lacks a common position to act strongly.

Also related to the relation between the USA and EU, it is important to underline the strong army of the USA and the weak European approach to the military field with the Western European Union. After the World War II, some parts of Western Europe were literally destroyed, and could not stand alone against the Soviet Army. The USA became the defender of the democratic and economic values of Europe deploying thousands of soldiers to avoid the Soviet intervention. The creation of NATO and the clear leadership of USA allowed the Europeans to invest their resources in other important areas and invest relatively little in the army.

After the collapse of Soviet Union, the world is facing a new situation, there is not a common threat to Europe, and so NATO has lost its main reason of being. At the same time, without an army is difficult to influence in many parts of the world, as

---

[22]http://en.wikipedia.org/wiki/Donald_Rumsfeld.

[23]http://ec.europa.eu/external_relations/occupied_palestinian_territory/index_en.htm.

Iran, where the economic sanctions have been going on for decades without success, or many other conflicts in Africa where the soft power of the European Union has been completely ineffective in order to solve the armed conflicts. The EU should have clear what it wants to be in order to act according to it. If it wants to become a world power, a European army is without doubts needed. If the EU wants to be the loyal ally of USA with some influence, just integration in the political sphere would be enough forgetting then the army and the entire problems link with it.

From Asia, the main partner of the EU is China; the European Union and China are two of the biggest traders in the world. China is now the EU's second-biggest trading partner behind the USA and the EU is China's biggest trading partner.

The EU is committed to open trading relations with China. However, the EU wants to ensure that China trades fairly, respects intellectual property rights and meets its obligations as a member of the World Trade Organization (WTO). Unfortunately, the relations of the EU and China are not dealing with the usual topics included by the EU, as human rights, democracy, national minorities, etc. It reveals a double standard of the EU that includes all these aspects in its relations with less powerful partners, but when it finds a powerful state as China, forgets all its principals. Alternatively, simply shows pragmatism, accepting China as a much more powerful state than the EU and all its members together.

The position of the EU in the trade war between China and the EU could determine the outcome, but it is still not clear if the Union will fully side with any contender.

Japan is another important partner of the EU in Asia; Europe has become the major source of foreign direct investment in Japan and the largest recipient of Japanese foreign investment, surpassing US and China, again economic relations of great importance, but lacking any political influence.[24]

Finally, the last important partner of the EU in Asia is India, a former colony of UK that still has cultural and population ties with UK. Nevertheless, the main aspects of the relations between the EU are also economic; the EU is India's biggest trading partner and provider of foreign investment, situation that could be affected by BREXIT.

Latin America is just an important partner for some member states of the EU, specially Spain and Portugal. All Latin American countries are now linked to the EU by association, cooperation or trade agreements. Also is important to light the promotion of areas of integration in America done by the EU, linking trade with integration with Mercosur, Central America and the Andean Community. Nevertheless, the EU focuses in other parts of the world, leaving its relations in this part of the world in the hands of USA and China, just Spain trying to increase the relations between both areas.[25] The main reason is the decline of the raw materials market of the European Union and the increased necessities of China in this field.

[24] Pawlas (2015).

[25] www.la-moncloa.es/.

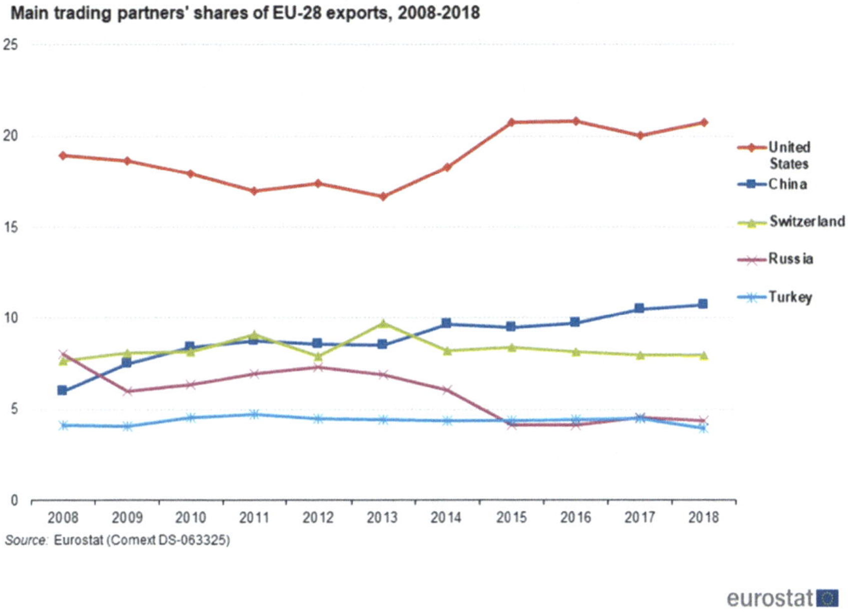

Source http://trade.ec.europa.eu/doclib/html/122530.htm

5 Politics and External Relations: Towards a Single Voice

Several international events, specially the 1970s oil crisis, encouraged the European member states to increase their political cooperation in order to increase their international influence and protect their national interests abroad. The conflict between Israel and the Arab countries meant an oil embargo over some of the members of the European Communities and a general increase of the prices all over Europe. The member states of the EEC did not act commonly and hence their influence was little. The crisis of the nationalization of the Suez Channel decided unilaterally by the Egyptian authorities, and the consequent invasion of French and British troops supported by Israel had also a big impact in the European international influence. USA saw Egypt as a key ally in the Cold War, and hence forced France and UK to withdraw, showing the weakness of the European powers.[26]

It was also a time when France and de Gaulle tried making the European Communities the third player in the context of the Cold War. The European Communities asked Étienne Davignon, the Belgian Foreign Office minister, to elaborate a draft on potential improvements on this field. The main conclusions of the report were:

[26]Martín de la Guardia and Pérez Sánchez (2001).

- Semester meetings of the Foreign Affairs Ministers. In the special case of problematic issues, the meeting could be done by the heads of the member states governments
- A Political Committee formed by the heads of cabinets of the Foreign Affairs ministers with meetings four times a year to prepare the meetings of their bosses
- A committee of high civil servants to discuss different problems
- The president of the Council of Ministers communicates once a year with the European Parliament about the political cooperation.

All these meetings and institutions were just a mean to achieve a single voice in the Foreign Affairs, and the embryo of the current Common Foreign and Security Policy.

The report was accepted by the member states and started working in 1970.[27]

The necessity to improve the external projection of the member states of the communities lead to a second Davignon report. It included:

- Intensification of the meetings of the heads of the member states
- Definition of the main goals of the common policy
- Creation of urgent meetings to respond to crisis with a common position
- Construction of a common foreign policy, each state compromise not to fix definitely its position without consulting the rest of the member states.

This report was also adopted by the European Union, deepening the cooperation in the political affairs. Another important measure taken in terms of international politics was the creation of the European Council, the regular meetings of the heads of the member states governments. Until 1974, there were seven meetings of this kind, but it was not official until 1974 when Giscard D'Estaigne, president of France, fathered the idea. Jean Monnet saw this Council as the provisional government of Europe. Monnet saw this institution as a leading political force in Europe with effect on the internal development and the external representation of the organization.[28]

The targets of the new Council were:

- Reinforce the working of the European institutions
- Increase the budgetary powers of the European Parliament
- Democratic elections for the European Parliament
- Increase the power of the European Commission
- Increase the political cooperation.

And the functions of the Council were:

- Take decisions about issues already discussed in other European levels
- Establish priorities in the European Building process.
- Declaration. Common positions of its members
- Coordination of the European affairs

[27] http://www.ena.lu/davignon-report-luxembourg-27-October-1970-020002259.html.

[28] Chochia et al. (2018).

– Develop a political cooperation[29]

The first official meeting of the European Council was in 1975 in Dublin. It was less pompous than the previous meetings, and more focus in problems, closer to a working meeting instead of a diplomatic meeting.[30]

The targets and the functions of the European Council showed that the political cooperation increased at 1970 but it was just the beginning, with an important need of further integration in this field. Following the European model of integration, normally the new policies start with cooperation, where the member states can accept or reject any action.[31] Afterwards, when the working system is improved, the cooperation evolves to mild integration with majority voting system in the decision-making with different alternatives of blockade, and at some point becomes full integration.

The steps taken in the political cooperation were based on different reports. Like the Tindemans report, made by the Prime Minister of Belgium after a request of the European Council. The report presented the fact that the idea of Europe was getting weaker, proposing different actions to strengthen it. In the field of the foreign affairs, the report accused Europe of looking inwards, and proposed a much more active role of Europe in the international affairs.[32]

The report of the three wise men drafted by Baren Biesheurel, former agricultural minister of Holland, Edmon Dell, former trade minister of UK and Robert Marjolin, a collaborator of Jean Monnet, was about the difficulties of the European Integration, outlining the main obstacles, specially the different interest of the member states and the need of deeper political cooperation. They proposed stronger European institutions to solve the problem.[33]

The Gensher-Colombo[34] project included political cooperation. Emilio Colombo was the foreign affairs minister of Italy, and Hans Genscher the foreign affairs minister of Germany and a very close collaborator of the German Prime Minister Helmut Kohl. Their report proposed to reinforce the political cooperation increasing the role of the European Union in the world. It relevant outlining that these reports were drafted around 1981, before the end of the Cold War, before the major changes in the world affairs consequence of the end of the world confrontation between USA and Soviet Union, but still, the report made clear that the European Union was weak internationally and should improve this aspect.

The Genscher-Colombo report proposed:

– Increase the political cooperation, including security and with its own secretariat
– Cultural cooperation

[29]http://www.ena.lu/interview-etienne-davignon-preparations-davignon-report-brussels-14-january-2008-022500863.html.

[30]Rosamond (2000), p. 77.

[31]Castro and Lago (2018).

[32]http://www.ena.lu/the-tindemans-report-020100267.html.

[33]http://www.jstor.org/pss/20081465.

[34]http://www.iuee.eu/pdf-dossier/20/A7XQ4Brly5FP7Dd7AQHB.PDF.

- Creation of a Law Union, same legislation in the main issues in all the member states
- Fight against terrorism, criminals or any other kind of violence.

European Council rejected the report, but it was the starting point of the Single European Act (1986) one of the most important Treaties in the European building process that created the Single Market and paved the way to the single currency.

The Spinelli report, made by a group of federalist of the European Parliament, proposed the creation of a European Constitution, with a European government, were all the policies and powers were clearly defined between the new European government and the member states governments, being the foreign affairs under the power of the new European government.[35] It was the first report that spoke about integration instead of cooperation in order to have an effective foreign affairs policy in Europe.

None of these reports were completely accepted by the European Council, but it created a debate leading to the creation of a new Treaty, the Single European Act.

Jacques Delors led the draft of the treaty, a French socialist and president of the European Commission. Two working groups created for the draft; the first one was in charge of developing the political cooperation in Europe, and entailed political experts from each member state. The final draft, adopted in 1986, included a compromise between the member states that wanted intergovernmental cooperation, and the states that wanted a common position, a European position.

The SEA created different institutions in the area of the political cooperation:

- Presidency of the EU
- Political Committee, with members from all the member states, with a fast working system, and it needs just the petition of three member states to meet in 48 h. Their targets are to impulse the cooperation and prepare the meetings of the ministers
- A group of European correspondents
- Different working groups
- Secretariat located in Brussels with the function to assist the presidency during all its term to prepare its activities
- The objectives of the European Political cooperation were extended to all foreign policy issues of general interest.[36]

The Single European Act made no mention to the development of the European defence.

The Treaty was more important in other fields, mainly economy. The political cooperation mainly focused on greater concentration on matters concerning security, and cooperation in the armaments sector.[37] However, it settled the first stone in the creation of a real common foreign policy including it in the sphere of influence of the European Union from the previous intergovernmental cooperation; it established the institutional basis required for further development.

---

[35] http://ec.europa.eu/research/social-sciences/news04_en.html.

[36] http://europa.eu/legislation_summaries/institutional_affairs/treaties/treaties_singleact_en.htm.

[37] Kerikmäe (2015).

6 The Roots of a Common External Position: The Creation of the Common Foreign and Security Policy

The Treaty of the European Union, the Treaty of Maastricht in 1992, also had different working groups before its draft. An intergovernmental group on political union was one of them. It led to the inclusion in the EU Treaty of a specific title on a Common Foreign and Security Policy (CFSP).

The TEU was divided in three main pillars including different policy areas, where the decision-making was the main difference. The first pillar included the so-called Communitarian policies, the second pillar the CFSP based on unanimity in the European Council, and the third one, Police and Judicial Cooperation in Criminal Matters based on intergovernmental cooperation.

The second pillar organized a common foreign policy of the European Union, of all its member states. The decisions are taken by unanimity, a logical step to avoid the concerns of some states. The unanimity meant, in reality, a capacity of veto of any member state; hence, no decisions might be taken against the opinion of any member state. Consultation and the search of a common agreement became the normal way to adopt a decision. This system protected the national sovereignty of the member states, but at the same time, it included the CFSP in the sphere of influence of the European Union.[38]

Nevertheless, a small improvement was included in the treaty as some issues could be adopted by qualified majority. The qualified majority protected big and small member states making the weighted of the votes and the majorities needed impossible for an alliance of big states or an alliance of small states to reach the minimum votes required.[39]

This process underlines the weakest point of the CFSP, the long and arduous way to take a decision makes ineffective the policy. When fast decisions are required, the CSFP is not able to provide them, when a problem needs to be solved, is hardly difficult to make all the member states agreeing on it. Therefore, the next logical step should be a restrictive qualified majority, in the sense of blocking minorities, following with a qualified majority without restrictions, simple majority and finally the creation of the European government that will take all the decisions on the foreign affairs of the Union. This is the logical development, but probably it will take many years. It is a main challenge for XXI century in the EU and a long process that depends on the European will to become a world power and on external influences as USA or the role of other states in the world affairs.

The Treaty on European Union, Article 11, defines and implements a Common Foreign and Security Policy that covers all areas of foreign and security policy, the objectives of which are to:

- Safeguard the common values, fundamental interests, independence and integrity of the Union in conformity with the principles of the United Nations Charter

[38]Outeda (2001).

[39]Kerikmäe (2019).

- Strengthen the security of the Union in all ways
- Preserve peace and strengthen international security, in accordance with the principles of the United Nations Charter, as well as the principles of the Helsinki Final Act and the objectives of the Paris Charter, including those on external borders
- Promote international cooperation
- Develop and consolidate democracy and the rule of law, and respect for human rights and fundamental freedoms.[40]

The Treaty also established two CSFP policy instruments:

- Common positions: these are adopted in the Council by unanimity (but with the informal constructive abstention rule applying) and require the member states to implement national policies that comply with the position defined by the EU on a particular issue. However, there are no legal sanctions for failing to comply with common positions. It means that the debates are long, tedious and slow, because nobody can be forced into an agreement, a not very effective way of decision-making.
- Joint actions: these are operating actions to implement common positions, and are adopted by the Council after the European Council has agreed that a matter should be the subject of a joint action, and may be adopted by a qualified majority (following a decision by unanimity that a qualified majority can be used). This was the first time that a Treaty provided for the use of qualified majority voting in the foreign affairs field. Also, joint actions are more binding than common positions. As with common positions, the member states are required to change their policies in accordance with a joint action, but under joint actions, they must also inform and consult the Council on how joint actions have been implemented. If a member state is unable or unwilling to implement a joint action, it must justify its position to the other member states.[41]

Another improvement introduced by the Treaty of Maastricht was the inclusion of the defence field in the European foreign affairs field. Already after the end of the World War II, France and UK signed the Dunkirk agreement, a military cooperation between these two countries to protect each other in case Germany could become again a threat for them. The developing of the Cold War made clear that the enemy was not Germany, and the essence of the Treaty changed, becoming a European Defence Community. More countries joined the organization, like the Benelux or even West Germany, and the organization changed its name to Western European Union.[42] It had its own institutions, but based on cooperation, never on integration. In 1950, René Pleven proposed the creation of a European Defence Community, in order to establish a European defence in the Cold War, and control the creation of Western German Army. Its members were West Germany, France, Italy and the Benelux countries. It was a very big step in term of integration, and signed by all

---

[40] http://europa.eu/legislation_summaries/economic_and_monetary_affairs/institutional_and_economic_framework/treaties_maastricht_en.htm.

[41] Hix (1999), p. 389.

[42] http://www.weu.int/.

the member states, but the French Parliament stopped its confirmation. An important question arose during the ratification process, if Europe was going to have a common army, who was going to control it, who was going to decide when to use the army, how to use it, and hence hold the responsibility for the casualties. The lack of democracy of the European Institutions made unable them to lead this process. The Italians then proposed the European Political Community, an important step in terms of integration, similar to the current European Union, pushing for a federal approach in the European integration. This was too aggressive for the French positions, who rejected the EPC and hence the EDC.

The creation of NATO, in 1949, and its further development finished with the possibility of developing a European Defence Community, and established a conflict between the European states that last until today. The European states are divided in three main groups, the neutral states, the pro-American states and the Europeanist. The USA European supporters want a tight cooperation with NATO in the field of defence; its main members are UK, the Netherlands and the Central and East European member states of the Union. The British supports this idea because of their historical links with USA and its repulse for further integration in Europe that will mean bigger losses of national sovereignty. On the other hand, the new members of the UE understand NATO as the only military institution that could defence them from a hypothetical aggression from Russia. Mainly because it was because of the Cold War and USA that Soviet Union collapsed and these countries got free from the Soviet occupation, and because USA at the moment is the only power with enough military strength to stop Russia. Europe has not the power and neither the will to play the role of USA against Russia. In that sense, it is interesting to point out that the European identity will increase if Europe could defend itself from threats from abroad. Currently, USA plays this role, but if Europe could assume it, the citizens of all these states will be identified much more with the European Union, and with the European values, and the European construction, because they will see it as the power that is protecting them. Nevertheless, BREXIT has weakened this group and it is still not clear whether they will still remain as an option in Europe or their alternative will just vanish with the British withdraw.

The Europeanist on the other side, led by France and Germany, favoured a European defence policy independent of NATO. The end of the Cold War meant the reactivation of the Western European Union as a platform to develop the European army, the threat that Russia represents is smaller than the Soviet threat, and some European countries thought that Europe could face this and other threats by itself, without the support of USA. The Treaty of Maastricht recognized the WEU as integral part of development of the EU and provided for the foreign and defence ministers of the WEU member states to discuss defence issues within the framework of the EU Council. In order to avoid conflicts with the Atlantics states, the treaty included the reaffirmation that the WEU will strengthen the European pillar of the Atlantic alliance. The creation of European armed forces is the main challenge of the European integration in the coming years, and it will define the capacity of the Union to act as an independent actor in the world affairs.

The next step to develop the CFSP was the treaty of Amsterdam, done just a few years after Maastricht to amend the previous treaty focusing, especially in the field of CFSP. It started working in 1999.[43]

The treaty made several significant changes:

- Common strategies: A new instrument where the Council sets out a particular issue's objectives, duration and means. Common positions, joint actions or legislation implement it. Its intention is to give a clear focus on the external affairs of the Union.
- Distinction between common positions and joint actions: Joint actions are supposed to be used when specific operational action is required, while common positions are meant for less clearly definable situations.
- Constructive abstention: CSFP decision-making is based on unanimity, it means that every member state has to agree with the action or at least they do not vote against it. It helped the CFSP to become faster, because states could not agree on some issue and just with their abstention will express their disagreement, but the action will go on, because the states that abstain are not bound to participate in the implementation of a decision. Therefore, they can show that they are against it and they are not forced to follow it, but they do not veto it.
- Qualified majority voting: Amsterdam includes this voting system in two areas, common positions or joint actions to implement a common strategy adopted by unanimity in the European Council. In addition, the decisions to implement a joint action or common position already adopted by the Council decided by qualified majority.
- High representative for the CFSP: The Treaty created a new position to assist the Council in matters within the scope of the CFSP, in particular through contributing to the formulation, preparation and implementation of policy decisions, and, when appropriate and acting on behalf of the Council at the request of the Presidency, through conducting political dialogue with third countries. The first man to hold this office was Javier Solana, a Spanish socialist politician that in his early years was campaigning against the Spanish membership of NATO, and afterwards became the Secretary General of NATO. This was the most obvious reform of the Amsterdam treaty for the Europeans, because he gave a face to the CFSP. Finally, it implicated, that the problem faced by Kissinger in the 1970s about finding a phone number to call Europe was past.[44]
- Enhanced strategic planning: A new planning and early warning unit, the Policy Unit, established in the secretariat general of the Council under the direction of the high representative for the CFSP.
- European Security and Defence Policy: The Amsterdam Treaty strengthened the defence policy cooperation, by granting the European Council the competence to elaborate and implement defence policies, particularly with regard to armaments. The treaty also expresses the will to collaborate with NATO, again a compromise to

[43] Hamulák (2018).

[44] http://www.allacademic.com/meta/p_mla_apa_research_citation/0/9/7/9/0/p97909_index.html.

the Atlanticist states, as the nomination of Solana to the post of high representative because his previous job was in NATO.[45]

All these reforms created a real framework for the CFSP, but still its work was not enough strong to play an active role in the world affairs. Too much compromise between the member states made impossible strong positions, fast resolutions and hence successful policies.

The Lisbon Treaty has been the last reform of the CFSP. It started working in December 2009, and mainly in terms of CFSP reformed the high representative office. In order to joint efforts and become more effective, most of the European actions for foreign policies were concentrated in this position. It was a merged of the previous high representative and the European Commissioner for external relations and European neighbourhood policy. It stopped a duality between the Council and the Commission in the external affairs, trying to improve the effectiveness and make clear which office is on charge was for the external relations of the Union.

The Commission contributes with the European policies, an important budget in the external relations field, and numerous civil servants. The high representative adds the political legitimacy given by the Council and the power of the member states.[46] The new High Representative also becomes a vice president of the European Commission, a very important though symbolic move, because it is the first step to accept the communalization of the CFSP, to finally make it European. It is important to remind that the European Commission is the executive arm of the European Union, a part of the European integration, including the high representative in the Commission means recognizing that the CFSP needs to change its current development from cooperation to integration. It will take some years, hard negotiations, and some setbacks, but the stream is leading the CFSP to the European arena, to the integration. It means that the member states will share sovereignty in the European Union, and the Union will be their voice abroad. It does not mean that the member states give up these powers, it just means that they will share this sovereignty between them according to the rules of the European Union. Therefore, maybe, the new high representative, and its inclusion in the European Commission could become an empty symbol, just a declaration of intentions without real consequences. It is yet to see how is going to develop, so far it is an important member of the Commission, one of the big four top positions, but more symbolic than powerful.

The high representative is also the administrator of the European Defence Agency, in charge of the development of supporting the member states and the Council in their effort to improve European defence capabilities in the field of crisis management and to sustain the European Security and Defence Policy as it stands now and develops in future.[47]

The High Representative for Foreign Affairs and Security Policy is in charge of an External Action Service created by the Treaty of Lisbon.[48]

---

[45] Hix (1999), p. 390.

[46] http://europa.eu/lisbon_treaty/index_en.htm.

[47] http://www.eda.europa.eu/.

[48] http://www.eurostep.org/wcm/dmdocuments/BP41_EEAS_080602.pdf.

Finally, the High Representative for Foreign Affairs and Security Policy lost the place, previously occupied by the former high representative, as Secretary General of the Council of Ministers, position occupied by the new Union Minister of Foreign Affairs.[49] It is another separation of the CFSP from the sphere of influence of the member states locating it in the European common frame. Nevertheless, the high representative takes part in the meetings of the European Council without any voting power, but at least there is some coordination between the European institutions and the member states in the external actions of Europe. The role of Borrell, the newly appointed Spanish for this position is crucial for the development of the political capacity of the Union in the external affairs. Perhaps, a politician with his experience will be able to transform the institution, or his age, weakness of the socialist family in the Council or other obstacles will reduce his time in charge of the CFSP in a transitional period.

7 Conclusions

It is clear that in its economic relations, the EU is a world power, however, the world is changing and the current economical privileged position of the EU is challenged by other parts of the world, as China. The EU needs to focus in its comparative advantages, a way that needs more efforts that are common. More integration is required in order to keep the economic status of the EU.

On the other hand, the economic position of the EU comes from the national economies and the development created with the Single Market. The most powerful economies of the EU are Germany and France, two important countries in Europe, but medium in the world scale. They alone could never play an important role by themselves in the world affairs against China, USA or India; just with all the members of the EU, they could become leaders in the current world. So, more integration is required in order to present a compact block able to compete with other areas of the world.

The common currency, the Euro meant the end in the economic integration with the current shape of the Union; further steps need the framework of a European federation. It means more political integration is basic in order to achieve deeper economic integration. A common public debt, or common economy minister, or a European Union Monetary Fund, or other different economical options, can just work with new common institutions to establish the rules and look after their fulfilment.

In addition, the economic power of the EU does not reflect in the world politics its stature because the economy is mostly under the surveillance of the national governments. The high representative and the president of the Council have no executive powers in this field and no control over the different commissars of the Commission who are working with economic matters.

[49]Troitiño (2017).

An interesting proposal would be to unite all under the power of one institution. Then Europe could speak with a single and strong voice, having much more power and influence in the world affairs. The possibilities are not clear, but strengthening the office of the president of the European Commission, taking the responsibilities of the president of the European Council, the supervision of the high representative office, and the coordination with the economical commissars, could be the way. This option would find the opposition of the member states that do not want to share more sovereignty.[50]

Then, the European dream of common foreign and security policy will be much closer, with a single head leading it, a single voice of Europe, and making also easier the communalization of this policy, mainly with a voting system based on majority ending with the control of the member states over it and making it real European. Then, the EU will be in a stronger position in the international arena, defending better the interest of the Europeans in the world.

The military field is another weak spot in the external relations of the EU, without more investment in future European army. Currently, the European states do not have the material transportation means to transfer their soldiers around the world, and they need the transportation provided by NATO. In addition, the EU should end with the problem of the neutrality of some of its members, because otherwise, it is going to develop an army in the framework of the Western European Union that is going to represent just some part of the EU.

Finally, the main problem is about the control of the army, because someone should decide when, where and how to use it, someone should accept the responsibility of the casualties, someone should explain the European public opinion the development of the operations, the possible mistakes, the targets and so on. Integration here means sharing; the federalist option seems the best, with a democratic office chose by the European citizens in charge of this sensitive policy.

The current confrontation between China and the USA is defining a new world of international relations. The position of the European Union is still not clear, but whatever the Union decides, will affect the external relations of Europe in the first half of XXI century and perhaps even beyond. Now all the possibilities are possible and the confrontation could mean the final blow to the European influence in the world or an opportunity to regain a privilege position in the world affairs.

References

Booker, C., & North, R. (2016). *The great deception: Can the European Union survive?* Bloomsbury Publishing.

Castro, L. D., & Lago, J. R. R. (2018). Educación y diplomacia cultural en la primavera de Europa (1948-1954) = Education and Cultural Diplomacy in the Spring of Europe (1948-1954). *Revista de educación, 383,* 63–84.

[50] Kerikmäe et al. (2019).

Chochia, A., Troitiño, D. R., Kerikmäe, T., & Shumilo, O. (2018). Enlargement to the UK, the Referendum of 1975 and Position of Margaret Thatcher. In *Brexit* (pp. 115–139). Springer, Cham.
Färber, K. (2017). Mitterrand and the Great European Design—From the Cold War to the European Union. *Baltic Journal of European Studies, 7*(2), 132–147.
Hamulák, O. (2018). La carta de los derechos fundamentales de la union europea y los derechos sociales. *Estudios constitucionales, 16*(1), 167–186.
Hix, S. (1999). *The political system of the European Union*. Macmillan International Higher Education.
Kerikmäe, T. (2015). European history and the future of legal freedoms. *Baltic Journal of European Studies, 5*(2), 3–4.
Kerikmäe, T. (2019). Euroopa Inimõiguste Konventsiooni tõlgendamisest. *Juridica. International, 2019*, 2.
Kerikmäe, T., Troitiño, D. R., & Shumilo, O. (2019). An idol or an ideal? A case study of Estonian e-Governance: Public perceptions, myths and misbeliefs. *Acta Baltica Historiae et Philosophiae scientiarum, 7*(1).
Leonard, M. (2005). *Why Europe will run the 21st century* (pp. 49–56). London: Fourth estate.
Martín de la Guardia, R. M., & Pérez Sánchez, G. A. (2001). Historia de la integración europea. *Ariel, Barcelona*.
Moravcsik, A. (2013). *The choice for Europe: Social purpose and state power from Messina to Maastricht*. Routledge.
Outeda, C. C. (2001). *El proceso de constitucionalización de la Unión Europea: de Roma a Niza* (No. 3). Univ Santiago de Compostela.
Pawlas, I. (2015, September). The Visegrad countries and European union membership-selected issues. In *Proceedings of International Academic Conferences* (No. 2704866). International Institute of Social and Economic Sciences.
Ramiro Troitino, D., & Pando Ballesteros, M. D. L. P. (2017). Churchill's European integration model. *REVISTA DE OCCIDENTE, 433*, 57–71.
Rifkin, J. (2004). The European dream: How Europe's vision of the future is quietly eclipsing the American dream Polity Press.
Rosamond, B. (2000). Theories of European integration.
Troitiño, D. R. (2017). Jean Monnet before the first European Community: A historical perspective and critic. *Trames, 21*(3), 193–213.
Troitino, D. R., & Faerber, K. (2019). Historical errors in the initial conception of the euro and its subsequent development. *Brazilian Journal of Political Economy, 39*(2), 328–343.

The NATO-Russia Council—An Assessment of the NRC Prior to the Ukraine Crisis

Alexander Antonov and Thomas Hoffmann

Abstract Before the NATO-Russia Council's cooperation with Russia was suspended in 2014 against the background of the Ukraine crisis, it contributed in various fields as a platform for various cooperation projects. However, little research has been achieved so far on the function of the NRC in terms of international relations theories. This paper intends to analyse the NRC from neorealism and liberal institutionalism perspectives, trying to elucidate and discuss whether NATO's cooperation with Russia within the NRC had benefitted their mutual security before the Kremlin's illegal annexation of Crimea in March 2014.

Keywords NATO-Russia Council · Realism · Liberal institutionalism

1 Introduction

Around 30 years ago, the Cold War came to an end with the fall of the Berlin Wall and the dissolution of the Soviet Union. Overnight, with the election of the pro-Western president, Boris Yeltsin, Russia, was considered a partner by its previous adversaries. While the counterpart to the Western military alliance, the Warsaw Pact was disbanded,[1] NATO survived and even enlarged from 12 to 28 states today, of which most new members are former Soviet satellite countries. Although, for the Kremlin, this was a breach with NATO's promises not to extend the alliance further than to Eastern Germany,[2] even under the incumbent Russian president Vladimir Putin, the institutional relationship between both parties had been gradually strengthened until the Ukraine crisis erupted in 2014. Due to Russia's illegal annexation of Crimea, in breach of the NATO-Russia Founding Act, the Helsinki Accords and the Budapest

[1]Today, NATO's rather marginal counterpart is the CSTO, see http://www.odkb.gov.ru/start/index_aengl.htm.

[2]Putin at the 43rd Munich Security Conference: http://www.washingtonpost.com/wp-dyn/content/article/2007/02/12/AR2007021200555.html.

A. Antonov (✉) · T. Hoffmann
Tallinn Law School, Tallinn University of Technology, Ehitajate tee 5, 19086 Tallinn, Estonia
e-mail: alanto@taltech.ee

D. Ramiro Troitiño et al. (eds.), *The EU in the 21st Century*,
https://doi.org/10.1007/978-3-030-38399-2_13

Memorandum, NATO decided to halt all practical civilian and military cooperation with the Kremlin.[3] Tensions between both parties have risen to such a point that the Russian premier minister Medvedev spoke of a "period of a new Cold War" at the Munich Security Conference in 2016.[4]

Formally, the relationship between the political–military organisation NATO and the Russian Federation commenced with the creation of the North Atlantic Cooperation Council, an initiative to establish links between Western, Central and Eastern European countries.[5] The "honeymoon period" of the 90s, during which, e.g. US Secretary of State James Baker shared the idea of Russia joining NATO,[6] abated quickly with Russia's resistance towards NATO enlargement and its general discontent with its "junior partner" status.[7] The Partnership for Peace Initiative (PfP), which is the first step to NATO membership, and the establishment of the Permanent Joint Council (PJC) based on the new "Founding Act" in 1997 did not satisfy the Kremlin's ambitions of being considered an "equal" partner by the West.[8] NATO's actions in Kosovo exacerbated distrust and rendered the PJC as a consultative forum for security issues obsolete, as an isolated Russia had to face the view of 19 united NATO members.[9]

The PJC was replaced by the NRC, envisaged to satisfy Russia's desire for "equality", "reciprocity" and "parity"; Russia wanted to be considered an "equal partner" in the NRC, where its voice would be finally heard and its great power status recognised.[10]

Against this background, we intend to scrutinise the effectiveness of the NRC prior to the Ukraine crisis. Drawing upon two international relations theories, neorealism and liberal institutionalism, the main purpose of this paper is to elucidate and discuss *whether NATO's cooperation with Russia within the NRC had benefitted their mutual security before the Kremlin's illegal annexation of Crimea in March 2014.*

Given the current stalemate of both parties, the unstable European security order and the increase of new threats posed by terrorism, the topic is highly relevant. Since both NATO and Russia share a common enemy, international terrorism, we intend to point out the successes and failures of the NRC conducive to a possible rapprochement between both parties in the future.

---

[3]NRC: http://www.nato.int/nrc-website/en/articles/20140327-announcement/index.html.

[4]Medvedev at the 52nd Munich Security Conference: http://government.ru/en/news/21784/.

[5]Foxall (2014): 4.

[6]Forsberg and Herd (2015): 44.

[7]Ratti (2013): 143; Pouliot (2011): http://www.nato.int/docu/review/2011/NATO_Russia/Symbolic-Irritant/EN/index.htm.

[8]Forsberg and Herd (2015): 45–47.

[9]Ibid.

[10]Foxall (2014): 4; Forsberg and Herd (2015): 46–47.

2 Theoretical Framework

Both neorealists as Walz or Grieco and liberal institutionalists as Keohane or Martin start from the assumption that the international system is governed by anarchy, defined as the "absence of a common inter-state government".[11] The main distinction between the two IR theories is their approach towards handling the security dilemma that results from an anarchical system.

Neorealists argue that states are the main actors that shape structure, guided by a rational reasoning of survival in a self-help manner and by the promotion of national interest.[12] Anarchy results in states being always selfishly preoccupied with their own agenda, fearing to lose to others relatively.[13] A zero-sum logic impedes the creation of mutual trust making win-win cooperation almost impossible as states are always wary of the others' intentions.[14]

Taking issue with the neorealists' pessimistic view, liberal exponents assert that institutions could help create a rather more cooperative environment in which states trust each other because relative gains thinking is transformed into mutual interests.[15] For them, the security dilemma could be overcome by cooperation within an institutional framework where parties share (secrete) information with each other.[16] In an environment in which reciprocity is valued and states' interest considered equal, trust might enable win-win policies.[17]

Keohane provides a valid argument questioning the neorealist assertion that institutions were only of a marginal value.[18] He wonders why states do actually invest so many resources in institutions, although, following the neorealist logic, they know that "these institutions will not have any impact on patterns of cooperation".[19] Hence, according to the neorealist logic, there would be no rational explanation for why the NRC was established. However, Waltz would counter Keohane's argument asserting that the effectiveness of institutions depends on what the states intentions are within the institutions.[20] Neorealism does not rule out cooperation within an institutional framework per se, as Waltz contends.[21] The theory differs from liberal institutionalism in the fact that in neorealist logic strong states exploit institutions for their own interest and free ride in situations where its national interest is at stake.[22]

[11] Grieco (1988): 497.

[12] Grieco (1988): 488.

[13] Ibid.

[14] Grieco (1993): 127–128 (ed. Baldwin).

[15] Grieco (1988): 486.

[16] Keohane and Martin (1995): 45–46.

[17] Keohane and Martin (1995: 50.

[18] Keohane and Martin, 1995): 47–48.

[19] Ibid.

[20] Waltz (2000): 35.

[21] Ibid.

[22] Ibid.

Strong states interpret laws in the "way that suit them".[23] Assuming that NATO did only survive because the organisation could project and maintain the US hegemony on the European continent, and providing the example of NATO "expansion", Waltz and Mearsheimer criticise Keohane for his naive view on positive cooperation within an institutional framework: "Realism reveals what liberal institutionalist theory obscures, namely that international institutions serve primarily national rather than international interests".[24]

Generally, both theories entail weaknesses and strengths, which render the following analysis and discussion more interesting. While neorealism is good at explaining the importance of power and states' interest, it reaches its limits when it comes to providing an account on states' actions of a benevolent character. Here, it is, *inter alia*, referred to the US's initiated "reset policy" in the second phase of the NATO-Russia relationship within the NRC. Liberal institutionalism fills this theoretical gap and can scrutinise why states might not always be guided by selfish ambitions. Nevertheless, by putting too much focus on cooperation and interdependence, liberal institutionalists can be criticised for their idealistic interpretation of power. Examples as the NRC's failure to prevent both the Georgian and Ukraine crisis render those exponents vulnerable to fierce criticism by neorealists. It is therefore necessary to consider both theories with distance, taking their most valid arguments and trying to find a balance between both views.

The following section continues with an analysis and discussion of the NRC, where I will apply the theoretical concepts with the purpose of answering the main research question and assessing the theories' applicability on the topic.

3 Analysis and Discussion

3.1 Rationale Behind the Creation of the NRC

Reiterating the principles and areas of cooperation of the Founding Act on Mutual Relations in which both parties stated they "do not consider each other as adversaries" and are intended to "overcome{...} the vestiges of earlier confrontation and competition {in order to} strengthen{...} mutual trust and cooperation", Russia's president Vladimir Putin and NATO leaders signed the Rome Declaration, "NATO-Russia Relations: A new Quality", on 28th May 2002.[25] An inherent element of the NRC was to create "a lasting and inclusive peace in the Euro-Atlantic area on

---

[23] Ibid.

[24] Waltz (2000): 29.

[25] NRC, Background: http://www.nato.int/nato_static_fl2014/assets/pdf/pdf_2017_02/20170206_1702-nato-russia-en.pdf; Founding Act: http://www.nato.int/cps/cn/natohq/official_texts_25468.htm.

the principles of democracy and cooperative security".[26] Headed by NATO's Secretary General, meetings between ambassadors and military personnel took place on a monthly basis within the NRC.[27] Twice a year, foreign and defence ministers of both NATO and Russia convened in Brussels, and occasionally, summits were hold.[28]

Intended to face "unprecedented new threats" together, especially global terrorism, the NRC replaced its predecessor, the PJC, as a consensus-building institution where Russia was attributed with a privileged status.[29] Different to the PCJ's bilateral NATO+1 format, Russia could meet the other NATO members as a more equal partner within the NRC.[30] NATO promised the Kremlin not to confront it with already "precooked" decisions but to allow it to actively shape NATO policies in common agreed areas.[31]

9/11 has disclosed that NATO needed to change its priorities from "conventional threats by sovereign states" to the "fight against terrorism".[32] The flagrant terrorist plots, leading to the invocation of Art. 5 for the first time in NATO's history, demonstrated that the unprecedented challenges could be addressed more effectively, if NATO and Russia unite in their efforts. A new institution as the NRC could create trust and establish a conducive environment for win-win policies, in liberal institutionalists logic. NATO and Russia recognised that they could mutually benefit from collaboration within a framework that serves as an inclusive forum for "consultation, consensus-building, cooperation, joint decision and joint action" in nine areas of common interest: struggle against terrorism, crisis management, non-proliferation, arms control and confidence-building measures, theatre missile defence, search and rescue at sea, military-to-military cooperation and defence reform, civil emergencies and new threats and challenges.[33] While especially through its perilous Southern borders in Chechnya and Dagestan, Islamic terrorists infiltrated Russia, NATO had to cope with terrorism originating from the Middle East, mainly from Al-Qaida affiliates and the Taliban government in Afghanistan.[34] Taking this into consideration, the parties' core interest lied in eliminating terrorism and stabilising Central Asia, primarily Afghanistan.[35]

Russia's main goal was finally to gain influence over the decision-making process of the Euro-Atlantic security institutions, NATO's former Special Adviser for Central

---

[26] Rome Declaration: http://www.nato.int/nrc-website/media/59487/2002.05.28_nrc_rome_declaration.pdf.

[27] About NRC: http://www.nato.int/nrc-website/EN/about/index.html.

[28] Ibid.

[29] Ibid.

[30] NRC: http://www.nato.int/cps/it/natohq/topics_50091.htm.

[31] Forsberg and Herd (2015): 48.

[32] Spota (2011b): https://www.fairobserver.com/region/europe/whats-happening-nato-russia-relations/.

[33] As listed in Rome Declaration: http://www.nato.int/nrc-website/media/59487/2002.05.28_nrc_rome_declaration.pdf.

[34] Sherr (2014).

[35] Ibid; Foxall (2014): 4.

and Eastern Europe, Willem Matser argued.[36] He expressed scepticism prior to the creation of the NRC that a new strategic partnership with Russia would automatically increase trust and result in win-win policies.[37] Especially Russia's reluctance to democratise and its imperialist ambitions stood in conflict with the core principles of the Founding Act. A strong and sustainable partnership requires compromising national interests.[38] If NATO and Russia were unwilling to do so, "the backlash could be serious and long-lasting".[39]

Although the first working period of the NRC was promising (2002–2008/08), it did not last long, until Matser was proven right with his neorealistic interpretation of powerful countries' national interest.

3.2 The NRC's Achievements Until Russio-Georgian War

In the first six years of NATO-Russia collaboration, both neorealistic and liberal institutionalist arguments can be applied. What speaks in favour of the latter exponents are, e.g. that Russia permitted NATO infrastructure to traverse its territory in support of the International Security and Assistance Force (ISAF) in Afghanistan.[40] Moreover, neorealism reaches its limits in explaining why Russia allowed the US to establish military bases in its neighbourhood, as in Uzbekistan.[41] If the neorealist's assertion, that states inherently distrust each other, was proven right, then Russia would have never let its main military and political adversary, the US, station fighter jets close to its borders. In liberal institutionalist logic, due to the new security guarantee by the NRC, Russia temporarily trusted in the US efforts to stabilise the Central Asian region. The example evidences that NATO and Russia believed that cooperation in the area of counterterrorism would mutually increase their security.

This paper argues that the struggle against terrorism yielded the most promising results within the NRC, because deterring terrorism was in both parties' core national interest. Neither Russia nor NATO could lose relatively to the other as terrorists presented a threat to both of them.[42] The Beslan school siege in Russia or the train bombings in Spain's capital in 2004 resulted in a common, comprehensive "Action Plan on Terrorism".[43] It laid out three strategic objectives: (1) preventing

[36]Matser (2001): 21.

[37]Ibid.

[38]Ibid.

[39]Ibid.

[40]Foxall (2014): 4.

[41]Sleivyte (2010), 38–39.

[42]Kulhanek (2011): 42–43.

[43]NATO-Russia Action Plan on Terrorism: http://www.nato.int/cps/on/natohq/official_texts_21003.htm?.

terrorism, (2) combating terrorist activities and (3) managing the consequences of terrorist acts.[44] In this regard, the "cooperative airspace initiative" was created with the purpose of increasing air safety and help deterring terrorist attacks as 9/11.[45] The initiative materialised and improved air-transparency, predictability and interoperability in the Euro-Atlantic airspace.[46]

A common project on counter-narcotics training for Afghan and Central Asian police forces or Russia's offer to contribute to NATO's maritime counter-terrorist operation in the Mediterranean, Operation Active Endeavour, can be all considered as strong signs of both parties' determination to cooperate in the area of counterterrorism.[47] A mix of neorealist and liberal institutionalist thinking guided former NATO Secretary General Jaap de Hoop Sheffer, who spoke of a "results-oriented partnership {between Russia and NATO} based on pragmatism and shared interest".[48] In general, the fight on international terror, consolidating and uniting both parties, became more and more the core driving factor of the NRC. Russia's former defence minister Sergei Ivanov evidences this claim calling the NRC the "New Anti-Terrorist Organization".[49]

Although also in other areas as in "theatre missile defence" or "search and rescue" joint exercises were practised in the context of confidence-building measures,[50] considerable disagreement remained regarding the US's withdrawal from the ABM Treaty and NATO's "open door" policy that resulted in further NATO enlargement to Russia's borders.[51] Putin's personal involvement in the Ukraine election in 2004, fearing to lose a key ally to NATO, testifies to the neorealist argument, that trust was still defined in Hobbesian terms despite cooperation within the NRC.[52] While in one area, the parties found common ground, in others the NRC could not overcome major differences between NATO and Russia, because of considerable lack of trust.[53] The liberal institutionalist argument, that interdependence would solve this dilemma, is rendered implausible in areas where the national interest of one party, Russia, ontologically conflicts with the other. Still thinking in zero-sum logic, the Kremlin criticised the incorporation of former Soviet ruled countries into NATO as it created an imbalance of power on the European continent, standing in conflict with Russia's security interest.[54]

---

[44] Ibid.

[45] Liik and Maigre (2016), ECFR: http://www.ecfr.eu/article/commentary_nato_russia_dialogue_and_the_future_of_the_nato_russia_council.

[46] Ibid.

[47] NATO-Russia, Forging Deeper Relations: https://scoalanato.files.wordpress.com/2010/03/nato-russia.pdf; Relations with Russia: http://www.nato.int/cps/en/natolive/topics_50090.htm#.

[48] Ibid.

[49] Sergei Ivanov's speech (13 July 2004) quoted by Ratti (2013): 144.

[50] NATO Russia, Milestones in Relations: http://www.nato.int/cps/en/natolive/topics_50090.htm#.

[51] Ratti (2013): 145.

[52] Nygren (2006): 141–142 (eds. Hallenberg and Karlsson).

[53] Averre (2014): 58 (eds. Michta and Hilde).

[54] Averre (2014): 56 (eds. Michta and Hilde).

In this regard, Russia's military actions in Georgia after the Bucharest Summit[55] are therefore to be considered as a red line setting to NATO. Russia's counter-attack on Georgian forces in the separatist region of South Ossetia and later on, on official Georgian territory, led to a destabilised European security order and a temporal freeze of cooperation within the NRC.[56] Neorealists were proven right that despite cooperation within an institutionalised framework, conflicts between powerful countries will remain. Moreover, assessing the crisis management of the NRC regarding the Georgio-Russian war, just as its predecessor, the NRC failed in confidence-building measures, as it could not establish "early warning mechanisms" to prevent such a crisis.[57]

To the detriment of both parties common security, this huge weakness of the NRC will also remain in the second phase of cooperation, between the "reset policy" and the Ukraine crisis. However, what is interesting to mention is that Russia remained cooperative in one "key area{...}"[58] of the NRC, namely counter-terrorism. For example, Russia continued to provide logistical support to ISAF and both parties maintained collaboration in counter-narcotics during the NRC's partial suspension.[59] This once again testifies to the great potential the NRC holds as an anti-terrorist organisation.

3.3 *The NRC's Achievements During the "Reset Policy"*

The fact that both parties' security is heavily intertwined and the big European powers Germany and France understood that with Russia in isolation, neither counterterrorism in Afghanistan nor strategic armaments issues as the CFE Treaty[60] or nuclear weapons could be discussed, efforts of de-escalation were quickly introduced by NATO.[61]

Moreover, informed by the newly elected president Obama about his intentions to reset relations with Russia, NATO foreign ministers decided to re-approach Moscow.[62] At that time, NATO remained hopeful to reengage Russia for the purpose of creating greater stability on the European continent and of deterring the

---

[55] Ukraine and Georgia have been promised to become NATO members in the future; this has resulted in Russia's foreign minister's and Moscow's 'bewilderment', 'regret' and 'alertness'; Forsberg and Herd (2015): 50.

[56] NATO Russia, Milestones in Relations: http://www.nato.int/cps/en/natolive/topics_50090.htm#.

[57] Averre (2014): 55 (eds. Michta and Hilde); Spota (2011a): https://www.fairobserver.com/region/europe/whats-happening-nato-russia-relations/.

[58] NATO Russia, Milestones in Relations: http://www.nato.int/cps/en/natolive/topics_50090.htm#.

[59] Forsberg and Herd (2015): 49.

[60] Russia abandoned the CFE Treaty in 2007 since new NATO countries did not join it, creating a security dilemma for the Kremlin: https://www.armscontrol.org/ACT/2015_04/News-Briefs/Russia-Completes-CFE-Treaty-Suspension.

[61] Forsberg and Herd (2015): 49.

[62] NATO Russia, Milestones in Relations: http://www.nato.int/cps/en/natolive/topics_50090.htm.

global terrorist threat together, building on the previous achievements within the NRC. 18 months after Russia's official recognition of South Ossetia and Abkhazia, the NRC resumed its work and initiated a Joint Review of Twenty-first Century Common Security Challenges.[63]

Neorealism reaches it limits in explaining the reset policy, because a powerful adversary as the US does not offer cooperation to Russia after a serious crisis if it would not gain something from it. For liberal institutionalists, the US's push for a new START Treaty, which led to the reduction of strategic warheads from 2200 to 1550 and enabled a verification regime of both parties' nuclear weapons,[64] was aimed at improving mutual trust. Nevertheless, one has to consider that the role of the NRC was marginal in the negotiation of this treaty since it was concluded in bilateral talks between the US and Russia.[65] This example illustrates the weakness of the NRC and takes issue with liberal institutionalist reasoning on the inclusiveness of institutions because it is mainly two powerful countries, the US and Russia, that shape the common security agenda. It also demonstrates the importance of the US within NATO and its powerful leverage over NRC decision making.

A crucial policy the parties had been failing to agree on despite common exercises was in the area of missile defence. On the initiative of the US administration, a ballistic missile defence (BMD) shield should be created to counter threats posed by rogue states. Mainly addressed against Iranian missiles, Russia was concerned with the new "phased adaptive approach" of the US, stating, in neorealist logic, that such a strategy would unbalance the European security order.[66] Despite the idea about creating a joint Missile Data Fusion Centre and Obama's decision to cancel the fourth phase of the BMD project, Russia's criticism remained as NATO did not provide a legal guarantee that the system will not be used against Russia.[67] The text of NATO's 2010 Strategic Concept, that included Russia as partner in the area of missile defence,[68] did not reassure the Kremlin.

In neorealist logic, it is understandable that Russia was reluctant to cooperate with NATO since the US administration wanted to create two different BMD systems, one NATO system stationed in Poland and the Czech Republic in reach of Russia's territory, and the other would be a Russian system.[69] The Kremlin's push for a joint missile shield ended to no avail, because NATO members did not want to share sensitive information with Moscow,[70] a typical characteristic of powerful states,

[63] Ibid.

[64] Johnson (2011): 2.

[65] Ibid.

[66] Averre (Averre 2014): 61 (eds. Michta and Hilde).

[67] Gates (2014): 531; Chicago Summit Declaration: http://www.nato.int/cps/en/natohq/official_texts_87593.htm?selectedLocale=en.

[68] NATO Strategic Concept 2010: http://www.nato.int/nato_static_fl2014/assets/pdf/pdf_publications/20120214_strategic-concept-2010-eng.pdf.

[69] Spota (2011a): https://www.fairobserver.com/region/middle_east_north_africa/nato-russia-relations-theatre-missile-defense/.

[70] Averre (2014): 62 (eds. Michta and Hilde).

neorealists would argue. Russia felt betrayed by NATO and thought that it relatively loses to the Western alliance in regard to its security. Liberal institutionalists were proven wrong that the NRC would increase trust between both parties despite partial achievements in the military-to-military area, such as in submarine search and rescue exercises,[71] and especially in counterterrorism.

Looking from today's perspective, the Lisbon Summit in 2010 could not significantly increase trust between both parties despite Russia's foreign minister Lavrov stating that "the logic of negative interdependence {has been transformed} to a logic of positive interdependence".[72] Although the NRC Joint Statement spoke of a "new stage of cooperation towards a true strategic partnership" and based on the negative experience in the first phase of the NRC the parties agreed that "the NRC is a forum for political dialogue at all times and on all issues, including where {they} disagree",[73] the lack of trust remained an ontological hurdle for the NATO-Russia relationship.[74]

Building on the achievements in the area of counterterrorism, common undertakings as counter-narcotics Training, the creation of a NRC Helicopter Maintenance Trust Fund to help improve Afghan Air Force capabilities[75] or a joint technology efforts to invent a machine called the "Stand-off Explosive Detection" system, that can detect terrorist bombs in mass transport,[76] support our main argument *that the NRC has been primarily a counterterrorism organisation* and helped improve both parties' security in this regard. The common fight on terrorism was the core area of shared interest where both could agree on without compromising their own security to the other. It is not without reason why Russia's ambassador to NATO called the cooperation a "success" in this area.[77]

Another example testifying to the authors' argument is the "Cooperative Airspace Initiative". Only months prior to Russia's illegal annexation of Crimea and NATO's decision to suspend all NRC cooperation, the parties undertook a comprehensive counterterrorism exercise ("Vigilant Skies") over Poland, Russia and Turkey with fighter jets controlled from the Arctic to the Baltic Sea, aimed at increasing NATO's and Russia's capabilities in the fight against air terrorism.[78]

Similar to the Russio-Georgian war in 2008, the NRC, conceived as a consultative and consensus-building forum, failed to prevent the Ukraine crisis. Retrospectively,

---

[71]NATO Review, Monaghan (2011): http://www.nato.int/docu/review/2011/NATO_Russia/Resuscitating-partnership/EN/index.htm.

[72]Lavrov, speech at the 47th Munich Security Conference: https://www.securityconference.de/Lavrov-Sergey-V.696.0.html?&L=1.

[73]NRC Joint Statement, Lisbon Summit (2010): http://www.nato.int/cps/po/natohq/news_68871.htm.

[74]NATO Review, Eggert (2011): http://www.nato.int/docu/review/2011/NATO_Russia/Step-forward/EN/index.htm.

[75]NRC, Trust Fund: http://www.nato.int/nrc-website/EN/articles/20130712-nrc-hmtf/index.html.

[76]NRC, STANDEX: http://www.nato.int/nrc-website/EN/articles/20121123-nrc-10-years-standex/index.html.

[77]Grushko (2014).

[78]NATO, Vigilant Skies: http://www.nato.int/cps/en/natohq/news_103663.htm?selectedLocale=en.

in addition to mutual distrust resulting from NATO's enlargement or the parties' disagreement on a missile defence shield, events as NATO's intervention in Libya or the US intention to oust Russia's ally Assad in Syria perpetuated mistrust and impeded the "reset policy".[79] Neorealists have therefore been proven right that cooperation between powerful actors is only possible in areas where they share most interest in. In regard to the NRC, this has been the area of counter-terrorism.

4 Main Criticism of the NRC and Concluding Remarks

Assessing the general goal of the NRC, namely to create "a lasting and inclusive peace in the Euro-Atlantic area",[80] we concur with the criticism shared by academics and state officials in regard to the NRC. This paper has shown that as a liberal institutionalist organisation, the NRC has failed to significantly increase both parties' security, create trust and/or at least minder the effects of distrust so as to allow cooperation in other eight key areas than only in one, namely counterterrorism.

Referring back to the quote mentioned in the beginning of the paper, Rasmussen is right to say that, on the one hand, the NRC holds great potential for Europe's security; on the other, this potential could not be materialised because of great disagreements in core political areas. His argument that "{o}ne major disagreement and {the relationship} would falter" was proven right by Russia's illegal annexation of Crimea just one month after his speech.[81]

Averre is right to criticise the NRC that it has not developed into a "forum for real deliberation over strategic issues"[82] but, in Trenin's logic, became more a "technical workshop—useful, but extremely narrow in scope".[83] Moreover, the NRC could not overcome the previous flaws of the PJC, as NATO members confronted Russia with an "already negotiated united position" in the Council.[84] This fact perpetuated distrust and impeded win-win policies in core security areas. Rogozin's statement, closely in line with neorealism's logic, one year after the Georgian crisis, supports our argument: "{N}o one should ensure their own security at the expense of others".[85]

Pouliot sheds light on the NRC's marginal achievements by asserting that both parties' "incompatible expectations" hindered mutually beneficial policies in various

[79] Averre (2014): 64–65 (eds. Michta and Hilde).

[80] Rome Declaration: http://www.nato.int/nrc-website/media/59487/2002.05.28_nrc_rome_declaration.pdf.

[81] Speech by NATO Secretary General Rasmussen (2014): http://www.nato.int/cps/en/natohq/opinions_106788.htm?selectedLocale=en.

[82] Averre (2014): 57 (eds. Michta and Hilde).

[83] Trenin (2009): 300.

[84] Rahr (2016): http://valdaiclub.com/a/highlights/russia-nato-forced-or-unforced-dialogue/.

[85] Rogozin (2009): 23.

core security areas.[86] While NATO offered Russia cooperation without providing the Kremlin a veto right over its decisions, Moscow sought an "exclusive forum" where it could significantly influence NATO's decision making over core European security matters.[87] NATO, however, guided by neorealist logic, recognised Russia's rational reasoning and remained sceptical in providing the Kremlin a right to complicate or even block NATO policies.[88]

With the help of liberal institutionalism, one can question neorealism and ask why Russia then still agreed to cooperate with NATO within the NRC, both before the Georgian crisis and even during the reset policy. This paper has disclosed the flaws of neorealism. States are not solely guided by their own power interests that block further cooperation. There remains always room for collaboration if states recognise goodwill of the other actor. The beginning of NATO's reset policy provides a tangible example to support this liberal institutionalist claim, which is also evidenced by Lavrov's hopeful statement characterising the relationship between NATO and Russia as transforming from "negative{…} to positive interdependence" months after the Lisbon Summit.[89]

A crucial aspect, which neither realism nor liberal institutionalism can explain, is the parties' disagreement on democracy and how their different perceptions of each other have resulted in distrust. Within the NRC, NATO as a democratic politico-military organisation has not achieved the aim of creating a lasting peace in Europe based on democratic principles laid out in the Founding Act. To cover this important issue, one could have applied a third IR theory, namely Constructivism. As a suggestion for future research on this topic, this approach could explain in detail how Russia's different interpretation of norms, values and its negative experience from the past have impeded trust and hindered NRC cooperation in areas of missile defence, in the reactivation of the CFR treaty or, as today's Ukraine crisis evidences, in resolving the division and imbalance of power in Europe by a mutually beneficial, equal dialogue in faith of "animus in consulendo liber".

---

[86]NATO Review, Pouliot (2011): http://www.nato.int/docu/review/2011/NATO_Russia/Symbolic-Irritant/EN/index.htm.

[87]Ibid.

[88]Ratti (2013): 159.

[89]Lavrov, speech at the 47th Munich Security Conference: https://www.securityconference.de/Lavrov-Sergey-V.696.0.html?&L=1.

Bibliography

Primary Sources

NATO Documents:

Chicago Summit Declaration. (2012). *Issued by the Heads of State and Government Participating in the Meeting of the North Atlantic Council in Chicago on 20 May 2012*. Accessed June 3, 2017. http://www.nato.int/cps/en/natohq/official_texts_87593.htm?selectedLocale=en.

Founding Act on Mutual Relations. (1997). *Cooperation and security between NATO and the Russian Federation Signed in Paris, France*. Accessed June, 3 2017. http://www.nato.int/cps/cn/natohq/official_texts_25468.htm.

NATO and Russia Hold Joint Counter-Terror Exercise 'Vigilant Skies'. (2013). Accessed June 3, 2017. http://www.nato.int/cps/en/natohq/news_103663.htm?selectedLocale=en.

Nato Russia relations: A new quality. Declaration by Heads of State and Government of Nato Member States and the Russian Federation. (2002). Accessed June 3, 2017. http://www.nato.int/nrc-website/media/59487/2002.05.28_nrc_rome_declaration.pdf.

NATO-Russia, Forging Deeper Relations. (2010). Accessed June 3, 2017. https://scoalanato.files.wordpress.com/2010/03/nato-russia.pdf.

NATO Russia Relations: The Background. (2017). Accessed June 3, 2017. http://www.nato.int/nato_static_fl2014/assets/pdf/pdf_2017_02/20170206_1702-nato-russia-en.pdf.

Strategic Concept for the Defence and Security of the Members of the North Atlantic Treaty Organization. (2010). Adopted by Heads of State and Government at the NATO Summit in Lisbon 19–20 November 2010. Accessed June 3, 2017. http://www.nato.int/nato_static_fl2014/assets/pdf/pdf_publications/20120214_strategic-concept-2010-eng.pdf.

NATO Online Resources:

NATO. (2010). *NATO-Russia Council Joint Statement at the Meeting of the NATO-Russia Council Held in Lisbon on 20 November 2010*. Accessed June 3, 2017. http://www.nato.int/cps/po/natohq/news_68871.htm.

NATO-Russia Action Plan on Terrorism. (2011). *Superseded by the NATO-Russia Action Plan on Terrorism Agreed Upon at the NATO-Russia Council Meeting in Berlin at the Level of Foreign Affairs Ministers—15 April 2011*. Accessed June 3, 2017. http://www.nato.int/cps/on/natohq/official_texts_21003.htm?.

NATO Russia Council. (2013). *Afghan Helicopter Trust Fund Set for Second Phase*. Accessed 3rd June 2017. http://www.nato.int/nrc-website/EN/articles/20130712-nrc-hmtf/index.html.

NATO Russia Council. (2013). *STANDEX counter terrorism project: 10 years 10 stories anniversary feature*. Accessed June 3, 2017. http://www.nato.int/nrc-website/EN/articles/20121123-nrc-10-years-standex/index.html.

NATO Russia Council. (2014). *Statement by NATO Foreign Ministers*. Accessed June 3, 2017. http://www.nato.int/nrc-website/en/articles/20140327-announcement/index.html.

NATO. (2017). *NATO-Russia Council*. Accessed June 3, 2017. http://www.nato.int/cps/it/natohq/topics_50091.htm.

NATO. (2017). *Relations with Russia. Milestones in Relations*. Accessed June 3, 2017. http://www.nato.int/cps/en/natolive/topics_50090.htm.

NATO Russia Council. (2017). About NRC. Accessed June 4, 2017. About NRC: http://www.nato.int/nrc-website/EN/about/index.html.

NATO Videos (Interviews):

Grushko, A. (2014). Video. *NATO and Russia: Uneasy partners?* 3:22–4:22. Accessed June 3, 2017. http://www.natolibguides.info/nato-russia/videos.

Sherr, J. (2014). Video. *NATO and Russia: Uneasy partners?* 2:46–3:03. Accessed June 3, 2017. http://www.natolibguides.info/nato-russia/videos.

Speeches:
Lavrov, Sergey. (2011). *Speech at the 47th Munich Security Conference*. Accessed February 9, 2011. https://www.securityconference.de/Lavrov-Sergey-V.696.0.html?&L=1.
Medvedev, D. (2016). *Dmitry Medvedev's Speech at the Panel Discussion of the 52nd Munich Security Conference*. Accessed June 3, 2017. http://government.ru/en/news/21784/.
Putin, V. (2007). *Putin's Prepared Remarks at 43rd Munich Conference on Security Policy*. Accessed June 3, 2017. http://www.washingtonpost.com/wp-dyn/content/article/2007/02/12/AR2007021200555.html.
Rasmussen, A. F. (2014). NATO and Russia—Time to engage. *Remarks by NATO Secretary General Anders Fogh Rasmussen at the 50th Munich Security Conference*. Accessed June 3, 2017. http://www.nato.int/cps/en/natohq/opinions_106788.htm?selectedLocale=en.

Secondary Sources

Academic Journals:
Forsberg, Tuomas, & Herd, Graeme. (2015). Russia and NATO: From windows of opportunities to closed doors. *Journal of Contemporary European Studies, 23*(1), 41–57.
Foxall, A. (2014). A fateful summit: The future of NATO's relationship with Russia. Russia Studies Centre. *The Henrey Jackson Society. Policy Paper No. 1*, 1–15.
Grieco, J. M. (1988). Anarchy and the limits of cooperation: A realist critique of the Newest Liberal Institutionalism. *International Organization, 42*(3), 485–507.
Johnson, J. D. (2011). Developing better relations with Russia. *Small Wars Journal., 7*(2), 1–6.
Keohane, R. O., & Martin, L. L. (1995). The promise of institutionalist theory. *International Security, 20*(1), 39–51.
Kulhanek, J. (2011). Russia's uncertain rapprochement with NATO. *The RUSI Journal, 156*(1), 40–45.
Matser, W. (2001). Towards a new strategic partnership. *NATO Review, 49*(1), 19–21.
Ratti, L. (2013). 'Resetting' NATO–Russia relations: a realist appraisal two decades after the USSR. *The Journal of Slavic Military Studies, 26*(2), 141–161.
Rogozin, D. (2009). On our terms. *World Today, 65*(4), 22–23.
Trenin, D. (2009). NATO and Russia: partnership or peril? The Atlantic Alliance and Russia need to decide, and soon, whether they want to build security with or against each other. Partnership would be far better for both sides. *Current History, 108*(720), 209–303.
Waltz, K. N. (2000). NATO expansion: A realist's view. *Contemporary Security Policy, 21*(2), 23–38.
Books:
Averre, D. (2014). Dealing with Russia. A new 2020 vision? In A. A. Michta & P. S. Hilde (Eds.), *The future of NATO. Regional defense and global* (pp. 55–75). Ann Arbor: The University of Michigan Press.
Gates, R. (2014). *Duty: Memoirs of a secretary at war*. New York: Alfred A Knopf.
Grieco, J. M. (1993). Anarchy and the limits of cooperation: A realist critique of the newest liberal institutionalism. In: D. A. Baldwin (Ed.), *Neorealism and neoliberalism. The contemporary debate* (pp. 116–140). New York: Columbia University Press.
Nygren, B. (2006). The implications for Putin's policy toward Ukraine and Belarus of NATO and EU expansion. In: Hallenberg, J., & Karlsson, H. (Eds.), *Changing transatlantic security relations. Do the US, the EU and Russia form a new strategic triangle?* (pp. 125–145). London: Routledge.
Sleivyte, J. (2010). *Russia's European agenda and the Baltic States*. London: Routledge.
Expert Opinions:
Eggert, K. (2011). One step forward. *NATO review*. Accessed June 3, 2017. http://www.nato.int/docu/review/2011/NATO_Russia/Step-forward/EN/index.htm.

Liik, K., & Maigre, M. (2016). *NATO-Russia dialogue and the future of the NATO-Russia Council*. European Council on Foreign Relations. Accessed June 3, 2017. http://www.ecfr.eu/article/commentary_nato_russia_dialogue_and_the_future_of_the_nato_russia_council.

Monaghan, A. (2011). NATO and Russia: Resuscitating the partnership. *NATO Review*. Accessed June 3, 2017. http://www.nato.int/docu/review/2011/NATO_Russia/Resuscitating-partnership/EN/index.htm.

Pouliot, V. (2011). Dealing with the symbolic irritant in NATO-Russia diplomacy. *NATO Review*. Accessed June 3, 2017. http://www.nato.int/docu/review/2011/NATO_Russia/Symbolic-Irritant/EN/index.htm.

Rahr, A. (2016). Russia-NATO: forces or unforced dialogue? *Valdai Discussion Club*. Accessed June 3, 2017. http://valdaiclub.com/a/highlights/russia-nato-forced-or-unforced-dialogue/.

Spota, A. (2011). NATO – Russia relations: Theatre missile defense. *Fair Observer*. Accessed June 3, 2017. https://www.fairobserver.com/region/middle_east_north_africa/nato-russia-relations-theatre-missile-defense/.

Spota, A. (2011). What's happening with NATO—Russia relations? *Fair Observer*. Accessed June 3, 2017. https://www.fairobserver.com/region/europe/whats-happening-nato-russia-relations/.

Other Online Resources:

Kingston, R. (2015). *Russia completes CFE treaty suspension*. Accessed June 3, 2017. https://www.armscontrol.org/ACT/2015_04/News-Briefs/Russia-Completes-CFE-Treaty-Suspension.

ODKB. (2017). *Basic facts*. Accessed June 3, 2017. http://www.odkb.gov.ru/start/index_aengl.htm.

Ukraine in European Human Rights Regime: Breaking *Path Dependence* from Russia

Iurii H. Barabash, Oleksandr V. Serdiuk and Volodymyr M. Steshenko

Abstract In this article, we use the notion of '*path dependence*' to explain, on the one hand, Ukraine's continuing dependence on Russia stemming from the hundreds of years that the Ukrainians were governed by the Russian Empire and later the USSR. Among other things, this dependence led to some parts of Southern and Eastern Ukraine being populated by Russian-born settlers and their descendants, which is still manifested in their historical and sociocultural orientation toward a closer integration with Russia. On the other hand, the notion of '*path dependence*' implies significant differences between Ukraine and Russia, especially due to many Ukrainians self-identifying as a European nation. The European self-identification of Ukrainians is apparent in the desire of the vast majority to overcome dependence on Russia through integration into the European political, legal, cultural, and economic system. We firmly believe that, to successfully overcome dependence on Russia, Ukraine and Ukrainians first need a fundamental recognition of European standards of human rights and the European human rights protection model in general. The success of the 2014–2018 democratic reforms in Ukraine is obvious, but no less obvious is the fact that the positive changes in Ukraine are far from irreversible. At present, the biggest threat to Ukraine is the 'force field' of the 'Russian World', and it is in being able to efficiently resist this threat that Ukraine needs Europe's support the most.

Keywords Path dependence theory · European Union · European integration · Ukrainian–Russian relations · 'Russian World'

1 Introduction

In 1991, Ukraine declared independence and founded a separate state. Ukraine is the only post-Soviet republic to hold a national referendum (December 1, 1991) in which

---

I. H. Barabash (✉)
Academic Affairs, Yaroslav Mudryi National Law University, Kharkiv, Ukraine

O. V. Serdiuk · V. M. Steshenko
International Law Department, Yaroslav Mudryi National Law University, Kharkiv, Ukraine
e-mail: steshenko_vm@ukr.net

D. Ramiro Troitiño et al. (eds.), *The EU in the 21st Century*,
https://doi.org/10.1007/978-3-030-38399-2_14

a clear majority expressed itself in favor of the Act of Declaration of Independence of Ukraine (August 21, 1991).[1] The referendum was seen as a sign of true democracy on part of Ukraine and its people, so the very next day, December 2, 1991, the European Council adopted a joint declaration on Ukraine, whereby the European Community and its member states in particular called upon Ukraine to honor all commitments under the Helsinki Final Act, the Charter of Paris, and other relevant CSCE documents.

For its part, Ukraine announced its intentions toward European integration in the Main Directions of Foreign Policy of Ukraine, adopted by the Verkhovna Rada (Ukrainian parliament) on July 2, 1993,[2] which specified as one of the long-term goals of Ukrainian foreign policy 'Ukraine's membership in the European Communities'.

An integral element of this course was recognizing the need for a new model of human rights protection. Article X of the Declaration of State Sovereignty of Ukraine of July 16, 1990,[3] recognized 'the prevalence of general human values over class values and the priority of generally accepted standards of international law over the standards of the domestic law'. This was the first step in the complex and controversial process of Ukraine's integration into the European system of human rights protection.

Ukraine's attainment of a formal status in its relations with the Council of Europe and the European Union (such as various membership options or relationship statuses) is not in itself a guarantee of organic and efficient implementation of the institutional and value-based human rights mechanisms that they have in place. Since 1991, Ukraine has seen a process of democratization, an element of which has been the creation of a system of human rights protection at least at the level of minimum standards enshrined in the form of a 'European consensus', whereby human rights are recognized as a key constituent of the European public order. The dragging out of these reforms and the numerous obstacles in their path have been a subject of continuing political dialogue between Ukraine and European institutions (particularly the Council of Europe and European Union authorities), with intermittent flare-ups of negativity dating back to the early 1990s.[4]

Since the end of the last century, it has become increasingly apparent that it is the human rights issue that poses the biggest obstacles to European integration. Let us recount the key dates in the relationships between Ukraine and the EU. On June 11, 1998, the President of Ukraine signed the Strategy of Integration of Ukraine into the European Union,[5] and on September 14, 2000, the Program of Integration of Ukraine into the European Union[6] was adopted. Article 11(2) of the Law of Ukraine 'On the Principles of Domestic and Foreign Policy' of July 1, 2010,[7] states that one of

---

[1] Akt proholoshennia nezalezhnosti Ukrayiny (1991).

[2] Pro osnovni napriamy zovnishnioyi polityky Ukrayiny (1993).

[3] Deklaratsiya pro derzhavny suverenitet Ukrayiny (1990).

[4] Petrov and Serdiuk (2009), pp. 189–220.

[5] Stratehiya intehratsiyi Ukrayiny do Yevropeyskoho Soyuzu (1998).

[6] Programa intehratsiyi Ukrayiny do Yevropeyskoho Soyuzu (2000).

[7] Zakon Ukrayiny 'Pro zasady vnutrishnioyi i zovnishnioyi polityky' (2010).

the fundamental foreign policy principles is ensuring Ukraine's integration into the European political, economical, and legal landscape in order to attain membership in the European Union.

Article 1(3) of the Law of Ukraine 'On National Security of Ukraine' of June 21, 2018,[8] states that Ukraine's integration into the European political, economical, security, and legal space and attaining membership in the European Union is one of the fundamental national interests of Ukraine.

Finally, the course toward integration into the European Union was set down in the ultimate document, the Constitution of Ukraine,[9] with the preamble now 'confirming the European identity of the Ukrainian people and the irreversibility of the European and Euro-Atlantic course of Ukraine'; Article 85 tasking the Verkhovna Rada with the 'realization of the strategic course of the state on acquiring full-fledged membership of Ukraine in the European Union'; Article 102 stating that 'the President of Ukraine is a guarantor of the implementation of the strategic course of the state for gaining full-fledged membership of Ukraine in the European Union'; and Article 116(1-1) stating that the Cabinet of Ministers of Ukraine 'provides the implementation of the strategic course of the state for gaining full-fledged membership of Ukraine in the European Union'.

To provide legal support for European integration, the Law of Ukraine of March 18, 2004, adopted the All-State Program of Adapting the Legislation of Ukraine to the Legislation of the European Union.[10]

On the bilateral level of Ukraine's integration into the EU, there is the European Neighbourhood Policy plus two major agreements between Ukraine and the EU. First came the Partnership and Cooperation Agreement between Ukraine and the European Communities and their member states of June 14, 1994,[11] which after September 1, 2017, was replaced with the current Association Agreement between Ukraine, of the one part, and the European Union, the European Atomic Energy Community, and their member states, of the other part, of June 27, 2014.[12]

Ukraine's performance in fulfilling its obligations under these agreements explicitly demonstrates the key obstacles on the path of European integration that still remain. As of autumn 2019, Ukraine has fulfilled most of the requirements in adjusting its legislation to EU legal framework. However, the public response to this harmonization has been very mixed. There were no significant difficulties in harmonizing provisions on technical regulations, economy, finances, etc. The implementation of European antidiscrimination standards, however, met a furious backlash. Pursuant to Annex XL to Chapter 21 'Cooperation on Employment, Social Policy and

[8]Zakon Ukrayiny 'Pro natsionalnu bezpeku Ukrayiny' (2018).

[9]Konstytutsiya Ukrayiny (1996).

[10]Zakon Ukrayiny 'Pro Zahalnoderzhavnu programu adaptatsiyi zakonodavstva Ukrayiny do zakonodavstva Yevropeyskoho Soyuzu' (2004).

[11]Partnership and Cooperation Agreement between the European Communities and their Member States, and Ukraine (1994).

[12]Association Agreement between the European Union and its Member States, of the one part, and Ukraine, of the other part (2014).

Equal Opportunities' of the Association Agreement,[13] Ukraine has introduced into its national legislation the relevant EU legal norms on combating discrimination and establishing gender approaches. Specifically, changes to the Labor Code of Ukraine[14] were approved in order to harmonize with the European Union law on preventing and counteracting discrimination. The law is aimed at bringing legislation of Ukraine in compliance with the provisions of the Council Directive 2000/78/EC,[15] which establishes the general framework of equal treatment in employment and occupation. In particular, Article 2-1 of the Code was supplemented with the list of grounds on which discrimination is prohibited, such as 'sexual orientation', 'gender identity', 'disability'. Even before that, in 2012, a framework antidiscrimination legislation was adopted under pressure from the EU and the Council of Europe. Clearly, Ukraine had never seen such widespread criticism and defiance toward legal novation. Ukraine was not exactly unique in this regard, since these issues also turned out to be rather sensitive for some other 'new democracies'. A good example is the similar public response in Georgia.

This phenomenon deserves a comprehensive explanation, but the first step is acknowledging the geopolitical and historical background.

Ukraine is a nation with a thousand-year history, famous for establishing Kievan Rus', the first Christian country in Eastern Europe and the largest European state of the early Middle Ages. During the rule of Grand Prince Yaroslav the Wise, Ukraine adopted the first codified legal document—the Rus' Justice, as significant for Eastern Europe as the Salic law was for Western Europe.

Due to the Mongol invasion of the thirteenth century, and afterward due to its closeness to the two neighboring empires, the Ottoman and the Russian, Ukraine lost its statehood, falling, since the mid-1600s, first under the 260-year yoke of the Russian Empire and then the 70-year yoke of a new Soviet empire—the former Soviet Union.

What makes the Ukrainian situation unique is the 'Russian factor', which should not be seen as an autonomous or situational force, i.e., a result of particular decisions or actions by individual politicians or political entities. A better explanation is to recognize the deep-seated commonalities, ones that can be conceptualized under the *path dependence* theory which seeks to explain certain aspects of the social modernization processes through 'process history'. This approach was first used in late-1980s macro- and microeconomic research as a methodological application of mathematical and evolutionary biology methods to study social phenomena.[16]

Path dependence offers an apt description of certain patterns of political and legal development that make any political processes dependent on a prior state, which exists as a sort of relic, a 'past in present'. Contrary to the more conventional

[13] Ibid.

[14] Kodeks zakoniv pro pratsiu Ukrayiny (1971).

[15] Council Directive (2000) establishing a general framework for equal treatment in employment and occupation.

[16] David (1985), pp. 332–337.

methodological traditions of social sciences that emphasize the importance of 'historical prerequisites', the *path dependence* theory outlines stricter conditions that act as a combination of contingency and self-reinforcing mechanisms and are very likely to determine the current state as something 'preprogrammed by factors from the past'. Understanding and critically evaluating the 'past' is not enough to break free of it. There are deep-seated irrational contexts of the present that stem from the (far or near) past and act independently of and contrary to understanding and acknowledgment. This methodological approach has been rather effective in explaining many political and social processes, especially with regard to conservative trends, opposition, and resistance to reforms.[17] For the past twenty years, scholars of post-socialist transformations have relied on this theoretical model to explain the most controversial processes in post-socialist countries, such as privatization and political reforms.[18] However, these studies have failed to look at the successes and failures in creating national models of human rights protection as part of these countries' integration into the European political and legal structure; the very complexity and inconsistency of these models require a highly specific and sensitive methodological approach.

Given the connection between political and legal processes, it makes sense to extend this concept to study the modernization of legal systems, as it would help explain complex and nonlinear phenomena of legal development.[19] Furthermore, it can be argued that the mechanisms of *path dependence* universally apply to legal development, which has relevance not only for legal studies but also for legal practices.[20]

Since Ukraine gained independence in 1991, the key tendency in the development of the Ukrainian legal system has been an implementation of European standards of democracy, the rule of law, and human rights. However, it has been nonlinear and inconsistent in character, with sporadic breakthroughs and setbacks leaving their mark on the nascent Ukrainian society and identity. These processes cannot be understood unless one accounts for Ukraine's 'balancing act' between Russia and Europe—the geopolitical context born of the longtime common historical background of Ukraine and Russia within the Russian imperial project, albeit one disguised as a 'union of fraternal peoples'.

Moreover, at various stages of Ukraine's recent history, and with varying degrees of intensity, the political elites took advantage of Ukraine's regional differences in their power plays, artificially exacerbating them to the point of creating vast divides between rival values and political orientations. Especially prominent was the reliance on pro-Russian historical and sociocultural orientations prevalent in some parts of Eastern and Southern Ukraine.[21] All this stemmed from the fact that Russia's political dilemma has been enormous: whether to construe itself as part of Europe or

---

[17] Alexander (2001), pp. 249–270.

[18] Hedlund (2000), pp. 390–407 and Stark (1992), pp. 17–29.

[19] Sourgens (2016).

[20] Hathaway (2003).

[21] Petrov and Serdiuk (2009), pp. 189–196.

as an independent civilization and even hostile to ('Romano-Germanic') Europe.[22] Objectively, anything that fell into the sphere of Russian influence came up against the problem of making a geopolitical or even civilizational choice.

Back in his day, Mykhailo Hrushevsky spoke of the need for Ukraine to escape the 'Slavic embrace', but he could never have foreseen the strength of this embrace, or the difficulty of finding a European identity for Ukraine.

In recent history, Ukraine's political elites differed on the exact format of 'divorcing the Russian Federation': from the cautious '*Ukraine is not Russia*' (President Leonid Kuchma's turn-of-the-century way of defending the 'multi-vector' nature of the Ukrainian political model) to the resolutely and unequivocally pro-European '*the only thing Russia and Ukraine have in common is the border, which must be brought back under [Ukrainian] control*' (said by President Volodymyr Zelensky, elected in 2019).[23]

Despite the increasingly obvious incompatibility of the Ukrainian and Russian models of political development, there are still reasons to believe that the *path dependence* factors of Russia or the common past continue to exert their influence, in particular when it comes to human rights protection.

Our study is an attempt to outline these dependence factors, identify their origins, and describe their current state.

2 Constitutionalizing the International Standards of Human Rights Protection

Provisions for human rights protections were enshrined in all constitutions of the USSR and its constituent republics. For example, Section 2 of the 1978 Constitution of the Ukrainian SSR, 'State and Individual', was almost entirely devoted to articles on human rights, with separate provisions also included in other sections. The Constitution of the Russian Soviet Federative Republic was similarly structured. In reality, however, all these constitutional provisions were no more than ideological decorations for the authoritarian political regime of the 'ruling Communist Party'. In the twentieth century, the former Soviet Union's communist view of the individual as an object of paternalism and a small cog in a giant state machine left the Ukrainians no chance to learn and use the universal or even the regional (Council of Europe[24]) catalogs and mechanisms of international legal protection of human rights. Let us not forget that the USSR abstained from voting for the adoption of the Universal Declaration of Human Rights (1948). And the USSR's participation in the International Covenant on Civil and Political Rights (1966) and in the International Covenant on Economic, Social and Cultural Rights (1966) was no more than a legal formality,

---

[22] Mälksoo (2015), p. 76.

[23] Zelensky rizko vidpoviv na zayavu Putina: zi spilnoho z Rosiyeyu u nas zalyshyvsya lyshe kordon (2019).

[24] Kerikmäe et al. (2019).

since the provisions of these Covenants were not implemented domestically. Furthermore, anyone who called for actual implementation of the Covenants' human rights provisions in the former USSR met with ruthless persecution, including long-term politically motivated imprisonment. By the way, the majority of Soviet dissidents were ethnic Ukrainians.

The collapse of the Soviet Union and the emergence of independent states from its ruins have led to different models of democratic transformation of the post-Soviet countries. An important aspect of this process was the creation of national systems of human rights protection, in which an essential part was played by the national constitutions. The constitutional enshrinement of international standards of human rights protection was a prerequisite for these countries' integration into the European Community: first into the Council of Europe and then, possibly, into the European Union. This is why European institutions were committed to making sure that such transformations represent not an 'updated' or 'humanized' version of socialism but rather a resolute break from the socialist past to build a society based on radically new principles. The paradox of these social transformations lay in the fact that human rights turned out to be a rather premature concern, as this concept was too foreign for these societies; thus, it was largely reduced to welfare demands or expectations in public consciousness—and the tendency of political elites—to implement not so much human rights as 'intended social policies'.

It makes sense to consider the processes that simultaneously took place in the post-socialist Central and Eastern European countries, most of which in just a few years would get a chance to become EU members. It was exactly the prospect of attaining EU membership that inspired the political elites to construct a national constitutional model of human rights protection. Some European scholars believe the EU at the time had no ambitions to 'impose its model of human rights protection', since there was no clear-cut, formalized, and enshrined model back then. The EU member states having 'common constitutional traditions' did not mean there was a universally accepted approach that served as a European Union (and not just Council of Europe) standard. Moreover, it has been said that 'the constitutional design of the would-be new EU members was often ahead of the general EU approach' since the catalog of rights—later defined in the EU Charter of Fundamental Rights—was very similar to the rights previously listed in the national constitutions of this region.[25] However, the constitutional practice in Ukraine and in Russia was fundamentally different.

The early 1990s' models of human rights protection established in Russia and Ukraine were nominally based on the new constitutional provisions, but in reality these provisions were 'imported goods' and boiled down to textual borrowings from international agreements (primarily UN treaties on human rights). Even the European Convention on Human Rights was largely disregarded.

While it can be easy to identify the conceptual or textual parallels between international treaties and the relevant constitutional provisions, it is much harder to appraise the protection model as a whole. In attempting to identify the core beliefs underlying

[25]Morlino and Sadurski (2010), p. 217.

the Ukrainian Constitution, V. Rechitsky concludes that they are closer to 'hastily reimagined Marxism' than Western values. He believes this to be the reason why the national constitutional model is rife with 'preserved socialism'.[26] In other words, the Soviet 'ideological and constitutional tradition' had an influence on the establishment of Ukrainian constitutionalism. Meanwhile, the view that Ukraine has a 'longstanding constitutional tradition', popular in the 1990s and still held by some today, is untenable. S. Holovaty, for instance, argued that Ukraine was one of the regions that 'not only stood at the origins of European constitutionalism but were active creators of the European constitutional heritage', citing various historical facts (the Constitution of Pylyp Orlyk, the political and legal practices of the Hetmanate, the 1918 Constitution of the Ukrainian People's Republic, and others).[27] All these facts are testament to a rich and colorful national history, but they could not have possibly had any effect on the constitutional process, since the normal pattern of historical development was violently interrupted by the Soviet period, which almost completely eliminated these traditions from the society's institutional memory and mentality.[28]

The constitutional process in the Russian Federation, on the other hand, had an undeniable effect on similar processes in Ukraine, especially with regard to the concepts and wording of the constitutional text, since the recommendations made by experts from the Council of Europe, which actively supported the constitutional process in Ukraine, were not always accepted in Ukraine.[29] The constitutional process in Russia was more similar conceptually and politically, and thus more understandable and reasonable as a role model. Consider the following case in point: To modernize the concept of constitutional wording, both Russia and Ukraine were advised to include in the text a separate section on civil society which, among other things, would outline some basic provisions on civil and political rights. However, the Russian framers' refusal to do so led to a similar decision in Ukraine.[30] Such technical influences are apparent in many other issues.

Overall, for Ukraine and Russia, the 'constitutional phase' of implementing international standards of human rights protection was synchronized not only in time (the first half of the 1990s) and particulars but also in the more fundamental issues of ideological principles and paradigms. The problem was finding a justification for human rights that would combine the patently incompatible: preserving the 'constitutional tradition' and carrying out a democratic modernization of both the state mechanism and the society in general. The political entities behind the constitutional process saw human rights as an essential component of state-building—but not as a

[26]Rechitsky (2018).

[27]*Konstytutsiya nezalezhnoyi Ukrayiny* (1998) knyha 2 chastyna 1, pp. 29–31.

[28]Serdiuk and Petrov (2010).

[29]A prime example is the harshly critical response by F. Burchak, a member of the Constitutional Commission, to the proposition of one of the Council of Europe experts to include a provision for the 'right to common freedom' in the Constitution: 'it's nonsense ... you can't just mechanically copy the norms of other legal systems' (*Konstytutsiya nezalezhnoyi Ukrayiny* (1998), knyha 3 chastyna 3, p. 83).

[30]*Konstytutsiya nezalezhnoyi Ukrayiny* (1998), knyha 3 chastyna 1, p. 27; Rechitsky (2018), p. 82.

priority. The emphasis was on creating a new institutional model of the state, so the top-priority issues were the mechanisms for the separation of power, identifying the role of the Councils and the status of the presidency, etc. One of the participants of the constitutional process in Russia recalled that the framing of the 'Human Rights' section was left to the supporters of liberal democracy, while the 'institutional part' was framed by the proponents of strong presidential authority, which created a certain discrepancy between the democratic and the authoritarian elements of the Russian constitution.[31]

The situation in Ukraine was similar. The minutes of the meetings of the Constitutional Commission and its bodies show that most discussions centered on the structure of power, while the constitutional provisions on human rights were created in a rather controversial way: The idea was to take the rights already enshrined in the 1978 Constitution of the Ukrainian SSR and add a catalog of 'new rights (right to life, freedom of expression, etc.)', which would be, first and foremost, an implementation of the provisions of UN treaties on human rights and the European Convention on Human Rights.[32] This method of creating constitutional norms, as noted by V. Butkevych (a member of the Constitutional Commission and later a Ukrainian judge at the European Court of Human Rights), was 'strictly mechanical', since 'some rights were copied with no consideration to their applications, turning them into political declarations, dubious and thus untenable legal constructs'.[33]

The Constitutional Commission was mainly concerned with the wording of the human rights provisions, although in fact it proposed something of a conceptual basis for constitutionalizing human rights: a doctrine of 'natural human rights' as opposed to the idea of 'state-granted rights'. In Ukrainian scholarly discourse, this doctrine is now shedding its 1990s 'quasi-religious' trappings, organically expanding to include new modern approaches, whereby these ideas are further developed and naturally combined with the recognition of the need for an 'international legal positivization of human rights'. An important part is played by the instrumental doctrines of the European Court of Human Rights, which make it possible to perceive human rights standards as 'living and effective instruments' rather than abstract ideas and values[34].

The doctrine of natural rights has had a very different fate in Russia, where it has been, contrary to the modern international human rights law, reframed as the natural law in its Orthodox Christian interpretation, whereby human rights are seen as natural to the degree that they correspond to 'God's law as interpreted by the early sermons'. This approach interprets human rights as 'responsibilities before God', which pits the Russian ideology of human rights against the European one to the point of complete incompatibility.[35] In a few years, this ideological incompatibility

---

[31] Kovler (1996), pp. 23–24.

[32] *Konstytutsiya nezalezhnoyi Ukrayiny* (1998), knyha 3 chastyna 1, p. 27. It should be noted that the sources of constitutional provisions on human rights cite UN treaties more frequently than the European Convention on Human Rights, which remained yet to be ratified.

[33] *Supra n*, knyha 3 chastyna 2, p. 284.

[34] Ramiro Troitino and Pando Ballesteros (2017).

[35] Kurkin (2008), p. 112.

led to an institutional clash between Russia and the European system of human rights protection: several years of refusing to ratify Protocol No. 14 and the consequent lack of reform of the conventional control mechanism in general; a refusal to enforce certain ECHR decisions due to their inconsistency with the constitutional framework, later culminating in a federal law codifying this approach.

Both in Ukraine and in Russia, to a similar degree, the natural-rights 'style' of constitutionalizing human rights was rather contradictorily combined with the Soviet legacy of 'preserved socialism' in the form of paternalism in social matters and constructing a number of social rights. The enshrinement of these rights took place under the influence of the normative constructs of the International Covenant on Economic, Social and Cultural Rights, which were seen as a sort of internal political and ideological compromise and a way to ensure the minimum social standards. This created the illusion of a 'social state': 'we have a special kind of public consciousness; the people would prefer deception to a lack of promises' (from the discussion at the meeting of the Constitutional Commission of the Verkhovna Rada of Ukraine).[36] Driven by these motivations, the reformers in Russia and Ukraine created what A. Sajó calls 'an overdose of human rights provisions', whereby the existing institutions and resources are insufficient for meeting the public expectations of social justice and the rule of law, which often are most prevalent among the parts of the population that are the most reliant on social support from the state.[37]

In fact, the wording of post-Soviet constitutions is at times rather odd, with the sanctity of private property being listed alongside an incredibly extensive catalog of social rights, as well as the provision that 'the content and scope of existing rights and freedoms shall not be diminished in the adoption of new laws or in the amendment of laws that are in force'. The latter provision was actively employed by the Constitutional Court of Ukraine to defend not only social rights but also the benefits established by the current legislation every time the parliament tried to limit these social security elements in adopting the annual state budget. Only the political pressure put on the Court by the government controlled by President Yanukovych managed to break down this impregnable protective wall of constitutional justice: The Constitutional Court granted the executive branch maximum discretion in social issues by prioritizing the principle of 'the financial security of the state' ('a balanced state budget') as opposed to 'the inviolability of social rights'.[38]

It should be noted that both approaches raised objections from the expert community. The citizens, meanwhile, welcomed the absolutization of the state's obligations enshrined as social rights (except the decisions of the Constitutional Court gave them no satisfaction in asserting their rights before the government for the simple fact that it would have taken about twice as much money as was available in the budget).

The Revolution of Dignity brought new people to the government and a new way of thinking to the consideration of many state issues. Thus, free of 'supervision' from the presidential administration, the Court took the position of its German counterpart,

---

[36] *Konstytutsiya nezalezhnoyi Ukrayiny* (1998), knyha 3 chastyna 3, p. 305.

[37] Sajó (1997), pp. 4–7.

[38] Rishennia Konstytutsiynoho Sudu (2012).

linking the doctrine of guaranteed social rights to the concept of human dignity as a basic constitutional value requiring unconditional protection, including within the system of social security.[39]

Nevertheless, the paternalist mind-set of the majority of the population has remained unchanged, bolstered by inadequate social security and widespread use of socially populist slogans in every election.

3 Pragmatism or Incompatible Values?

The constitutionalizing of international standards of human rights protection was accompanied by an important 'external process'. The early 1990s was a period when the post-Soviet countries were actively joining the European political and legal landscape, in which human rights are the very *backbone*. There were also important changes in the European system of human rights protection, first and foremost the reformation of the oversight mechanism of the European Convention on Human Rights to make it more efficient and responsive to issues that could potentially arise from the expansion of the Council of Europe to include post-socialist countries.

Both for Ukraine and for the Russian Federation, the European political and legal landscape was not something radically new: At the behest of the Committee of Ministers of the Council of Europe, the Soviet Union had already joined several Council of Europe conventions that did not require mandatory membership (Protection of Architectural Heritage, Protection of Archaeological Heritage, Protection of Animals during International Transport, etc.) but created a basis for limited cooperation within the framework of an international organization built on principles of the rule of law and human rights.

Membership in the Council of Europe and the ratification of major conventions, especially the Convention for the Protection of Human Rights and Fundamental Freedoms, were important milestones in 'parting with the Soviet past'. However, with regard to Russia, the situation was difficult: Internally, concerns were immediately raised about retaining sovereignty in the face of the perceived risks stemming from such membership, while for the West, a constant source of anxiety was the Chechen War and the resulting widespread violations of fundamental human rights.

B. Bowring notes a special subtext of the Russian Federation's accession to the European system of human rights protection, since one of the main internal arguments in favor of membership in the Council of Europe was the opportunity to use the existing instruments of human rights protection to protect the rights of 'Russian speakers' in post-Soviet countries.[40] So the imperial ambitions and the idea of the '*Russian World*' were already manifested at the early stages of state-building, and although they were not always proclaimed as such, they carried more weight than did the need for a democratic reformation of Russia.

---

[39] Rishennia Konstytutsiynoho Sudu (2018) and Barabash (2016).

[40] Bowring (2013), pp. 140–173.

Ukraine's accession to the Council of Europe required it to settle the important geopolitical issue of the 'external development vectors' and determine the format of relationships within the Commonwealth of Independent States (CIS). It is in this context, apparently, that the problem of Ukraine's orientation toward a specific model of human rights protection was for the first time formally expressed as a choice of alternatives at the geopolitical or even civilizational level, demanding political decisions.

The CIS was already establishing its own model of human rights protection based on the CIS Convention on Human Rights; thus Russia, in its quest to reanimate the Soviet Union, sought to create a regional system of human rights protection that would be nominally harmonized with its European counterpart. For this reason, even the wording of the CIS Convention replicated that of the European Convention on Human Rights.

Ukraine and the Russian Federation underwent the procedure for attaining the Council of Europe membership almost simultaneously. However, there were significant differences not only in their positions and motivations, but also in the Council of Europe's approach; they were important symptoms of the problems that would become apparent ten years later in Russia's clear challenge to the foundations of the European model of human rights protection.

In May of 1996, Ukraine refused to sign the CIS Convention on Human Rights. According to paragraph 12 of the PACE Opinion 190 of September 26, 1995, on the application by Ukraine for membership of the Council of Europe, 'Ukraine ... intends not to sign the Commonwealth of Independent States (CIS) Convention on Human Rights and other relevant CIS documents' pending research on their compatibility with the Council of Europe conventions, 'given the fact that individual applications submitted under this convention might render impossible the effective use of the right to individual application' under the European Convention on Human Rights and Fundamental Freedoms.[41]

The Council of Europe's stance toward Russia was somewhat different. When the PACE considered the application by the Russian Federation, the main issue under discussion was the compatibility of the two conventional systems—the CIS Convention and the European Convention on Human Rights. The PACE Opinion 193 of January 25, 1996, on the application by Russia for membership of the Council of Europe, mentions the possibility of applying the two conventions in parallel and notes Russia's intent to ensure that the application of the CIS Convention does not in any way interfere with the procedure and guarantees of the European Convention.[42] In Russia, the PACE position was met with criticism because it was perceived as disrespectful toward the CIS Convention and dismissive of the possibility of creating a system of human rights protection independently of European institutions. At the same time, Russian political elites changed their tune regarding Russia's possible EU membership, becoming more critical, talking of sovereignty risks, and discussing

[41] PACE Opinion 190 (1995).

[42] PACE Opinion 193 (1996).

the possibility of reanimating the Soviet Union in the form of the Commonwealth of Independent States.

4 Cloning the Instruments of Restricting Civil and Political Rights: An 'Internal Matrix' of Post-soviet Political Elites?

State-building in the post-Soviet region has always been accompanied by the political elites' fear of massive protest movements. The responses to it have been different: from populist promises and manipulating public consciousness to paternalist and untenable social laws, to repressive measures. In the post-Soviet world, civil and political rights were seen as the biggest challenge to 'national security and stability'.

On the other hand, restricting democratic freedoms can be a way of protecting democracies.[43] The fact that the line between protecting and curbing democracy is way too thin and very often determined only by the specific details is evident from the ECHR practices, whereby an obligatory criterion for assessing the legitimacy of restricting human rights is its 'necessity for a democratic society', which is always based on analyzing facts rather than declarations.

An exception to this general rule in the Ukrainian constitutional practice was the effective ban of the Communist Party on ideological grounds (interestingly, the war with Russia-backed separatists in Eastern Ukraine has shown the party that had always questioned the independent Ukrainian statehood to be an active supporter of the 'Russian World').[44] And although the final court ruling on banning the Communist Party is yet to be made, its activities are completely halted by the Ministry of Justice and the Central Election Commission on the basis of the relevant law.

For the systems both in Russia and in Ukraine, civil and political rights in their classic form were 'new', since they demanded not just a declaration but actual guarantees and real legal remedy, including applications to the ECHR. Given the cyclic (in Ukraine) and continuous (in Russia) setbacks in democratic standards and the slide toward a more authoritarian political regime, the curbing of these rights became objectively inevitable as a prerequisite for preserving the regime. As early as 2013, the prominent Russian political scholar L. Shevtsova was predicting that 'the agony of the Russian political regime has all the classic hallmarks. For Putin's regime, a transition from façade democracy to a repressive regime is only possible through conflict—including armed conflict with the outside world'.[45] Such a conflict could be used not only to justify restrictions on civil rights and liberties but also to render the regime legitimate in the eyes of the public. It is what Ivan Krastev wrote about:

---

[43] Barabash (2013).

[44] Kazansky (2014).

[45] Busygina (2013), pp. 111–121.

'what distinguishes the new authoritarianism in Russia is that Russia has lost not only its status as a great power but also the "air of mysteriousness" that it once had'.[46]

The curbing of democratic freedoms in Russia had two objectives: (a) to squash the internal opposition by restricting civil and political rights that form the basis of a functioning civil society, and (b) to create a myth of a sacral political regime that exists in the midst of a hostile environment and protects the national identity and sovereignty, all of which forces it to deploy such extraordinary measures. A distinct characteristic of Russian society was a rather low public demand for civil and political rights, which the majority of the population saw largely as a means of petitioning the government to provide social justice and well-being. As long as the government did, these rights were considered *not important enough* to risk losing social stability over. The positive dynamics of the Russian economy (albeit achieved via the export of primary resources) and a relatively high standard of living, real social security all these worked to quell public resistance to the restrictions on civil and political rights. The Russian practice of restricting these rights is pretty varied in its objectives, ways, and scale.

A very serious development of recent years has been the ongoing persecution of Russian NGOs (nongovernmental organizations), which started in July 2012, whereby the organizations that receive foreign donations and engage in 'political activity' must register as 'foreign agents'. This is the *Foreign Agents Law*.[47]

Almost synchronously, the Ukrainian government started planning its own steps to restrict the civil society, borrowing the techniques, methods, and rhetoric from the Russian political regime. But in late 2013 the situation changed dramatically. The widespread protests in response to the government's refusal to sign the EU Association Agreement saw millions of people take to the streets of Ukrainian cities and towns, and the government promptly moved to carry out its plans that were inspired by the Russian experience and simply sought to clone the repressive instruments of Putin's authoritarian regime. In a very short time (over just a few days), the 'January 16, 2014, laws' were adopted (12 in all) and immediately became known as 'dictatorship laws' because of the restrictions on civil rights and liberties they contained: the introduction of the concept of 'foreign agents', which referred to any nongovernmental organizations receiving foreign funding; restrictions of the right to assembly and demonstration, including harsher punishments for unauthorized public events; restrictions of access to Internet resources and communication networks; harsher punishments for violating laws on media activities; criminalization of libel; control over mobile communications, etc. Altogether, the laws contained over 30 restrictions of rights, and most of them were not of the kind that the ECHR found legitimately 'necessary for a democratic society'.

The simplest and seemingly most reasonable explanation for this similarity of behavior displayed by political elites in restricting civil liberties would be that such restriction is a universal instrument of protecting authoritarian political regimes from risks posed to them by democratic institutions.

[46]Krastev (2011), p. 39.

[47]*Rossiyskaya Gazeta* (2012).

This assumption, however, is somewhat refuted by the Ukrainian experience of recent years (2014–2018), when the political regime showed no obvious signs of authoritarian transformation that were so apparent under President Viktor Yanukovych. The idea of restricting democratic liberties was reanimated in a new public context and with new motivations. For one, the idea of recriminalizing libel (defamation) is constantly present in the Ukrainian political discourse. Another symptom of 'dislike' toward the civil society and the civil liberties it represents was manifested in the amendments to the Law of Ukraine 'On Preventing Corruption' that required civil anticorruption organizations and certain categories of activists to declare their income. The negative and rather concerted reaction of all the European institutions was largely ignored for more than two years. Moreover, cases of EU member states imposing restrictions on civil rights at various points and in various contexts were cited as justification for this approach.

5 Traditional Values: The Last Bastion?

It is obvious that one of the biggest problems facing Ukraine today is its capability to actually implement (and not just formally include in the legislation) the European antidiscrimination standards as stipulated in the current EU Association Agreement. All public debate on this matter is centered around the doctrine of 'traditional values', which emerged in full force in the early twentieth century, when the main and the most controversial area of progress in the European system of human rights protection centered around the issues of personal development, associated with the right to privacy, the right to physical integrity, the freedom of expression, and so on. New biological and medical technologies, new forms of social bonding, family life, and realizing one's personal potential created a radically new context, wherein the traditional civil and political rights gained new meanings, sparking controversy and fierce public dispute.

In Ukraine, 'traditional values' have always been somewhat relevant, especially for radical Ukrainian nationalists, but it is fair to say this issue has been blown out of proportion under Russian influence as a way of obstructing the European integration of the Ukrainian society.

Since the late 1990s, Russian scholars have been increasingly uniform in their view of 'the new European ideology of human rights' as 'the amoral expansion of human rights',[48] 'Western ideological manipulations', and 'the degeneration of the European philosophical and sociological thought'.[49] Human rights were perceived as an element of the 'liberal political ideology' and interpreted as incompatible with Russian values, since 'they are a utopia driven by the pathos of disavowing all that is indigenous' and run counter to 'the Christian model of human rights'.[50]

[48] Krasnov (2013), pp. 465–477.

[49] Rogozhin (2001), pp. 31–37.

[50] Kurkin (2008), pp. 115–116.

All this theorizing, however, was no marginal scholastics: It reflected the deep transformations within the Russian society, ones that created a radically new context vis-à-vis the European system of human rights protection and had an undeniable influence on Ukraine. Clearly, it is at this plane that the difficulty of Ukraine's getting out of the 'Russian rut' is the largest and the risks for implementing European standards the highest—especially given the pan-European populist trends, the spread of various conservative ideologies, and the rise of right-wing parties.

In one way or another, the doctrine of traditional values almost always came up whenever the Russian Federation deliberately chose to oppose the European system of human rights. This was especially prominent in Russia's dealings with the ECHR, which were increasingly confrontational: the case of *Markin v. Russia* and the final judgment of the ECHR Grand Chamber finding the 'traditional [for Russia] distribution of gender roles' to be incompatible with European values; the[51] ruling by the Constitutional Court of the Russian Federation allowing to disregard ECHR decisions if they fail to conform to basic constitutional norms (2015); the adoption of a federal law outlining the terms and procedures enabling Russia not to enforce ECHR decisions; the political declarations regarding the inevitability of Russia's exit from the system of human rights protection under the Convention on Human Rights and Fundamental Freedoms.

The response of the legal doctrine has been mixed. The issue touched upon one of Russia's sore points: the problem of retaining sovereignty in the context of interaction between national and international law.[52] Most scholars felt 'mobilized' to provide theoretical arguments in support of the Russian government's position. It became popular to talk of the 'overall European and worldwide tendency of states to resist the judicial activism of international courts (most notably, the ECHR), which increasingly overstep the boundaries of authority that had been presumed by the states when they created the oversight mechanisms via multilateral agreements'.[53] Other researchers used more elaborate arguments, painting this position as a refusal to engage in a dogmatic and pointless discussion on the interrelation between national and international law and a move toward 'methodological pragmatism', whereby everything is determined by context.[54] The Russian practice is another example of the vulnerability of the European system of human rights protection when it comes to dealings at the national level.

A formal risk factor is the primacy of the Constitution, which puts Ukraine in the risk zone. In new democracies, constitutional courts are politically sensitive, so a 'Russian model' is always possible. If the principle of the constitution taking priority over international treaties is extended beyond the specific issue of the Convention's legal force, it could destroy the entire national model of interacting with European institutions. Constitutional identity can be interpreted in many ways, and the Russian experience of recent years shows that a perceived threat to 'traditional values' can be

[51] Troitiño et al. (2018).

[52] Zorkin (2010).

[53] Ispolinov (2018).

[54] Vaypan (2014), pp. 133–138 and Budylin (2013).

ruled unconstitutional. In other words, the balance between the European consensus on human rights and the 'traditional values' is likely to shift toward the latter.

Russian criticism of the European consensus on human rights (as doctrinal/official approach and general public discourse) is actually inspired by the 'desecularized' doctrine of human rights, which was offered by the Russian Orthodox Church to 'remove the defects of the world order and prevent a conflict of civilizations'. It states, in particular: 'no human rights standards but faith and traditional values should have the highest authority for the people'; Orthodox Christianity is basically a state religion. However, there is no evidence that the majority of the population in Russia is religious; actually, there is no 'internal value consensus', to which the critics of the 'European consensus on human rights' often refer. Perhaps there is an aggressive minority and a silent majority.

Religious doctrine and legal doctrine (and practice) do not exist as parallel realities. They work closely and there is a unique Russian context. There were clear signs of the 'desecularization ideology' at work during Russia's initial (and, so far, nominal) accession to the European system of human rights protection in the second half of the 1990s. Back then, many Russian scholars and practitioners found the requirements in the codes of judicial ethics 'alarming and dangerous', seeing in them a 'secularization of the judicial process' because they 'banned [religious] icons in the courtroom and ritualistic acts by judges (such as crossing themselves)'.[55] Over time, the outward elements became discarded, but the ideology of desecularization extended to the underlying structures of the legal doctrine and practice: worldview, legal culture, methodologies, and so on.

The period of formation of the Orthodox doctrine of human rights has coincided with the beginning of active promotion by the Russian Federation of the doctrine of 'traditional values' in the UN system, resulting in the adoption of UN Human Rights Council Res. 16/3, 'Promoting Human Rights and Fundamental Freedoms through a Better Understanding of Traditional Values of Humankind' (2011). In fact, it was proposed to replace the European consensus on human rights by a general civilization consensus (based on 'traditional values'). And then there is reason to talk about the 'messianic role of Russia', which, unlike Europe, has preserved traditional values.

However, history shows that the myth of exceptional spirituality only emerges in nations that lag behind their neighbors both economically and in protecting human dignity. This is the compensatory function of the myth, which is supposed to demonstrate that special spirituality comes from a special standing in the world and a special historical mission. The biggest flaw in this mythology is not even the utopian (mythical) nature of its key premise but the presumption of a 'golden age' and the attempt to solve modern-day problems by returning to traditions. And once a vessel of these traditions is identified, it gives rise to the idea of a messianic nation that has preserved the things it now must help others to understand (say, the value of a true marriage as a union of man and woman). Thus, Russia's special way and special mission can be explained via the modernization theory as an attempt to find a different, non-Western way of modernizing the preserved relics, i.e., to adapt archaic institutions to

[55]Pashin (2014), pp. 78–91.

modern conditions. This rejection of organic modernization is a long-standing tradition of the Russian sociocultural ethos. Back in the early twentieth century, Dmitry Merezhkovsky came to a sad conclusion: 'we sit in a puddle and comfort ourselves that it is not a puddle but the "Russian idea"'. More than a century later, almost nothing has changed, except the puddle may have grown bigger.

In 2005, the World Russian People's Council[56] set to the task of creating a truly Christian concept of human rights. The key issue was whether some values are above human rights. The next year the Council rolled out the 2006 Declaration of Human Rights and Dignity which sought to 'remove the defects of the world order and prevent a conflict of civilizations'. This is when it became evident that the positions of church and state became consistent, with Foreign Minister Lavrov saying that 'Russia must become the spiritual power that will save the world order'.

The Orthodox human rights doctrine deprived human rights of any inherent meaning and was based on recognizing a different consensus: the traditional values held by the majority of the population.[57]

The key premise of the Declaration reads: 'We must not allow situations to occur in which the realization of human rights tramples upon religious or moral traditions, insults religious or national feelings or sacred objects, or threatens our homeland's existence. It is dangerous to "invent" such "rights" which make legal that behavior condemned by traditional morality and all historic religions'.

The Russian Orthodox Church's Basic Teaching on Human Dignity, Freedom and Rights (2008) states that 'human rights cannot be superior to the values of the spiritual world'; 'it is not so much secularized standards of human rights as the creed and traditions that have the ultimate authority'; 'one's human rights cannot be set against the values and interests of one's homeland, community and family'. The teaching differentiates between manmade traditional values, which are transient, and God-given values, which form the basis of human life.[58]

In Ukraine, the category of 'traditional values' long ago found its way into legal terminology. The 2003 Law of Ukraine 'On Protection of Public Moral' determines 'public moral' as based on 'the traditional cultural and spiritual values' that dictate ethical norms, behaviors, etc.[59] This institutionalized system of protecting public morals turned out to be untenable and was soon marginalized by public rejection.

Overall, the 'traditional values' doctrine found no legal recognition or formal acknowledgment. Instead, it thrived in the realm of politics as part of the idea of the 'Russian World' and the 'unity of the fraternal peoples of Russia and Ukraine' based on common faith and a shared system of traditional values. The most notorious was the initiative by Member of Parliament V. Kolesnichenko, who in 2010 prepared a Draft Declaration of the Verkhovna Rada of Ukraine 'On Dignity, Freedom and Human Rights', which in wording and content followed the Russian Orthodox Church's Basic Teaching on Human Dignity, Freedom and Rights (2008), nominally

[56] A typical example of trying to imitate civil society.

[57] Troitiño (2017).

[58] *Tserkov i vremya* (2014).

[59] Zakon Ukrayiny 'Pro zahyst suspilnoyi morali' (2003).

adapted to the Ukrainian context. The key premise of this document was the rejection of the universal nature of human rights and contrasting the ‘Ukrainian model of human rights’ with the relevant international and European standards. In the contemporary political context, such a position served to provoke anti-European sentiment and could have been used to justify restrictions on civil and political liberties (such as freedom of expression and freedom of assembly) by framing them as a threat to ‘traditional values’. Tellingly, the act of Russian aggression in 2014 revealed a powerful organizational infrastructure that had been created in Ukraine on the pretext of protecting ‘traditional values’ to serve as a ‘fifth column’ in Vladimir Putin’s geopolitical strategy.

The Kolesnichenko Declaration was rejected by both the Verkhovna Rada and the public. That did not mean, however, that there was no public support for its basic ideological premises, since they were later reused by those who had publicly criticized the Declaration. The reason was different: What had been unacceptable initially was the ‘primitive source of these ideas’ and the overly direct association of this initiative with other instruments of Russian influence.

European institutions (first and foremost, the institutions and political leaders of the EU and the leading EU member states) have praised the 2014–2018 democratic reforms in Ukraine. But the positive institutional changes overshadow the risks of rejecting some formally recognized standards of human rights which not only remain but grow bigger. This pertains first and foremost to the antidiscrimination instruments, the creation of which was one of the key conditions of the EU Association Agreement. Among the ruling political class, a preference toward conservative ideology is becoming increasingly apparent. It is under the auspices of this ‘moderate conservatism’ that the powerful ideological construct of viewing human rights through the lens of traditional values is making a comeback. The state and politicians cross a kind of axiological line in their dealings with the church by recognizing its doctrine as a point of reference when it comes to the most sensitive and controversial human rights.

A case in point is the position of governmental institutions regarding the cooperation between the state and the church in ‘protecting the family and family values’. The IV All-Ukrainian Family Forum that took place in March of 2019 was attended by top government officials (the President, the Prime Minister, the Head of Parliament, the key ministers, and so on) and the leaders of the major political parties. The key ideas of this event, openly proclaimed or supported by representatives of the government and political parties, were as follows: ‘a number of bills were proposed to remove gender terminology from legislation and administrative practices, ban surrogate maternity, expand the participation of church officials in activities of the state authorities; the state must be built with consideration to and on the basis of church principles; the principle of the “separation of church and state” should be reconsidered to combat the godlessness of power; the Parliamentary Committee on Health has laid out the groundwork for rejecting the gender approach in public administration; state offices responsible for gender policies need to be abolished (in particular, that of the Government Commissioner for Gender Policy); the Istanbul

Convention is unacceptable for Ukraine since it runs counter to the traditional values of the Ukrainian society'.[60]

At this point, it is hardly surprising to see the ease with which Ukraine's political elites discard the standards of human rights protection that were only recently, and with great difficulty, enshrined in the antidiscrimination legislation; the adherence to these very standards is seen, within the political dialogue with the EU, as a prerequisite for not only settling the narrow issue of visa liberalization but also any further integration. To explain it we should turn to, among other things, the phenomenon of path dependence in the relationships between the state and the church. Of paramount importance is the position of the Orthodox Church, whose conservatism is widely known. To a large extent, however, it is fueled and enhanced by the influence of the Russian Orthodox Church, which is used by Vladimir Putin's regime as an instrument of 'soft power' in establishing the 'Russian World' and in geopolitics in general.

It makes sense to draw an analogy to the situation in Georgia, where the Orthodox Church has historically served as one of the key instruments in maintaining national identity. This led to a distinct model of relations between the church and the state after Georgia gained independence, whereby the church was given the opportunity to interfere in secular life not typically seen in modern democracies, which was even reflected in the Georgian constitution. However, the European choice of the Georgian democracy found no support from the church, whose criticism of European values basically regurgitates the Russian Orthodox Church's ideological clichés of 'civilizational incompatibility'. This was especially apparent in the extremely negative and public reaction to the antidiscrimination bill that Georgia was required to adopt under the 2014 EU Visa Liberalization Action Plan. The arguments used were identical to the views espoused by the Russian Orthodox Church and the Ukrainian orthodoxy and its political allies ('combating homosexuality'; 'removing the gender approach from the legislation'; 'threats to national identity'; and so on). A somewhat softer version of the 'Georgian scenario' is being played out in Ukraine.

Today, following the presidential (March and April 2019) and parliamentary (July 2019) election, a new configuration of political processes is emerging in Ukraine, whereby the post-Soviet tradition of governance and all its attendant risks may cease to matter. However, it is very difficult to predict the relationship with the church and the position on the 'traditional values' issue. We cannot disregard the existence of political movements which consciously and systematically employ religious beliefs and institutional resources to achieve their own goals or at least mobilize their voters. This rivalry between ideological and political strategies will doubtlessly be influenced by the 'Russian factor' and have a significant effect on relationships with the European system of human rights protection. This applies especially to the most controversial and sensitive part of the 'European catalog of human rights' (right to life, privacy, religious freedoms, freedom of expression, etc.).[61]

---

[60] Delegaty 4 vseukrainskogo foruma semyi trebuyut likvidirovat dolzhnost upolnomochennogo po voprosam gendera (2019).

[61] Which reminds us of an apt Soviet-era joke: 'What do you need for art to flourish and for religion to decline? Free art from the state and make religion state-mandated.'

Following the 2019 presidential and parliamentary elections, the first events on the political landscape suggest that the political movements are leaning more toward a modernization of the political system and democratic institutions. The ideological issue of 'traditional values' will very likely remain, except not on the surface (as before) but rather as a subtext; still, that does not negate the risks it intrinsically poses to retaining and strengthening the current model of human rights protection.

6 In Conclusion: What's Next?

The key issue for Ukraine's organic and successful integration into the European model of human rights protection is identifying the necessary degree and the most viable ways of breaking free from the Russian model, and acknowledging the risks it will pose.

The limits to Ukraine's implementation of European political and legal standards of human rights protection are only slightly objectified by the legislation. Indeed, Ukraine has many examples of backpedaling or resistance, and often merely passive and totally unmotivated expectations, when it comes to ratifying certain European conventions. The most notorious is the unwillingness of the parliament to ratify the Council of Europe's Istanbul Convention and the aggressive attacks on it. Many of the Convention's provisions, however, are in fact already implemented in the national legislation. For example, the laws were amended to criminalize certain acts as stipulated by the Convention. This is an example of a selective and narrowly pragmatic perception of international standards. But the Istanbul Convention, just like any other international statute on human rights protection, is an integral document based on a certain ideology. It is no coincidence that the punitive provisions in European conventions are rather limited and largely technical in nature.

The codification of the European standards of human rights protection in the norms and institutions of national and international law is only one of the prerequisites for their actual use in the national system of justice. A bigger threat to these standards and the worldview they are based on is to be found on deeper social planes: in social structures, public consciousness, ideologies, and social interactions. This is where Ukraine has the hardest time escaping the 'force field' of the 'Russian World'.

The paradox of the Ukrainian situation is apparent when one compares the degree of success of the formal implementation of European standards in 2010–2014 (under President Yanukovych) and 2014–2019 (under President Poroshenko). Under strong pressure from European institutions, Ukraine under Yanukovych managed to significantly reform its antidiscrimination legislation and introduce radically new approaches in one of the most sensitive areas of human rights; however, in the more favorable political climate following the Revolution of Dignity, the political elites basically began to block these new legal instruments, demonstrating their allegiance to a different value system and unexpectedly acknowledging the 'acceptability of the system of ideas and values', which is used by the aggressor state in its attempts to undermine the European identity of the Ukrainian society.

Another noteworthy fact is that the previous administration, acting on its campaign promises, managed to amend the Constitution to require that any foreign policy decisions made by the parliament or the head of state must be in line with Ukraine's strategic course toward NATO and EU membership.[62] This is rather unique for post-Soviet systems of law, because, despite a lack of necessary consensus among the ruling elites and the majority of voters regarding the permanency of such course, it was still enshrined at the highest possible level of the Constitution. Stranger still, the key political actors refrained from making any radical revisions of the effectively socialist 1996 Constitution (it should be emphasized that when the Constitution was being adopted, the pro-Communist parliamentary majority of the time—which, as later events showed, had good reasons to hope for a resurrection of the Soviet Union in one form or another—managed to completely 'amorphize' Ukraine's civilizational choice at the constitutional level) but simply added a mention of 'the path toward NATO and the EU', with no guarantees for market economy or true democratic parliamentarianism.

The scale, the success, and the consistency of integration into the European system of human rights protection are ultimately determined by the degree to which Ukraine can overcome its dependence on Russia. In this case, the important thing is not even overcoming direct dependence per se (political influence, economic dependence, etc.) but rather overcoming the deep commonalities that hamper modernization efforts both in Ukraine and in Russia (and to a similar degree). For Ukraine, this will mean breaking path dependence from Russia; for Russia, the creation of a new path—possibly the only path of organic integration into Europe.

References

Akt proholoshennia nezalezhnosti Ukrayiny. (1991). https://zakon.rada.gov.ua/laws/show/1427-12.

Alexander, G. (2001). Institutions, path dependence, and democratic consolidation. *Journal of Theoretical Politics, 13*(3), 249–270.

Association Agreement between the European Union and its Member States, of the one part, and Ukraine, of the other part. (2014). https://eur-lex.europa.eu/legal-content/EN/TXT/PDF/?uri=CELEX:22014A0529(01)&from=EN.

Barabash, Y. (2016). Bezzakhysni prava chy neobgruntovani spodivannia. *Holos Ukrainy* vid 5 travnia. http://www.golos.com.ua/article/268300.

Barabash, Y. (2013). Konstitutsionnaya kharakteristika ukrainskoy demokratiyi: ideologicheskiye osnovy i mehanizmy samozashity v svete yevropeyskogo opyta.

Bowring, B. (2013). Human rights in the yeltsin period. In *Law, rights and ideology in Russia: Landmarks in the destiny of a great power* (pp. 140–173). Abingdon: Routledge.

Budylin, S. (2013). Konventsiya ili Konstitutsiya? Mezhdunarodnoe pravo i predely gosudarstvennogo suvereniteta. *Zakon*, No. 12.

Busygina, I. (2013). Kak rossiyskiy politicheskiy rezhim dokazyvayet svoyu privlekatelnost. *Otechestvennye zapiski, 6,* 111–121.

[62] Ukraine's parliament backs changes to Constitution confirming Ukraine's path toward EU, NATO (2019).

Council Directive. (2000). Establishing a general framework for equal treatment in employment and occupation. https://eur-lex.europa.eu/legal-content/EN/TXT/?uri=celex%3A32000L0078.
David, P. A. (1985). Clio and the economics of QWERTY. *American Economic Review Proceedings, 75,* 332–337.
Declaration on Ukraine. (1991). http://aei.pitt.edu/3242/1/3242.pdf.
Deklaratsiya pro derzhavny suverenitet Ukrayiny. (1990). No. 55–XII. https://zakon.rada.gov.ua/laws/show/55-12.
Delegaty 4 vseukrainskogo foruma semyi trebuyut likvidirovat dolzhnost upolnomochennogo po voprosam gendera. (2019). https://censor.net.ua/photo_news/3114428/delegaty_iv_vseukrainskogo_foruma_semi_trebuyut_likvidirovat_doljnost_upolnomochennogo_po_voprosam_gendernoyi.
Hathaway, O. A. (2003). Path dependence in the law: The course and pattern of legal change in a common law system. John M. Olin Center for Studies in Law, Economics, and Public Policy Working Papers, 270.
Hedlund, S. (2000). Path dependence in Russian policy making: Constraints on Putin's economic choice. *Post-Communist Economies, 12*(4), 390–407.
Ispolinov, A. (2018). Osobye mnenia v mezhdunarodnyh sudah: doctrina i practika. https://istina.msu.ru/publications/article/108980749/.
Kazansky, D. (2014). Yak KPU spryyaye separatyzmu. https://tyzhden.ua/Politics/120457.
Kerikmäe, T., Troitiño, D. R., & Shumilo, O. (2019). An idol or an ideal? A case study of Estonian e-Governance: Public perceptions, myths and misbeliefs. *Acta Baltica Historiae et Philosophiae scientiarum, 7*(1).
Kodeks zakoniv pro pratsiu Ukrayiny. (1971). https://zakon.rada.gov.ua/laws/show/322-08.
Konstytutsiya nezalezhnoyi Ukrayiny v troh knyhah. Dokumenty ta stenogramy. (1998), Kyiv.
Konstytutsiya Ukrayiny (1996). https://zakon.rada.gov.ua/laws/show/254к/96-вр.
Kovler, A. (1996). Konstitutsionnye osnovy novoy rossiyskoy gosudarstvennosti. In *Stanovleniye novoy rossiyskoy gosudarstvennosti: realnost i perspektivy* (pp. 23–24), Moscow.
Krasnov, M. (2013). Khristianskoye mirovozzreniye i prava cheloveka. *Lex Russica, 5,* 465–477.
Krastev, I. (2011). Paradoxes of the new authoritarianism. *Journal of Democracy, 22*(2), 39.
Kurkin, B. (2008). Ideologema prav cheloveka i yeyo interpretatsiya v otechestvennoy pravovoy nauke. *Pravo, 2,* 112–116.
Mälksoo, L. (2015). *Russian approaches to international law.* Oxford: Oxford University Press.
Morlino, L., & Sadurski, V. (Eds.). (2010). *Democratization and European Union. Comparing Central and Eastern European Post-Communist Countries.* London: Routledge.
PACE Opinion 190. (1995). Application by Ukraine for membership of the Council of Europe. https://assembly.coe.int/nw/xml/XRef/Xref-XML2HTML-en.asp?fileid=13929&lang=en.
PACE Opinion 193. (1996). Application by Russia for membership of the Council of Europe. https://assembly.coe.int/nw/xml/XRef/Xref-XML2HTML-EN.asp?fileid=13932&lang=en.
Partnership and Cooperation Agreement between the European Communities and their Member States, and Ukraine. (1994). http://ec.europa.eu/world/agreements/downloadFile.do?fullText=yes&treatyTransId=659.
Pashin, S. (2014). Sudebnaya sistema Rossii: perelitsovka. *Otechestvennye zapiski, 3,* 78–91.
Petrov, R., Serdiuk, O. (2009). Ukraine: The quest for democratization between Europe and Russia. In L. Morlino, A. Magen (Eds.) *International actors, democratization and the rule of law. Anchoring democracy?* (pp. 189–220). London, New York: Routledge.
Pro osnovni napriamy zovnishnioyi polityky Ukrayiny. (1993). No. 3360–XII. https://zakon.rada.gov.ua/laws/show/3360-12.
Programa intehratsiyi Ukrayiny do Yevropeyskoho Soyuzu. (2000). No. 1072/2000. https://zakon.rada.gov.ua/laws/show/n0001100-00.
Ramiro Troitino, D., & Pando Ballesteros, M. D. L. P. (2017). Churchill's European integration model. *Revista de Occidente, 433,* 57–71.
Rechitsky, V. (2018). *Neformalny konstytutsionalizm* (pp. 74–84). Kharkiv: Prava Lyudyny.

Rishennia Konstytutsiynoho Sudu vid 22.05.2018 No. 5-r/2018. https://zakon.rada.gov.ua/laws/show/v005p710-18.

Rishennia Konstytutsiynoho Sudu vid 25.01.2012 No. 3-rp/2012. https://zakon.rada.gov.ua/laws/show/v003p710-12.

Rogozhin, S. (2001). Prava cheloveka kak ideologicheskiye manipulyatsii Zapada v Rossii. *Moskovskiy zhurnal mezhdunarodnogo prava, 2*, 31–37.

Rossiyskaya Gazeta. (2012). *Federal Law of July 20, 2012, No. 121-FZ*, 23 July. https://rg.ru/2012/07/23/nko-dok.html.

Sajó, A. (1997). Universal rights, missionaries, converts, and 'local savages'. *East European Constitutional Review, 6*(1), 4–7.

Serdiuk, O., & Petrov, R. (2010). Ukraine: A constitutional design between façade democracy and effective transformation. In Morlino L., & Sadurski V. (Eds.). Democratization and European Union. Comparing Central and Eastern European post-communist countries (pp. 170–175). London: Routledge.

Sourgens, F. G. (2016). The virtue of path dependence in the Law. *Santa Clara Law Review, 56*, 2.

Stark, D. (1992). Path dependence and privatization strategies in East Central Europe. *East European Policies and Societies, 6*(1), 17–29.

Stratehiya intehratsiyi Ukrayiny do Yevropeyskoho Soyuzu. (1998). No. 615/98. https://zakon.rada.gov.ua/laws/show/615/98.

Tserkov i vremya. (2014). No. 2.

Troitiño, D. R. (2017). Jean Monnet before the first European community: A historical perspective and critic. *Trames, 21*(3), 193–213.

Troitiño, D. R., Kerikmäe, T., & Chochia, A. (Eds.). (2018). *Brexit: History, reasoning and perspectives*. Berlin: Springer.

Ukraine's parliament backs changes to Constitution confirming Ukraine's path toward EU, NATO. (2019). https://www.unian.info/politics/10437570-ukraine-s-parliament-backs-changes-to-constitution-confirming-ukraine-s-path-toward-eu-nato.html.

Vaypan, G. (2014). Acquiescence affirmed, its limits left undefined: The Markin judgment and the pragmatism of the Russian Constitutional Court vis-à-vis the European Court of Human Rights. *Russian Law Journal, 2*(3), 133–138.

Zakon Ukrayiny 'Pro natsionalnu bezpeku Ukrayiny'. (2018). No. 2469–VIII. https://zakon.rada.gov.ua/laws/show/2469-19.

Zakon Ukrayiny 'Pro Zahalnoderzhavnu programu adaptatsiyi zakonodavstva Ukrayiny do zakonodavstva Yevropeyskoho Soyuzu'. (2004). No. 1629–IV. https://zakon.rada.gov.ua/laws/show/1629-15.

Zakon Ukrayiny 'Pro zahyst suspilnoyi morali'. (2003). No. 1294–VI https://zakon.rada.gov.ua/laws/show/1296-15.

Zakon Ukrayiny 'Pro zasady vnutrishnioyi i zovnishnioyi polityky'. (2010). No. 2411–VI. https://zakon.rada.gov.ua/laws/show/2411-17.

Zelensky rizko vidpoviv na zayavu Putina: zi spilnoho z Rosiyeyu u nas zalyshyvsya lyshe kordon. (2019). https://www.unian.ua/politics/10536321-zelenskiy-rizko-vidpoviv-na-zayavu-putina-zi-spilnogo-z-rosiyeyu-u-nas-zalishivsya-lishe-kordon-video.html.

Zorkin, V. (2010). Predel ustupchivosti. *Rossiyskaya Gazeta*, October 29.

The EU's Common Security and Defence Policy in Facing New Security Challenges and Its Impact on Cyber Defence

Agnes Kasper and Holger Mölder

Abstract The chapter focuses on the perspective of emerging liberal democratic security communities in the post-Cold War European security environment. Does EU's emerging security community complement NATO or makes it weaker? The focus on a European Army, independent from NATO, seems recently become a priority for the EU, but it faces numerous challenges as how to deal with the neutral member states, how the relations will be with NATO, also with Russia, does Europe really needs an army and why. The impact of Brexit on the future CSDP development will be analyzed as well. Specifically, the chapter focuses how EU's Common Security and Defence Policy is prepared in standing against new security challenges, especially cyber threats, which influence to the future CSDP developments will be discussed as well. In order to successfully oppose new security challenges, the European Union has to build up its cyber capacity compatible with other major powers.

Keywords cyber defence · European integration · European challenges · European e-development

1 Introduction

When World War II was over, the Western Europe has developed a successful peace project where the possibility for interstate wars has been effectively minimized. The comprehensive European integration process has been built on the idea of consciously increasing economic interdependence among its members. In the post-Cold War security environment, this peace project has been expanded to the major part of European continent, and with the exception of former Soviet Union and former Yugoslavia, long-standing interstate conflicts very common in Europe for centuries became almost unthinkable in the present-day security environment.

A. Kasper (✉) · H. Mölder
Ehitajate tee 5, 19086 Tallinn, Estonia
e-mail: agnes.kasper@taltech.ee

H. Mölder
e-mail: holger.molder@taltech.ee

D. Ramiro Troitiño et al. (eds.), *The EU in the 21st Century*,
https://doi.org/10.1007/978-3-030-38399-2_15

Nevertheless, this does not mean that Europe today is more secure and would have fewer security concerns. In order to maintain their core values, EU nations should be prepared to stand against various kinds of attacks against integrity and unity of the European Union. Multiple new status seekers—China, Russia, Iran, India, Brazil, Saudi Arabia, Turkey, and others—are offensively challenging the post-Cold War world order. The current wave of populist and extreme nationalist trends has pushed the world away from the course of global integration. The European dependence on US military capabilities has been a cornerstone of security and Defence policies of Western European countries since the end of World War II. Now, under the Trump presidency, the USA is retrenching its presence in Europe. Moreover, after the Brexit process in progress and UK possibly leaving EU after being the integrated part of the Common Security and Defence Policy (CSDP), the capability of EU to stand against its security challenges is more topical than ever.

EU's High Representative of the Union for Foreign Affairs and Security Policy Federica Mogherini stated in her foreword to the renewed EU's security strategy:

> Our wider region has become more unstable and more insecure. The crises within and beyond our borders are affecting directly our citizens' lives. In challenging times, a strong Union is one that thinks strategically, shares a vision and acts together. This is even more true after the British referendum.[1]

Against the background of economic prosperity following the Treaty of Paris of 1951, the development of information and communication technologies throughout the last decades facilitated the emergence of new threats and has a tendency to disrupt classic Defence paradigms into the radically transformed strategic environment. Not a long time ago states attempted to militarily destroy their adversaries by fighting wars. The direct military threat coming from other states has been tremendously reduced, but we are facing various other security challenges like trade wars, uncontrolled migration, refugee crisis, cyberattacks, spread of culture of fear, influence operations, status conflicts, social unrests, international terrorism and criminality, and control over weapons of mass destruction among others. These new strategic challenges make the European security environment even more unstable and insecure than it was throughout the Cold War, and therefore, the European Union should foster alternative Defence strategies which assist to maintain the community-building process based on shared liberal democratic values.

While conventional security threats still remain a core issue in strategic Defence planning, it is important to highlight that new technologies, which apply equally to civilian and military sectors, play a significant role in the recent paradigm shift in the CSDP. In the light of the growing volume of international cyber incidents, data and information security as a vital resource in contemporary conflict may be the twenty-first century's new equivalent to concerns over coal and steel competition, which once launched the European integration process.[2] Several signs indicate that EU considering comprehensive economic and social interdependence of its member

---

[1] Shared Vision (2016), p. 3.

[2] Kasper and Vernygora (2019) NB!!! We are still waiting for the review of this publication. Details will be added if accepted.

states should take the development of independent Defence capabilities more seriously. This chapter analyzes the perspective of the European Union to build up its own Defence capabilities complementary to NATO, which, in times of crisis, would be able to act independently.

2 Building Security Community in Europe

Lessons learned during the long process up to reaching the Common Security and Defence Policy have demonstrated that a successful cooperation network is incomplete without its security dimension. Therefore, CSDP is a rational outcome of comprehensive and complex integration the European liberal democratic countries had over the last 70 years. With launching a security dimension, the European Union has adopted the main principles accredited to the classical concepts of security communities based on "we-feeling," trust and mutual responsiveness by presuming that transnational value-sharing communities can shape the identities of people.[3] The concept of security communities was first developed by the US Political Scientist Karl Deutsch in the 1950s, when many integration processes have been initiated in Europe. Deutsch believed that the community will offer a solution to common social problems must and can be solved by institutionalized procedures of peaceful change by which he meant "without resort to a large-scale physical force."[4]

The idea of building security community in Europe is not a newborn initiative. After World War II, the Western European political elites understood that integrated Defence capabilities would help Western European countries to stand against military threats primarily from the Soviet Bloc at this time. In 1950, Prime Minister of France René Pleven proposed a plan for the European Defence Community (EDC). Pleven's initiative aimed to involve the Western European countries, particularly West Germany, France, Italy, Belgium, Netherlands, and Luxembourg in uniting their military capabilities into an integrated pan-European military force, which was a little bit more than just evolving another traditional military alliance. The European Defence Community could have offered a credible alternative to Germany's accession to NATO. By the Pleven's plan, the EDC would have joint budget, arms, institutions, and procurement, but the pan-European military force would comprise national components, which would report to their national governments. The only exception was the German contingent, which would be directly subordinated to the EDC. Fear that the German militarism will return was still strong five years after the war. However, the proposal failed after the French Parliament did not ratify the treaty in 1952.

Two years later, in 1954, seven Western European states—the UK, France, West Germany, Italy, Belgium, Netherlands, and Luxembourg—initiated a new institution the Western European Union (WEU), which was initially not only to cooperate in a Defence sector but primarily to promote social, economic, and cultural collaboration between Western European nations. In the 1950s, the main objective of WEU was

[3]Adler and Barnett (1998), p. 8.

[4]Deutsch et al. (1957), p. 2.

the control over the rearmament of West Germany.[5] After West Germany joined the Alliance in 1955, WEU played only a minor role in the European security architecture during the Cold War. The enhanced focus of Western European integration has been focused on the extension of economic integration through the European Economic Community (EEC). However, the EEC members gradually started to build up a more comprehensive cooperative framework. In 1984, the Foreign Minister of West Germany Hans-Dietrich Genscher and his Italian colleague Emilio Colombo advocated the plan to move toward a well-integrated federalist union in multiple areas including security and Defence sectors.

The post-Cold War international system demonstrated its ability to operate as the first stable international system in the world history, which was built on conflict prevention, security governance, and cooperative security regimes by focusing on complex interdependence between states, institutionalization, and consolidation of principles of democratic peace.[6] During the entire decade of the 1990s, it seemed that value-sharing security communities conceptualized by Karl Deutsch[7] will progress without any remarkable opposition in the new political environment. First of all, these principles have been primarily accepted by the Western democracies—the USA, Canada, and Western Europe, which were willing to keep a peaceful change from the Cold War system to the new one. The important executive role of the new international system after the end of the Cold War has become visible by the continued salience of international institutions.[8] In the new situation, international organizations played a crucial role in international security governance and started to embody principles of cooperative security "by adopting Immanuel Kant's recipe for perpetual peace: representative democracy; international law and organizations i.e. enlargement of existing institutions by new members; and the development of free trade."[9]

Cooper[10] claims that security in the new post-modern society is based on transparency, mutual openness, interdependence, and mutual vulnerability. By enhancing integration from economics to multiple fields of cooperation, EU successfully contradicted the realist expectations of Europe's quick return to the nineteenth-century multipolarity with the balance of power politics as successful implementation of the European Union has prevented the restoration of great power competition in Europe (Jepperson et al. 1996, 64). Moreover, in 1990, a European Commissioner from the UK Leon Brittain declared that "now is the time to develop a security dimension to the European Community."[11] The Maastricht Treaty of 1992 and launching the

[5]Laursen (1996), p. 172.
[6]Mölder (2010), pp. 101–105.
[7]Deutsch et al. (1957).
[8]Baldwin (1993), p. 288.
[9]Lucarelli (2002) p. 4.
[10]Cooper (2000), pp. 19–20.
[11]Brittain (1990).

Common Foreign Security Policy (CFSP) made a step forward in the European security community-building process emphasized by a shared identity, norms, and values accepted by every member of the Union.[12]

Similar values concerning political ideologies but also economic and religious (cultural) values together with the formation of a common sense of us are among the main criteria that makes a distinction between security communities and military alliances.[13] Emmanuel Adler[14] settled a general principle required for successful existence for security communities, "it is not enough to behave like us, you have to be one of us." By the Copenhagen criteria of 1993, the European Union elaborated a mechanism to define, which countries would be eligible to access the European Union:

> Membership requires that candidate country has achieved stability of institutions guaranteeing democracy, the rule of law, human rights, respect for and protection of minorities, the existence of a functioning market economy as well as the capacity to cope with competitive pressure and market forces within the Union. Membership presupposes the candidate's ability to take on the obligations of membership including adherence to the aims of political, economic and monetary union.[15]

It would also explain current tensions around the future of EU as many nations have had difficulties to accept the core idea of shared values.

A significant step toward the consolidation of the European liberal democratic security community has been made in the British-French summit of 1998 in Saint-Malo. French President Jacques Chirac and British Prime Minister Tony Blair agreed that the EU is expected to play a major role in international stage and concluded the European Union ought to build up the credible military capability able to conduct autonomous actions. The Saint-Malo's declaration was a starting point of the Common Security and Defence Policy, during which WEU's capabilities have been included in one integrated system.

> In order for the European Union to take decisions and approve military action where the Alliance as a whole is not engaged, the Union must be given appropriate structures and a capacity for analysis of situations, sources of intelligence, and a capability for relevant strategic planning, without unnecessary duplication, taking account of the existing assets of the WEU and the evolution of its relations with the EU.[16]

A long-time backstage player in the European security architecture, the WEU became a cornerstone of the new EU's security and Defence pillar. Already in 1987, the WEU declared that the member states intend to assume their responsibilities in a greater role of Defence.[17] In 1992, the WEU made a step forward by adopting the Petersberg tasks,[18] a list of military and security priorities to deploy troops and

[12] Mölder (2010), pp. 195–198.

[13] Deutsch et al. (1957), p. 6.

[14] Adler (2005), p. 190.

[15] Presidency Conclusions (1993).

[16] Joint Declaration (2002).

[17] Laursen (1996), p. 173.

[18] After the Petersberg Hotel near Bonn where the WEU ministerial summit took place.

resources from across the whole spectrum of the military capabilities under the authority of the WEU. These tasks settled a possible WEU involvement for a wide range of international military operations and to deploy military capabilities and resources for conducting peace operations under the authority of the WEU (i.e., humanitarian, rescue, peacekeeping, and crisis management tasks). In June 1999, the European Council decided to incorporate the WEU within the European Union and the same year, the EU's members signed the Helsinki Headline Goal, the first military capability target that focused on building up rapid reaction forces and implement the full range of Petersberg tasks.

The European Security Strategy of 2003 defined strategic objectives and security implications for the European Union. In 2016, the EU adopted a new strategic document "The Global strategy for the Foreign and Security Policy of the European Union." The purpose to review security strategy was related to recent challenges in wider security environment in the age of increasing insecurity and instability when crises have been easily emerged, but much harder to solve. The European Union does not have a history of success stories in crisis management, and CSDP deployments have diminished after the Lisbon Treaty came into force.[19] The EU Battlegroup initiative has reached its full operational capacity in 2007, but since then did not participate in any military operation. There is an obvious need to further develop the CSDP pillar for securing the European Defence space, but mainly political objections have prevented the further integration in this field.

3 European Union Versus NATO—Alternative or Complementary Bodies in Building the European Defence Capabilities?

The claim that the Europeans do not spend much to their own Defence and prefer to rely on US military capabilities has been immediately appeared in major narratives circulated around the European Defence prospects after the Cold War ended. In the 1990s, the USA actively encouraged the enhanced contribution of European partners to NATO. Before the establishment of the EU's own Defence structures, the idea of the European Security and Defence Identity (ESDI) came out during the Bosnian crisis. At the 1996 NATO's ministerial meeting in Berlin, the ministers made a conclusion that the WEU will play more significant role in the European security architecture, would replace tasks omitted to the ESDI, and should give to the EU's members the access to NATO's military capabilities. Strategic partnership between EU and NATO has been specified by two basic documents—The "NATO-EU Declaration on ESDP" agreed on December 16, 2002, and the "Berlin Plus agreement" adopted on March 17, 2003, which covered the exchange of classified information, EU access to NATO's planning capabilities and common assets, and joint consultation mechanisms. The

[19]Marrone and Nones (2013), p. 15.

European Union has achieved the right to use NATO's assets in conducting their peace operations.

Despite the comprehensive integration process started, the European nations have remained different in their unity claims. During the Bush administration, the European Union was split between trans-Atlanticist nations (notably the UK, Denmark, and Poland, but also the Baltic states and most of East European countries), which still emphasized the need for a strong alliance with the USA particularly in security and Defence matters over the EU security and Defence cooperation and euro-centrist nations (notably Germany, France, and Belgium), which became open to more independent solutions and have focused on stronger European integration as well in security and Defence matters.[20] The gap between EU's leading nations Germany and France from one side and the United States from another side showed its strength after 2003, when the "schism" over the Iraqi operation threatened the Western unity with strategic decoupling of the Europe and the United States.[21] Trans-Atlanticist nations strategically emphasize a central role of national security over more integrated Defence cooperation between EU nations.[22] Especially Denmark keeps distance on further EU integration and practices intensive opt-out policy concerning EU policies in relation to security and Defence, citizenship, police and justice, and the adoption of the common currency.

Fear that the developing independent military capabilities within EU framework will weaken NATO's military capabilities has been widely discussed all these years EU started to develop its security and Defence pillar. So far, there has been less political will to develop independent Defence capabilities and too many claims, which emphasize that CSDP is useless to comprehend the effective mechanism established already by NATO. These misperceptions have been tightly connected with the particular position of security guarantees from the USA and stem from the realist logics of international relations, which does not take into account the ability of international institutions to produce efficient security regimes and security governance. Having 22 of the 28 EU member states also as NATO members should provide a credible mechanism to prevent any competition between EU and NATO. So far as much both organizations share the same liberal democratic values and proceed from shared identity adopted by the member nations of both organizations, there should be no any serious ideological or cultural gap between EU and NATO, and both institutions can be easily adapted into one integrated system. These organizations represent different political frameworks, but develop similar goals by cooperating closely to each other. Therefore, further security and Defence integration of EU members are most obviously not to replace NATO capabilities, but it manifests rather complementary processes.

The fact that NATO has adopted the principle of collective Defence and the EU has not has sometimes been mistakenly interpreted. A claim that NATO's membership would be more trusted applies to the anarchical security environment as well the logic of military alliances is different from the logic of security communities. Indeed, the

[20] Mölder (2010), pp. 125–126.

[21] Krastev (2006), p. 2.

[22] Mölder (2018), p. 161.

Treaty of Washington fixes the principle of collective Defence under the paragraph 5 as a security guarantee from the organization to its members. However, in 1949 NATO was created as a military alliance of independent nations where mutual obligations had to be fixed in the Treaty. If the institution will adapt a security community perspective, the demands for additional security guarantees can be abandoned. The European Union followed the different logic of community-building based on similar values and shared identity, by which the principle of collective Defence has been naturally integrated into the EU founding documents.

Paradoxically, the ongoing Brexit process if it finally takes place may even fasten security and Defence integration in the European Union. Since World War II, the UK has been keener to develop strategic partnership with the USA than to contribute to the further European integration.[23] The UK has always loosely integrated with the European Union, and either way practiced opt-outs from EU policies or took part at its own speed and extend.[24] Brits have been probably the staunchest opponents to EU's military initiatives despite the fact that the conceptual idea of the European Union as a liberal democratic security community was once declared by the British Commissioner Leon Brittan.[25] It will be also worth to mentioning that the UK and particularly Tony Blair were related to the birth of the Common Security and Defence Policy. The post-Brexit EU may be more open for further integration, especially if Donald Trump will be re-elected in 2020 and the USA continues to develop its protectionist foreign policy by destroying the post-Cold War world order.

The most widely used argument used against building EU's independent Defence capabilities is based on the tradition of US responsibilities over the European security architecture. Military disadvantages of the European Union and its dependence from the military contribution of the USA in security and Defence enable for NATO to play continually an important role in the European security environment.[26] Indeed, the USA remains being the biggest military contributor to NATO, military capabilities of the European Union are much weaker than that of NATO, and Europe does not have a strong centralized government, which may negatively affect the decision-making process during crisis.[27] Therefore, the development of its own military dimension has been not commonly welcomed among the EU members. Leon Brittan[28] pointed out that the European reluctance in abandoning security dependence from the USA and to build an independent security community is stemming from a long tradition of thought that "Europeans have had neither the desire to finance their own Defence; the purpose to devise a common strategy; nor the temerity to risk destabilizing a structure which was serving them so well."

Misbalance between military capabilities of the USA and NATO's European allies and a wish from the US side to decrease their military presence in Europe caused

[23] Ibid., p. 154.

[24] Riedel (2018), p. 103.

[25] See Footnote 11.

[26] Mouritzen and Wivel (2005), p. 28.

[27] Marrone and Nones (2013), p. 6.

[28] Brittain (1990).

the recent increase of Defence expenditures in Europe. Since 2015/2016, European allies of NATO turned from post-Cold War decline of their Defence budgets. There are currently five EU's NATO members that overcome a 2% benchmark—UK, Poland, Lithuania, Latvia, Estonia, and Greece, but just Belgium and Spain have their Defence budgets less than 1% of GDP. While the average Defence expenditure 1.44% is still below 2% of GDP (the recommended threshold for NATO members), the gap between US and European members expenditures is coming closer (US$102 billion now). In 2017, the European Union initiated the European Defence Fund, which aims to increase its resources to €5.5bn with the expected investments from member states.[29] Additionally, a new off-budget funding mechanism, the European Peace Facility, has been proposed by High Representative Federica Mogherini. The majority of these new funding mechanisms should focus on developing capabilities in the weakest areas of the European Defence sector as research and development or new equipment acquisition.[30]

It will be genuinely wrong to see the further European integration in security and Defence issues as alternative to NATO if both organizations will continually follow the security community perspective based on liberal democratic values. Influential outside powers forced by protectionist policies of Donald Trump in the USA and Vladimir Putin in Russia have effectively promoted the European disintegration and attempted to return to more anarchical security environment with less international security governance. The inconsequent policy performed by Donald Trump has significantly raised tensions around the world as well-produced misperceptions between the USA and its major allies in Europe. Changes in political rhetoric of the US administration naturally caused discussions in the future of EU's security guarantees and reducing its dependence from the US capabilities.

4 European Army

The concept of the European army has been strongly advocated by the French President Emmanuel Macron and supported by the German Chancellor Angela Merkel. Recent shifts in US policies during the Trump presidency may cause the need for the EU nations to reduce their dependency from the US military capabilities. President Trump has several times expressed his concerns about NATO's future, which certainly might require preparing alternative framework for the occasion NATO is not able or willing to solve any security issue related to the European Union. In his speech at the Sorbonne University in 2017, Macron called the European nations to join the European Intervention Initiative (E2I), which is a joint military project outside of NATO and EU framework of 10 EU nations (France, Germany, Denmark, Belgium,

[29] Pothier (2019).

[30] Ibid.

the Netherlands, Spain, Estonia, Portugal, the UK, and Finland) to develop a mutually shared strategic culture by focusing on enhanced interactions on intelligence sharing, scenario planning, support operations and doctrine.[31]

After President Trump pulled out of a 1987 nuclear treaty banning medium-range ground-launched missiles with Russia, Macron made a further step forward and made a proposal for joint military forces within EU framework—called the European army. He declared that Europeans cannot be dependent on US precarious willingness to defend them, while Russia may still pose constant security threat for Europe.[32] Fabrice Pothier[33] pointed out that the successful implementation of President Macron's vision of a European Army requires first of all comprehensive reforms of EU institutions. However, critics to Macron's initiative have been treated it as an alternative to NATO destroying the Western unity. Peck (2018)[34] brings up primarily political obstacles which may undermine building a successful operational capability by claiming that EU is not a unitary actor. Under the current division of EU countries in which several nations showed up a strong critic against liberal democratic values, overriding structural reforms seem to be hardly achievable at least in the near future. Moreover, despite the US President Donald Trump several times mentioned the opportunity of withdrawing his country from NATO and accused the European allies in freeloading of the US capabilities, the current US administration has been deeply concerned on the viability of the European army.[35] Tocci[36] pointed to three structural factors that underlie the need for a more integrated security and Defence union in Europe: NATO security umbrella cannot be taken for granted indefinitely; sharp increase of insecurity within and beyond the EU; financial and technological implications of high interdependence point to a rational response of acting together.

Considering strong anti-institutionalist views of the current US administration and the influence of President's Hawkish National Security Adviser John Bolton,[37] these statements cannot be completely ignored. Trump has openly questioned a number of military and economic partnerships, the Paris climate accord, the Asia-Pacific trade pact, military alliances with South Korea and Japan, and returned the American troops from the coalition to defeat the Islamic State Syria without consulting allies. Ahead to NATO summit of 2018, Trump delivered an opinion that NATO is "a drain on the United States."[38] Trump constantly complains that the European allies do not spend enough money for their Defence. President Trump has growing a deeply negative attitude against the European Union, calling EU as a "trade foe" for the

---

[31] Letter of Intent (2018).

[32] BBC News (2018).

[33] Pothier (2019).

[34] Peck (2018).

[35] Ibid.

[36] Tocci (2018), pp. 132–33.

[37] John Bolton is a vocal critic of the European Union. He has often criticized the EU for pursuing liberal policies, fervently supported Brexit and accused EU in "the endless process of diplomatic mastication"… (Bolton 2008).

[38] Barnes and Cooper (2019).

USA, openly supported Brexit and several times he praised the President of Russia Vladimir Putin. Former chief strategist of Trump Steve Bannon after resigning from Trump's team started a dissolution campaign against the European Union.[39] In such competitive environment, it becomes questionable if Europe can trust the USA on the same level as it has been trusted during the Cold War.

However, if EU builds up its own military capabilities, it does not necessarily mean confrontation with NATO, but these capabilities may be arranged as complementary to each other. There is neither NATO army nor EU army today. The Defence capability of both organizations relies on national components trained and accustomed to operating together.[40] All member states of the European Union are members or partners to NATO—those EU members not joining NATO (Finland, Sweden, Ireland, Austria, and Malta)[41] participate in the Partnership for Peace program. In response to more protectionist policy of the USA, European leaders have declared their willingness to take more responsibility in Defence matters. Angela Merkel emphasized the European army is not against NATO, but a complement to NATO. Merkel addressed in her speech to the European Parliament:

> The times when we could rely on others are over. This means nothing less than for us Europeans to take our destiny in our own hands if we want to survive as a Union. This means, in the long run, Europe has to become more capable to act. We have to reconsider our ways of deciding and to renounce the principle of unanimity where the European treaties allow and wherever this is necessary. I proposed a European security council, in which important decisions can be prepared faster.[42]

The same logic can be followed in developing the Common Security and Defence Policy within the European Union, which does not pose any threat to NATO as these two institutions share the same values. There are already some evidences which indicate progress by launching the Permanent Structured Cooperation (PESCO) mechanism, where twenty-five EU nations have united their national armed forces under the joint command in order to pursue further structural integration. The agreement was signed by 23 member states on November 13, 2017, while Ireland and Portugal joined in the next month. There were three opt-outs performed—the UK, Denmark, and Malta. The PESCO process was partially forced by the inconsistent policy of Donald Trump, by which the US commitment to the European Defence became more vulnerable. The initiative was backed by leading EU nations like France and Germany, while both of them had slightly different purposes—France aimed to strengthen organization's military capabilities while Germany focused on reinforcing unity between EU nations.[43] PESCO has been seen as a framework and a process driving deepening integration in the Defence field by focusing on undertakings in the field of capability

---

[39] De La Baume and Sciorilli Borrelli (2019).

[40] BBC News (2018).

[41] Except Cyprus, which is an aspiring member, but constantly vetoed by Turkey.

[42] De La Baume and Herszenhorn (2018).

[43] Pothier (2019).

development and operational areas like Cyber Rapid Response Teams and Mutual Assistance in Cyber Security, upgrading Maritime Surveillance and others.[44]

5 The European Commission and Recent Security and Defence Challenges

After the European Defence Agency (EDA) was established in 2004, there is a responsible EU body, which focuses on developing joint Defence capabilities for crisis management tasks, armament cooperation, Defence technology, and industrial base as well as Defence research and technology issues as well to establish an internationally competitive European Defence Equipment Market. EDA[45] underlined that "... while military operations will not change [...] the conduct of future operations cannot be discussed without consideration of the political, social, cultural and technical contexts. In this technology requires a special mention. [...]The ability to plan, prepare and conduct knowledge-based operations will be fundamental for the future." In addition, an overall trend can be pointed out, that "the need for developed concepts, doctrine, procedures, training and architectures to generate the future new, enhanced and interoperable capabilities is more dominant than the perceived requirement to acquire hardware."[46]

Adaptation to the changing role of force and adapting to the technological revolution was seen as the two key issues for Defence, and "[t]he objective is not 'victory' as traditionally understood, but moderation, balance of interests and peaceful resolution of conflicts—in short, stability."[47] The EDA's predictions seem to have materialized in a number of ways: algorithmic solutions are transforming the practice of security,[48] states are increasingly developing their cyberwarfare capabilities,[49] the EU's strategic documents declare resilience building against internal and external challenges as an overarching goal, and strategic autonomy as a concept is resurfacing due to Washington's demands.[50]

Although Article 24 of the Treaty on European Union (TEU) clearly lays down that decision-making powers in the policy areas of CSFP remain with the Council and its preparatory bodies, numerous studies have pointed toward the Commission's strong influence in some areas of this intergovernmental domain.[51] The Commission's influence in the CFSP by leveraging its budgetary powers suggested by Dijkstra[52] became

[44] EEAS (2018).

[45] EDA (2008).

[46] Ibid.

[47] Ibid.

[48] Amoore and Raley (2017), p. 4.

[49] Domingo (2016).

[50] Shared Vision (2016).

[51] Riddervold (2016), p. 354.

[52] Djikstra (2013), p. 9.

a palpable reality with a "game-changer" move of the Juncker Commission prioritizing Defence. In June of 2017, the European Commission surprised the member states by launching a proposal for the European Defence Fund (EDF), a supranational body touching upon an area that was considered the domain of the intergovernmental method.[53] Arguably, with the EDF initiative the Commission was able to expand supranational governance to Defence by exploiting the functional connection between its own economic competences and the pressures to increase cooperation in the Defence industry, while exploiting the dysfunctional features of intergovernmental cooperation.[54] Hence, the same argument applies to cyber defence-related areas of the EDF and the Commission gained a powerful tool to steer the directions of cyber defence cooperation among EU member states.

Another line of argument put forth by Riddervold[55] emphasizes the role of institutional features and the Commission's expertise as important factors in the Commission's *de facto* influence over CSDP areas, such as the broadening of the scope of the Maritime Security Strategy and facilitating an agreement to launch the Atalanta mission. After vetoing the initial 2010 attempt of the European External Action Service (EEAS) to draw up a military-oriented EU Maritime Security Strategy, two years later, the Commission redefined the strategy from a security and Defence-oriented strategy to a cross-sectoral one.[56] The Commission helped to create a legal framework to deal with suspected pirates, which was a controversial issue, turning member states to prefer an EU mission to a NATO one, hence "[t]he main source of the Commission's influence on Atalanta was, in other words, that it drew on its competences and expertise to make an agreement on an EU mission possible despite initial disagreements among the Member States."[57]

From this institutional perspective, the Commission was set to its position for a brave move in the field of cybersecurity by three events. Firstly, the 9/11 attacks raised EU-wide security concerns prompting overview of the critical infrastructure policy in the EU, and then, the 2007 cyberattacks against Estonia raised awareness about the vulnerability of nation states and societies dependent on information and communication technologies. Thirdly, the discovery of the Stuxnet incident also blew away illusions and demonstrated about the potential physical harms of cyberoperations. While the EU's cybersecurity strategy is rooted in data protection ideals and in the fight against cybercrime starting in the twentieth century, the Juncker Commission's prioritization of Defence domains is well detectable in the 2017 revised cybersecurity strategy, which marked a turning point in moving from a comprehensive approach toward an integrated, truly horizontal one. In 2017, the Commission redefined the strategy from a market-oriented one to a cross-sectoral strategy that also covers a wide number of Community policy areas falling under Commission competences and establishes clear links to areas of the CFSP, including the CSDP.

---

[53] Haroche (2019), p. 4.

[54] Ibid., p. 8.

[55] Riddervold (2016), p. 366.

[56] Ibid., p. 361.

[57] Ibid., p. 362.

The Commission's relevance is also remarkably present in the context of EU-NATO relations; for example, the Joint EU-NATO Declaration was signed by the President of the European Council, the President of the European Commission, and the Secretary General of the North Atlantic Treaty Organization in Warsaw on July 8, 2016. The declaration emphasized two areas of cooperation most relevant to cyber defence: countering cyber and hybrid threats. Implementing measures focus on information sharing, training, education, exercises, fostering research and innovation, as well as mainstreaming cyber into crisis management. The EU-NATO cooperation and potential division of labor in cyber issues were discussed already in 2011, suggesting that EU focus on "resilience"—on its cybercrime and critical information infrastructure (CIIP) policy—NATO focus on "deterrence"—military-related cyber issues. This has significant disadvantages in relation to the questionable concept of cyberdeterrence, inclusion of non-NATO nations, EU's own credibility in demonstrating cyber power and autonomy, functioning of the EU's communications resources.[58] However, what is clear that the core mandates of the EU and the NATO differ, hence interlocking and complementary functions can provide the best synergies in cyber defence, which in turn likely to take the two partners to uncharted territories in terms of cooperation both within and inbetween them.

6 CSDP and New Logics in cyber defence

While the EU's security actorness in the field of cybersecurity has been established by proclamations in areas of Common Security and Foreign Policy, as well as mandates given to EU institutions in areas that largely correspond to the European Communities in the old pillar system,[59] until 2016 the resources allocated to this security area had been extremely low and a significant gap existed in doctrine implementation.[60] However, the years of 2016–2017 were a turning point in many respects both for the overall CSDP and cyber defence policy, as well as for the cybersecurity posture of the EU as a whole.

To the extent policy makers might overestimate the strengths and direction of cyber-kinetic relationship,[61] there are arguments to make why and how the EU can weigh in and complement NATO cooperation in the field of cyber defence. However, there may be a need to re-evaluate the EU's options, clarify what is the meaning of strategic autonomy in this domain, how it relates to cyber resilience, and how to achieve it. This leaves us with a few contradictory rationales for cyberoperations: Although current experience does not generally seem to support a clear justification claiming short term military advantage,[62] cyberweapons still enjoy a somewhat

[58] Klimburg and Tiirmaa-Klaar (2011), p. 36.

[59] Trimintzios et al. (2017), p. 9.

[60] Barrinha and Carrapiço (2016).

[61] Kostyuk and Zhukov (2019), p. 340.

[62] Kostyuk and Zhukov (2019).

preferred status as a first-strike capability[63] despite the disconnects from physical violence, and cyberoperations beyond the boundaries of armed conflict may be seen as useful for their long-term political effects (propaganda, deterrence) and for reconnaissance. It is also important to emphasize the exposures to cyberattacks, where military systems are not spared, although international maturity in this field is questionable. While cyber dominance remains with the USA and US-based companies, the US government is concerned about the diffusion of Defence technologies across the globe and devises new ways to use innovative technologies, such as cyber, to maintain its military edge, which has an impact on Defence innovation in the EU.[64] As Tocci[65] explained it in plain words, the European Security and Defence Union means thinking, buying, and acting together and cyber is a significant factor in all these three pillars, demonstrating the linkages between strategic questions, Defence capabilities, and industrial issues.

Fiott[66] suggests to conceptualize the EU's goal of strategic autonomy as a scale measuring operational and industrial dependencies, ranging from autonomy as responsibility (freedom to operate regardless of the origin of tools), through autonomy as hedging (freedom to operate and reducing industrial dependencies as an "insurance policy"), to complete emancipation. Cybersecurity and cyber defence as part of strategic autonomy, however, do not fit well into this framework for several reasons. First, cyber defence operations cannot be confined to missions and operations of the EU, unless we equate cyber defence with passive, internal defensive network operations that merely aims to prevent incursions, but exclude activities outside the defended networks. Even then the nature and operation of cyber tools are quite different from those of kinetic Defence equipment, because their separation from the worldwide Internet turned out to be illusory and intention behind any attack can be difficult to decipher.[67] Secondly, cyber tools tend to need maintenance, updates—attackers can use known or zero-day vulnerabilities, and the target needs to recognize and patch their systems, which creates an indivisible and continuous link between operation and industry dimensions. Thirdly, the private sector provides a fertile ground for finding delivery methods for cyberattacks, be it a popular webmail service or social media—too many of them provided by US firms. Instinctively one might sense that autonomy as responsibility and continued dependence on the USA, as well as complete emancipation in terms of operational and industrial terms carry significant risks, can be undesirable in policy terms or plainly impossible given the global dominance of the USA in information and communication technologies.

Although there is a legal separation between the established security and Defence union, cybersecurity—along with migration—is a field that cuts across both.[68] This distinction is, however, not always well reflected in the terminology used to describe

---

[63] Leuprecht et al. (2019) pp. 382–383.

[64] Fiott (2017), pp. 6–7.

[65] Tocci (2018) p. 135.

[66] Fiott (2018).

[67] Leuprecht et al. (2019), p. 385.

[68] Bendiek (2017), pp. 14–16.

civilian and military aspects of the cyber domain, since the term cybersecurity is used in the sense that it refers to civilian context, as well as the global context encompassing all sorts of cyber threats regardless of their characterization of civilian or military, while the term cyber defence is generally used for military cyber aspects. The distinction between legal regimes might be unsustainable in the long term, given the entanglement of domains, sectors, and architecture of cyberspace. In addition, the EU's overall cyber policy is based not only on the 2013 and 2017 cybersecurity strategies that emphasizes resilience to cyberattacks and integrates internal and external security and Defence aspects, but also on the 2015 Strategy for Digital Single Market, thus including areas where neofunctionalist integration theory has provided ample explanations for EU's governance dynamics. In our view in the particular field of cybersecurity, the established invariants such as the dual nature of cyber defence, the synergies between civilian and military approaches in protecting critical cyber assets,[69] and that both cybersecurity in the civilian context and cyber defence in the military context often address the same threats, follow the same basic principles and require very similar measures and procedures,[70] channel elements of the neofunctional logic into areas of the EU's Defence policy.

The central concept of resilience, where classic domestic policy domains gain high relevance in the CFSP/CSDP, also has a tense relationship with the idea of multilateralism and weakens the distinction between the EU's legal and political community,[71] therefore implies new logics in the CSDP. Technology's overarching transformative power in these domains manifests in the "loss of location" and pressure for increased operational tempo in cybersecurity and cyber defence and shakes up past logics of integration and action in the EU. Indeed, examining the EDF's innovative features and its links to economy-dominated rationale, Haroche[72] argued that a "new type of offensive spillover from economy to Defence" can be detected and new intergovernmentalism and neofunctionalism offer potentially "complementary sets of empirical hypotheses on the evolution of EU governance." cyber defence is a constitutive element of the EU's holistic cybersecurity policy and as such, despite belonging to the system based on intergovernmental customs, is unlikely to escape alignment with the EU's neofunctionalist dynamics.

7 Functional Discrepancies and Rationales in the Field of cyber defence

Interdependencies in the field of cyber defence stem from the heavy focus of cybersecurity policies highlighting the need to protect the vital functioning of society, often referred to as critical or essential areas and infrastructures, hence reflecting a

[69]Trimintzios et al. (2017), p. 15.

[70]Powell (2018), p. 36.

[71]Bendiek (2017), p. 28.

[72]Haroche (2019).

broader, societal understanding of Defence, where military operations are a component thereof.[73] The reviewed EU cybersecurity strategy of 2017 moves toward an integrated approach and emphasizes that "[o]ur future security depends on transforming our ability to protect the EU against cyber threats: both civilian infrastructure and military capacity rely on secure digital systems."[74] The strategy *expressis verbis* recognizes that "EU cyber preparedness is central to both the Digital Single Market and our Security and Defence Union,"[75] turning cybersecurity into a truly horizontal policy area. The strategy was released with a number of accompanying proposals, legislative and non-legislative, including the recently adopted Cybersecurity Act (Regulation (EU) 2019/881), which establishes the European Union Agency for Cybersecurity with a rather modest advisory role in CSFP and CSDP areas.

Recognizing the emergence of new security challenges and the interlinked internal and external security environment, in 2013 the EU Council called for an EU Cyber Defence Policy Framework,[76] which was indeed established in 2014. In the end of 2018, the Council updated the 2014 EU Cyber Defence Policy Framework reiterated the goal of the EU's enhanced strategic autonomy and that also in the context of cybersecurity and cyber defence. This requires more cooperation in capability development, promoting effectiveness and interoperability, and primary focus is on the development of cyber defence capabilities, as well as the protection of the EU CSDP communication and information networks. Other priority areas include training and exercises, research and technology, civil-military cooperation and international cooperation.[77] In 2017, after the Council adopted a PESCO mechanism and identified first 17 collaborative PESCO projects, the projects developed under PESCO currently include such as Cyber Threats and Incident Response Information Sharing Platform and Cyber Rapid Response Teams and Mutual Assistance in Cyber Security.[78]

The functional discrepancies and links between the need to achieve a high level of security of network and information security—which the NIS directive identified as essential for the smooth functioning of the internal market (Directive (EU) 2016/1148)—and the EU's cyber defence policy are highlighted by recent state-sponsored cybersecurity incidents. Both the WannaCry and NotPetya cyberattacks spread out across the EU in 2017 summer, causing losses measured in billions of euros, and exploiting the same NSA-built "EternalBlue" tool for propagation to unpatched Windows systems despite the availability of a fix issued by Microsoft months earlier.

The WannaCry attack, which also features in the European Parliament resolution of June 13, 2018, on cyber defence, showcases the need for common EU responses, since the private sector was heavily impacted by these large-scale malicious cyber

[73] Griffith (2018), p. 18.

[74] European Commission (2017).

[75] Ibid.

[76] European Council (2013), p. 9.

[77] Council of the European Union (2018a).

[78] Council of the European Union (2018b).

activities and it is also often better placed to provide deep technical analysis of these operations, while it is mostly beyond the capabilities and mandates of single private sector entities as well as single EU member states to address such threats effectively. The WannaCry ransomware attack leveraged a vulnerability in common Microsoft products, one that was stockpiled by NSA and stolen in 2017,[79] encrypted data in computer systems Europe and worldwide, including that of Deutsche Bahn, Renault, Telefonica, several UK hospitals, and demanded ransom payments in Europe and worldwide Bitcoins.[80] The attack was attributed to North Korea by the USA and UK in 2017, and concern was expressed about the WannaCry and other cyberoperations used to generate illicit revenues in violation of sanctions against the DPRK.[81]

A few weeks after the WannaCry attacks, the NotPetya malware rampaged across the world, masquerading as the Petya ransomware, yet the code was built to destroy, not to extort.[82] Although most victims were based in Ukraine, its indiscriminate design caused it to spread affecting European businesses and the UK publicly attributed the attack to Russia, more specifically to the Russian military.[83] The USA followed suit blaming the Russian military in a statement issued by the White House indicating that it was the most costly cyberattack in history, "[it] was part of the Kremlin's ongoing effort to destabilize Ukraine and demonstrates ever more clearly Russia's involvement in the ongoing conflict" and will be met with international consequences.[84]

While the EU as such never publicly attributed the attacks, but condemned them in more abstract words, the cases illustrate the interdependencies and blurred boundaries between organizational, state, and supranational levels. The attacks affected and entangled a variety of state and non-actors, clearly demonstrating that similar techniques, tactics, and procedures can be used by cybercriminals, terrorist groups, as well as states, while hostile actors easily hide behind anonymity-enabling features of cyberspace and/or plausible deniability. Potential and actual responses mirror this diversity, ranging from the need to address market dynamics, incorporate the security by design approach and setting product standards in the industry, establishing effective frameworks for vulnerability discovery and disclosure, controlling foreign acquisition of critical cyber technologies, to being able to swiftly and reliably collect and act upon information for containing ongoing attacks, identifying perpetrators and where appropriate, devising responses to state actors in accordance with international law. Detection and full understanding of their impact, attribution, and response imply unique operational challenges in cyber defence, including in terms of threat intelligence capabilities in the large attack surface expanded by technological factors,[85] whereas paradoxically cyber activities mostly take place in infrastructures that

[79] Christensen and Liebetrau (2019).

[80] Ghosh (2017).

[81] US Department of Justice (2018).

[82] The Register (2018).

[83] Foreign & Commonwealth Office (2018).

[84] White House (2018).

[85] Griffith (2018), pp. 6, 26.

are owned and operated by private businesses, representing both a vital component of military operations and a critical vulnerability.

While the original objective of incorporating network and information security issues into EU regulations, as well as the establishment of the European Network and Information Security Agency in 2004 served the purposes of completing the internal market in the area of electronic communications,[86] technological diffusion created a new environment where cyber (existential?) threats emanating from state or non-state actors represent a serious obstacle for the functioning of the (digital) single market. The 2017 WannaCry and NotPetya cyberattacks could have been easily avoided by basic security practices, such as stop using the obsolete systems containing critical vulnerabilities, however governments' practices of stockpiling and exploiting vulnerabilities for building cyberweapons and spying tools instead of reporting them to those who could fix them also gives rise to serious concerns. The challenges in the field of market-focused cybersecurity policies, and the vulnerabilities present in the dominantly private "territory" of cyberspace—the fifth domain of military activity—lead to mutual tensions that are unlikely to be resolved without further integration in the field of cybersecurity and cyber defence.

Arguably, with the above background of the cybersecurity policy area and expertise accumulated by supranational actors, particularly ENISA's (now European Union Agency for Cybersecurity) and the Commission's role as well as complex interdependencies between economy, society, and national Defence, a purely intergovernmental approach in the CSDP is unsustainable and member states are unlikely to be able to bypass EU institutions and Commission's role if the overarching goals of building resilience against internal and external challenges are to be achieved. Once the Commission has access to the de facto decision-making arenas, it is able to leverage several tools—procedural, budgetary, or competence powers—to influence the traditionally intergovernmental decision-making processes, as it has already done so in areas neighboring cyber defence, while the actual role and powers of the EU Agency for Cybersecurity remain to be seen given its newborn status as such with new competences. However, the Commission's strong role as a policy entrepreneur in areas of cybersecurity and lifting several aspects of cyber defence onto the supranational level appears to confirm that neofunctional and intergovernmental logics are not mutually exclusive, but rather complementary in the cyber domain.

The EU 2017 Cybersecurity Strategy added a significant modification to the European conceptualization of cybersecurity and bases its deterrence paradigm on the theory of criminal law and closely links it with criminal justice with the goal to maintain an effective deterrence posture by strong responses aimed have the offenders and aggressors recalculate their intentions.[87] In the EU's framework, this may be better understood in terms of coercive capacity and the Weberian notion of states' monopoly on legitimate use of violence, rather than pure military might, reflecting the EU equivalent of "whole-of-government deterrence" approach: "whole-of-integration deterrence." However, this line of logic is not consistently expressed in the

[86]European Court of Justice (2006), p. 66.

[87]Tor (2017) pp. 94–95.

strategy, since it also uses rhetoric reflecting the dichotomous deterrence perspective: "As long as the perpetrators of cyber-attacks—both non-state and state—have nothing to fear besides failure, they will have little incentive to stop trying,"[88] implying that deterrence is not about moderation of the adversary's behavior, but mitigation of cyber risks to near to zero—a goal that may be ill-fit in cyberspace.

8 Conclusion

The enhanced cooperation and integration in multiple areas will inevitably lead to the situation in which community members are paying more attention to security and Defence cooperation. The European Security and Defence Policy is the ultimate result of the comprehensive integration process and the community-building in Europe. Therefore, the advancement of CSDP cannot be interpreted as the alternative process to any existing security cooperation framework, including NATO. The US responsibility over the Defence of European nations helped to successfully survive the Cold War, which was structurally well controlled and stable system. In the ongoing age of instability and insecurity, we are facing new hybrid security challenges including information warfare, psychological warfare, cyber threats, electronic warfare, energy security among others, and many of them are result of ongoing global social processes like technological progress, the intervention of artificial intelligence, environmental problems, revolution of communication networks, and others. Consequently, Europe might need alternative mechanisms that might be more flexible and suitable in the present security environment, in which statuses of powers are constantly changing. The comprehensive security approach sets much different criteria for Defence cooperation that depart from the narrow definition of military security. The extensive cooperation EU members practice in numerous areas sets an unwritten requirement for much broader Defence cooperation because without respective security guarantees the whole integration process becomes extremely vulnerable.

First mismatches between the USA and leading powers of the European Union appeared already during the George W. Bush administration, but after the US elections of 2016 during the Donald J. Trump administration, rivalry gap between USA and the European Union has increased significantly. Therefore in this new environment, the US security guarantees may become not credible enough during the potential crisis. If the Brexit process will be finalized and the UK leaves the European Union, EU may need such independent decision-making mechanisms even more. Moreover, a stronger pillar of EU's Common Security and Defence Policy may force the European nations to build stronger independent (EU's) Defence capabilities often complained by the Trump administration. Today, the European army may seem unnecessary duplication to NATO, but what about tomorrow?

In the EU's approach to cyber defence boundaries between internal and external dimensions are blurred by the nature of the cyber domain where actors, structures, and

---

[88] European Commission (2017).

functions are interdependent. Although the NATO and EU cyber defence cooperation has come a long way, outsourcing cybersecurity, cyberdeterrence, and cyber defence as a whole to the NATO is not a viable option. Considering the potential political prerequisites and consequences of the above, even a mildly put EU cyber defence strategy implies joint cyber capabilities for the use of full spectrum of cyber powers and force—in terms of legal force, technological force, and potentially kinetic. Given the outspoken posture of the UK in cybersecurity, as well as its ìinfamous competences and capabilities in intelligence gathering, the likely Brexit has the potential of adverse impact on EU cybersecurity if, i.e., intelligence sharing practices are disrupted as a consequence of a no deal or for other reasons. This increases the EU's need for strong and practical cooperation with the NATO states, as well as strengthening its own capabilities in operational terms.

The EU's current role as an advisor and lack of strategic and operational mandate in cyber defence leave gaps and inefficiencies and are incompatible with a "whole-of-integration" approach predicated upon cyber resilience building and strategic autonomy. The dual nature of cyberoperations and entanglement of civilian and military sectors makes cyber defence a good candidate for stronger cooperative effort in the EU, not only in terms of trust and sharing responsibilities, but also as an issue that cannot be addressed in isolated fashion. The primary responsibility of member states for cybersecurity and cyber defence can be complemented by entrusting an EU institution with coordinating as well as complementary operational tasks in cyber defence and integrated within the institutional framework responsible for the broader cybersecurity field. A potential solution could be the creation of an EU Algorithmic Defence Force within the new European Union Agency for Cybersecurity, thereby emphasizing its core mandate rooted in economy-driven security integration, and the nature and place of EU cyber defence vis-à-vis NATO and third states.

References

Adler, E. (2005). *Communitarian international relations*. Routledge, London, New York: The Epistemic Foundations of International Relations.

Adler, E., & Barnett, M. (Eds.). (1998). *Security communities*. Cambridge: Cambridge University Press.

Amoore, L., & Raley, R. (2017). Securing with algorithms: Knowledge, decision, sovereignty. *Security Dialogue, 48*(1), 3–10.

Baldwin, D. (Ed.). (1993). *Neorealism and neoliberalism: The contemporary debate*. New York: Columbia University Press.

Barnes, J. E., & Cooper, H. (2019). Trump discussed pulling U.S. from NATO, aides say amid new concerns over Russia. *New York Times*, January 14, https://www.nytimes.com/2019/01/14/us/politics/nato-president-trump.html. Accessed June 30, 2019.

Barrinha, A., & Carrapiço, H. (2016). The EU's emerging security actorness in cyber space: Quo vadis? In L. Chappell, J. Mawdsley, P. Petrov (Eds.), *The EU, strategy and security policy* (pp. 104–118). London: Routledge

BBC News. (2018). *France's Macron pushes for 'true European army'*, 6 November. https://www.bbc.com/news/world-europe-46108633. Accessed July 2, 2019.

Bendiek, A. (2017). *A paradigm shift in the EU's common foreign and security policy: from transformation to resilience*. Berlin: SWP Stiftung Wissenschaft und Politik, German Institute for International and Security Affairs.

Bolton, J. (2008). *Surrender is not an option: Defending America at the United Nations*. Threshold Editions.

Brittan, L. (1990). A European security community? *Extracts from a speech delivered to the British Atlantic Group of Young Politicians*, London, May 17.

Christensen, K. K., & Liebetrau, T. (2019). A new role for 'the public'? Exploring cyber security controversies in the case of WannaCry. *Intelligence and National Security, 34*(3), 395–408. https://doi.org/10.1080/02684527.2019.1553704

Cooper, R. (2000). *The postmodern state and the world order*. London: Demos, The Foreign Policy Centre.

Council of the European Union. (2017a). *Draft council conclusions on a framework for a joint EU diplomatic response to malicious cyber activities* ("Cyber Diplomacy Toolbox")—Adoption, 9916/17, Brussels, 7 June 2017.

Council of the European Union. (2017b). *Draft implementing guidelines for the Framework on a Joint EU diplomatic response to malicious cyber activities*, 13007/17, Brussels, October 9, 2017.

Council of the European Union. (2018a). *EU cyber Defence policy framework (2018 update)*, 14413/18, Brussels, 19 November 2018. https://www.consilium.europa.eu/media/37024/st14413-en18.pdf. Accessed June 30, 2019.

Council of the European Union. (2018b). COUNCIL DECISION (CFSP) 2018/1797 of 19 November 2018 amending and updating Decision (CFSP) 2018/340 establishing the list of projects to be developed under PESCO.

De La Baume, M., & Herszenhorn, D. M. (2018). Merkel joins Macron in calling for EU army to complement NATO. *Politico*. https://www.politico.eu/article/angela-merkel-emmanuel-macron-eu-army-to-complement-nato/. Accessed June 10, 2019.

De La Baume, M., & Sciorilli Borrelli, S. (2019). Steve Bannon's stuttering European adventure. *Politico*. https://www.politico.eu/article/steve-bannon-european-parliament-the-movement-stuttering-european-adventure/. Accessed June 10, 2019.

Deutsch, K., et al. (1957). *Political community and the North Atlantic Area*. Princeton: Princeton University Press.

Dijkstra, H. (2013). Approaches to delegation in EU foreign policy: The case of the Commission. In M. Wilga & I. Karolewski (Eds.), *New approaches to EU foreign policy*. London: Routledge (Forthcoming). https://ssrn.com/abstract=1452726. Accessed June 30, 2019.

Domingo, F. C. (2016). Conquering a new domain: Explaining great power competition in cyberspace. *Comparative Strategy, 35*(2), 154–168. https://doi.org/10.1080/01495933.2016.1176467.

EEAS. (2018). Permanent structured cooperation—PESCO, deepening Defence cooperation among EU member states. *Factsheet on the permanent structured cooperation (EEAS)*. https://eeas.europa.eu/sites/eeas/files/pesco_factsheet_05-03-2018.pdf.Accessed June 30, 2019.

European Commission. (2017). Joint communication to the European Parliament and the Council, resilience, deterrence and Defence: Building strong cybersecurity for the EU. *JOIN(2017) 450 final*, Brussels, 13.9.2017

European Commission. (2019). Stepping up the EU's role as a security and Defence provider—Supporting European Defence in the current EU budget. *Ref. Ares(2019)1797828 - 19/03/2019*. https://ec.europa.eu/docsroom/documents/34510/attachments/1/translations/en/renditions/native. Accessed June 30, 2019.

European Council. (2013). European Council 19/20 December 2013 conclusions. *EUCO 217/13*, Brussels, December 20, 2013.

European Court of Justice. (2006). Judgment—02/05/2006—United Kingdom v Parliament and Council. *Case C-217/04*.

European Defence Agency. (2008). *Potential trends in future military capability characteristics*. https://www.eda.europa.eu/docs/documents/CDP_brochure. Accessed June 30, 2019.

Fiott, D. (2017). The EU, NATO and the European Defence market: Do institutional responses to Defence globalisation matter? *European Security, 26*(3), 398–414. https://doi.org/10.1080/09662839.2017.1352582.

Fiott, D. (2018). Strategic autonomy: towards 'European sovereignty' in Defence? *EUISS brief*, November, 2018. https://www.iss.europa.eu/sites/default/files/EUISSFiles/Brief%2012__Strategic%20Autonomy.pdf. Accessed June 30, 2019.

Foreign & Commonwealth Office. (2018). *Foreign Office Minister condemns Russia for NotPetya attacks*, 15.02.2018. https://www.gov.uk/government/news/foreign-office-minister-condemns-russia-for-notpetya-attacks. Accessed June 30, 2019.

Ghosh, A. (2017). WannaCry: list of major companies and networks hit by ransomware around the globe. *International Business Times*, 16 May 2017. www.ibtimes.co.uk/wannacry-list-major-companies-networks-hit-by-deadly-ransomware-around-globe-1621587. Accessed June 30, 2019.

Griffith, M. K. (2018). *Strengthening the EU's cyber Defence capabilities*. Center for European Policy Studies (CEPS), Brussels. https://www.ceps.eu/wp-content/uploads/2018/11/CEPS_TFR%20on%20Cyber%20Defence_1.pdf.Accessed June 30, 2019.

Haroche, P. (2019). Supranationalism strikes back: A neofunctionalist account of the European Defence Fund. *Journal of European Public Policy*. https://doi.org/10.1080/13501763.2019.1609570.

Jepperson, R. L., Wendt, A., & Katzenstein, P. J. (1996). Norms, identity, and culture in national security. In P. J. Katzenstein (Ed.), *Culture and national security* (pp. 33–75). New York: Columbia University Press.

Joint Declaration on European Defence. (2002). http://www.fco.gov.uk/resources/en/news/2002/02/joint-declaration-on-eu-new01795. Accessed February 17, 2009.

Kasper, A., & Vernygora, V. (2019). *Towards a 'cyber Maastricht': Two steps forward, one step back*. IN: Forthcoming. NB!!!!.

Klimburg, A., & Tiirmaa-Klaar, H. (2011). *Cybersecurity and Cyberpower: Concepts, conditions and capabilities for cooperation for action within the EU*. European Parliament, Ref.: EP/EXPO/B/SEDE/FWC/2009-01/Lot6/09.

Kostyuk, N., & Zhukov, Y. M. (2019). Invisible digital front: Can cyber attacks shape battlefield events? *Journal of Conflict Resolution, 63*(2), 317–347. https://doi.org/10.1177/0022002717737138.

Krastev, I. (2006). *NATO in the age of populism*. http://www.gmfus.org/doc/A4_Krastev_d.pdf. Accessed September 4, 2007.

Laursen, F. (1996). The common foreign and security policy of the European Union: Words vs deeds. In I. Peters (Ed.), New security challenges: The adaptation of international institutions. New York: St. Martin's Press.

Letter of Intent between the Defence ministers of Belgium, Denmark, Estonia, France, Germany, The Netherlands, Portugal, Spain and the United Kingdom concerning the development of the European Internvention Initiative (EI2) (2018).

Leuprecht, C., Szeman, J., & Skillicorn, D. B. (2019). The Damoclean sword of offensive cyber: Policy uncertainty and collective insecurity. *Contemporary Security Policy, 40*(3), 382–407. https://doi.org/10.1080/13523260.2019.1590960

Lucarelli, S. (2002). *Peace and democracy: Rediscovered link*. The EU, NATO and the European System of Liberal-Democratic Security Communities. http://www.nato.int/acad/fellow/00-02/Lucarelli's.pdf. Accessed March 23, 2018.

Marrone, A., & Nones, M. (Eds.). (2013). More Europe on Defence or no Europe. Istituto Affari Internazionali.

Mölder, H. (2010). *Cooperative security dilemma—practicing the Hobbesian security culture in the Kantian security environment*. Doctoral dissertation, University of Tartu, Tartu.

Mölder, H. (2018). British approach to the European Union: From Tony Blair to David Cameron. In A. Chochia, T. Kerikmäe, D. Ramiro Troitino (Eds.), *Brexit: History, reasoning and perspective* (pp. 153−173). Springer International Publishing. https://doi.org/10.1007/978-3-319-73414-9_9.

Mouritzen, H., & Wivel, A. (Eds.). (2005). *The geopolitics of Euro-Atlantic integration*. New York: Routledge.
Peck, M. (2018). Why a European army would be a total disaster. *The National Interest*, December 4. https://nationalinterest.org/blog/buzz/why-european-army-would-be-total-disaster-37817. Accessed June 10, 2019.
Pothier, F. (2019). *A European army: Can the dream become a reality?* https://www.iiss.org/blogs/analysis/2019/01/macron-european-army-reality. Accessed June 10, 2019.
Powell, N. (2018). Military concept for cyber Defence in CSDP. In J. Rehrl (Ed.), *Handbook on cybersecurity, the common security and Defence policy of the European Union*. Federal Ministry of Defence of the Republic of Austria. https://doi.org/10.2855/240212.
Presidency Conclusions, Copenhagen European Council. (1993). 7.A.iii. http://www.europarl.europa.eu/enlargement/ec/pdf/cop_en.pdf. Accessed April 27, 2010.
Regulation (EU). (2019). 2019/881 of the European Parliament and of the Council of 17 April 2019 on ENISA (the European Union Agency for Cybersecurity) and on information and communications technology cybersecurity certification and repealing Regulation (EU) No. 526/2013 (Cybersecurity Act).
Riddervold, M. (2016). (Not) in the hands of the member states: How the European commission influences EU security and Defence policies. *JCMS: Journal of Common Market Studies, 54*, 353–369. https://doi.org/10.1111/jcms.12288.
Riedel, R. (2018). Great Britain and differentiated integration in Europe. In: Chochia, A., Kerikmäe, T., Ramiro Troitino, D. (Eds.), *Brexit: History, reasoning and perspective* (pp. 99–112). Springer International Publishing.
Shared Vision, Common Action: A Stronger Europe A Global Strategy for the European Union's Foreign And Security Policy. (2016). http://eeas.europa.eu/archives/docs/top_stories/pdf/eugs_review_web.pdf. Accessed 10 June 2019.
The Register. (2018). *Everything you need to know about the Petya, er, NotPetya nasty trashing PCs worldwide. This isn't ransomware—it's merry chaos*. 28.06.2018. https://www.theregister.co.uk/2017/06/28/petya_notpetya_ransomware/. Accessed June 30, 2019.
Tocci, N. (2018). Towards a European Security and Defence Union: Was 2017 a Watershed? *JCMS: Journal of Common Market Studies, 56*, 131–141. https://doi.org/10.1111/jcms.12752.
Tor, U. (2017). Cumulative deterrence' as a new paradigm for cyber deterrence. *Journal of Strategic Studies, 40*(1–2), 92–117. https://doi.org/10.1080/01402390.2015.1115975.
Treaty on European Union. https://europa.eu/european-union/sites/europaeu/files/docs/body/treaty_on_european_union_en.pdf. Accessed 10 June 2019.
Trimintzios, P., et al. (2017). *Cybersecurity in the EU common security and Defence Policy (CSDP)—Challenges and risks for the EU, EPRS/STOA/SER/16/214N*. https://doi.org/10.2861/853031.
United States Department of Justice. (2018). *North Korean regime-backed programmer charged with conspiracy to conduct multiple cyber attacks and intrusions*. Press release of 6.9.2018, https://www.justice.gov/opa/pr/north-korean-regime-backed-programmer-charged-conspiracy-conduct-multiple-cyber-attacks-and. Accessed June 10, 2019.
White House. (2018). *Statement from the Press Secretary, 15.02.2018*. https://www.whitehouse.gov/briefings-statements/statement-press-secretary-25/. Accessed June 10, 2019.

The Leadership of the EU in Shaping the International Ocean Governance: Fighting Against IUU Fishing

Carlos Aldereguía Prado

Abstract Seas and oceans play an important role on human's life; they regulate our climate and are a primary source of food, being therefore essential in food security. In recent times, the pressure on the seas has been increased considerably, provoking a number of negative effects, such as decline of marine ecosystems and fisheries resources. Thus, elements such as the overexploitation of fish stocks, the maritime pollution or IUU fishing, among others, have become part of the International Political Agenda, and in 2015, UNGA approved the 2030 Agenda for Sustainable Development. The agenda proposes 17 sustainable development goals (SDG), urging all countries, to take action. In this context, SDG 14 aims to conserve and sustainably use the oceans, seas and marine resources, and under it, one of the main targets is to end IUU fishing. The EU is leading this international objective, not only through the Common Fisheries Policy, but also from a holistic approach.

Keywords IUU fishing · Ocean Governance · Sustainable development goal 14 · EU leadership · International Fisheries Governance

1 Introduction

Seas and oceans cover more than 70% of the earth's surface, regulate our climate and supply 50% of the oxygen we breathe, being therefore essential in climate change. In addition, it is a primary source of food, from which it deduces its important role in food security, as a sustainable food.

However, aspects such as climate change, overexploitation of fisheries resources, maritime pollution, or illegal, unreported and unregulated fishing, (IUU fishing), endanger both the sustainability of the oceans and the people who depend heavily on them.

It is important to underline that the EU is the main market in the world for fishing products, and it cannot remain outside the international management of the fisheries

C. Aldereguía Prado (✉)
Fisheries Attaché of the Spanish Permanent Representation to the EU, Bd. Du Régent 50-52, 1000 Brussels, Belgium
e-mail: caldereg@gmail.com

D. Ramiro Troitiño et al. (eds.), *The EU in the 21st Century*,
https://doi.org/10.1007/978-3-030-38399-2_16

resources, nor, of course, the International Fisheries Governance. Thus, the Common Fisheries Policy and the Integrated Maritime Policy establish, in the European Union, the framework to enhance the sustainable development of maritime activities. These are complemented by various commitments acquired internationally.

With a world population of more than 7000 million people, with forecasts of reaching more than 9000 million by 2050,[1] the pressure on the oceans is increasing, and the European Society demands from their political leaders a strong commitment for sustainable development, not only in the European Union, but internationally.

On 4 March 2019, in an open letter to EU citizens,[2] the French President, Mr. Emmanuel Macron recalled the main problems and challenges of the International Governance, noting that Europe has a moral duty to act, proposing a "*Renaissance*" around three objectives, freedom, protection and progress, highlighting the fight against climate change and sustainable development.

The President of the German government party, the CDU, (Christian Democratic Union), Ms. Annegret Kramp-Karrenbauer, replied to President Macron,[3] only five days later, indicating her full agreement with him, advocating for a greater European construction and underlining that the world is changing and Europe faces a choice.

In this chapter, it will analyse how the EU works to end with a global problem in the Ocean Governance, i.e. IUU fishing.

2 International Ocean Governance

– *Definition*

From an academic point of view, governance could be defined as the set of rules, practices and institutions that interact at all levels to provide equity and sustainability in the allocation and management of the resources and spatial planning of seas and oceans.[4]

That is, a system of "government" in which formal and informal rules would have a place, presence of old and new power structures (institutions from administration and other stakeholders organizations, such as environmental NGOs, fisheries producers, sea workers, women networks), efficiency and equity in resources management and mechanisms to solve conflicts regarding access to the ocean, especially taken into consideration that the problems are more acute in an area where actors are interdependent.[5]

---

[1] http://populationmatters.org/the-facts.

[2] Macron (2019).

[3] Kramp-Karrenbauer (2019).

[4] Mann Borgese and Saigal (1996).

[5] Friedheim (1999).

Therefore, it could be said that International Ocean Governance consists of managing and using the world's oceans and their resources, while maintaining healthy, productive, safe, protected and resilient oceans.

– *The EU leadership on the International Ocean Governance*

In September 2015, the United Nations General Assembly approved the 2030 Agenda for Sustainable Development,[6] which is basically an action plan in favour of the people, the planet and the prosperity.

The agenda proposes 17 sustainable development goals (SDG), urging all countries (developed and developing) to take action (call of action). In this context, SDG 14 aims to conserve and sustainably use the oceans, seas and marine resources.

In particular, SDG 14 includes three specific targets related to the sustainability of fisheries resources:

- *"Target 4: By 2020, effectively regulate harvesting and end overfishing, illegal, unreported and unregulated fishing and destructive fishing practices and implement science-based management plans, in order to restore fish stocks in the shortest time feasible, at least to levels that can produce maximum sustainable yield as determined by their biological characteristics.*
- *Target 6: By 2020, prohibit certain forms of fisheries subsidies which contribute to overcapacity and overfishing, eliminate subsidies that contribute to illegal, unreported and unregulated fishing and refrain from introducing new such subsidies (…).*
- *Target 14.b (9): Provide access for small-scale artisanal fishers to marine resources and markets".*

On 10 November 2016, the European Commission and the EU High Representative launched a joint communication on International Ocean Governance,[7] which is the EU's agenda for the future of our oceans.

The Joint Communication proposes that the EU should lead this process, and it establishes three priority areas:

- Improving the International Ocean Governance framework;
- Reducing human pressures on the oceans and creating the conditions for a sustainable blue economy; and
- Strengthening international ocean research and data.

The Joint Communication is the EU response to the SDG14.

– International Fisheries Governance[8,9]

[6]UN 2030 (2015).

[7]JOIN (2016) 49.

[8]Laxe et al. (2018).

[9]Gray (2005).

Fisheries are one of the main maritime activities, and the concept of "Ocean Governance" cannot be understood without it. Its importance is not only economic but also social, and it is pursued in a framework of the ecosystems and the living resources sustainability, that is, respecting the environmental dimension.

The scope of fisheries is particularly suitable for addressing the governance, since there are numerous actors directly (fishermen, ship-owners, processing companies and even administrations) and indirectly involved (consumers, environmental groups, scientists, mass media, etc.).[10]

The different socio-economic and environmental protection elements make the fisheries a very complex sector.

At the international level, the main elements that make up the legal framework of Fisheries Governance are as follows:

- The United Nations Convention on the Law of the Sea (UNCLOS 1982)
- UN Fish Stocks Agreement (1995)
- United Nations General Assembly Resolution on Sustainable Fisheries
- Regional Fisheries Management Organizations regulations.
- FAO Guidelines and Agreements on sustainable fisheries and the fight against IUU fishing.

In the Fisheries Governance, one of the main issues (which is also a priority in the 2030 Agenda) is the fight against IUU fishing, and throughout this chapter, it will analyse what it is about, what is its impact and its global cost, as well as the actions carried out, at international level, in general, and those developed by the EU, in particular, given that the EU leads Fisheries Governance at international level. Actually, the Joint Communication is based on the political mandate given by the President of the European Commission, Mr. Jean Claude Juncker, to the Commissioner for Environment, Maritime Affairs and Fisheries, Mr. Karmenu Vella, to take part in the configuration of the International Ocean Governance at the United Nations meetings, as well as in other multilateral forums and, bilaterally, with key partners at global level.

3 IUU Fishing

- *Definition*

In the 1970s, the global fishing capacity was considerably increased, mainly because of the technological advances that allowed fleets to operate further, deeper and catch the fish more easily, which, together with the improvements in on board freezing systems, resulted in a crisis of lack of fishing resources, which led to the need for regulation of fishing activities at the international level.

International community was aware about the need to update the use of the oceans, and that is why the III United Nations Conference on the Law of the Sea was held,

[10]Symes (1997).

which began in 1973, and lasted until 1982. As a result, on April 1982, the United Nations Convention on the Law of the Sea (UNCLOS) was adopted, which constitutes an essential milestone in improving legal security in the uses of the seas and oceans.[11]

In 1992, the Cancun Conference on Responsible Fisheries and the UN Conference on Environment and Development, held in Rio de Janeiro, warned and alerted to the depletion of global fisheries and called for responsible and sustainable long-term fishing.

Up to this moment, the debate was about the improvement of fisheries management and the long-term sustainable development, but the concept of IUU fishing is more modern and appears first time ever, in 1997, within the work of the Commission for the Conservation of Antarctic Marine Living Resources (CCAMLR), during its 16th annual meeting.[12]

Later on, in 1999, FAO includes it in the Rome Declaration on responsible fishing. Nowadays, the most complete and widely used definition is contained in the FAO International Plan of Action to Prevent, Deter, and Eliminate Illegal, Unreported and Unregulated Fishing (IPOA-IUU).[13]

Thus, *"illegal fishing refers to activities*:

- *Conducted by national or foreign vessels in water under the jurisdiction of a state, without the permission of that state, or in contravention of its laws and regulations;*
- *Conducted by vessels flying the flag of states that are parties to a relevant regional fisheries management organization but operate in contravention of the conservation and management measures adopted by that organization and by which the states are bound, or relevant provisions of the applicable international law; or*
- *in violation of national laws or international obligations, including those undertaken by cooperating states to a relevant regional fisheries management organization.*"

It basically covers activities that go against the legislation of the coastal countries in areas under national jurisdiction, and on the high seas, against the regulations of the RFMOs or against international law in the absence of an RFMO.

"Unreported fishing refers to fishing activities:

- *which have not been reported, or have been misreported, to the relevant national authority, in contravention of national laws and regulations; or*
- *undertaken in the area of competence of a relevant regional fisheries management organization which have not been reported or have been misreported, in contravention of the reporting procedures of that organization*".

Consequently, undeclared fishing can be considered an illegal type of fishing, given the negative impact of not recording catches in the general context of fisheries management.

And, finally, *"Unregulated fishing refers to fishing activities:*

[11] Pastor Ridruejo (2009).

[12] CCAMLR (1997).

[13] FAO (2001).

- *in the area of application of a relevant regional fisheries management organization that are conducted by vessels without nationality, or by those flying the flag of a state not party to that organization, or by a fishing entity, in a manner that is not consistent with or contravenes the conservation and management measures of that organization; or*
- *in areas or for fish stocks in relation to which there are no applicable conservation or management measures and where such fishing activities are conducted in a manner inconsistent with state responsibilities for the conservation of living marine resources under international law".*

This part of the definition sets limits for RFMOs, considering that illegality occurs in the event that a rule of International Law is violated, and it is applicable to any flag state, regardless of whether or not they belong to an RFMO.

However, the differentiation of concepts is not that important in practical terms, since the three concepts are applied cumulatively.[14]

- *IUU as a wider transnational crime*

The concept of IUU fishing is usually associated with the management and the conservation of marine living resources. However, in recent years, the notion is that it has been the subject of a broader debate in the field of maritime security, as it has sometimes been used to refer to a wide range of criminal activities at sea.[15]

IUU fishing is characterized by its total lack of transparency, which can provide opportunities to cover up other types of more complex transnational crimes, such as drug and arms trafficking, smuggling of people and serious human and labour rights abuses[16,17] as well as related crimes, such as fraud and tax evasion.[18] There are countries with weak governance, and therefore, it is difficult to identify the owners of the fishing companies, in addition to the almost impossibility of controlling and monitoring the vessels activities at sea.

Some countries, such as Norway, defend the path of criminalization of the IUU fishing and even the consideration of transnational organized crime in cases that meet the criteria established by the United Nations Convention against Transnational Organized Crime.

Neither the EU nor the FAO shares this systematic criminalization approach to IUU fishing, considering that IUU fishing and transnational organized crime have different legal regimes applicable under international law.[19] However, the debate exists on the international agenda.

- *Global cost and dimensions of its impact*

---

[14]Treves (2009).

[15]Roselló (2019).

[16]EJF (2010).

[17]EJF (2013).

[18]OECD (2013).

[19]UN A/RES/73/125.

The magnitude of IUU Fishing is a global threat, with a negative impact on fisheries resources and ecosystems, food security or coastal communities, so it can be said that the consequences of IUU fishing are environmental, social and economic.

In the economic dimension, the global losses as a result of IUU fishing are estimated between 10 and 23.5 billion dollars as per year.[20] The NGO Environmental Justice Foundation (EJF) estimated in 2005 that the European fishing industry had a profit of approximately 1.5 billion euros, and almost 50% would come from illegal sources.[21]

In an increasingly populated world, the pressure on the oceans is also growing, actually, according to FAO, in 2016, world fisheries production amounted to 171 million tons (of which 47% came from the aquaculture) while in 2000, production was 41.6 million tonnes (17 from capture fisheries and 24.6 from aquaculture).[22] Regarding the state of stocks, the proportion of fish stocks that are within biologically sustainable catch levels has shown a downward trend from 90% in 1974 to 66.9% in 2015. Instead, the percentage of populations exploited at biologically unsustainable levels increased from 10% in 1974 to 33.1% in 2015.[23]

The costs of IUU fishing from a social perspective are also enormous, to the loss of jobs related to the fishing and the processing industry, and it is added to the negative impact on ecosystems, which jeopardizes the sustainability of resources, and in addition generates problems in other fields, such as tourism, as well as compromises seriously the food security and the livelihoods of coastal communities.[24]

Some of these costs are difficult to quantify, but there are mathematical models to calculate the cost of the reduced catches, the job losses and the reduction of fish stocks generated by IUU fishing.

If the impact on the environment is analysed,[25] it can be talked about the reduction of fish stocks, distortion of fisheries data, resulting in less effective management and the possible extinction of sensitive species, or general damage in ecosystems and biodiversity.

IUU fishing vessels compromise the health of fisheries ecosystems and the marine environment and cause damage to bottom habitats, and there is a high level of by-catches, which includes vulnerable marine life, such as sharks or turtles.

These kinds of vessels work with less production costs, breaking the leverage, unfairly competing with legal operators. They also operate in closed areas, displacing artisanal fishermen to river areas, where numerous stocks spawn, reducing their reproductive capacity. Moreover, IUU fishing can also be called to the one carried out by vessels that do not comply with the safety measures on board, do not use legal fishing gear, do not apply to the fisheries management regulations, including limitation of catches, fishing areas, temporary closures or catching prohibited species.

---

[20] Agnew et al. (2009).

[21] EJF (2005).

[22] FAO (2002).

[23] FAO (2018).

[24] Gameiro and Wilson (2003), Bostock et al. (2009).

[25] Sander et al. (2014).

The damage caused by this activity is especially dramatic in developing regions,[26] where there are the highest levels of IUU fishing worldwide. The living and working conditions on board of the crews of IUU fishing vessels (mostly from those developing countries with few job opportunities) do not even apply the minimum standards of safety and health for seafarers provided by the ILO,[27] taking advantage of the lack of effective control by its flag states.[28]

Fishing is a common resource, which belongs to humankind, and should be managed in a sustainable and legal way, to ensure the future of coastal communities, the food security and the health of the oceans, notably in the context of the current climate crisis. Therefore, addressing the impact of IUU fishing is an essential part of the International Fisheries Governance,[29] and the European Union has emerged as the main driver of its constitution and improvement.[30]

4 International Milestones in the Fight Against IUU Fishing

- *Evolution*

In the decades of the 60s and 70s, with the improvement of the technologies, the long-distance fleets of the main fishing countries increased the pressure on the oceans, increasing the world fishing production from 26 to 46 million tons reported between 1958 and 1972, causing a major overfishing crisis.[31]

The world is worried about the state of the stocks, and that is why in 1973 the third United Nations Conference on the Law of the Sea begins, which will be finished 10 years later with the signing of the Law of the Sea in 1982. There is a period of debate in the search for a fisheries management that reverses the global overfishing trend. Thus, in 1992, the Cancun Conference on Responsible Fisheries and the Rio Declaration, introduced in the International Political Agenda, the concepts of precautionary approach and sustainable development, which represent a turning point in the International Fisheries Governance.[32]

The search for a proper management in the use of the oceans and seas is reinforced with the appearance of the FAO Code of Conduct for Responsible Fisheries, in 1995,[33] and of course, to a greater extent, with the United Nations Agreement on fish stocks, also in 1995,[34] which is the UNCLOS application tool, and it is legally binding.

---

[26] Weldemichael (2012).

[27] C188 (2007).

[28] Politakis (2008).

[29] Garcia et al. (2014).

[30] Troitino et al. (2017).

[31] Garcia et al. (2014).

[32] Garcia et al. (2014).

[33] FAO Code of Conduct (1995).

[34] UN Fish Stocks Agreement (1995).

The concept of "IUU fishing" does not appear until the CCAMLR 16th annual meeting, in 1997 (as it was mentioned previously).

In 1999, during the 23rd meeting of the Committee on Fisheries (COFI) the FAO examined deeply the need to fight against IUU fishing. There was a big concern about the increase of this activity, carried out, mainly, by vessels with "flags of convenience", since the "registration countries" did not exercise any control over their fleet, undermining the global efforts in the fight against IUU fishing and allowing a very negative behaviour of their fleets.[35] At the same time, in many cases, it was almost impossible to find out who were the real ship-owners of those vessels.[36]

Hence, in the year 2000, the FAO International Plan of Action to Prevent, Deter and Eliminate Illegal, Unreported and Unregulated Fishing (IPOA-IUU) is approved. Its main goal was to achieve its objectives through coordinated activities between the countries, the FAO, the RFMOs and other international organizations such as the IMO.

– FAO International Plan of Action to Prevent, Deter, and Eliminate IUU Fishing.[37]

This plan is the starting point of a new era in the international commitment to the sustainability of marine resources. It was approved on 2 March 2001, at the 24th session of the COFI and ratified in June, the same year.

This is the first text where the problem of IUU fishing is formally addressed, understanding that *"(…) Existing international instruments addressing IUU fishing have not been effective due to a lack of political will, priority, capacity and resources to ratify or accede to and implement them"*, (paragraph 1, IPOA).

Its main objective is *"To Prevent, Deter and Eliminate IUU Fishing by providing all states with comprehensive, effective and transparent measures by which to act, including through appropriate regional fisheries management organizations established in accordance with international law"* (paragraph 8).

This meant that the plan acted as a "toolbox", which will be used according to the needs of each case. In addition to the application of these measures, the plan establishes competences between the different actors/players, highlighting the roles of the flag, coastal and Port States. Today, we can also include the concept of the "state of commercialization", due to the evolution of this issue.[38]

For the success of the plan, it is essential that a first implementation at the national level by the countries followed by a good coordination at the international level, through bilateral, multilateral collaboration, or through existing structures, such as RFMOs or FAO itself.[39]

Furthermore, it should be applied transparently in accordance with the provisions of the FAO Code of Conduct, without discrimination between any States.

---

[35]Gianni and Simpson (2005).

[36]OEDC (2003).

[37]FAO IPA-IUU (2001).

[38]Treves (2009).

[39]Castro and Lago (2018).

In summary, it is a non-binding text, adopted in the context of international fisheries legislation and, specifically, under the 1982 United Nations Convention on the Law of the Sea (UNCLOS) and the 1995 United Nations Agreement on fish stocks (UNFSA) and by which, all States have a duty to take appropriate measures to ensure the sustainable management of marine resources and to cooperate in the fight against IUU fishing.

– *Agreement on Port State Measures (PSMA).*[40]

In 2007, at the 27th annual meeting of the COFI, it was set up the work schedule related to the establishment of a legally binding international instrument based on the IPOA-IUU, which was intended to compiled measures for the Port State to fight against IUU fishing.

Thus, on 22 November 2009, after a hard work by the designated working groups, the Agreement on Port State Measures was approved by the FAO Conference at its 36th session, which would enter into force once was ratified from 25 countries, which happened on 5 June 2016, and it can be considered as the first legally binding international treaty specifically focused on IUU fishing.

The main objective of the PSMA is to fight against IUU fishing by preventing that the vessels involved in IUU operations could use any port to land their catches. So, this tool searches to ensure, in the long term, the conservation and sustainable use of fisheries resources and marine ecosystems. The PSMA seeks to clarify the jurisdiction of States, and requires them—under the authorization of customary international law—to take appropriate measures within their ports to strongly deter IUU fishing activities.[41]

These measures will be taken just against vessels with a flag different from the one of the Port State.

The Agreement has ten parts (37 articles) and five annexes.[42] Throughout, 37 articles are established the general provisions of application, the procedures for entering the port and the cases in which it will allow or deny it, as well as the conditions of use of the port services, the criteria related to inspectors and the inspection process. Additionally, there are some other elements, such as the special needs of developing countries, the cooperation between countries, the flag state competencies, or the procedures on resolution of disputes.

There is a global concern on IUU activities among society, and most of the International NGOs encourage countries worldwide, which have not yet done so, to ratify the PSMA, and implement it in their national legislation, which would allow not only the improvement of their domestic governances, but also greater and better international coordination, to address these challenges more directly and efficiently.[43]

In conclusion, the closure of ports around the world to the vessels involved in IUU fishing activities prevents the fruit of their infractions from being in legal markets,

[40]FAO PSMA (2016, revised edition).

[41]Kuemlangan et al. (2010).

[42]FAO (2016). PSMA.

[43]SWAN (2016).

which contributes to discourage this type of fishing. Therefore, the more the countries ratify this agreement, the more effective its application will be.

– *FAO Global Record of Fishing Vessels, Refrigerated Transport Vessels and Supply Vessels*

During the FAO Ministerial Fisheries Meeting in 2005, the Rome Declaration on IUU fishing was approved, and, in the same meeting, through a recommendation, the bases of the Global Record program were also agreed.

From then on, through an expert consultation process, progress is being made, while seeking the support of the countries during the annual sessions of the COFI. So, in 2016 a Pilot Project is launched, with the participation of 11 countries (among them, one EU Member State: Spain).[44]

In April 2017, less than one year after the entry into force of the PSMA, and thirteen years after the FAO indicated the need to have all fishing vessels registered in a single census, the Global Record is launched in the framework of the 33rd session of the FAO Fisheries Committee (COFI), in Rome.[45] This tool is developed as a "powerful weapon"[46] against IUU fishing. Currently, it is accessible to the public in general, after more than one year of restricted use, exclusively to the countries taking part in Pilot Project, above mentioned.

From this moment, everyone can be aware of the circumstances surrounding a particular vessel, as the Record provides a lot of information, such as the name of the ship-owner, its fishing authorizations, a record of its activity, including its compliance history, since the Global Record collects "certified and unambiguous" information concerning vessels and their activities, and it is important to underline that this data comes from the flag state authorities, hence its great value.[47]

One of the main obstacles in the fight against IUU fishing is the lack of transparency and information not only about the operations, but also on the ownership of the vessels involved in these kinds of activities.[48] Therefore, the Global Record has a huge potential in practice, for example, to perform risk analysis and determine inspection plans. In addition, it is very useful to Port States, since it can help as a basis for authorizing or not authorizing foreign flag vessels to land their catches in their ports or even to check their historical activity to know if their flag states are reliable or not.[49] It may also be used by civil society organizations (like NGOs) or even for the public in general, to check the background of a particular vessel.

Each vessel is assigned a Unique Vessel Identifier (UVI) which is a global number, which ensures traceability through reliable, verified and permanent identification of the vessel. Currently, it has been restricted to ships of more than 24 m length, or more

[44] http://www.fao.org/global-record/background/history/es/.

[45] Kerikmäe et al. (2019).

[46] COFI/2018/6.

[47] FAO (2015).

[48] EJF et al. (2016).

[49] FAO (2018).

than 100 gross tonnage (GTs) which matches with those that have a unique number of the International Maritime Organization (IMO).

Initially, the registration was planned in three phases, the first one, as it was already mentioned, focuses on vessels of 100 GTs or of 24 m length, or above, the phase two was intended to introduce those of more than 18 m and 50 GTs, and finally, the phase three would incorporate the units of more than 12 m and 10 GTs. However, currently the main criteria is to have an IMO number, regardless of the dimensions of the vessel, so that there are already units of less than 10 m (but operating in international waters), in the Global Register.[50] By mid-2019, there were around 23,000 fishing vessels registered, from more than sixty countries.[51]

To sum up, the Global Record is a tool of great importance to boost the PSMA.

– *Multilateral approach: The role of the RFMOs in fighting against IUU fishing*

The Regional Fisheries Management Organizations (RFMOs) are international organizations formed by countries that have fishing interests in a given area.[52] Some RFMOs have the mandate to manage all the fish populations under a specific area, and some others are aimed to manage just some stocks, usually highly migratory species (tuna and tuna-like) in wider geographical areas.

These organizations are open, both to the coastal states of the region, as well as to those who have direct fishing interest. Some of these organizations have a purely consultative nature, and are called Regional Fisheries Bodies (RFBs), while others are legally binding and can adopt conservation measures, and these are known as RFMOs.

The 1995 UN Agreement on fish stocks refer to the RFMOs as a basic instrument to achieve the long-term sustainability objectives of the fishery resources under their control and constitutes, together with UNCLOS, the legal basis that makes their decisions legally binding.[53]

The evolution of the function of the RFMOs is closely linked to the awareness of the need to sustainably manage fish stocks. The main issues of these organizations deal with, including fisheries management, the application of the ecosystem and precautionary approaches, the management of by-catches, the science and research, the strengthening of international cooperation, promoting transparency, and the improvement of monitoring, control and surveillance (MCS) measures, including the implementation of the Vessels Monitoring Systems (VMS), the adoption of regional schemes to implement the PSMA, its internal functioning, and of course, fighting against IUU fishing.

The International Community recognizes the continuous need to strengthen cooperation, both at the international level, and also among the institutions working at the regional level, so as to increase the coverage under the RFMOs mandates, which

---

[50] https://bit.ly/2K774pM.

[51] Source: FAO.

[52] With the exception of the International Whaling Commission, (IWC), which covers the whole world.

[53] UN Fish stocks Agreement (1995).

would ensure greater protection (it would cover more species and zones) and interaction between organizations. To make this possible, the strengthening and coordination of the states involved would be essential.[54]

The RFMOs constitute the ideal framework to fight against IUU fishing, and most of these organizations have approved measures designed to discourage the activity of these harmful practices. These measures are primarily intended to prevent IUU vessels from obtaining an economic gain to ensure that this illegal activity is not profitable.[55]

The measures agreed in a multilateral framework, like those within the RFMOs, are more effective in preventing or deterring the trade of illegal fishing products, and are more respectful with the international trade rules, than those adopted unilaterally by some states.[56] Actually, the World Trade Organization (WTO) does not oppose, in principle, that RFMOs impose trade restrictions for environmental reasons, including those related to the conservation and sustainable management of marine living resources.[57]

Among the main measures adopted with the aim to fight against IUU fishing, it is important to highlight some as the lists of IUU vessels, which can be positive (white lists) including vessels authorized to operate in the regulated area, or negative (blacklists) with those not allowed to operate and are also part of any other IUU lists in any other international organization.[58] The application of PSMA in the RFMOs is one of the main milestones in the fight against IUU fishing. Some RFMOs have also established joint inspection programs, in order to monitor compliance by the contracting parties with the measures approved by them. Also within the framework of the RFMOs, it is necessary to highlight the catch certification schemes, which seek to limit the market access only to those fisheries products accompanied by a catch certificate validated by the competent authorities of the flag state. This document certifies that the catches in question have been made in accordance with international laws, regulations and fisheries conservation and management measures.[59]

International cooperation is essential under this scenario, just as each party has to be committed to the final objective. It is not that difficult to understand the consequences of the inaction of a flag state against illegal activities of a vessel within its fleet, and in this sense (as it will be seen later), the EU has been the main player worldwide which has resorted, more decisively, to take restrictive trade measures against non-cooperating third countries, including the total import ban of fisheries products.[60]

– *Voluntary Guidelines for Catch Documentation Schemes*

[54]Pawlas (2015).

[55]OECD (2005).

[56]Urbina (2017).

[57]Art. XX Gatt (1994).

[58]Lobach (2010).

[59]OECD (2005).

[60]Pons Rafols (2016).

The Voluntary Guidelines for catch documentation schemes were officially approved by the FAO Conference in July 2017, after a very long working process.

These guidelines were designed to assist not only the states authorities, but international organizations, such as RFMOs, regional economic integration organizations and some other intergovernmental organizations in the development and implementation of catches certification systems or in the harmonization or revision of existing ones.[61]

The harmonization of the information on the catch certificates, or even, in the templates, would facilitate the work to the Port States.[62]

5 The Eu Approach

– *Introduction*

The EU fishing sector has a very high level of external dependence, being EU the main market for fishery products worldwide, and so, being also very attractive for the IUU operators.[63]

In the framework of the International Fisheries Governance, IUU fishing is one of the main threats for reaching a sustainable exploitation of living aquatic resources, jeopardizing the international efforts to achieve a proper management of them.

The EU Council, in the 2002 Conclusions on IUU fishing, invited the Commission to lead the fight against this type of fishing, in the scope of the RFMOs.[64] So, in the same year, the European Commission approves the Community Action Plan against IUU fishing, inspired by the FAO IPOA-IUU.

However, the plan was not as effective as expected, which led to a proposal from the European Commission for the establishment of a specific regulation on IUU fishing. It was presented in October 2007, and it was launched together with a Commission Communication on an Integrated Maritime Policy for the EU.[65] The IUU Fisheries Regulation was approved by the Council of EU Fisheries Ministers on 24 June 2008 and was formally adopted on 29 September 2008, being in force since 1 January 2010.

It is important to underline the fact that the proposal for a regulation against IUU fishing was presented together with the communication on the Integrated Maritime Policy of the EU, which implies a recognition of the need to jointly apply all the policies related to maritime activities to obtain the results we are looking for. It is a clear statement of intent to attack IUU fishing from a holistic and comprehensive approach.

---

[61] FAO (2017).

[62] FAO (2018).

[63] Tinch et al. (2008).

[64] Council Conclusions (2002).

[65] COM (2007) 574.

The International Ocean Governance is the most holistic approach possible, and it is a priority element in the EU Political Agenda,[66] since the EU is one of the main international players committed to the conservation and sustainable use of the oceans. Hence, in November 2016, the European Commission and the EU High Representative for Foreign Affairs and Security Policy launched the Joint Communication to the European Parliament, the Council, the European Economic and Social Committee and the Committee of the Regions on "International Ocean Governance: an agenda for the future of our oceans".[67]

In this section, it will be seen as the IUU Fisheries Regulation, as well as some other elements from other EU policies that contribute to the fight against IUU fishing, and its success and effectiveness are confirmed by the achievements made in recent years.

– *EU Council Regulation 1005/2008*

Council Regulation (EC) No 1005/2008 of 29 September 2008 establishing a community system to Prevent, Deter and Eliminate Illegal, Unreported and Unregulated Fishing, entered into force on 1 January 2010.[68] It is a transparent and non-discriminatory instrument, which has a clear expansionist vocation, and underlines the relationship that the EU has with third states, both as an importer and exporter of fisheries products.[69]

The EU has adopted a quite innovative approach to combat IUU fishing by not allowing fisheries products to access the EU market, unless they are certified as legal. It must be recalled that the EU is the main world market on fisheries and imports 60% of domestic consumption.[70]

The regulation applies to all trade in marine fisheries products, processed or not, from a third country fishing vessel and exported by any means of transport to an EU Member State and to catches of EU fishing vessels to be exported to third countries.

The main elements of this tool are the catch certification scheme, the procedures against third countries (carding system) and the penalties for EU operators.

The EU works to close the loopholes that allow illegals to get any profit from their activities. Through a catch certification scheme, it is intended for the flag states to certify the legal origin of the catches. In the event that third countries do not cooperate, measures can be taken against them, and the regulation establishes a carding system: In those cases in which the dialogue with a third country has not allowed to solve the deficiencies detected, the European Commission warns of a risk of being identified as a non-cooperating country in the fight against IUU fishing ("yellow card").[71] This procedure creates a framework for collaboration to achieve

[66]Troitino (2017).

[67]JOIN (2016) 49.

[68]Council Regulation 1005/2008.

[69]Hamulák (2018).

[70]Tsamenyi et al. (2010).

[71]Art. 32 R1005/2018.

better fisheries governance.[72] If the differences are not solved, the next step would be the "red card", that is, the identification and subsequent inclusion in the blacklist of third countries. This decision has commercial consequences, including a ban on importing fisheries products into the EU.

The main measures adopted in the framework of the regulation are the development of a list of IUU fishing vessels, which includes vessels identified as such by a RFMO, a blacklist of non-cooperating countries and the application of sanctions to EU fishermen and operators, who are involved in any IUU activity anywhere in the world and under any flag.

The Alignment of the IUU Regulation with the International Law

The regulation relies on the responsibility of the Port State, and Article 73 of UNCLOS states that the coastal State has the right to enforce its laws and regulations related to fishing and conservation in its exclusive economic zone (EEZ) and in its section 1, authorizes the coastal state to adopt the necessary measures to guarantee compliance with the national legal framework.[73] In addition, Article 23 of the 1995 UN Agreement on fish stocks establishes the right and duty of a Port State to promote the effectiveness of sub-regional, regional and global measures on conservation and management of marine resources, denying, among other things, access to port facilities for landings and transhipments, when it has been demonstrated that the catches have been taken in a way that undermines the effectiveness of these conservation and management measures on the high seas.[74]

Moreover, as it was stated before, the WTO does not oppose to the countries or the RFMOs from imposing trade restrictions for environmental reasons, which would cover the measures established by the regulation in this regard.[75]

Results/Achievements

In 2015, five years after its entry into force, the commission issued a communication on the application of Council Regulation (EC) No 1005/2008.[76] The main conclusion was that the regulation has meant an important mechanism for improving the cooperation between states, and it has fostered the willingness of some countries to fulfil their international obligations and commitments towards better management of fishing resources and sustainability through a more effective and global fight against IUU fishing.

As for the next steps forward, the European Commission is working to simplify, harmonize and modernize the application of the regulation,[77] improving the traceability and using the possibilities offered by new technologies. In this regard, it should

[72] EJF et al. (2016).
[73] Art. 73 UNCLOS (1982).
[74] Art. 23 UN Fish Stocks Agreement (1995).
[75] Art. XX GATT (1994).
[76] COM/2015/048.
[77] Kerikmae (1997).

be noted that the commission, in May 2019, launched CATCH,[78] an IT system, which aims to digitalize the currently paper-based EU catch certification scheme. In parallel, it has been published the proposal to modify the control regulation, and one of the main amendments proposed is to digitalize (compulsory) all these processes,[79] which would mean a huge advance in the effectiveness of the system to combat IUU fishing.

From the day the regulation entered into force until 2018, 25 third countries have been pre-identified, of which six received the red card and were included in the black list of third countries, three of them have already been delisted.[80]

The European Commission is working to adapt the control system to fight against IUU fishing in the context of the improvement of the International Ocean Governance.

– *Holistic Approach: Improving Fisheries Governance*

The EU is one of the international players most committed to the conservation and sustainable use of the oceans, something that is clearly stated in the 2016 Joint Communication on International Ocean Governance, in which it has highlighted the EU aspiration to contribute to the development of the Governance based on its own experience.[81] In this sense, in addition to the Common Fisheries Policy itself (which includes the regulation 1005/2008 as well as the fisheries control framework), it is necessary to highlight the environmental and transport policies, and above all, the Integrated Maritime Policy (IMP), and within of the latter, the Blue Growth, which is the contribution of the IMP in achieving the objectives of the Europe 2020 Strategy for a smart, sustainable and integrated growth.

To protect the oceans from current threats (among which IUU fishing stands out), there is a need for good cooperation between states at the international level. In addition, having accurate and reliable information on the state of stocks and ecosystems would allow for an improved adaptation of the measures to be taken.

The UN 2030 Agenda addresses the goal of achieving the conservation and sustainable use of the oceans, through the SDG 14, and it has already been said that the Joint Communication means the EU response to this challenge, which establishes three priority areas of action.

These actions cannot be taken just in the scope of a single EU policy;[82] therefore, we can talk about the fact that the Joint Communication represents the holistic and comprehensive approach of the EU to address this issue, and the fight against illegal fishing is not excluded from this approach.

On 15 March of 2015, the European Commission published the Joint Report to the European Parliament and the Council on the achievements of the first two years

---

[78] https://ec.europa.eu/fisheries/cfp/illegal_fishing_en.

[79] COM/2018/368.

[80] https://ec.europa.eu/fisheries/sites/fisheries/files/illegal-fishing-overview-of-existing-procedures-third-countries_en.pdf.

[81] JOIN (2016) 49.

[82] Outeda (2001).

of the implementation of the plan to improve the International Governance, called "Improving International Ocean Governance—Two years of progress".[83]

Let us see the achievements reached in fighting IUU fishing through this innovative approach:

– *Achievements*

As we have seen before, one of the main international tools to fight against IUU fishing is the RFMOS, and the EU, in addition to leading the regulatory and operational development of these organizations and supports their funding. On the other hand, with the funds provided to UNCLOS and the 1995 UN Fish Stocks Agreement, the EU supports as well the reinforcement of the governance of the current fisheries management structure in areas beyond national jurisdictions (ABNJ).

The international dimension of the CFP entails the promotion of its principles in the international fisheries management. It must be recalled that Fisheries Governance is a relatively new concept, and the EU approaches it comprehensively, through all maritime activities, thereby improving the capacity to influence.

As an example, in West Africa the EU searches to improve the governance in the region, by uniting synergies between all available instruments, with the aim to strengthen management. In this context, just make mention the Sustainable Fisheries Partnership Agreements (SFPAs) that the EU signs with third countries, which include a financial contribution called "sectorial support" which aims to promote sustainable fisheries development in the partner countries, by strengthening their administrative and scientific capacity through a focus on sustainable fisheries management, monitoring, control and surveillance. The "sectorial support" is also complemented with some other actions or projects, such as PESCAO project.[84]

The general objective of the PESCAO project is to strengthen the contribution of fisheries resources to sustainable development, food security and poverty alleviation in West Africa. The specific objective is to improve regional Fisheries Governance in the region through better coordination of national fisheries policies. The European Fisheries Control Agency (EFCA) cooperates very actively with two international organizations in the region, the Sub-Regional Fisheries Commission (SRCF/CSRP) and the Fisheries Committee for the West Central Gulf of Guinea (FCWC/CPCO), for improving their capacities in fighting IUU fishing.[85]

As a frontrunner in the fight against IUU fishing, since adopting the IUU Regulation, the EU has entered into dialogues on IUU fishing matters with more than 50 countries, and as a result of these dialogues, some countries have successfully reformed their control and management system.[86]

The EU has made meaningful progresses through the dialogue with third countries.[87] But it is interesting to briefly analyse the holistic approach in the case of

[83]JOIN (2019) 104 final.

[84]Commission Decision C (2017) 2951, April 2017.

[85]Press release DG MARE 9/10/2018.

[86]Troitino and Faerber (2019).

[87]Martín de la guardia and Pérez Sánchez (2001).

the partnership with China. China is the world's leading fish producer, accounting for around 18% of fish catches.[88] Looking to these figures, it is easy to imagine the importance of this country being engaged in the fight against IUU fishing; however, China has always been reluctant to join any international initiative on this problem. The EU has recently signed an ocean partnership with China,[89] and the most difficult aspect of the negotiations was to include sustainable fisheries and IUU fishing. But through the integrated approach, it was finally possible to introduce these references. It is an important achievement at international level, and some other important global players, like the USA or Norway, have recognized it and congratulated the EU for this agreement.

It should also be noted the role played by the EU in the agreement to prevent unregulated high seas fisheries in the Central Arctic Ocean,[90] which will allow for sustainable development of the area.

These are just few, but there are a lot of more examples of the success of the EU plan to improve International Governance. It is important also to highlight the permanent investment to improve the knowledge of the impact that climate change has on the distribution of fish stocks, which will lead to the changes in management. Other elements, such as the EU role on the BBNJ negotiations would be subject of a lot of studies, but it has been clearly stated that the integral EU approach is being very successful for the time being.

6 Final Remarks

The latest FAO report on the State of World Fisheries and Aquaculture 2018 points out, regarding IUU fishing, specifically, on goal 14.6: "*Almost all respondents to the 2015 CCRF survey reported having taken measures to combat IUU fishing, most importantly through the improvement of coastal State controls and monitoring, control and surveillance (MCS) and legal frameworks. The percentage of respondents identifying IUU fishing as a problem dropped from 90 percent in 2013 to 79 percent in 2015. Of these countries, 69 percent have drafted a National Plan of Action on IUU fishing (NPOA-IUU), and 84 percent of countries with an NPOA-IUU have started implementing it*[91]".

In many of these cases, the role of the EU has been essential to reverse the trend, and it can be said that the EU IUU fishing regulation has been the turning point to cure a disease that affects the entire globe.

In the short and medium term, the improvement in cooperation with the main global players, like the USA, China or Japan, will be very important. In addition, new

[88]FAO. SOFIA 2018.

[89]Blue Partnership for the Oceans UE/China. 16/07/2018.

[90]Final text available in https://bit.ly/2GBNwL7.

[91]FAO. SOFIA 2018.

elements will be included in the concept of IUU fishing, such as working conditions on board.

At European level, to underline that the review of the control framework has already begun, and the simplification, harmonization, centralization and digitalization of the process will make impossible the entry of IUU fishing into EU market.

Finally, recall that the governance of the oceans has been included in the political priorities of the G7[92] (it was a France's proposal, and with the strong support of the EU), which makes clear the strong commitment to leave clean, healthy and sustainable oceans to the future generations.

Bibliographic References

Publications

Agnew, D. J., Pearce, J., Pramod, G., Peatman, T., Watson, R., Beddington, J. R., et al. (2009). Estimating the worldwide extent of illegal fishing. *PLoS ONE, 4*(2), e4570. https://doi.org/10.1371/journal.pone.0004570.

Bostock, T., & Walmsley, S. (2009). *Enough to eat? Fisheries and Food Security.*

Castro, L. D., & Lago, J. R. R. (2018). Educación y diplomacia cultural en la primavera de Europa (1948-1954) = Education and Cultural Diplomacy in the Spring of Europe (1948-1954). *Revista de educación, 383,* 63–84.

EJF. (2005). *Pirates and profiteers: How pirate fishing fleets are robbing people and oceans.* Available at www.ejfoundation.org/report/pirates-profiteers.

EJF. (2010). *All at sea—The abuse of human rights aboard illegal fishing vessels.* London: Environmental Justice Foundation.

EJF. (2013). *Sold to the sea—Human trafficking in Thailand's Fishing Industry.*

EJF, Oceana, Pew, & WWF (2016). "Improving performance in the fight against IUU fishing". Report available at www.IUUwatch.eu (consulted on 15th June 2019).

Friedheim, R. (1999). *Ocean governance at the millennium: Where we have been—Where we should go.*

Gameiro, M. F. S., & Wilson, J. D. K. (2003). *The importance of marine fisheries to coastal community livelihoods in SADC countries.* Maputo: Kusi Consultores Ltd.

Garcia, S. M., Rice, J., & Charles, A. (2014). *Governance of marine fisheries and biodiversity conservation: The integration challenge. Part I: Governance Trends and Challenges.* Wiley Blackwell.

Gianni, M., & Simpson, W. (2005). *The changing nature of high seas fishing: How flags of convenience provide cover for illegal, unreported and unregulated fishing.* Australian Department of Agriculture, Fisheries and Forestry, International Transport Workers' Federation, and WWF International.

Gray, T. S. (2005). *Theorising about participatory fisheries governance. Participation in Fisheries Governance.* Berlin: Springer.

Hamulák, O. (2018). La carta de los derechos fundamentales de la unión europea y los derechos sociales. *Estudios constitucionales, 16*(1), 167–186.

Kerikmae, T. (1997). European convention on nationality and states' competence: The issue of human rights. *Juridica Int'l, 2,* 25.

[92]From the report of the G7 Summit in Halifax, (Canada). 20th September 2018.

Kerikmäe, T., Troitiño, D. R., & Shumilo, O. (2019). An Idol or an Ideal? A case study of Estonian e-Governance: Public perceptions, myths and misbeliefs. *Acta Baltica Historiae et Philosophiae scientiarum, 7*(1).

Kramp-Karrenbauer, A. (2019). *Getting Europe right* (09.03.2019).

Kuemlangan, B., & Press, M. (2010). Preventing, deterring and eliminating IUU fishing: Port state measures. *Environmental Policy and Law.*

Laxe, F., & Martín Bermúdez, F., Martín Palmero, F., & Novo-Corti, M. I. (2018). Governance of the fishery industry: A new global context. *Ocean and Coastal Management.*

Lobach, T. (2010). Combating IUU fishing: Interaction of global and regional initiatives. *VIDAS*, op. cit., 123.

Macron, E. (2019). *Pour une Renaissance européenne* (04.03.2019).

Mann Borgese, E., & Saigal, K. (1996). *Managerial implications of sustainable development in the ocean.*

Martín De La Guardia, R. M., & Pérez Sánchez, G. A. (2001). *Historia de la integración europea.* Barcelona: Ariel.

Outeda, C. C. (2001). *El proceso de constitucionalización de la Unión Europea: de Roma a Niza* (No. 3). Univ Santiago de Compostela.

Pastor Ridruejo, J. A. (2009). "El Derecho Internacional del Mar y su evolución incesante" La cooperación internacional en la ordenación de mares y océanos. Ed. Iustel.

Pawlas, I. (2015, September). The Visegrad Countries and European Union Membership-selected issues. In *Proceedings of International Academic Conferences* (No. 2704866). International Institute of Social and Economic Sciences.

Politakis, G. P. (2008). From tankers to trawlers: the international labour organization's new work in fishing convention. *Ocean Development & International Law, 39*(2), 119–128.

Pons Rafols, X. (2016). El protagonismo de la Unión Europea en la lucha contra la pesca ilegal, no declarada y no reglamentada. Thomson Reuters Aranzadi, Cizur Menor (Navarra), 2016, p. 194.

Roselló, M. (2019). *Maritime crime and the role of insurers.* From the blog https://houseofocean.org/.

Sander, K., Lee, J., Hickey, V., Mosoti, V. B., Virdin, J., & Magrath, W. B. (2014). Conceptualizing maritime environmental and natural resources law enforcement—The case of illegal fishing. *Environmental Development, 11*, 114.

Swan, J. (2016). *Implementation of port state measures—Legislative template, framework for procedures, role of regional fisheries management organizations.* Rome: FAO Publications.

Symes, D. (1997). Fisheries management: In search of good governance. *Fisheries Research.*

Tinch, R., Dickie, I., & Lanz, B. (2008). *Cost of IUU fishing in EU fisheries.* PEW Environmental Group, November 2008.

Treves, T. (2009). *La pesca ilegal, no declarada y no reglamentada: Estado de pabellón, estado costero y estado de puerto.*

Troitiño, D. R., Färber, K., & Boiro, A. (2017). Mitterrand and the great European design—From the Cold War to the European Union. *Baltic Journal of European Studies, 7*(2), 132–147.

Troitiño, D. R. (2017). Jean Monnet before the first European Community: A historical perspective and critic. *Trames, 21*(3), 193–213.

Troitiño, D. R., Kerikmäe, T., & Chochia, A. (Eds.). (2018). *Brexit: History, reasoning and perspectives.* Berlin: Springer.

Troitino, D. R., & Faerber, K. (2019). Historical errors in the initial conception of the euro and its subsequent development. *Brazilian Journal of Political Economy, 39*(2), 328–343.

Tsamenyi, M., Palma, M., Milligan, B., & Mfodwo, K. (2010). The European Council regulation on illegal, unreported and unregulated fishing: An international fisheries law perspective. *International Journal of Marine and Coastal Law, 25*(1), 5–31.

Urbina, J. J. (2017). *La cooperación internacional en la aplicación de medidas comerciales para luchar contra la pesca ilegal, no declarada y no reglamentada.*

Weldemichael, A. T. (2012). Maritime corporate terrorism and its consequences in the western Indian ocean: Illegal fishing, waste dumping and piracy in twenty-first-century somalia. *Journal of the Indian Ocean Region, 8*(2), 113.
WWF, EJF, Oceana, & the Pew Charitable Trusts. (2016). *The EU IUU Regulation: building on success EU progress in the global fight against illegal fishing.*

Legislative Acts and Official Reports From Official Institutions

Agreement to prevent Unregulated High Seas Fisheries in the Central Arctic Ocean. (2019).
CCAMLR. (1997). *Report of the sixteenth meeting of the Commission XVI* (p. 79) 16.8. Available at www.ccamlr.org/en/ccamlr-xvi, consulted on June 21, 2019.
COFI. (2018). *Report thirty-third session COFI, Rome*, 9–13 July 2018 (COFI/2018/6). Available at http://www.fao.org/3/MX190EN/mx190en.pdf, consulted on 14th June 2019.
Council Regulation (EC) No 1005/2008 of 29 September 2008 establishing a Community system to prevent, deter and eliminate illegal, unreported and unregulated fishing, amending Regulations (EEC) No 2847/93, (EC) No 1936/2001 and (EC) No 601/2004 and repealing Regulations (EC) No 1093/94 and (EC) No 1447/1999.
Declaration on the establishment of a Blue Partnership for the Oceans: Towards better ocean governance, sustainable fisheries and a thriving maritime economy between the European Union and the People's Republic of China. Signed in Beijing, 16th July 2018.
DG MARE. (2018). Press release DG MARE "EFCA—A cornerstone of ocean governance in EU and beyond, 9/10/2018.
European Council. (2002). Council conclusions on illegal, uncontrolled and unregulated fisheries, 11.VI.2002.
European Commission and the EU's High Representative. (2016). Joint Communication to the European Parliament, the Council, the European Economic and Social Committee and the Committee of the Regions. International Ocean Governance: An agenda for the future of our oceans (JOIN(2016) 49 final).
European Commission. (2007). Communication from the Commission to the European Parliament, the Council, the European Economic and Social Committee and the Committee of the Regions—An Integrated Maritime Policy for the European Union (COM(2007) 574 final). Brussels, 10/10/2007.
European Commission. (2015). Communication from the commission to the European Parliament and the Council on the application of Council Regulation (EC) No 1005/2008 establishing a community system to prevent, deter and eliminate illegal, unreported and unregulated fishing. COM/2015/048.
European Commission. (2017). The project 'improved regional fisheries governance in western Africa (PESCAO)' was adopted by Commission Decision C (2017) 2951 of 28 April 2017.
European Commission. (2018). Proposal for a Regulation of the European Parliament and of the Council amending Council Regulation (EC) No 1224/2009, and amending Council Regulations (EC) No 768/2005, (EC) No 1967/2006, (EC) No 1005/2008, and Regulation (EU) No 2016/1139 of the European Parliament and of the Council as regards fisheries control. COM/2018/368 final (adopted on 30/05/2018).
European Commission. (2019). Joint Report to the European Parliament and the Council improving International Ocean Governance—Two years of progress. JOIN/2019/4 final.
FAO. (1995). Code of conduct for responsible fisheries was adopted in Resolution 4/95 by the FAO Conference on 31 October 1995.
FAO, Rome. (2001). *International plan of action to prevent, deter, and eliminate illegal, unreported and unregulated fishing.*
FAO. (2002). *The state of world fisheries and aquaculture 2000.*

FAO (2015). Fisheries operations. Best practices to improve safety at sea in the fisheries sector. *FAO Technical Guidelines for Responsible Fisheries, 1* (Suppl. 3). Rome, 196 pp.
FAO. (2016). *Agreement on Port State measures to prevent, deter and eliminate illegal, unreported and unregulated fishing* (Revised edition). Rome: FAO.
FAO. (2017). *Voluntary guidelines for catch documentation schemes*, Rome, 20 pp.
FAO. (2018). The State of World Fisheries and Aquaculture 2018—Meeting the sustainable development goals. Rome.
GATT. (1994). From the general exceptions in the art. XX of the General Agreement on Tariffs and Trade (GATT) (1994).
G7 Report. (2018). Report of the G7 Summit in Halifax, (Canada), September 20, 2018.
ILO C188—Work in Fishing Convention. (2007). Convention concerning work in the fishing sector (Entry into force: 16 Nov 2017).
OEDC. (2003). *Ownership and control of ships* (pp. 23–34). OEDC Publishing, Maritime Transport Committee.
OECD. (2005). *Why fish piracy persists: The economics of illegal, unreported and unregulated fishing* (pp. 41–42). Paris: OECD.
OECD. (2013). *Evading the net: Tax crime in the fisheries sector.*
UN. (1982). United Nations Convention on the Law of the Sea (UNCLOS) of 10 December 1982.
UN. (1995). 1995 UN Fish Stocks Agreement. The Agreement for the Implementation of the Provisions of the United Nations Convention on the Law of the Sea of 10 December 1982 relating to the Conservation and Management of Straddling Fish Stocks and Highly Migratory Fish Stocks, signed in 1995 and entered into force on 11 December 2001.
UN. (2015). *United Nations "2030 Agenda for Sustainable Development".*
UNGA. (2018). United Nations General Assembly, (UNGA), Resolution on Sustainable Fisheries, December 11, 2018. A/RES/73/125.

Websites

http://populationmatters.org/the-facts.
http://www.fao.org/global-record/background/history/es/, Consulted on 14th June 2019.
Interview to a FAO Fisheries Officer, Ms. A. Mosteiro, (30/07/2018), available at https://bit.ly/2K774pM, consulted on 3rd May 2019.
DG MARE website: https://ec.europa.eu/fisheries/cfp/illegal_fishing_en.pdf (consulted on 24th June 2019).
DG MARE website: https://ec.europa.eu/fisheries/sites/fisheries/files/illegal-fishing-overview-of-existing-procedures-third-countries_en.pdf (consulted on 15th April 2019).
DG MARE website: https://ec.europa.eu/maritimeaffairs/index_en.
https://www.fao.org.
https://houseofocean.org/.

The manufacturer's authorised representative in the EU is Springer Nature Customer Service Centre GmbH, Europaplatz 3, 69115 Heidelberg, Germany. If you have any concerns regarding our products, please contact ProductSafety@springernature.com

Printed and bound by CPI Group (UK) Ltd, Croydon, CR0 4YY
30/09/2026
02225647-0010